THE SMALL GARDEN

THE SMALL GARDEN

C. E. LUCAS PHILLIPS

FRANCES LINCOLN

Frances Lincoln Limited
4 Torriano Mews
Torriano Avenue
London NW5 2RZ
www.franceslincoln.com

First Frances Lincoln edition 2006
First published as *The Small Garden* 1952
Published as *The New Small Garden* 1979

British Library Cataloging in Publication data
A catalogue record for this book is available
from the British Library

ISBN 10 0-7112-2482-X
ISBN 13 978-0-7112-2482-7

Printed in England

9 8 7 6 5 4 3 2 1

CONTENTS

Part Four: Know Your Enemy

Part Five: The Year's Work

FOREWORD

Of the vast number of books on gardening, fat, shiny and heavy with photographs, which fill our shelves, this has long been my favourite. First published in 1952, it met a post-war enthusiasm for beautifying your plot. This reprint is good news indeed.

The author was a handsome soldier, decorated for distinguished service in both world wars. He was also an inspired writer, an original who holds the attention of the reader in his instructions on even the duller aspects of gardening.

He tells us he is an amateur writing for amateurs. Too modest, but it is an encouragement to beginners and succeeds in making us happy to try to get it right.

It is nothing if not thorough. The basics are explained, and the reasons for the various operations (stages, steps), leading to the pleasures of growing whatever your fancy, for anyone who knows one end of a hoe from the other.

There is a glossary and a cultural calendar (it is a comfort to see 'cultural' used in this context and not coupled with 'heritage', describing some outrageous kind of art). He tackles the vexed problem of plant names in the same robust way as the other difficulties met in learning how to deal with the vegetable kingdom.

Some of his instructions are positively poetic. Compost, its components and how to mix them, and the value of liquid manure of a 'deep tawny hue' (but when it comes to adding 'a trifle of soot' you may have to admit defeat, should your house be without coal fires). Other unlikely subjects are so well described they carry you along with intense pleasure.

There is much to go into before you dig. Fifty pages go by till he puts spade, fork and hoe to ground. There are some surprises in the chapter on tools (The Armoury) – 'the dibber should be handled with care ... in unskilled hands it is a menace to the infant plant.' I never looked on the good old dibber as a menace, but his reason for the warning is logical.

The seasons and the reasons for the work they bring are explained in simple language you can't forget. Digging and manuring in the autumn allow the frosts to break up newly dug clods, working on particles of soil moisture as it does on water pipes, bursting and crumbling a heavy soil into a fine tilth with great efficiency. The comparison to burst domestic pipes brings this process of nature home to every British householder. Early spring east winds with their 'harrowing breath' bring you to the coming of summer when he begs you not to disturb the roots of established plants when keeping the ground clear of invaders, but a little light hoeing 'to slaughter the weeds' is in order.

The author is at his most lyrical describing the plants he loves. Species anemones, for instance, 'have a chaste and porcelain beauty, fragile and virginal'. Eremurus are 'elegant ladies of hyacinthine appearance of 6 foot stature and more. Expensive. Beware slugs.' The best he can say of the easily grown valerian is 'Beloved by Winston Churchill.'

He does not spare us his dislikes and warns that after flowering in 'barbaric splendour' in late spring the Oriental poppy is a 'grisly mess'. You can't have one without the other. *Salvia splendens* is a 'pillar-box red bedding plant which startles the optic nerve in August'. Cecil Beaton had the same anti-scarlet prejudice and called this salvia and its colour-mates 'retina irritants'.

The pages on roses produce their own loving descriptions. How he would have enjoyed the modern tribe of new/old roses which answer all needs with their scent, vigour and complicated beauty. Looking to a brighter future, he barks out orders to amputate newly planted ramblers to within fifteen inches of the ground, thus preventing any flowers in their first year, and makes sure we obey by adding that this is 'a cardinal injunction not to be funked'.

Much of the Brigadier's writing is delightfully dated to half a century ago. Many bright little plants are 'gay' and in my old battered paperback he recommends a dependable insecticide DDT – edited out now it is illegal. Slugs, bugs and bacteria are likened to fifth columnists. The new generations of gardeners may wonder at the meaning of that.

Weeds are classed in three degrees of abomination, the worst being the tap-rooted varieties – 'underground creeping horrors'. Couch grass and ground elder are 'vegetative serpents, brutes which laugh at the hoe as love laughs at the locksmith'.

I know of no other gardening book which engages our interest in subjects dull as ditch water and vaguely unpleasant as well, apt to be skipped in search of something more attractive. You have to read on for fear of missing some descriptive gem, and you remember what he says because of how he says it.

The chapter on the kitchen garden takes us steadily along with all the favourites and their needs clearly described. It is embellished with simple line drawings (we have already seen a little masterpiece entitled 'How not to water'), one page ending with 'a gallery of oddments' showing their age as they are no longer odd but fashionable – kohlrabi, celeriac and salsify.

Having profited by the Lucas Phillips wisdom and followed his ways in making a new garden or improving an old one to our (and his) liking, we arrive at the last chapters where he excels himself. We are jolted into full attention by the originality and often hilarious descriptions of 'Friend and Foe' and, best of all, 'The Enemy in Detail'.

Who else but our now beloved author would describe the larva of the ladybird (a friend) as 'agile, torpedo-shaped, resembling a minute crocodile'?

You have got to know the difference between the 'brisk' centipede (friend) and a millipede (foe). The latter has 'innumerable very small legs and, when worried, gives off an obnoxious smell from his stink glands'. The idea of a worried millipede is something I have never considered, but I will now – assuming I can tell the difference from its fewer-legged rival, the friendly centipede – and I will do my best to give the wicked millipede a nervous breakdown. I am afraid the children's dear old tortoise is entirely an enemy.

The worst garden pest by a long way is Man ('ignorant and lazy'), led in his assault on nature by the Jobbing Gardener. (Fifty years on would the worst pest be the strimmer?) Birds are in a special category and have become 'a serious problem ... pestiferous to fruit'. RSPB please not.

His language becomes better and better. Cuckoo spit: 'inside a mess of frothy spittle is a curious soft creature which, on disturbance, will attempt to escape by weak hops'. You can't beat it.

'Know Your Enemy', something he studied in his military career and brought so forcibly to the deceptive calm of the garden, is the old soldier's title for the introduction to the last chapter. Who could forget the picture conjured up by scab and canker 'going hand in hand', asking for a drawing by Edward Lear of these brotherly pests advancing on your apple trees? He quotes Erasmus Darwin in 1790: 'Crack follows crack, to laws elastic just, And the frail fabric shivers into dust.'

Dip into this book and you will find yourself digging. Dig and you will be rewarded.

The Dowager Duchess of Devonshire
January 2006

PUBLISHER'S NOTE

'Peter' Lucas Phillips was born in 1897 and educated at St Lawrence College and King's College, London University. In the First World War he served in the Royal Artillery in France and Flanders, becoming a major before he was twenty-one. During the Second World War he fought in the campaigns of Dunkirk, the Western Desert and Italy. He became a brigadier, was awarded the MC, the OBE and the Croix de Guerre, and was the author of several war books. Of these, *The Cockleshell Heroes* remains his most popular and renowned work. Describing himself as a 'passionate gardener', he lived in Surrey, where his own 'small garden' was an inspiration to many visitors, and wrote a string of gardening titles, including *Roses for Small Gardens, Climbing Plants for Walls and Gardens, Ornamental Shrubs* and *The Modern Flower Garden*. He died in 1984.

The Small Garden was originally published in hardback in 1952 and subsequently in paperback. It underwent six revisions and seventeen reprints. In 1979 the author revised it extensively and it was reissued as *The New Small Garden*. It is this text that is reproduced here. For this edition all botanical names have been updated and where plants are no longer available either they have been deleted or substitutes have been supplied. Proprietary products and chemicals have been replaced by modern, legal equivalents. Otherwise, apart from a few other minor changes for ease of use by today's reader, the book is as the original.

GARDENERS' JARGON

This very brief dictionary of gardening terms is included 'by special request' as a means of ready reference. It cannot hope to be complete, but numerous other definitions are given in the text and can be dug out by means of the Index. Terms specially used in pruning are in Chapters 7 and 20. A bare minimum is included of the Latin and Greek terms most commonly used in plant names, and these are in italics. Of adjectives, the masculine form only is given. Thus *albus* is *alba* in the feminine and *album* in the neuter; *officinalis* is both masculine and feminine, but *officinale* in the neuter. Don't ask me why cotoneaster is masculine, berberis feminine and rhododendron neuter.

   n = noun; v = verb.

Acid soil. Soil with a low lime content.
Albus. White.
Alkaline soil. Opposite to acid.
Anther. The pollen-bearing part of the stamen (the male organ).
Anthus. Flower; as in polyanthus and polyantha, many-flowered; or macrantha, large-flowered.
Atro-. Deep in colour, as in *atropurpureus*.
Axil. The angle between a stem and a branch; hence axillary.
Bed out, *v.* To plant out a whole flower-bed according to a set scheme with plants already well advanced in growth; e.g. 'geraniums' for summer bedding, or wallflowers for spring bedding.

A shoot showing: **a**, *terminal or extension bud;* **b**, *leaf axil;* **c**, *axillary bud, important in sweet peas, chrysanthemums, tomatoes etc.*

Bolt, *v.* To run to seed prematurely.

Bract. Leaves at the base of a flower, sometimes very colourful, as in poinsettia.

Brassica. A vegetable of the cabbage family.

Breastwood. On wall-trained fruits, shoots that grow outwards from the wall; also called 'fore-right' shoots.

Bud, *n.* There are flower- or fruit-buds, and wood- or growth-buds; horticulturally, the term is used not only of a well-developed bud, but also from the moment when there is a tiny mark or swelling on the stem.

Bud, *v.* To propagate a desired variety by inserting a bud of that variety into a suitable root stock.

Calcareous. Chalky, of soil.

Calyx. The circlet or whorl of sepals that enclose a flower-bud before it opens.

Chamae-. Close to the ground, as in *chamaecyparis*.

Chlorosis. Loss of green pigment (chlorophyll) in foliage.

Chrys-. Golden.

Coccineus (pronounced 'koksineus'). Scarlet.

Collar. The junction of stem and root.

Compost. Has two meanings – a special mixture of soil components made up for pots or seed-boxes; and decomposed organic matter from a 'compost heap' used as manure.

Corm. A bulb-like swelling of a stem underground, e.g. gladiolus and crocus.

Corolla. The whole circlet or whorl of petals in a flower.

Crock. A piece of broken flower-pot, or other stony material in lieu, laid in the bottoms of pots or seed-boxes for drainage.

Cultivar. Orthodox term for the named variety of a species, occurring in cultivation, not the wild.

Cutting. A portion cut from a living plant from which a new plant can be grown; usually a small stem or branch; but sometimes a root or leaf.

Dead-head, *v.* Gardeners' colloquialism for removing spent flowers from a plant.

Dentatus, Denticulatus. Toothed.

Disbud, *v.* Usually, to remove a certain number of small flower-buds below or around the main one so that it may develop to its best.

Drill, *n.* A tiny trench, maybe only ¼ in. deep, made in the soil for sowing seed.

Eye. A rudimentary bud.

Fastigiate. Tall, slender, the branches erect and pressed closely together.

Fibrous. Of roots; thin, hair-like roots, more or less dense. 'Fibrous loam' is old turf with plenty of dense grass roots.

Fl. Pl. = Flore Pleno. Double-flowered. *See* 'Single'.

folius. Leaved, as in *longifolius*, long-leaved.

Fruticosus. Shrubby.

Fulgens. Shining, glowing.

Glabrous. Smooth, hairless.

Glaucous. Sea-green.

Harden off, *v.* To accustom a non-hardy plant, raised under glass, to outdoor conditions gradually.

Heavy soil. One preponderating in clay.

Heel in, *v.* To make a rough trench, put the plants in semi-erect, and cover their roots with soil as temporary protection until ready to plant; or, as with spent tulips and other bulbs that have to be got out of the way, to allow them to complete their cycle of life.

Humus. *See* Chapter 3.

Inflorescence. The method in which flowers arrange themselves on a stem, whether 'solitary' (one flower per stem, as in the pansy), or numerously in a 'spike', a 'raceme' (a spike on which each floret has a short stem, as in the lupin), a domed 'umbel' (several flowers springing from one point, as in the polyanthus), a flattish 'corymb', etc. These terms are often used inexactly.

Japonicus. Japanese.

Lati-. Broad, as *latifolius*, broad-leaved.

Legume. A plant that forms its seeds in pods, as in peas, beans, lupin, laburnum, broom.

Light soil. One predominating in sand.

Loam. A blend of clay, sand, and humus.

Macro-. Large or long, e.g. *macrocarpus*, large-fruited, and *macrantha*, large- or long-flowered.

Micro-. Small.

Mulch, *v.* To cover the soil with leaves, grass-mowings, manure, etc., either to conserve moisture, or to provide a food for the plants, or both (Chapter 5).

Multi-. Many.

Nanus. Dwarf.

New wood. A shoot (branch or twig) that has sprouted and grown in the current season.

Node. The joint on a stem, often slightly swollen, from which a leaf-stalk will sprout or has sprouted.

Nursery. A small reserved part of the garden, especially the kitchen garden, in which young plants are reared; it has a seed-bed and a pricking-out bed.

Officinalis. Commercial, medicinal.

Old wood. A shoot that grew last year or earlier.

Open weather. Weather in which the soil is neither frost-bound nor saturated with rain.

Pan. A shallow pottery vessel in which seed is sown, often in preference to a seed-box; also a hard, compressed substratum of soil.

Perennial. A plant that lives on from year to year (Chapter 2).
Peri-. Around; e.g. perianth, the roundish combination of calyx and corolla in a narcissus and other plants.
Persicus. Persian – i.e. Iranian
-phyllus. Leaf, e.g. *microphyllus*, small-leaved.
Pinch, *v.* To nip out, commonly with the finger-nails, the growing point of a plant or one of its shoots.
Pistil. The female organ of a flower including stigma, style, ovary.
Poly-. Many, e.g. *polyanthus*, many-flowered.
Pot on, *v.* To move a plant from a small pot into a larger one as it grows.
Praecox. Early, precocious.
Prick in, *v.* To work fertilisers etc. into the top inch or two of soil with hoe or fork.
Prick out, *v.* To transplant seedlings from their seed-bed or box into another bed or box, at wider spacing to allow healthy development.
Repens, Reptans. Creeping.
Rhizome. A prostrate, fleshy stem, on or just below ground level, emitting roots below and leaves above, most familiar in flag irises; sometimes an underground stem. Pronounced 'ryzome'.
Runner. A prostrate shoot thrown out by some plants, which roots at several points and forms new plants, e.g. strawberry.
Sax-. Rock, as in saxifrage and the adjective saxatile.
Scaber. Rough.
Schiz-. Split. Pronounced 'skitz'.
Scion. A cultivated variety of a tree, shrub, etc., that has been grafted or budded on to a different root stock, often of a wild species, as in roses, fruit trees, lilac, etc.
Seed-bed. Any strip or patch of soil specially prepared for the sowing of seed, whether in the nursery or the open ground.
Self-coloured. Of one colour throughout.

The sepals, which collectively form the calyx, unfolding to disclose the flower-bud that they have been protecting.

Sepal (to rhyme with petal). One of the leaf-like members that collectively form a calyx.

Serratus, **serrate.** With saw–edged leaf.

Serrulatus, **serrulate.** Finely saw–edged.

Sessilis. Sessile, stalkless.

Sinensis, **Sino–.** Chinese.

Single. A flower that has only one ring of petals, as in the wild brier or dog rose, and the common buttercup. Cf. single and double chrysanthemums, asters, etc.

South wall. That side of a wall which faces South.

Spectabilis. Showy.

Spit. The depth of one spade in digging (10 in.).

Spur. A fruit–bud or cluster of several on fruit trees (Chapter 20).

Stamen. The whole male organ of a flower.

Standard. Of trees, an erect stem without branches below a certain height.

'Start', *v.* To start a plant into early growth before planting out, e.g. dahlia and begonia, by planting it under glass.

Steno–. Narrow, e.g. *stenophyllus,* narrow–leaved.

Stigma. The sticky part of the pistil or female organ of a flower; it receives the pollen.

Stock. The rooted growth, often of a wild species, on which a cultivated scion is grafted or budded.

Stop, *v.* To remove the growing tip of a plant to induce branching.

Strictus. Erect and slender.

Sub–. Semi, as in subsessile, *subserrulata.*

Sucker. A shoot springing from the root formation of a plant, usually noxious, as in the rose and lilac, where a cultivated variety is budded on other stock; but in the raspberry and blackberry they are the normal means of multiplying.

Tap-root. A thick tapering root growing straight downwards.

Tilth. Cultivation. A 'fine tilth', as of a seed-bed, is soil worked down to small, loose, fine crumbs, or particles.

Tomentosus. Downy.

Transpiration. The giving-out of moisture by a leaf.

Tuber. A fleshy underground stem, as in the dahlia and potato.

Vegetative propagation. The raising of plants by cuttings, budding, division, etc., not by seed.

Vulgaris. Common.

Whorl. A ring or circlet of petals, leaves or sepals springing from the same level on a stem.

PRESENTATION

This is a book by an amateur for amateurs. In presenting it I have thought chiefly of those of us who have only small gardens, as most of us understand the term, who have no time or inclination for mixing ounces of this or that per square yard, but who would like, with small resources, to turn out a garden in which we can take pleasure and pride.

I myself began gardening just fifty years ago in complete ignorance, making my first attempt by sowing sweet pea seed six inches deep under an elm tree, and having to contend with the problems of catching the 8.30 a.m. daily. Remembering my own early tribulations, therefore, I have devised this book for those who have little or no experience, but who do at least know which end of a hoe is which. It will also, I hope, be a help to those who have passed their novitiate and are anxious to make progress in the craft, and to all who wish to grow, for their own delight, good roses or clematis or peas, and to make their gardens, however small, an integral part of their homes, as full of pleasure and of practical usefulness as their houses.

Space (which means money – your money) has obliged several limitations. Therefore do not look in here for any guidance on how to grow for exhibition – no legendary beans or parsnips, no solitaire roses of splendid size and substance.

Nor, unfortunately, will there be anything about heated greenhouses, orchids, cacti, large trees or water gardens. And in the lists of flowers and vegetables I have omitted anything 'precious' or unduly difficult, and have, moreover, been highly selective in all these lists, aiming, in the first place, at dealing with the better of the usual things that most people will want to know about and 'look up', and, secondly and specially, at pointing to some worthy and unhackneyed things which though not in the least 'rare' to a horticulturist, are for some reason seldom seen in small places. Where 'new-made gauds' are rapidly superseded by others (as in chrysanthemums and dahlias) I have usually made no selections at all, for most are quickly out-of-date.

What has been more difficult than selection has been compression. Most of these chapters are fit subjects for a whole volume, some of them for several volumes. Besides having to shun that friendly discursiveness that makes gardening books agreeable, I have also had to omit all those qualifications, those ifs and buts, that books on gardening ought to contain but seldom do. For in gardening, as in law, dogmatism and downright mandamus ought to be guarded against. The doctors of gardening, on some matters, disagree as much as others. Listen to them, if you ever have the chance, on lilies! One man's experience is not another's. Moreover, soil, climate, situation and aspect have such infinite variations that what is right treatment in one instance is not necessarily right in another, and the local knowledge of the old hand may be worth more than many written words. One must not too far dogmatise, for example, on the pruning of apples and roses. One can only guide. Every gardener finds his own way of doing things and where I have found a particular method good I advocate it. I am convinced, for example, that, where things are permanently planted, we worry the soil too much. And there are many popular misconceptions about roses. Labour-saving has been much in my mind, and, as compared with technical books, I have simplified appreciably in matters of fertilisers, insecticides and so on. Where orthodoxy is safest for the apprentice, however, I have followed that path.

What is a 'small' garden? The City Magnate would have an idea quite different from his clerk's. There are the handkerchief gardens of cottage and town house, and the rather larger gardens of the suburbs and the country. I have borne in mind a limit of about an acre, but with special considera-tion for the suburban garden of much less than that size. The limitation, of course, applies in no way to cultural requirements, and what is good for the rose and the daffodil in the cotter's plot is equally good for the Magnate's demesne.

Most people who possess anything like an acre, or half of it, contribute weekly to the support of a gentleman known as Jobbing Gardener. You are warned of the danger that he may prove to be Garden Pest No. 1. I have come across a few good ones and, very rarely, one or two very good ones, who have been brought up on the staff of some big establishment or who have taken the trouble to train themselves properly. If you have one of these, reward him well. Usually, however (leaving aside those who are just downright bad or bone-idle), Jobbing Gardener's ability is limited to keep-ing the place tidy, trimming hedges (often wrongly), making a bonfire, mowing the lawn and, sometimes, the raising of the simpler vegetables. Such a man should not be allowed on any kind of flower-bed. Put a pair of secateurs or any kind of pruning tool into his hand and he is likely to become like Milton's 'blind Fury with th' abhorred shears that slits the thin-spun life'.

I hope that these pages will help you to be independent of him, and that the bug of gardening will bite you 'good and proper'. Adventure for-ward on your own. But remember that real gardening is sometimes hard work. If you are no longer young, don't overdo it, though personally I have always found it a happy slavery, overcoming even the lure of golf (after cricket had been left far behind !). Learn all you can from living examples. Go to Kew Gardens, the Royal Horticultural Society's Garden at Wisley, the Royal Botanic Garden in Edinburgh, Harlow Carr at Harrogate, and

Roath Park in Cardiff and visit the better nurseries. Haunt all the flower shows that you have time for, but don't go by looks alone, for the beauty that allures you on the bench may not be hardy, may grow too big, may fear lime or be otherwise fastidious. Collect all the catalogues you can and compare one with another, though not all nowadays are informative on cultural needs and many are plastered with too much 'glorious technicolour' at the expense of factual information.

Many good old nurseries have now been crushed out of existence by economic burdens and those that remain often impose irksome restrictions on their customers in addition to heavy charges for packing and carriage. To some extent the place of the good old retail nurseries has been taken by the new 'garden centres', which have sprung up all over the place. Most of these are no more than shops, not growing their own produce but merely buying them in from wholesale nurseries, often foreign ones. You cannot place any orders and can buy only what they have in stock, and it is rare indeed to find anyone at hand who can give you horticultural advice. Better conditions usually prevail at garden centres run by nurseries themselves and the best that I know, though of modest size, is the one recently set up by the Royal Horticultural Society at Wisley. On the other side of the coin, however, are the facts that at garden centres you have no charges for packing and carriage and that their container-grown plants can often be planted out of season, though it is not always wise to do so, especially when the roots are tightly packed in the containers and have to be teased out.

You will get great benefit also from joining the Royal Horticultural Society and the specialist society of any particular flower that appeals to you, such as the Royal National Rose Society, the Alpine Garden Society, the Scottish Rock Garden Club, and those dedicated to the delphinium, sweet pea, iris, dahlia, etc. RHS Fellowship gives you free admission to their numerous shows and to their gardens at Wisley in Surrey, where you may learn a lot and where many specialists are at your service, by post or otherwise, to diagnose your problems and give professional advice.

I have included in this book most features that my friends exhorted me to cover, such as a glossary and a cultural calendar, What I have *not* been able to do, or only in part, is to avoid 'those awful Latin names'. It's not so easy.

Most of us, I am sure, would prefer to use English names, many of which have a native charm and euphony. Sweet William, Canterbury bell, larkspur, love-in-a-mist, columbine and many another are delectable. Not all, however; sneezewort and fleabane make no appeal to me, and Venus's navel-wort is a thought too intimate. Three kinds of trouble can arise from 'popular' names. One occurs when there is more than one sort of sage or marigold, a second when there is more than one popular name for the same plant, and a third when we find the same popular name being given to different plants. The 'bluebells of Scotland' are not those of England. The *Nigella* may indeed be love-in-a-mist, but it may also be devil-in-the-bush.

(Is there a difference?) 'Winter cherry' may mean the red-fruited pot plant of Christmas time (*Solanum capsicastrum*), or it may mean the *Physalis* with scarlet bladders (also called Cape gooseberry!), or it may mean, and should only mean, the real cherry tree that blooms in winter.

One pair of misleading popular names are 'sun rose' and 'rock rose'. Both are applied indifferently, even in nurserymen's catalogues, to either the helianthemum or the cistus, though, since 'helios' means the sun, there is no excuse for confusion.

More troublesome are those instances where the authentic botanical name for one plant is popularly applied to another. Nasturtium, which legally is a name for watercress, doesn't matter a great deal, but other instances definitely lead to confusion. A glaring one is 'geranium'. The real geranium is a hardy perennial with deeply cut leaves and dainty blossoms, often blue or mauve, spreading widely and densely and used in the herbaceous border and rock garden. The more effulgent creature used for summer 'bedding out' or window-sill pots is no 'geranium' at all, but a *Pelargonium*. If we so miscall it, what shall we call the true geranium?

Likewise, *Syringa* is the authentic name for lilac, and not for that white-flowered bush of spicy fragrance which is properly *Philadelphus*. An odd confusion. By all means call *Syringa* lilac, but don't call *Philadelphus* 'syringa', or the nursery will send you what you don't want.

Another little oddity is *japonica*. This word, of course, merely means Japanese, and we have a long and varied list of plants called so-and-so japonica. Popular taste, however, has attached the name specifically to the Japanese quince. So inconsistent are we, indeed, that we have often abandoned a perfectly good English name in favour of a foreign one, as in cranesbill, mullein, meadow saffron, meadow rue, stonecrop. And there is also, of course, a long, long list of importations from abroad that have never had any English names – *Chrysanthemum, Dahlia, Rhododendron* and a host of others. So why make a fuss about other Greek or Latin names?

So far the weight of argument has been mainly in favour of the classicists. The purpose of the botanical name is, of course, to identify every plant precisely all over the world, so that there shall be no confusion, and that you, Reader, may be sure of getting exactly what you want from the nursery. On the other side of the House, we argue that botanical names are so constantly changed by the meddlesome people that order these matters, nearly always to something even more tortuous to the tongue than the old name, that there is a great deal of confusion, and a lot of alternative names are bandied about. Nurserymen very frequently use invalid ones. Thus it would save a lot of bother if, generically, we called the 'japonicas' Japanese quinces, and the true geranium by its good English name cranesbill. Moreover, no one, I hope, will ever be coerced into calling the sweet pea, sweet William, Canterbury bell, daffodil, and other dear delights by any other names.

A nodding acquaintance with the method of forming these plant names is necessary for understanding garden literature. We may ignore the higher botanical classifications, dealing only with names as they appear in catalogues. First in the name-group comes the GENUS, then the SPECIES, a sub-division of the genus, then, maybe, sub-divisions of the species known as CULTIVARS or VARIETIES, often having fancy names in English or other languages.

Thus, to take an example, we have the genus Rosa, the rose. Of this, one of the species is R. x *centifolia*, the rose of a hundred 'leaves' (our ancestors called petals 'leaves'). Of this in turn there is a cultivar called R. x *centifolia* 'Muscosa', which is the hundred-leaved rose with mossy sepals. Note that the genus and species are abbreviated after first mention. Plants named after persons, either by right of discovery or merely for compliment, are written as in *Berberis darwinii*, Darwin's barberry, or in *Syringa vulgaris* 'Madame Lemoine', a variation, named after Mme Lemoine, of the common species of lilac. Many are named after a country or town (with no capital letter), as in *Berberis japonica*, the Japanese barberry and in *Cytisus kewensis*, the broom raised in Kew Gardens.

You pronounce all these names in a simple Anglicised manner, not à la modern Latin, since thousands of them are not Latin but Greek, or mixtures of the two, or sometimes Arabic, Japanese, or even Red Indian.

Now for the method I shall normally employ in this book for plant nomenclature. With respectful apologies to the orthodox, the rule as far as possible will be convenience, suitability and normal usage among laymen. Those names of plants will be used which seem to be the most in common use. Snowdrop and hollyhock will be found under those names, but snapdragon under antirrhinum. Moreover, I shall use English names even if not in common use, when it seems good to encourage them. Thus, generically, I shall write cranesbill and Japanese quince, but when it is necessary to identify a particular species or variety, then the forms will be *Geranium dalmaticum* and *Chaenomeles superba*. Many orthodox names, in addition to those used in the text, will be found in the index.

PART ONE: FUNDAMENTALS

I

FIRST STEPS

LAYOUT

The first task in any new garden is planning and design. The two are
closely interrelated, planning or layout being part of the practical craft and
management of gardening, and design the art of it. I shall have room for
only a few general suggestions later on about design, which is perhaps the
most fascinating of any garden exercise, but not really one to tackle at the
beginning of a novitiate. Layout is less difficult.

A garden may be new in the sense of being a vacant plot of ground,
but more often the 'new' house is an old one with an existing garden. In
both places the problems of layout are the same, but old gardens too often
have their paths and trees in the wrong places, and the impress of neglect
is manifest on many sides. Whatever the condition, formulate a permanent
plan, even if your bank manager allows you to execute it only in stages.

First, a clear purpose. Is the garden to be a pleasaunce only, 'to weave
the garlands of repose', or shall fruit and vegetables predominate, or shall
there be something of all? Space may govern one's decisions. In an invio-
late acre wonders can be done, but in smaller suburban and cottage gardens
something usually has to be sacrificed. Economic brutalities are an impulse
to grow at least some vegetables in any garden that is not more than a
handkerchief, but the kitchen plot needs far more time and labour than any
other part of the garden, apart from the aesthetics of the matter. In any
restricted space potatoes are the last thing to grow, for they are relatively
uneconomic, so is the mere odd row or two of peas, highly desirable but
all too quickly gobbled up. Selection of vegetables needs care, and we shall
consider it fully in the appropriate chapter.

In no garden, however, omit fruit, especially the small bush fruits.
Gooseberries, raspberries, and so on are as easy as anything, are good
economics, take up very little space when properly laid out, and are acceptable to the eye, or should be; apples and pears, though sorely tortured and
of little profit in most private gardens, have at least some decorative value,
while cherries are very much at home on house walls. Says Thomas Tusser,
of Elizabethan days:

> The Gooseberry, Respis, and Roses, all three
> With strawberries under them trimly agree.

Apportion the space, therefore, according to such broad considerations. The first things actually to be sited, however, are those to which as a rule last thought is given – namely, what I call the workshops of the garden. These are the greenhouse and frames, the tool-shed, compost bins, bonfire, and perhaps chicken-house. The greenhouse must usually go in the sun, the compost heap in the shade, and the bonfire must not give offence to oneself or neighbours; but, if you possibly can, group all these things together. They are closely complementary to each other, and if well placed will save an awful lot of traipsing to and fro.

If you decide to grow vegetables at all, do not stint them for space. Ten rods (roughly 300 square yards or 250 sq. m.) is supposed to be sufficient ground for providing a family of four with enough vegetables for about nine months; a useful guide in calculation. Your small fruits can well share the kitchen garden if space compels, using fences or walls for loganberries, blackberries and tomatoes, and for gooseberries and red currants grown as cordons; but your apples and pears, unless grown as cordons or espaliers, ought to be kept out, for you can *not* grow acceptable vegetables under spreading trees. Given enough space, all or nearly all fruits are better in a small orchard apart and protected against birds by a cage of small-mesh netting. In the typical small garden, rather narrow and long, all these comestibles must of course go at the end furthest from the house, but in plots that have breadth of frontage use a side strip instead, so that the pleasure garden may benefit by the utmost length available.

If you wish to acquire merit and praise, one small but important detail is to site your beds for herbs – parsley, mint, and so on – and perhaps some lettuces, as close as possible to the door of the kitchen, so that the genius thereof can pop out quickly for a plucking.

ASPECT

So much for apportionment and layout on broad general lines. But there is one factor that may have a decisive influence on the garden as a whole or parts of it – aspect.

Observe the points of the compass fairly carefully. Note that the term 'south wall' means the side of it that *faces* south, and that the other side of it is consequently a north wall. Much of a gardener's skill is revealed by how he handles aspects. A south wall, or even a fence or hedge, is of precious value for sheltering anything on the doubtful side of hardiness, whether tomatoes or ceanothus; but a north wall, so often a place of gloom, does, as I shall show, also offer unexpected opportunities for adornment and use. On the other hand, an open northerly or easterly aspect is exposed to strong and biting winds, and nothing of flower, fruit, or vegetable may be grown there that is not resistant to them. Normally, therefore, you must begin by reserving the sunniest parts of the garden for whatever you decide to make your main show – herbaceous border, rose garden, carnation beds, etc. – and for vegetables and fruit. For roses, other than ramblers or climbers, the site reserved should be out in the open, not closely shut in by walls, fences or high hedges. If there is a wall facing S, W, or SE, don't waste it by running a path close to it, but make there the widest border that you can.

The cosiest wall, after the south one, is a SW wall. There is a special catch about east and SE walls not usually discovered without experience – namely, that right up to the end of May the early morning sun will beam upon blossom or fruitlet encrusted with frost, and, by the sudden thawing, rupture them; whereas on a SW or west wall the thaw is gradual. Large trees, or even those of medium size, may also strongly influence layout. If they are retained for their own merit and virtue – and no good tree should be committed to the axe without strong cause – face the fact that very little will grow beneath them, certainly no vegetables or fruit.

DESIGN

Now a word or two about design, but only, I am afraid, a few pointers.

Design should be studied from the windows of the principal living-rooms overlooking the garden. The view as a whole – the 'garden picture' – is the thing. Length of perspective is much to be desired and a focal point to which the eye is instinctively attracted will help to form a basis of design, such as a seat, a sundial, a prominent tree, a distant feature.

The apparent length can often be artificially increased with dramatic effect by slanting the main axis, as for example, from SE to NW. On the other hand, in gardens that are not too minute, a charming series of pictures can be devised by dividing the plot into several compartments, each having its own special character, but without entirely blocking the end prospect. In every kind of design be especially careful to keep the centre open; do not clutter up the middle distance. In most gardens this means grass, which provides the stage for the whole coloured drama, but in tiny town gardens paving or gravel make good, trouble-free substitutes.

If you aim at a very formal design, straight lines are the thing, but otherwise think in terms of soft, smooth-flowing curves, which are easy on the eye as well as on the mower. Curves greatly increase the apparent size of a small garden; but no snaky wriggles, please.

Trees, lawns and paths are the dominant features in creating a garden atmosphere. Trees, especially those in the background and on the perimeter, provide the chief architectural element and they may be needed also to screen oneself from neighbours or to hide some hideous feature outside one's own domain. Paths should be as few as possible and should follow the general rhythm of the overall design, straight or curved; do not bend or wriggle a path unless there is a physical reason for so doing. If a very long straight line imposes too great a strain on the eye, create some justification for a bend by placing a shrub, pool or other artifice that the path must avoid.

Surprise is a factor as important in garden design as in war. Some sudden twisting in a path, a hedge tactically sited, disclosing unexpectedly some embowered place, a retired rose garden, a pool, give charm and variety to the otherwise commonplace. Alexander Pope very aptly enjoined us—

> Let not each beauty ev'ry where be spy'd,
> Where half the skill is decently to hide.
> He gains all points, who pleasingly confounds,
> Surprises, varies and conceals the Bounds.

Garden and house being one, the house itself must be included in the design. If the style of the house permits, some sort of paved terrace, however small, will give an architectural unity to the whole. The style of house may also dictate whether the garden shall be formal – of geometrical outline, maybe embellished with a sunken enclosure – or naturalised, simulating a slice of nature. The latter course is seldom practicable in small places, and a mort of skill and judgment is needed to save any such attempts from looking sham. In the very wee plot of a town house, an all-paved garden, if it suits the style of house, is often a happy answer, enamelled with rock plants and adorned with trees in tubs. But whatever the *motif*, avoid fussiness and too much fragmentation. Simple and bold effects are best. Shun all bearded gnomes, giant frogs, and reflective storks. Shun oddities and beds of horrid shape.

Factors that may influence design are the nature of the soil, the climate, and the nature of the site. Their importance is felt more when we come actually to consider what is to be grown, but it is convenient to mention them here. The merits of soils are dealt with in Chapter 3, and climate is often related to it. It is no use attempting to grow in the Midlands or in Aberdeen the more tender flowers, fruits and vegetables that may flourish in Cornwall or even Ayrshire (for parts of Scotland are bathed by the Gulf Stream, and are much milder than more southerly latitudes). The sea is also a mellowing factor, but creates its own problems of violent, salt-laden winds. Obviously, also, Norfolk is less suitable than Wales for plants that require abundant summer moisture. Therefore, 'consult the genius of the place in all', and don't be satisfied merely to copy stereotyped notions.

Related to both these factors is site – whether hill-top or valley, meadow, heath, or woodland. The top of a hill will be windswept and perhaps acid, but will be more free of frost than a valley bottom, and, in spite of previous teaching, you can often grow peaches there in the open. In marshy bottoms brooms will fail, but some spiraeas and primulas flourish. In large towns the impregnation of the atmosphere by sooty chemicals will tax the functioning of the leaf-organs of many plants – a study that we shall come to immediately in the next chapter. I have dealt fully with these and other related matters in *The Design of Small Gardens*.

2

THE PLANT

ROOT AND BRANCH

The plants that adorn our gardens or feed our bodies have come to us from all over the world, and gay strangers from China and Peru, Persia and Africa, mingle cheerfully with our own natives. The tomato and potato go into the same pot as our coastwise cabbage and seakale. The foxglove and the heather dwell at peace with the rhododendron and the dahlia. Their origins are as mixed as their nationalities – stony mountain-top, lush meadow, chalky down, shadowy woodland, the dry and open moor, and many other diverse conditions.

These mixed origins have through the ages caused many plants to evolve special characteristics to ensure their survival, conditioned by more or less heat, more or less water, more or less lime, and so on. The cactus and the water lily, the buttercup basking in the sun, and the ivy creeping in the shade bear witness to a wonderful adaptability. Yet, if we except such freaks as the mushroom, all plants clamour in common for certain essentials. It is the gardener's business, if he hopes to be successful in his occupation, to know a little about both these diversities and these common factors, which form what I call the social science of plant life, so that he shall not torture waterside primulas in roaring sun or brooms in water-laden hollows, and so that he shall intelligently practise the simple arts of planting and propagating.

The plant derives its health and nourishment principally through two organs – the root and the leaf.

Through its roots it obtains its food from the soil, which it absorbs in the form of soluble salts, i.e. through the agency of water. The root may be a 'tap' root – a thick member growing straight downwards, as in the lupin and the dandelion and the carrot. Or the root may branch and re-branch in the same manner as the leaf-system above ground; of such nature are 'fibrous' roots, as in the rose and many others. These are the methods by which the plant explores for its food. Absorption is not, however, by the larger visible roots, but by minute, almost invisible root-hairs which form as a fine down near the tips of the roots. Thus it is important to damage the roots as little as possible when transplanting and to lift them with a 'good ball of soil'.

Through its leaf, which is pitted with an immense number of tiny pores, the plant performs a much more involved and indeed mysterious process. It transpires or sweats, getting rid of excess water in its system; it breathes, taking in those gases it needs and rejecting others; and, through the agency of the vital green substance known as chlorophyll, it transmutes the elements of the air into carbohydrates, its energy food.

From this much-simplified outline of plant processes, we see that there are five elementals for healthy growth, and some important lessons emerge for the practical gardener.

ELEMENTAL NEEDS

First, like human beings, plants need *air*; therefore they must not be overcrowded. Competition is a law of nature's life.

Secondly, *light*, in order that the leaves may absorb the radiant energy of the sun. A film of dirt on the leaf or the obscurity of overhanging trees restricts light radiation. Most plants require light all day, but many have conditioned themselves to living in the diffused light of partial shade, notably plants with large, thick, extra-green leaves such as the rhododendrons and the laurel. A very few are accustomed to even deeper shade. The riddle of the shady border or corner to be found in nearly every garden is often a tough one to solve, but there are several degrees of shade. There is the 'high' or 'dappled' shade in which rhododendrons, camellias, and most lilies rejoice; the oblique shade cast by a building, wall, or fence which we can embellish with many delights – pyracantha, camellia, clematis, winter jasmine, several roses, etc.; and the more extreme problem of the dense shade immediately beneath a large tree, for which there are few enlivening themes except in the leafless days of early spring, when many of the bulbous plants will gaily enamel the bare earth.

Third and fourth needs are *heat* and *water* in varying degrees according to the source of origin of the plants. These need not be emphasised, but what is less obvious is that the process of transpiration may be critically affected by excessive heat, by wind, and by a dry atmosphere. All these may cause the plant to transpire faster than it can take in water by the roots; and it then droops, just as a man droops in the tropics if he drinks less than he sweats. It is for this reason that the gardener must: (a) keep the atmosphere of his greenhouse damp in hot weather; (b) when raising new plants from cuttings, protect them with shade and with a 'close' atmosphere that checks transpiration; and (c) transplant all large subjects when transpiration has ceased altogether or is at its lowest. Thus, deciduous shrubs are planted in winter, when they have shed their leaves, and evergreens either at the same time in mild climates or in mid-April in others, when the soil is thoroughly moist but the temperature high enough to promote rapid new root growth though not high enough for fast transpiration.

Here again many plants have specially conditioned themselves. The cactus, with thick, fleshy stem and leaves reduced to mere needles, is an extreme example of a plant conditioned to prolonged drought and heat. Less extreme examples are our own gorse and broom, stonecrop and house leek. These can 'drown' in water-logged ground, just as shade lovers can die from sunstroke if planted in intense light. At the opposite extreme of the scale are the water lilies and their kind.

Last, the *soil* must be the right one for whatever is grown, which means that the gardener must choose the right families of plant. There is no collectivism or communism in the vegetable world. But whatever the classification of the soil – sandy or marly, acid or alkaline, and so on – the essential constituents for healthy life should be present, and in the right proportion and balance. A pronounced deficiency may cause a premature discoloration of the leaf, which is thus prevented from doing its job. By no means all plants like a rich diet, but we may say that the highest common factor is a medium loam, dark in colour and slightly on the acid side. This is dealt with more fully in the next chapter.

THE BLOSSOM

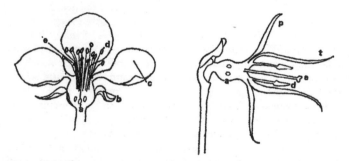

Sectional sketches of apple blossom and daffodil, showing: **a**, *ovary;* **b**, *sepal;* **c**, *petal;* **d**, *anther;* **e**, *stigma;* **p**, *perianth;* **t**, *trumpet-shaped corolla.*

I have no room for a chapter on botany, and would urge those who have not learnt this subject to get a small elementary book about it. But, to make other chapters intelligible, I must say a brief word about the blossom.

Flowers vary greatly in their construction, but in a normal one there will be several 'whorls', or rings, of different members. Immediately below the bud may be a ring of rudimentary leaves called bracts, which, in some flowers, as in the poinsettia, form the chief object of beauty rather than the flowers, but usually they are insignificant.

The bud itself is encased in a ring of protective sepals, collectively called the calyx. This likewise may be the plant's decorative feature, as in the clematis and anemone, which have sepals but no petals. Within the calyx is normally a further ring, this time of petals, known collectively as a corolla. A term that is used of the narcissus in particular is 'perianth', which is a calyx and corolla joined together, forming the round shield behind the trumpet.

Within the corolla appear the creative organs of the plant. The male organ is collectively known as the stamen, crowned with an anther loaded with brightly coloured pollen. The more complicated female organ is known collectively as the pistil, its most prominent part being the stigma, and when the male pollen falls upon the stigma, germination takes place and a seed is formed.

Many plants carry separate male and female blossoms, as in sweet corn, and others bear males on one plant and females on another. In general, self-fertilisation is abhorrent to nature. Thus if the holly fails to berry, it is not because of any occult prescience about the approaching winter, but merely because the female flower has not been successfully pollinated by a nearby male. Similarly, many fruit trees, especially the sweet cherries and many popular apples (including 'Cox's Orange Pippin'), are self-sterile and need a close companion of another brand to form their fruits. Even when both male and female organs are carried in the same flower there is often a device to forestall self-fertilisation.

TENDER AND HARDY

Besides these quiddities, plants have diversities of even greater general importance to the practical gardener.

One such diversity is in their resistance to frost, and in this characteristic we classify them thus:

A **tender** plant is one that at all times requires warm and genial conditions; we shall have few dealings with them here.

A **half-hardy** plant may stand fairly low temperatures, or possibly a light ground frost, such as antirrhinums.

A **hardy** plant is one that can stay outdoors all its life, enduring hard frosts, some more than others. This is all that 'hardiness' means in this country. It does *not* mean that you can treat the plant roughly, stick it anywhere without proper cultivation, and leave it to fend for itself. This misconception explains why thousands of pounds' worth of good seed is wasted every year, especially in 'hardy annuals', by those who imagine that the seed has merely to be broadcast lightheartedly anywhere. One has only to contrast, say, clarkia carelessly sown on untilled soil with the same plant thinly sown on well-dug, manured soil, to realise both how poor and how splendid this ill-used flower can be. Of only very few plants is it true that they thrive in poor and rough conditions.

THE SPAN OF LIFE

Our next classification for garden purposes is according to the span of life.

An **annual** is a plant which germinates from seed, flowers, dies, and reproduces its seed again all in one year or season. It may be hardy, half-hardy, or tender. Most vegetables are annuals, and there are annual forms of several longer-lived flowers, such as the annual chrysanthemum, the annual lupin, and the annual larkspur. We gardeners also in practice treat as annuals some plants that by nature would live longer, e.g. antirrhinum.

A **biennial** is a plant that germinates from seed this year, and blooms and dies next year. Sweet William, wallflowers, and Canterbury bell are examples. Here again there are hardy ones and others.

A **perennial** has a continuous life over a period of years, and it may be hardy or otherwise. A very large group, varying from the oak to the violet.

A **herbaceous** perennial is one which hibernates by shedding all its upper growth in winter, stem and leaf alike, right down to ground level, but retains life in its roots and crown. This class includes all the popular families that dwell in the 'border', from the delphinium downwards, as well as the humble rhubarb. In fact, however, a few plants classed as herbaceous do retain their foliage all winter, as in violas, pinks and primroses.

Another special category of perennial is the large and assorted congregation of **bulbs** and their kind, such as the daffodil and the dahlia.

3

MOTHER EARTH

TOP SOIL AND SUBSOIL

What goes on underground?

Since plants imbibe food through their roots, this enquiry should be the first and constant concern of the gardener, to an extent far greater than most of us realise. Earth is the mother of all, and her children's health depends on her own. Understand your soil and keep it in good heart and sweet temper. This is the beginning of wisdom. Project your thoughts underground, and ponder what is happening around the roots and whether the feeding and physical condition and drainage of the soil are adequate and balanced. 'Whoever begins a garden,' said Sir William Temple as far back as 1685, 'ought in the first place, and above all, to consider the soil, upon which the taste of not only his fruits, but his legumes and even herbs and salads, will wholly depend.'

Over most of the land formations of the earth the forces of nature have since times of pre-history gradually manufactured a thin film of soil compounded partly of pulverised rock surfaces and partly of the decayed vegetable and animal wastes of countless centuries. This film we call top soil or fertile soil. It is not a lifeless mass, but teems with tiny organisms, which we may refer to as bacteria. Among them are bacteria whose purpose is to transmute the elements that are in the earth into soluble forms which plants can imbibe through their roots. Thus the ammonia contained in dung is converted by degrees into nitrates.

To retain fertility, top soil needs aeration by some means, as by digging, and it needs replenishment in some degree with animal and vegetable wastes. Thus when we put dung or decayed vegetable matter into the earth we are feeding the soil, whereas artificial or chemical fertilisers merely feed the plant. We say of a soil, therefore, that it contains, or does not contain, a high proportion of organic matter – that is to say, matter which has originated from some order of creation having the organs of life and growth.

Below this thin film of top soil there is a subsoil. It may be only an inch or two below the surface, as on chalky downs, or it may be some feet below. Relatively it is a stolid and inert mass, and its lack of organic matter is shown by its lighter colour. For this reason subsoil should not be brought to the surface, except by the experienced hand who knows how to deal with it, but should be kept at its proper level. Builders are notorious authors of this infamy. It can, however, be made fertile by creating those conditions that will encourage the bacteria to explore it, namely, by letting in air and digging in organic matter. When therefore we speak of a 'good depth of soil' we mean one that has been deeply worked by man or nature, and unobstructed by rock, gravel, chalk, water, and so on.

TYPES OF SOIL

We should accordingly look first of all at the physical structure of soil. The main classes of soil ingredients for our purpose, in addition to a certain amount of air and of water, are: sand, clay, lime (as in chalk, oolite, lime-stone), and humus.

To be useful to man's husbandry two or more must be blended together. Thus chalk and clay together form marl, famous for making a hard, enduring cricket pitch. Sand, clay, and humus form loam, the essential type of soil needed for nearly all crops. The characteristics of these soil con-stituents which it is important for the gardener to understand are briefly these.

Sand, being composed of relatively large, rough, and loose particles, holds air (and therefore warmth) but not water. It makes a soil 'light' and easily workable, but it has no food value and its properties are purely phys-ical or mechanical. Soils containing too much sand 'dry out' quickly, and are said to be 'hungry', needing frequent feeding with organic matter. There are a great many types of sand; builder's sand is of little use to the gardener, who wants it sharp and rough, and 'sharp, silver sand' is a com-modity he will constantly need, especially for potting and for raising seedlings.

Clay, by contrast, is a tightly bound mass of tiny particles. There are several types of it, including the boulder clay of the North and the yellow clay of London. It holds water too much and obstructs the passage of air. It is cold, stiff, sticky, and stubborn to the spade. When really dry it becomes brick-like and cracks. But it is chemically active and itself provides plant food. Clay and sand together thus balance and correct each other's faults. Soils preponderating in clay are called 'heavy'.

Lime is a very versatile factor and is sufficiently important to have a section to itself, but we may note here that pure chalk requires large quan-tities of organic matter to bring it to fertility.

Humus is the precious element, so elusive of easy definition, that is the product of the decomposition of vegetable and animal (i.e. organic) matter. It is the heart and soul of soil, which, without it, would be an aggregation of lifeless mineral particles. You can, however, have too much of it, as man can of rich foods, and a few families of plants prefer a spartan diet poor in humus. Humus darkens and warms the soil.

Peat is vegetable matter long decayed in waterlogged conditions. The peats that are used for horticultural purposes are 'acid', and therefore palat-able to plants that dislike lime. Peat is by no means the only or the best form of acid soil, but it has a great many horticultural uses. It holds moisture in the manner of a sponge without clogging drainage, is a marvellous conditioner of clay soil, provides a soft, easy root-run for young plants and is a component of many 'composts' for pots and boxes. For general purposes one uses a 'granulated' peat of medium grade, but other grades are available for special purposes. Using peat has negative environmental consequences and you may prefer to use one of the peat substitutes that are available for some uses.

Tree bark (as in the proprietary 'Forest Bark') is an alternative to peat for some uses. It de-nitrifies, which is not a problem if the bark is used as a mulch, but is it the mulch is dug in.

We see from the above brief classification, therefore, that in all types of soil we require as a rule ample humus, that the best soil for general purposes is a well-balanced loam and that certain plants (called 'calcifuges') regard lime with marked distaste. A special form of loam that will be often referred to is 'fibrous' loam, which is a loam containing many fine fibrous roots in decay, as of old turf – a grand plant food.

CHEMICAL ELEMENTS

As important as the physical properties of a soil are its chemical qualities. The principal are: nitrogen, phosphates, potash, and calcium.

There are several others, but they are matters for the specialist, and should not be monkeyed with. The importance of these four is that they need constant renewal in cultivated soil. The qualities in them that we should specially note are:

Nitrogen improves foliage, making the plant large and leafy and a lush green. Therefore it is specially good for 'greens', and in the young period of plant life generally. It is apt to be deficient in regions of heavy rainfall, especially on the tops of hills (as is lime).

Phosphates are specially valuable for root crops and roots generally, and for the ripening of seed.

Potash is noted for its effect on fruit, and is also good for foliage, which becomes scorched at the edges under a potash deficiency; in shrubs it ripens the wood and promotes the formation of flower-buds.

Calcium is the element found in limestone and chalk; it is a plant food and promotes the decomposition of vegetable matter.

The important thing in a soil's chemical make-up, as in its physical structure, is correct balance, though not always a balance in the same proportions. An excess of nitrogen may be as harmful as a deficiency of potash (a subject dealt with shortly in Part 4). We come now, therefore, to the means by which any such unbalance, or wastage, in the soil's condition can be made good. The deficiency may be on nature's part, as when there is a lack of lime, or it may be caused by the exhaustion of one of the soil elements by a particular crop. In cultivated places a certain amount of wastage is always going on, for the soil is being eaten by what grows in it, though certain plants provide valuable secretions in the soil, such as peas and lupins, which develop nitrogen-bearing nodules on their roots.

The chief method by which nature herself corrects this wastage is by leaf-fall and other forms of decay, returning to the soil what came out of it. I am not going to indulge in any fanciful or pseudo-psychical transports on a subject essentially earthy but which some writers have made so delightfully esoteric, nor shall I disparage the virtues of chemical fertilisers, but I do insist that the basis of all good feeding is the liberal return to the soil of a certain amount of organic waste. We will therefore consider these first before going on to the inorganic foods, after which we will look at the versatile properties of lime separately.

ORGANIC FOODS

Compared with the chemical fertilisers, the organic ones are slow in action but enduring in effect. Most have also a physical or structural use to the soil, as well as their convertible chemical values. The outstanding ones for general use are old turves, animal manures, 'compost', and leafmould; and bonemeal is a commodity the gardener should never be without.

Manure generally, but not always, means animal dung. The best are those of the cow, horse, and pig, but the droppings of poultry, sheep, goats, and rabbits are also valuable. They vary greatly in merit. The dung of the corn-fed hunter and of the brewer's dray horse have greater value than that of the tradesman's nag. That of cake-fed cows is better than that of pasture-fed cows. Moreover, animal manures may also bring with them the seeds of weeds, insect pests, blow-fly grubs, and a smell, unless well rotted.

Cow manure is the best all-rounder, but horse manure is very good for heavy clays and pig manure for light (sandy) soils, but very smelly. For most purposes all animal manures should be 'short', referring to the length of the straw or other litter with which they are mixed. They should also be well rotted. Fresh manures liberate excess acids harmful to plant life. A raw, stiff clay is the exception; fresh horse manure with plenty of long straw is then an advantage, as the tubes of straw help to aerate and open-up the compacted mass of soil. Heavy clays are similarly benefited by digging in vegetable matter while still undecomposed, such as pea and bean haulm and soft, non-woody flower stems, in the lowest 'spit' of the soil.

Animal manures should not be left standing out in the open for any length of time. Their vitality is thus washed out by rain or evaporated by sun. If manure has to be kept in the open, stack it into a ridged or pointed pile, firmly compacted, and cover it with a large sheet of black polythene in a shady place; clouds of steam will be given off and it will shrink in volume. Manure may also be 'composted' either by itself or mixed with other refuse.

The method of applying manure to the ground is dealt with in Chapter 5.

Good animal manure is notoriously difficult to get nowadays in urban areas, but 'composted manure' of various brands can be bought in bags; most come from old mushroom beds and so contain some lime, and should not be used for lime-haters. The following organic manures are valuable:

Poultry manure is best used in the compost heap, where it is of great value. If used separately, apply it to the ground dry, partially or wholly decomposed, preferably in spring. Used raw, it tends to burn. Keep it under cover and dry. It is deficient in potash.

Dried blood. Nitrogenous; quick-acting; not cheap. Reserve it for the more precious plants. Two oz per square yard (70 gm per sq m) in spring or early summer.

Bonemeal. Mostly phosphatic. Good for almost everything; but it contains some lime. Apply in autumn or winter on the surface at about 4 oz. per square yard (140 g. per sq. m.). Bone flour is quicker-acting and more quickly exhausted.

Compost. The compost heap or pile has attained special favour because of the increasing difficulty of obtaining animal manures. Volumes have been written about it and fierce battles waged by the advocates of one system or another. We are even told that what seems a mere heap of decomposing refuse must be in tune with the Infinite. I fear that many people make it only into a mess.

The word 'compost' is itself ambiguous, for it also means a composition, or mixture, of soils for potting and seed-boxes. The compost heap is really a decomposition heap, for it is made up of vegetable and animal wastes in the process of decay. It is a humus factory. The only thing that is new about it is the notion of applying some special agent, uncouthly called an activator, for the purpose of hastening decomposition.

I shall not attempt to examine the numerous methods of activation. It is far better for the busy amateur to buy one of the proprietary activators and follow the manufacturer's directions. There are several good ones, such as Garotta.

The general idea is to heap up different types of refuse in a confined space. Heat must be generated. Thus the heap should hold a certain amount of air and not be too squashed, and it should be moist but not wet. Exposure to sun, drying winds, and heavy rain are all alike to be avoided. Choose a site in natural or artificial shade, such as the north side of a large tree, with free circulation of air round the sides, and with a base of plain earth or brick rubble, not anything impermeable.

The materials to be used are dumped into a 'compost bin'. I have tried advertised ones and found all wanting. The best are simple, home-made ones, using slats of timber, say 3 in. wide, with a spacing of about half an inch between them, set vertically like the palings of an old cottage garden, but without their points, or horizontally like a gate. Make it 3 or 4 ft. square and about 3 ft. 6 in. high. The front panel must be removable, so that the compost can later be dug out and this is easily done if at each end it has a pointed leg, which is driven into the soil and pulled out at need, hurdle-wise. Cover the whole bin with a loose, but close-boarded wooden lid, hinged about the middle for easy access; alternatively, use a cover of weighted black polythene, but rig up some device to prevent it from sagging in the middle and collecting rain-water.

Several small heaps are better than one big one, for the heap must be built up quickly – within a fortnight in summer and six weeks in autumn or winter. In fact the small villa garden hardly provides enough material, other than grass, to make orthodox composting practicable and grass alone simply makes a squashy mess; but what can be done, with good but not best results, is to collect stuff gradually and then make a proper heap all in one day.

The stuff that can go into the heap comprises: (a) any soft vegetable matter from flower or kitchen garden, hedgerow or common, especially nettles, *green* bracken, pea and bean haulm, lawn mowings; (b) household refuse such as fruit and vegetable peelings and pods, vacuum cleaner contents, tea leaves and egg shells (these contain lime and should not be too numerous if the compost is to be used for lime-hating plants); (c) the dung of horse, cow, pig, chicken, etc; (d) fresh bonfire and wood ashes.

Do *not* use: hard-wooded stuff such as rose prunings or twigs; virulent or tough weeds such as dandelion, dock, couch grass, and ground elder; coal ashes or cinders; sawdust; nor any leaves of trees, which must be decomposed differently. (*See under* Leafmould.)

The vegetable matter should be well mixed up; grass mowings especially should be mixed with other components, or they will make a thick, slimy blanket, obstructing air. Bash cabbage-stumps with a heavy implement or underfoot, and roughly break up into short lengths the semi-woody stems of herbaceous plants. Separate animal matter from the activator by a layer of vegetable matter. Makers of some activators claim that it is unnecessary to turn the heap once made, but it is usually best to do so at least once, bringing what was formerly on the outside into the centre. An easier method than turning the heap *in situ* is to fork it into an empty second bin, turning the while, and cover up again with polythene.

Test when the material is ready by taking out a spadeful. When completely decomposed it will be black-brown, slightly moist, friable, and crumbly, slightly sweet-smelling, and bearing no recognisable trace of the original structure of leaf, grass, or stem. Such material is dug into the top spit only of the soil several inches below ground level. Really well-made compost, in which all weed seeds are destroyed, can be used as a top dressing.

Fish wastes. Not so easy to get in proprietary forms as it used to be.

Green manure. This means a crop of some quickgrowing plant dug straight into the ground while growing. Quickest and cheapest is mustard, which may be sown in August for autumn digging. Rape and annual lupin should be sown before the end of July. Not a complete food.

Hoof and horn meal. Used as for dried blood, and valuable for potting and for brussels sprouts. Slow.

Hops. Available in two commercial forms. Spent hops, which are the wastes from brewings, have little food value but are excellent for improving the texture of heavy soils. Dig in liberally at, say, 1 cwt. per 15 sq. yd. (or 50 kg. per 14 sq. m.) after weathering for a few months. Not so easy to get as formerly.

'Hop manure', in which the hops have been used as a vehicle for chemical fertilisers, is a first-class plant food for all purposes in which manure or compost are advocated. Easy to handle and to store. Apply to the top spit only, in early spring, according to maker's directions.

Leafmould. Nature's own method of feeding her plants is by leaf-fall. Man cannot do better (in general) than follow her example, in the manner that I discuss in the section on Mulching in Chapter 5. The leaves of some trees can also very profitably be composted and, as such, are valuable for potting as well as providing humus and physical properties to all kinds of soil. They must, however, be composted separately, being much slower to decompose than the softer wastes.

Use only oak, beech, or hawthorn. Stack them in autumn under alternate thin layers of soil until June, then 'turn' the heap and treat with an activator. Most other tree leaves are best burnt, especially those with tough stalks and midribs, such as chestnut, sycamore and ash, which take ages to decompose. Conifer leaves are useless. Leaves of roses and the larger fruit trees should also be burnt, for fear of disease. Tough leaves, such as those of the rhododendron, laurel and holly, are no good and can be either left to lie or burnt.

Liquid manure. A valuable means of feeding plants while in growth, either in the ground or in pots. Fill a small sack or sandbag with rotted, not fresh, animal manure, add a trifle of coal-soot if available and suspend it in a tub or tank of water. When the resultant solution is of a deep tawny hue, draw off a small quantity, dilute it to the colour of straw and apply through a watering-can when the soil is moist. There are also some very good proprietary liquid fertilisers, such as Maxicrop, Liquinure and Sangral.

In addition, there are the modern 'foliar feeds', which are liquid manures applied to the leaves by syringe or watering-can. The chemicals in these feeds are very quickly absorbed by the leaves. Useful for nearly all kinds of plant, especially those that are hanging fire, but are not easily absorbed by leaves with polished surfaces (such as those of camellias and rhododendrons) unless applied with a fine, misty syringe or unless sprayed on to the under-surfaces.

Seaweed. One of the oldest manures known, specially rich in potash and salt and a traditional fertiliser for asparagus. The best is the kind with long, broad ribbons or streamers and crenellated edges. Next best are the 'bladder' seaweeds that children like to pop. The smaller, bushy kinds, often coloured, are of least value. Weed thrown up early in the year is better than summer or autumn weed, and dried weed is more valuable than wet. Use fresh at about 1 cwt. for 6 sq. yd. (50 kg. per 5 sq. m.) or less than half that quantity dry. Dry it under cover, not in the open. You can also compost it, but it should be mixed with other materials, especially animal manure.

Seaweed is also the main constituent of some proprietary fertilisers, such as Maxicrop and Marinure.

Top spit or turf-loam is decayed turf from old pastures, or from one's own lawn, full of fibrous roots. Quite first-class for almost all purposes, it gives substance to a light soil and porosity to a heavy one. One can scarcely use too much of it. Stack it upside down, with a sprinkling of animal manure between the turves if available. For rhododendrons and other calcifuges, order lime-free turf-loam.

Wood ashes from hard-wood provide some potash. Useless if allowed to get wet. Of most value on heavy clays and peats; it may make other soils sticky. Apply lavishly. Nice for tomatoes and onions.

INORGANIC FOODS

The majority of these are what are called artificial or chemical fertilisers. They are quick-acting, easy to handle, carry no pests, and in experienced hands can be nicely adjusted to the needs of a particular crop. But their effect is not enduring, they feed the plant only and not the soil, they have as a rule little physical or mechanical influence on soil structure. Many are caustic to foliage, should therefore not touch any portion of the plant and should be applied when there is little wind. Their best use is as a supplement to organic foods, and they are of particular value in the vegetable garden.

The artificials are pretty strong meat. The golden rule in their application therefore is 'little and often'. They are applied in spring and summer, and they have merely to be 'pricked' into the top inch of soil with a fork or hoe.

Be particularly careful to store all chemical fertilisers in a really dry place and raised off the floor, so that there is ventilation beneath. The chief artificials are:

∾ sulphate of ammonia, which provides nitrogen;
∾ superphosphate of lime, which provides phosphate;
∾ sulphate of potash, which provides potash.

There are many others. With one or two exceptions, however, I don't advise anyone who is not experienced, or who is not a chemist, to use any of these or other chemicals singly, nor to do his own mixing. They are tricky things. Nitrate of soda, for instance, makes sticky soils stickier, and sulphate of ammonia makes acid soils more acid. Moreover, there is always a danger of the soil's essential balance being upset. Therefore, whatever the experts of the press or the air may say, it is far sounder for the amateur to buy only proprietary fertilisers, of which there are many excellent brands.

For general use he should get a 'complete' or balanced fertiliser made by a firm of established repute, while Growmore, though devised for the vegetable garden, is good for flowers, too (though not for rhododendrons and others allergic to lime). For special purposes there are excellent preparations to be had, such as Tomorite for tomatoes, and Tonk's formula for roses. It is only for exhibition that you need to fiddle about with odd ounces of nitro-chalk or whatnot.

The following, however, need special mention:

Basic slag is a by-product of blast furnaces in the manufacture of steel, and combines phosphates with lime. If finely ground, it is a valuable fertiliser where the need might be to convert an acid soil to a limy one. In contrast to other artificials, it is slow-acting and should be applied in the autumn at about 5 oz. per sq. yd. (150 gm. per sq. m.).

Soot from **coal** fires provides some sulphate of ammonia, but in variable degrees. Its fertilising value depends on how much sulphate of ammonia it contains. Darkens and so warms the soil. Good general stimulant with wide uses, especially for onions. Used fresh, is a repellent for slugs and other soil pests, but should not be applied to growing crops till at least three months old. Almost useless if it is allowed to get wet. 'Soot-water' is also useful, and is made in the same way as liquid manure. Never use soot from an oil-fired boiler.

Foliar feeding is a good and quick acting method of feeding plants of all sorts through their leaves instead of by the roots. See under Liquid manure, page 29.

LIME

Lime occupies a mid-way position between the organics and the artificials. It has several interesting properties, and its correct management is of great importance. It has both mineral and chemical qualities. It has a marked physical effect on the structure of heavy soils. It provides a plant food in a form of calcium. It cures club root in cabbages and allied plants. It promotes the decomposition of organic matter. It breaks down sticky clay to loose crumbs. It encourages worms, so should be used more sparingly on lawns than elsewhere. In excess its effects are harmful, and to a fairly wide range of plants, headed by the rhododendron, it is highly dangerous. Its chief uses are for vegetables and fruit, but carnations, flag irises, clematis and many other flowers also enjoy it.

The acidity factor

A soil may be already well endowed with lime by nature, as in the locality of limestone hills or chalky downs, and even far away from such features it may have been spread by glacial action. If so, you can do nothing to take the lime away, should you want to do so, except in small pockets, and even then it may seep back. If, on the other hand, the soil is not naturally rich in lime, its requirements by way of man-made application will depend on what you want to grow in it, and if you want to grow rhododendrons, azaleas, pieris, witch-hazel or the summer heathers you will use none at all.

Soils that are short of lime are termed *acid* – a term that will constantly recur in this book – and those that are well supplied are *alkaline*. Degrees of acidity vary greatly. They are measured by what is known as the pH symbol, followed by an indicative figure. There is nothing abstruse about it. Neutrality in a soil is represented by pH 7; figures below 7 represent increasing degrees of acidity, figures above it the opposite. For general garden purposes in this country best results come from a neutral or slightly acid pH reading – say from 6.5 to 7. Below 5.5 acidity may be so pronounced as to cause a 'sour' soil; in such a condition it smells unpleasant and becomes green, slimy, and mossy, and a heavy dressing of lime is at once called for.

The amateur can test the acidity of his soil by one of the outfits sold in garden shops or he can send specimens to the RHS. The tests often recommended by hydrochloric acid, or litmus paper, are not much use.

The application of lime
As lime has a chemical action, it should *never be used at the same time as any other soil dressing, especially animal manures*. With animal manures and sulphate of ammonia, in particular, it causes the loss of nitrogen. Apply it (if needed) at least a month before or three months after manuring and at least fourteen days before chemicals; keep it similarly well clear of the application of any soil fumigant (Part 4) and of soot. A convenient rule is to manure in autumn and to lime about February, but a better practice still, especially in the kitchen garden, is to do the operations in different years as described in Chapter 21.

Except as shown below, lime is applied by merely spreading it on the surface. Clays and peats absorb it easily, and can therefore take large but infrequent dressings. In areas of heavy rainfall, however, and on thin sandy soils, dressings should be relatively more frequent but less in quantity.

Forms of lime
For carnations, many rock and other plants, lime can be supplied in permanent form by limestone chips or dust. Another very valuable form in the flower garden and the orchard is old lime-mortar rubble; but, with the modern building practice of using cement instead of lime-mortar, it is now as difficult to get as horse manure. Good substitutes are roughly ground chalk or ground limestone as sold for poultry grit. These forms of lime should be applied at root level (for plants that need it).

For more general and widespread use the busy amateur will be content to buy a bag or two of hydrated lime, which is readily available. The real enthusiast will make his own by getting some quicklime fresh from the kiln (if he can) and 'slake' it by pouring water over it, when the lumps will disintegrate into powder. This is the real thing, hot and strong.

On light, sandy soils, carbonate of lime is better, being less easily washed through by rain.

4

THE GARDENER'S ARMOURY

So far we have not put spade or hoe to ground, and before doing so in the next and following chapters we ought to see what tools are needed for the job, with a few words on their correct usage.

Buy the best tools that you can afford, of good steel and strong ash; it is better to make do with a few high-quality ones than a multitude of second-rate articles that break in one's hand. Avoid all gimmicky, new-fangled tools. I have tried nearly all and have found them a waste of money, except as I shall show. Otherwise, the long tried and proved traditional tools are still the best.

The spade is the most important of all garden weapons. Get a size suited to your strength, but have a blade with a flange on the top edge to protect your boots. There is no room to examine the various methods of handling this weapon, except to say that the best and least fatiguing is with the left or lower hand palm downwards, acting merely as a fulcrum, while the right hand is used as a lever.

Forks are of two kinds – a potato fork with broad tines for lifting crops, and one with finer, round tines for digging. A long-handled 'lady's-sized' fork is a great blessing, having many uses and saving the pangs of 'gardener's back'.

Hoes are several and various. Most widely useful is the Dutch hoe, available in blades of different widths; the well-equipped garden will have several. The correct action is, walking backwards, to slide the blade to and fro at a shallow angle to and just below the surface, using both the 'leading' and the 'trailing' edges, as the RAF would say, in order to slice off weeds just below their crowns.

Next come 'draw' hoes, with the blade either close-coupled to the shaft or set on a swan-necked shank. With these you work forward, using a chopping or drawing motion. Used also for drawing a 'drill' or minute trench in which seed is sown, and for earthing up potatoes, but for the former purpose a triangular hoe is better.

A special form of draw hoe is the Canterbury hoe, having three short prongs instead of a blade. Valuable for breaking down the upper crust of stiff, heavy soils, using swinging blows as you work forward. The short-handled onion hoe is handy for working close to plants.

A rake is a vital tool for working surfaces to a fine tilth, especially when making seed-beds. The proper action is both backwards and forwards, pushing as well as pulling, with long strokes. Rubber rakes are first-class for gathering up leaves on lawns, paths and flower-beds. With circumspection,

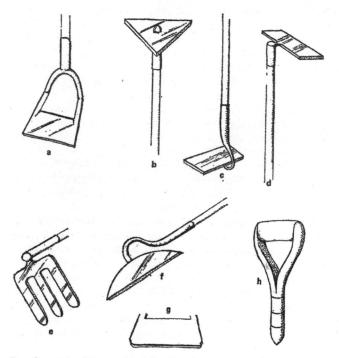

Some hoes and a dibber: **a**, *Dutch hoe (this shape, narrow-necked, is best);* **b**, *triangular;* **c**, *draw hoe, swan-necked;* **d**, *close-coupled;* **e**, *Canterbury;* **f**, *onion hoe;* **g**, *hoes should not get round-pointed, as this;* **h**, *a dibber marked off in inches.*

you can draw them right over growing plants without hurt; for this I use a rake cut down to about 8 in. wide.

A Springbok rake, splay-headed, has springy metal teeth for scarifying or aerating turf; plastic-headed rakes of similar shape are very light and useful for gathering leaves. The bamboo Hong Kong rake is crudely made and quickly wears out.

A companion to the rake is a little godsend named the Anita garden grab for lifting up gathered leaves or other trash. It consists of two pieces of curved aluminium attached to handles. You can lift a single leaf or a whole trugful without stooping. Obtainable from E. O. Culverwell Ltd, Brooks Road, Lewes, East Sussex BN7 2AY.

Trowels, which are used for planting small things, are best short-handled, and they must be strong, preferably with a curved shank, and of stainless steel if you can run to it. When using a trowel, always make the hole a little wider and at least as deep as the roots of the plant it is to hold. There are special trowels for rock work and for bulb-planting.

The dibber, simple though it is, is a tool to be handled with care. Use only one with a rounded point, or an air-pocket may be left beneath the seedling. Usage – make the hole, put in the seedling with the other hand, then make a slanting jab with the dibber 2 in. from the plant and lever the soil forward so that the seedling is properly embedded. See sketch, page 53. Firm lightly with toe or knuckle. To help in planting at correct depths, mark the dibber in inches, or centimetres if you like.

A garden line is essential for sowing seed, for transplanting seedlings in straight lines and for other jobs. It is easily homemade with two short pegs and strong cord, but the skirret type, with a revolving centre pin, is a great help. As you draw the hoe along it in making a 'drill', keep a foot on the line, or it will belly out. A measuring rod of some sort goes with it.

Cultivators usually have five springy prongs on swan-necks. Use only for rough work on unplanted land, otherwise it simply tears up roots. Not necessary.

The turfing-iron is a large, heart-shaped blade for lifting sods. Cut parallel lines in the turf with an edging-iron a foot apart or as needed, slide the turfing-iron forward under the turf between the lines about ½ in. (1.25 cm.) deep, thrusting with the thigh, and roll up the sod like a Swiss roll. Only occasionally needed and can sometimes be hired from a nursery. An extra-broad hoe or a spade can be used instead but makes harder work.

Of wheelbarrows, the old-fashioned wooden sort, fitted with extension pieces for loads of leaves and grass, is still best but pneumatic tyres will save damage to lawns. Avoid small iron horrors with handles so close together that your legs will not go between them.

Watering-cans are available in several sizes and shapes. The Haws type with long neck and two interchangeable roses is best. Always keep the rose on unless there is a very good reason for leaving it off. For pot-plants in the home get a miniature can with very thin spout and no rose. Be awfully careful to wash out very thoroughly any can that has been used for weed-killer; and preferably keep a special one for this purpose and put a dab of red paint on it.

A hose will be necessary, together with some sort of sprinkler. Never use a hose without one and get one that projects a fine mist, not large drops. See Chapter 5. One or more standpipes tactically sited will save much trouble. They can be fed by an alkathene main fitted by oneself.

Mowers are numerous in make and design. I can only say get the best you can afford; a good small one is better than a large cheap one. Cylinder machines with rollers back and front are best, and of course a motor-mower is highly desirable, together with a little transporting cradle on rubber tyres.

Rotary mowers should be assessed with caution. One popular type can easily cut off your toes; our local hospital has two such cases a week. One with a box or bag to collect the grass clippings is very desirable, for those that throw the clippings all over the lawn are damaging to it, clogging drainage and suffocating the roots; they also throw the clippings over beds and paths.

Rollers are rarely necessary in gardens today except for building paths and the like.

Syringes will be needed for spraying liquid insecticides, fungicides and foliar feeds. They must be capable of delivering a fine mist, and, if the purse will run to it, get one that works continuously, either from a knapsack on your back or from a bucket. It is essential also that the syringe should have a bent nozzle capable of being pointed upwards to spray the undersurfaces of leaves.

Other tools that may be needed are hand shears for clipping hedges and awkward spots of grass, long-handled edging shears for cutting the whiskers of a lawn, a crescent-shaped edging-iron for trimming grass edges, besoms, a daisy-grubber, a crowbar for handling rocks and making holes for posts, a heavy rammer and mattock for removing roots and stumps and making paths and steps, and other tools for specialised jobs. Weapons for pruning are dealt with in the chapter on that subject.

I have dealt here only with basic tools. Electricity comes to our aid for trimming hedges and the edges of grass, but at a price. There are also many motor-driven machines that plough, hoe, sow and mow. Whether you treat yourselves to one of these will depend on your pocket and whether the size of your garden justifies the expense.

5

GARDEN OPERATIONS

CULTIVATION IN GENERAL

Good cultivation and management of the soil are to the garden as diet, grooming, and exercise are to the horse or greyhound. Much depends on the beast itself, but the trainer must fit him for the stakes.

Cultivation begins with drainage, a *sine qua non;* in most established gardens it exists satisfactorily already (but by no means always), and if that is so, this chapter's next section, which is unlikely to arouse any transports of delight, can be skipped. After that, cultivation primarily implies digging, feeding, hoeing, weeding, and the creation of those conditions that will intimidate pests and perplex the agents of disease. Good mechanical cultivation of the soil will indeed by itself alone go far, without manuring and even with imperfect drainage. Listen to the No-Digging Brigade with the attention expected from an open-minded people, but remain sceptical. Remember that soils differ enormously from one another, and what may be acceptable treatment in one garden may be quite unsuitable for another.

Until the garden is established, the normal round of the cultural year is to dig the ground in autumn with the spade, manuring as necessary, to fork it over lightly in early spring, maybe adding lime, then to sow and plant. Afterwards, during the growing season, there is frequent harassment of weeds, fertilising perhaps, and of course various other chores. This is certainly the outline routine for the kitchen garden, and for the flower garden, too, when new beds have to be made or when crops of annuals or biennials have to be put into the line and replaced on becoming casualties. A virtue of autumn digging – in which the soil should always be left in large lumps or clods, not broken down – is that frost is able to bite in deep; and frost, working on particles of soil moisture as it does on water-pipes, will burst and crumble a heavy soil into fine tilth more efficiently than man can do. Newly-broken and neglected soils of obstinate clay may have to be 'ridged'. Afterwards, by the ordinary laws, east winds should come in early spring and with their harrowing breath drive off the surface moisture, leaving the soil in the condition most fit for sowing seed – moist below but dry and of a fine tilth on the surface – with the expectation of sun to come. If it could only be so always!

Circumstances may forbid this normal routine – a mort of rain in autumn, or occupation of the new house at the wrong time of the year. If so, the preliminary digging can be done at any time of year while the soil and weather are suitable. Never dig a soil when it is sodden, nor when it is frost-bound, but a light surface frost is no objection.

In established beds where some sort of perennial plant is already growing – herbaceous borders, rose-beds, shrubbery, orchard – the procedure is different. Here there is no autumn digging. A mere scratching of the surface, as by hoeing, raking, or the lightest possible pricking over with the fork of the top inch only, is all that should be tolerated, and even that is usually unnecessary. Any deeper disturbance serves merely to tear up roots and to disturb or mutilate lilies and other bulbs. I writhe, as the roots themselves must do, when I see Jobbing Gardener driving spade or fork deep into someone's rose-bed. What is far more valuable in autumn rather than digging, is the practice of mulching – loosely blanketing the soil with leaves or other organic matter in decay.

Of course, keep all beds, and indeed the whole garden, physically clean. Gather cabbage and other leaves, sticks, twigs, and prunings and all refuse. All are breeding places for slugs, bugs, bacteria, and other fifth columnists.

Now for the various garden operations *seriatim*.

DRAINAGE

The first necessity of good cultivation. To all normal garden plants a water-logged soil is fatal. The soil must, of course, be capable of holding such moisture as plants need – and some need a lot – but excess water must be able to drain away. In most existing gardens today there is little that need be done, but in new ground, or in major operations such as terracing, a drainage operation is likely to be necessary.

Pools of water lying on the surface for protracted periods after rain show a need for drainage; but often the necessity is less obvious. Tests should be made in any new garden by digging holes about 3 ft. deep in different parts of the garden, and if the level of water – or 'water table' – appears to remain permanently nearer to the surface than 18 in., then there is a need for drainage, either in that part of the garden – or throughout it.

The first problem – often very difficult in small gardens – is to decide where the waste water is to be directed. Very often the only thing to be done is to dig a sump-pit or soak-away.

A sump is a large hole dug at the garden's lowest level and filled with loose objects which will hold water in their interstices without allowing earth to fall through and fill them up. For a small job a hole about 6 ft. in diameter and 6 ft. deep will meet the need. The greater portion of the hole is filled with large lumps of clinkers, breeze, broken bricks, tin cans, etc. – any objects which will not set tightly together. Nearer the surface smaller materials should be laid in – such as angular stones and small brick, to the intent that water shall pass through but not earth. The top 12 in. is finished off with topspit earth, and it can be turfed over or used for the cultivation of shallow-rooting subjects.

Excess water from the garden is fed into the sump by means of one or more drains, which are narrow and shallow trenches containing some drainage agent. The depth of the trench will depend on the depth at which lies the stratum of impervious subsoil, or 'pan', that is obstructing the escape of the water. This pan is usually quite easily identifiable, often about 2 ft. down, and it is at exactly this level that the drain should be laid. The 'fall' of the drain from the highest point to the sump-pit need not be more than about 1 ft. in 50 ft., and the trenches, of course, must be straight. The main drain is fed by tributary drains running into it herring-bone fashion, and a main drain will be needed about every 5 yards in a clay soil, and about every 10 yds. in lighter soils.

Of drainage agents there are several varieties. A cheap and very effective method for a small job is to lay a course of twiggy faggots, preferably of hazel, in the bottom of the trench, 6 to 12 in. thick, according to the depth of the trench, cover with turves laid upside down, and fill with top soil.

A second method is to use clinkers or coarse rubble on the same principle as in the sump, graduating them from coarse to fine before filling in.

The best, but most expensive, method is to use earthenware field drains, which are short lengths of pipe laid simply end-to-end. They are embedded all round with a few inches of clinkers to prevent soil from silting up the pipes.

DIGGING

Four kinds of digging jobs have to be expounded – plain surface digging, trenching, bastard trenching, and ridging. There is also, of course, mere forking, which may be needed on vacant ground in spring, and is certainly required after lifting one crop of vegetables or flowers and before replacing it with a new crop, but this needs no description.

To simplify matters, here are three canons that apply to all these tasks when they are something more than a small or casual job:

First, keep the top spit at its proper level; never bury it, nor bring a lower spit to the top (though the expert can and sometimes does). On the other hand, each spadeful, after it is lifted out, should be roughly turned over with a twist of the wrist.

Secondly, work methodically row by row in clean, straight lines. If the plot is broad, divide it into strips.

Thirdly, at the head or start of each plot or strip take out an initial trench (of variable width) across the breadth of the job, and wheel the spoil away to the tail end of the plot. When one has dug through to the end, a vacant trench will confront one, and into this goes the spoil from the first trench. In deep trenching both top and second spits are wheeled away, but must be kept separate.

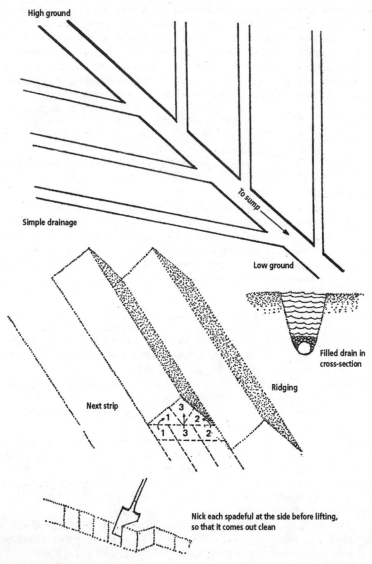

High ground

To sump

Simple drainage

Low ground

Filled drain in
cross-section

Ridging

Next strip

Nick each spadeful at the side before lifting,
so that it comes out clean

Drainage, ridging, and a digging trick.

Plain digging

This is a turning-over of the surface soil one spit deep (10 in.). Make the
initial trench about 15 in. wide, then dig out the next row of soil and throw

it forward into the empty trench – and so on, row by row. If manure is to be applied, lay it in the bottom of the initial trench, but in subsequent rows throw it on the sloping surface of the spoil in the previous row, so that it is distributed throughout the spit but with none exposed on the surface. Dig in young unflowered weeds without tap-roots but remove all flowered or seeded weeds and search to the uttermost extremity for tap-rooted ones, couch grass and other abominable 'underground movements'.

Bastard-trenching, or 'double digging'

Proceed as in plain digging, but fork over the bottom or second spit of each trench. Drive the fork down and turn the soil over. Bastard-trenching is almost invariably accompanied by manuring, and the manure should go into both spits, subject to what crop you will be growing.

Trenching

In this operation the soil is disturbed to the depth of three spits. It is hard work, considered by some people today to be unnecessary, and should be undertaken by less robust people in small doses, but it is of great and lasting value, expecially in the vegetable garden or where permanent and deeprooted plants requiring good drainage and plenty of bottom food are to be established. Manuring always accompanies it. The 'drill', illustrated overleaf, is as follows:

(a) At the head of the plot take out the usual initial trench or trough of *top* spit, a width of about 2 ft. being the minimum for convenience.

(b) Divide the trough by eye or measurement into two long strips. Dig out the front strip of this *second* spit and wheel away the spoil, keeping it separate from the top spit.

(c) Fork over the *third* or bottom spit, incorporating manure as necessary.

(d) Dig out the back strip of the initial trough and throw it forward to replace the second spit of the forward strip, incorporating manure.

(e) Fork over the bottom spit of the second strip.

(f) Return to ground level. Take out a new trough of top spit, half the width of the initial trough, and throw it right forward to top up the vacant front strip of the initial trough.

(g) Dig the second spit of the second trough and throw it into the vacant second spit of the first.

(h) Fork over the bottom spit of the second trough.

(i) Start the third strip, throwing the top spit forward on to the still vacant top spit of the second strip of the initial trough. The initial trough has now been completely rebuilt, each spit kept in its right place.

In any of these operations the top and second spits are usually the more important ones for manuring. If the ground to be treated was previously grassed, as for example when making a new bed in a lawn, then there is no more valuable food for the new bed than the old turf chopped up. But old

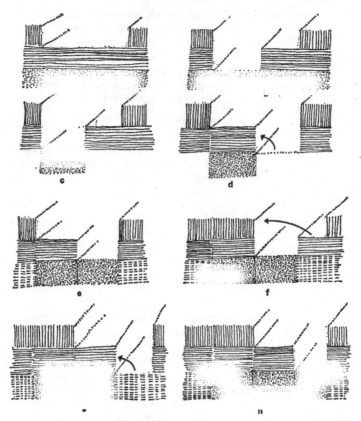

Trenching, the full operation: **a**, *initial trench about 2 ft. 6 in. wide, the spoil wheeled away;*
b, *second spit of front strip taken out and away;* **c**, *bottom spit of front strip forked over;* **d**,
second spit of back strip replaces that of front strip; **e**, *bottom spit of back strip forked over;* **f**,
top spit of second trench replaces that of front strip of initial one; **g**, *second spit of second
trench replaces second spit of initial one;* **h**, *bottom spit of second trench forked over.*

rough pasturage, if it contains couch, docks, dandelions and other horrors,
must be pared off with a turfing-iron and burnt.

RIDGING

This is an autumn or winter operation for heavy clay soils, the object being
to expose as large an area as possible to the pulverising action of frost and
wind.

Mark out the plot into 3 ft. strips, and suppose that we are working
from north to south.

At the head of the first 3 ft. strip take out a trench one spit deep and wheel the spoil away. Working backwards down the strip, throw the spoil from a second trench forward into the first but at the left and right edges of the strip turn the spadefuls inwards towards the centre, to the intent that a ridge shall run north and south down each strip, as though ploughed or as though roughly earthed-up for potatoes. (Sketch, page 40.) Leave the clods large and rough – and weather will do the crumbling better than you can.

MANURING

We have seen how to incorporate animal or vegetable organic matter in digging jobs. Rough and unrotted stuff should go into the bottom spits in full trenching or bastard-trenching, but the top spit should have only fully or nearly decomposed stuff, whether rotted animal manure, compost, leaf-mould, hop manure, peat, and so on.

Serious and often deadly injury is done to a great many plants if their roots have direct contact with fresh *animal* manures. If dung is applied in the autumn, planting in the spring will be safe for most things, but if planting is to follow soon after manuring, then 2 in. or so of fine soil or peat should intervene between dung and root; normally the bottom of the first spit is deep enough for manure. Remember not to apply lime at the same time as animal dung.

Granular or powdery manures or fertilisers, organic or otherwise, go into the top spit. The quick-acting chemicals and fish manures are spread on the surface and 'pricked in' by hoe or other implement into the top inch or two of soil either just before planting or during the season of growth. Slow-acting stuff such as bonemeal can go in at any time, but the most convenient is during autumn digging.

WEEDING

Weeds can be attacked by either physical or chemical weapons.

For a small infestation the human hand is best. For larger areas put the hoe to work, skimming just below the surface. If the soil is dry and the weather warm, fibrous-rooted weeds that have not yet flowered can be left to wither on the surface, but those that have seeded, or even flowered, you must rake together and either put on the compost heap, if you are skilful at that job, or else burn. Having thus got the ground clean, you can then prevent the germination of fresh weed seeds for long periods by treating the soil with a weed-inhibitor, such as Casoron G.

On paths, drives and terraces of stone or gravel Pathclear is very efficient and long-lasting, killing growing seeds, and stopping seed germination.

Tap-rooted weeds such as dandelions, underground creeping horrors, and 'vegetative serpents' such as couch grass and ground elder, and a few bulbous weeds defy the hoe. Any fragment of their roots left in the ground sprouts afresh, and there are only two ways of extermination – by poison or by burrowing patiently to their uttermost extremities.

Dandelions are effectively disposed of by painting the leaves with a glyphosate weed-killer as used on lawns, being careful not to make the solution stronger than advised by the manufacturers. A dab from a 'spot weeder' will also do the trick. Glyphosate can also be used to eradicate couch grass.

Bindweed, once such a curse to gardeners, is now also very easily disposed of. Just paint the tips or dip them into a jam-jar of a weedkiller containing 2, 4-D plus other translocated herbicides and the whole plant will die (but not its seeds). Should the wretched thing be found snaking itself through cultivated plants, untwine it and keep the painted portion away from its host by a piece of sacking.

The garden's most vicious delinquents are ground elder and marestail. The best antidote so far is Amcide (its active ingredient is ammonium sulphamate) if you can get it, but ground elder often yields to repeated attacks by a lawn hormone solution. In either case a dressing by a weed-seed inhibitor (mentioned above) should follow. The roots of ground elder are very brittle, snap easily, and any fragment left behind means a new plant. They love worming their way into the roots of your choicest plants, and if chemical attack fails there is only one remedy – lift the plant in autumn or spring, shake the earth out of the roots, and sort out the horrid tangle. If this happens to a bush or tree too large to lift, persecute the weed with relentless hoeing or plucking, and in time it will die from lack of the energy foods it needs from the air.

Two other methods of weed destruction are available if one is confronted with an inpenetrable jungle – the flame-gun and mass poisoning. The flame-gun is not nearly so alarming as it sounds, and will cremate all top growth but not all roots and, until you have learnt the technique, you are likely to make the air lurid with oaths. Good for paths.

The most virulent weed-killer is sodium chlorate, which will kill nearly everything. Use it only for mass weed clearance. About 6 oz. in two gallons of water does 10 sq. yds. (140 ml in 9 litres will do about 8 sq. m.). It goes fairly deep into the soil and can imperil the roots of underlying shrubs. If used on open ground you can grow nothing there for six months. For weeds in lawns see Chapter 19.

WATERING

All watering of plants must be *gentle* and must be *thorough*. So that it may be gentle, never use hose or can without a rose, sprinkler or similar fittings. Be especially careful when watering flower-pots not to wash out a hole in the soil.

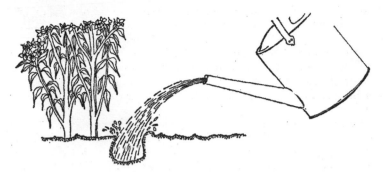

How not to water

Thoroughness also, when using a hose, can only be achieved by the use of a rain- or mist-forming fitting. Give a steady, gentle and prolonged soaking, instead of playing about by holding the hose in your hand. A surface wetting merely draws the fine rootlets to the surface and causes excessive transpiration. Test for penetration with fingers or a tool.

In the south and east of England we do not water our gardens nearly enough. In my own garden the hoses come out if there has been ten days without rain.

Some plants, such as hydrangea and rhododendron, need repeated heavy waterings in dry weather. Sweet and garden peas also dislike cold tap water, and if no rain-water is available a large tub may be filled from the tap and left outdoors in the sun for at least twenty-four hours. Rain-water is, of course, preferable for all watering operations when possible.

STAKING

Staking is necessary for non-rigid plants not of a lowly stature in order to prevent damage by wind and rain. It is rather a bore, and nowadays there is a tendency to stick as far as possible with plants that don't need it.

Delphiniums, gaillardias, peas and sweet peas, carnations and a few other things need staking early, but generally the right time is when a plant has made about three-quarters of its full growth. Staking must also be thorough and tidy; a large clump of chrysanthemums tied with string to a single stake is a horticultural Belsen.

For general work the easiest, neatest, and least conspicuous stakes are twiggy pea-sticks. Cut them to the required height, and plant them firmly so that they completely surround the plant or plants, with one or two extra in the middle of large clusters. The growing foliage will soon hide the sticks.

Less decorously, one may use bamboo canes instead, several to a plant, with string or raffia tied round at perhaps 15 in. intervals. Tomatoes need

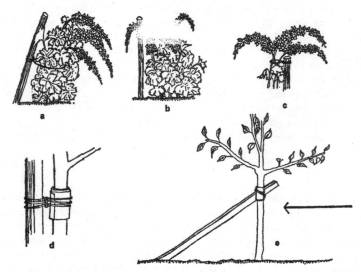

Staking: **a** *and* **b**, *how not to do it – the Weary Willy and the Hangman's Noose methods;* **c**, *delphiniums need one cane per flower-stem, not as here;* **d**, *staking a tree, showing band of sacking etc., and a simple method of tying to prevent chafing;* **e**, *another method, appropriate to fruit trees.*

something stronger, and square-cut posts are sold for this purpose; dahlias are often over-staked and usually four 4 ft. bamboo canes are enough.

Delphiniums are dealt with in Chapter 11.

MULCHING

This is the process of spreading a thick layer of leaves, manure, compost, peat or lawn mowings on the surface of the soil. It is highly beneficial.

Mulching with autumn leaves is particularly valuable, especially for shrubs, trees and hedges. They do four jobs in one – they keep the roots warm in winter, cool and moist in summer, deter the emergence of nearly all weeds and finally rot down into a rich humus. Undoubtedly mulching is the thing. Use only the leaves of oak, beech, hawthorn or soft leaves such as those of hydrangeas. Leaves with tough footstalks and veins, such as those of chestnut, sycamore, plane and ash, will not serve; nor will thick leathery ones, as of rhododendrons and laurel. Leaves of roses and the larger fruit trees, all of which may carry fungus diseases, should be gathered up and burnt.

Mulch really deeply: not less than 6 in. of leaves, 2 in. of peat (which has limited food value). It is a positive command that, *underneath* leaf and peat mulches, you apply a liberal sprinkling of a good organic fertiliser, especially one containing nitrogen. Contrary to what is often said, apply all mulches, other than of animal manures and grass, in autumn. Leave animal manures till spring, or their properties will be washed out before root systems are in active growth and ready to absorb them. Keep all animal manures clear of the stems of plants.

Grass mulches, applied during the mowing months, ought to be free of seed and occasionally stirred, for they get very hot. Do not use grass that has recently been treated with a 'hormone' weed-killer.

Do *all* mulching while the soil is moist and warm.

Do not mulch carnations, flag irises, or any very dwarf, low-growing plants, such as helianthemums, heathers and thymes.

PLANTING

Slovenly planting is the cause of many a good young plant growing into a straggly weakling. The operation of starting off a plant really well in its new home is of critical importance to its future.

In general terms the requirements are − a well-worked soil, friable, damp but not sodden; a hole slightly deeper and slightly wider than would appear necessary; an arrangement of the roots in the hole so that they are let well down or spread well out and not crowded, twisted or cockled-up; a fairly firm treading or pressing-down of the soil with hand or foot; and a good watering-in, using rain-water if available.

A few plants have their special requirements, of course, and some, especially carnations, and all the cabbage tribe, need especially firm planting. Roses need not be watered-in. Depth of planting is also often critical. Generally it suits the need barely to cover the crown, but carnations and rhododendrons should be planted very shallow, phloxes rather deeply, roses covered by just about an inch, peonies not more than 2 in. and so on. All trees and shrubs should be planted to exactly the depth of the old 'soil mark' showing on the stems, and the method I use for ensuring this is to lay a hoe or rigid stick across the open hole, so that when the plant is lowered into the hole the soil mark should be level with the stick and the roots only barely touching the bottom and sides of the hole.

Whenever in doubt about the right tool to use, choose the larger − a trowel rather than a dibber, a spade rather than a trowel.

Plant always in what is called 'open' weather − that is, when the ground is neither frost-bound nor saturated. The soil should be damp, but not so wet that the boots clog. If, as often happens, planting has to be done in a dry summer spell, soak the ground thoroughly the night before with the hose if the job is a big one, or water the plants in extra thoroughly as you plant. I often put a little water into each hole with a thinspouted can before popping in the plant, and the effect is excellent. Of course, if planting a large number of seedlings one can't afford to be so finicky.

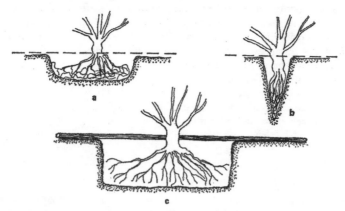

Wrong and right planting: **a**, *roots crowded, cockled up and crossing, crown above ground;* **b**, *ditto, crown too low;* **c**, *right, showing use of rigid stick to keep correct depth.*

Some plants, especially 'flag' irises and asparagus, need a slight refinement that we call 'saddle planting'. Having made the hole, shape the soil in the bottom of it roughly into a saddle, ridge or gentle mound below ground level, and lay the roots astride it. Leeks also expect a different technique.

In heavy clays work some peat or fine, loose soil into the hole before watering, to give the roots an easy start.

Trees and shrubs, including fruits, need rather more care than smaller growths. The plant having been 'offered up' correctly to its soil mark, partially fill the hole with fine soil and give the plant a little up-and-down shake to make sure that there are no air pockets in the roots. Then fill the hole, adding some fertiliser, firm the soil lightly, water and firm again an hour or more later when the water will have gone well down. In heavy soils do not overdo the firming, or compaction will result.

Plants in pots or other containers are often 'pot-bound', having a mass of coiled roots. Give a gentle squeeze to the ball of soil, tease out the roots and cut them back if excessively long. Evergreens often arrive in a ball of soil wrapped in sacking; remove this sacking with reasonable care, disturbing the ball of soil as little as you can. Sacking of a very open mesh, like netting, need not be wholly removed, but cut it off just below ground level. Balled plants can be settled straight into their prepared holes without any shake-up.

Trees and some shrubs need strong stakes. Drive them in before planting, making sure that they are straight.

When plants come from a nursery get them in their homes as soon as possible. If delay is unavoidable, they should be unpacked and 'heeled-in' somewhere convenient. This simply means making a rough hole or shallow trench in which the roots are laid, covered up with earth, and watered. Don't lose the soil mark of trees and shrubs by covering them too deeply. The plants are then safe for as long as you like. Those that arrive in time of severe frost are reasonably safe in their packings for probably a couple of weeks, but should be put in a shed and their foliage and roots moistened frequently.

6

BE FRUITFUL AND MULTIPLY

PROPAGATION GENERALLY

Virtually all plants can be grown from seed. In practice, however, there are often objections to this method of propagation, either because germination is difficult, or because growth is slow, or because the offspring may not resemble its parent. Nature herself employs other methods, as by stolons or suckers, by layers, by the formation of new bulbs, and so on. The tips of blackberries and loganberries, drooping to the earth, will take root and form new plants. The strawberry sends out its 'runners'. The stems of jasmine, hydrangea, clematis, and many other plants, laid on the ground, may take root anywhere along their length. The gardener takes advantage of these propensities of nature, and has invented some other methods himself. By his choice of method he is able to perpetuate a particular strain or to develop new ones.

Thus, moreover, will he save himself many bawbees. To buy the best stock his bank manager will allow in the first place, then to cause it to increase and multiply, is the way of the good gardener. Naturally it is slower than buying the full tally of ready-made plants, but from a small initial stock of the best quality he can fill his garden in a year or two and will very soon indeed, find himself with plenty over.

The several methods of propagation otherwise than by seed are called 'vegetative' as a useful distinctive term. A prime merit of plants so raised is that to all intents and purposes they are certain to be exactly like their parents, whereas seed, especially of the highly cultivated modern hybrids, may produce something quite different.

Broadly speaking, annuals and biennials, including virtually all vegetables, are raised from seed, and other categories of plants are more usually multiplied by one or other of the vegetative means. Thus the typical method of increasing carnations and rhododendrons is by layers, shrubs by cuttings or budding, fruits and roses by budding or grafting, many herbaceous perennials by division of roots, while some begonias will take root merely from a leaf laid flat on the soil. I am not in this book dealing with methods of grafting and budding, which usually require some experience and for which there is only very limited use in small gardens.

PLANTS FROM SEED

Quite a wide range of plants, however, can be raised perfectly easily from seed besides annuals and biennials, if one is content to wait a bit. Thus among hard-wooded shrubs broom seeds very easily; so does *Daphne mezereum*, and often with delightful results. Among herbaceous perennials the opportunity is still wider. Delphinium seed from high-class nurseries such as Blackmore and Langdon will readily produce first-class plants often quite comparable with expensive named varieties, though the bag will be a mixed one. Thus if one has the patience to wait a year the perennial border can be filled at very little cost.

The three main methods of raising plants from seed are by sowing by one of the following means:

Outdoors, direct into the plant's permanent quarters (*in situ*); many vegetables and hardy annual flowers are so raised.

Outdoors, but in a seed-bed in a special 'nursery', whence they are moved on into their permanent quarters, or often into an intermediate station, as soon as they are large enough to handle; this is the usual method for the cabbage family, for hardy biennials such as wallflowers and sweet William, and for hardy perennials such as delphinium and lupin.

'Indoors' in a greenhouse or frame, the seed being sown in boxes, or earthenware pans, or in pots; this is the characteristic method for starting half-hardy plants (e.g. antirrhinum and stock) and for tender subjects, but hardy plants may also be so started for special purposes. The wide, shallow 'half-pots', of clay or plastic, are very handy if only a small number of plants is needed.

The beginner should note carefully that only hardy plants can be sown direct outdoors, unless left so late in the season as to be hardly worth the trouble of sowing, but cloches often enable one to steal a march on nature for plants on the borderline of hardiness, such as zinnias, schizanthus, and nicotiana.

It is a broad general rule that plants do best if sown where they are intended to remain, without the wrench of transplanting; and for root crops – carrots, turnips, etc. – this is obligatory. Flowers with tap-roots, e.g. larkspur, similarly dislike being shifted, and so do some others.

Two golden rules of sowing, whether out or indoors, should be taken to heart early:

Sow sparsely (the parsnip is an exception);

Sow not too deep; large seeds such as broad beans go in 3 in. down, but very fine ones should have no more than a sprinkling of fine soil or sand over them, applied for preference through a sieve; on heavy soils seed is sown even less deeply than on light or thin soils.

Sowing outdoors

Whatever method of sowing is adopted – whether in a nursery bed or *in situ*, and if *in situ* whether in long straight ranks or broadcast – a fine 'seed-bed' must first be prepared. The soil must have been dug at least a few weeks beforehand according to normal methods of cultivation and allowed to settle. Preparation of the seed-bed then consists in reducing the top 2 or 3 in. to a good tilth; the smaller the seed, the finer the tilth.

First, lightly fork over the top few inches only, or hoe deeply. Next, lightly tread down the soil with the feet to crush lumps, moving along the row sideways. Then rake thoroughly to-and-fro, removing stones. Repeat the process of treading and raking as often as may be necessary, according to whether the soil be light or sandy or a heavy clay. The heavier the soil the more the treatment required. The last process is always raking.

This work should be done when there is plenty of moisture below ground but when the surface is sufficiently dry for the hoe to work easily without soil sticking to it. Conditions are generally just right after the east winds of early spring have dried off the surface moisture. 'The beginning of March,' says old Thomas Tusser 'or a little afore is time for a wyfe to make her garden, and to get as many good seeds and herbs as she can, and especially such as be good for the potte.' It is equally a mistake to do the work when the soil is dust-dry right through, and in a dry summer it may be necessary to make a shallow trench with the hoe overnight, fill with water and draw the soil back again when the water has drained through.

Having worked up a good tilth, make a 'drill' for reception of the seed. A drill is a tiny trench, which for very fine seed will be no more than ¼ in. deep. To make, or 'draw', the drill, set out the garden line, and, keeping one foot on it to hold it taut, draw the hoe along it, canting the hoe so that only a point of it penetrates the soil; a little V-shaped trench results. For very fine seed a pointed stake does well.

For large seeds such as beans and peas normal practice is to make a broad drill the full width of the draw hoe, using the hoe in its natural plane, or to use a spade. In the kitchen garden and the nursery, seed-beds should be neat, orderly and parallel; in the nursery the rows are usually about 4 in. apart. In clay soils a sprinkling of peat in the bottom of the drill will help germination.

The seed is now sown along the drill, either by pouring it gently out of the packet, or a pinch at a time with finger and thumb, or by means of a seed-sowing gadget. In the best conditions one seed every inch should normally be enough – larger seeds even more sparsely. The finer seeds may be mixed with sand for easy handling and even distribution. More detailed notes are given in the chapter on vegetables.

After sowing, cover the seed with the little ridge of spoil from the trench by drawing the back of a rake or edge of a hoe gently over the surface. Very fine seed can be covered by sprinkling fine potting soil or sand from a fine-mesh sieve. A sprinkling of coarse sand on the surface will help deter slugs. Label each row, not forgetting the date.

No further attention should be necessary until after germination, except for a watering with Cheshunt Compound for plants subject to the

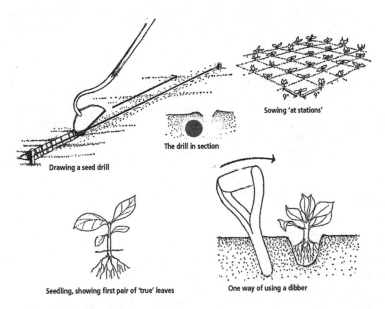

Drawing a seed drill

The drill in section

Sowing 'at stations'

Seedling, showing first pair of 'true' leaves

One way of using a dibber

Sowing outdoors and planting out seedlings.

damping-off disease. In prolonged dry spells a cautious watering through a fine rose may be necessary.

Seed may also be sown by broadcasting – sprinkling more or less at random. This is often done with annuals, but is not a method I care for. It is preferable to sow in irregular drills – serpentine, circular, as you will. Better still, however, not only for annual flowers but also when sowing vegetables *in situ*, is the method of sowing 'at stations'. This means dropping two or three seeds at selected spots, according to the ultimate spacing necessary, and subsequently thinning the seedlings to the most promising one when large enough. This method has all sorts of merits – it is economical, it is quick, it enables seedling weeds to be more easily identified and the hoe plied with greater safety. A good and quick way of sowing flower annuals at stations is to scratch a rough criss-cross pattern, like squared paper, on the soil, and to sow at the intersections of the lines, the lines being at distances apart suitable to the size of the plant – about 9 in. for the general run of medium-sized annuals.

When the seedlings have fully developed their second pair of leaves – i.e. the first pair of true leaves after the cotyledons or seed-leaves – they must be 'thinned out' if they have been sown in their permanent quarters, or 'pricked out' if they have been sown in a preliminary nursery bed. Thinning means reducing them so that those that remain stand at their final distances apart; or they can be reduced first to half-distances and later to full distances. Thus one may reduce carrot seedlings first to 3 in. apart and finally to 6 in. The thinnings can often be used – the baby carrots you would eat, the baby marigold you could transplant elsewhere; but some, such as the parsnip, are useless.

'Pricking-out' simply means lifting the seedlings from this nursery bed (or seed-box) – all of them – and replanting them more widely somewhere else, either into their permanent quarters or into some intermediate quarters. Lift them gently on to a pointed garden label, or similar small implement, with a little soil adhering to their roots, and get them into their next quarters as soon as possible. Do the job when the soil is moist but not sodden. Always handle seedlings by their leaves not their stems.

Be most particular to thin and prick out while the nurselings are still quite small; if left crowded together they will become weak and leggy and will never be of strong constitution. The way a plant begins its life is critical to its whole future.

Seedlings that cannot normally go into their final homes for some time, such as biennials (wallflowers, Canterbury bell, etc.) and perennials (delphinium, columbine, etc.), are pricked out into a nursery bed. This is a vital period for them. Give them a bed generously treated according to their kind, in an open position, not under trees; some will appreciate a degree of shade. In this bed they are planted out at distances suitable to their nature – wallflowers at about 4 in. apart, delphiniums at 8 in. or so. A typical course of events is for, say, wallflowers to be sown in June, pricked out when an inch or two high into a nursery bed, and transplanted into their permanent stations in the autumn.

Sowing indoors

For the general run of plants requiring to be started indoors wooden seed-boxes or shallow earthenware seed-pans are used, but sometimes pots instead. The same principles apply to all methods. If home-made boxes are used they should be about 2½ in. deep, and the bottom, if there are no gaps between the boards, should have plenty of holes for drainage. All receptacles must be clean. Old ones should be scrubbed with hot water and soda, or a fungicide, and dried before use. New clay pots should be soaked for some hours and then dried off.

The receptacles must then be 'crocked' – their drainage holes or slits layered with pieces of broken flower-pot or stones other than flat ones, to provide controlled drainage. On top of the crocks sprinkle some half-decayed leaves, or scraps of coarse fibrous soil to prevent the fine soil above seeping down and clogging the drainage.

The next task is to fill the receptacle with a satisfactory soil for young plants. For this you use the John Innes Seed Compost (a non-proprietary formula). Get it from firms of high repute only; its viability is limited. The prescriptions for it and other JI composts are given in Appendix 3 and you can make them yourself if you have the facilities.

Alternatively, use one of the proprietary composts based on peat or a peat substitute, sold in bags in shops. They are pretty reliable for ordinary things, but for lime-haters you must try to get a specially formulated one. These 'soilless' composts, if allowed to get dry, must be thoroughly moistened, but not saturated.

Fill the receptacle to within ¼ or ½ in. of the rim. Make the surface quite level by pressing it down rather firmly with a flat pressing-board, or a round one for pots. Then partially immerse the receptacle in water so that the water seeps up from below and nearly reaches the surface of the soil.

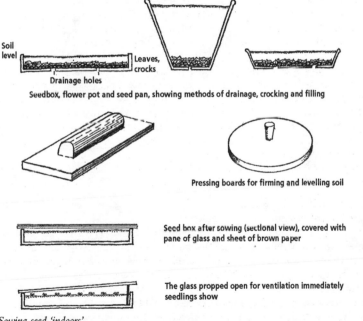

Soil level

Leaves, crocks

Drainage holes

Seedbox, flower pot and seed pan, showing methods of drainage, crocking and filling

Pressing boards for firming and levelling soil

Seed box after sowing (sectional view), covered with pane of glass and sheet of brown paper

The glass propped open for ventilation immediately seedlings show

Sowing seed 'indoors'.

Treat with Cheshunt Compound. Proprietary composts, if fresh from the bag, should not need soaking or treatment.

Broadcast the seed thinly on the soil, lightly sprinkle a little compost over it through a fine sieve, cover the receptacle with a sheet of glass and on top of it a sheet of brown paper. Wipe the glass dry every day, reverse it and replace the paper. As soon as the seedlings show their noses, remove the paper, tilt or shift the glass slightly to give more ventilation, and put the

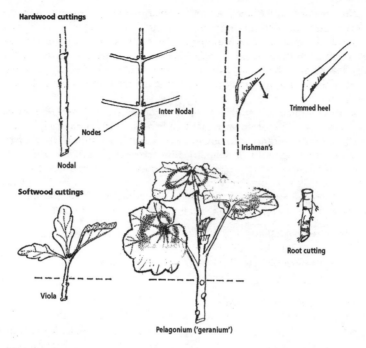

Hardwood cuttings

Nodes

Nodal

Inter Nodal

Irishman's

Trimmed heel

Softwood cuttings

Root cutting

Viola

Pelagonium ('geranium')

Taking cuttings.

receptacle close up to the roof of the greenhouse (*see figure*). After a few days remove the sheet of glass altogether.

This is the traditional method, but I find a piece of slate, or even hardboard, just as good. I am relieved of the daily turning of the glass, but must remove the cover immediately the seedlings show and shade them for a bit.

From now on see that the soil is kept fairly moist, preferably by immersion as before.

When the youngsters have developed their first pair of true leaves, prick them off into other boxes or pots, handling them by the leaves. If into a box, I like it to be 3 to 4 in. deep, instead of the shallow trays into which most nurseries crowd their seedlings. Use the same compost as before, treated likewise with Cheshunt Compound. Do not crowd the seedlings when pricking off. I like antirrhinums, if grown this way, to be about 3 in. apart instead of the usual jungle. Keep them well watered and as close to the light as possible.

CUTTINGS

It was a fortunate day when someone discovered that by sticking a twig into the ground a new plant would be born.

Not, of course, all plants, but a very great many, from pygmies of the rock garden to big trees. Cuttings are a very cheap and often (but not always) an easy method of multiplying. A cutting (by which is usually meant a stem cutting), is simply a limb removed from a living plant at the right time of year, and plunged into suitable soil. The base of the cut stem after insertion forms a callus or healing tissue over the wound and from this roots form.

It is not so easy to generalise about cuttings as it is about seed, since some plants need special treatment, but observance of general principles sees one through. Only perennials can be so multiplied, not annuals (except by experts); though some of those plants which are usually treated as annuals but botanically are really perennial grow admirably from cuttings if one is so disposed. Thus, if you grow antirrhinums from seed and one of them turns out to be particularly attractive, you can perpetuate it by cuttings.

The dominant considerations when growing from cuttings are:

∾ Selection of the right 'wood' or branch.
∾ Selection of the right spot to cut it.
∾ A soil in which it will 'strike', or take root.
∾ A shady site and a moist, close atmosphere (usually).

Selection of the right wood
Cuttings may be either of 'hard wood' or of 'soft wood'.

A **hardwood** cutting is a mature or nearly mature shoot of the current year's growth (what one might call a young adult shoot), taken from an established plant in autumn, or sometime when the plant is quite dormant and leafless. Plants for which the use of this kind of cutting is typical are shrubs, bush fruits, and roses – though not all of them by any means. The word 'mature' applies to texture and substance, not length. Side-shoots rather than 'leaders' are generally best, especially shoots springing from the base. Shoots growing on the shady side of the parent, or from a parent growing in light shade, are better than those in full sun.

Half-ripe cuttings, usually taken in early July are side-shoots (or maybe tips) which have sprouted during the current season and are beginning to get firm and woody at the base but are still soft and growing at the tip. A great many shrubs are so propagated, especially evergreens.

A **softwood** cutting may be either a young growth from a hard-wooded plant taken while the plant is actively developing in spring or early summer (as for fuchsia), or it may mean a cutting of a soft-wooded plant, such as viola, 'geranium', chrysanthemum, penstemon. Here again, on soft-wooded plants the nearly ripened shoots are usually the best; but several, of which chrysanthemum, dahlia, delphinium, and lupin are characteristic, require very young shoots taken when a few inches high early in the year, preferably cut off below ground level.

The cutting point

For our purposes there are three main types of stem cutting:

Nodal – those cut precisely below a node or joint or leaf-junction (examples of a node are the swollen rings of a carnation or bamboo). The term 'tip cutting', often used, implies a nodal one taken from the tip of a stem.

Internodal – used typically for clematis.

Heel – those made by cutting or plucking a side branch at the point of junction with its parent branch, and taking a strip, or heel of the parent with it.

As a rule, the best cutting is the nodal cutting, the cut being made cleanly with a very sharp blade horizontally, without slope. A safety-razor blade is just the thing if the wood is not too tough. Heel cuttings, however, are also extremely good. A heel is made by simply plucking a side-shoot from the parent stem by a smart downward pull, one's thumb being inserted in the angle between stem and side-shoot, but for a proper job you must make it into a 'trimmed' heel by paring off the frayed end cleanly with a sharp knife.

Except for those plants in which young growth is best, as noted, cuttings are usually best taken when the plants are nearing maturity, or at the end of their first flowering. Thus spring-flowering plants such as aubrieta and alpine phlox can be treated in June, and shrub cuttings in July

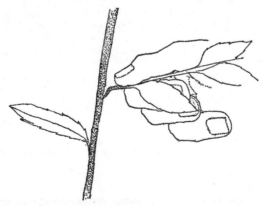

Taking a heel cutting: the thumb is inserted in the axil and the branchlet for propagation is severed by a downward snap.

or later. Sometimes the job can be done when pruning; gooseberry, black-currant, and forsythia prunings, for example, root easily in the open ground (in shade) as hardwood cuttings.

The Wisley pot: a polythene envelope is slipped over the wire frame and fastened below the rim of the pot by a rubber band.

Preparation of the cutting

The length of the cutting depends, of course, on the plant, but, whatever the length, 'short-jointed' cuttings are best – those with their nodes or leaf-joints relatively close together. A rose cutting is best about 9 in. long; camellias and azaleas a few inches, forsythias about 2 in., hydrangeas 5 to 12 in., heathers a mere inch or two. If the limb selected is too long, shorten from the tip, not the base; the base of a shoot is always better for rooting than the tip.

As the cutting has to be inserted in soil, all leaves are removed from the lower end for a distance of about one-third of the cutting. A good rule of thumb is to leave only two pairs of leaves above ground, but there is no need to be fussy about it, the purpose is to reduce transpiration until roots are formed. Heathers need no trimming.

Treat all cuttings, except very easy ones, with one of the root-forming 'hormones'.

Soil and atmosphere

Softwood cuttings, taken with their foliage on and the sap running, require a moist, close atmosphere in the shade. Sun, wind, and a dry atmosphere cause rapid transpiration.

For normal amateur work all that is needed is a deep box with a close-fitting glass lid, stood in full shade. Grey-leaved plants do not need these close and moist conditions, but do need shade. Specially designed propagating boxes of plastic can be bought in shops and garden centres at no great cost, and the prospects of success are widely enlarged if, at a price which is also enlarged, they are fitted with soil-heating cables, a subject which is discussed in the last section of the chapter on greenhouses.

Insert the cuttings in pots or half-pots, in a compost made up usually of one part medium loam, two parts peat (or peat substitute), and three parts sharp sand. The peat and loam parts can be varied. You may use one of the proprietary composts if you like, but I have not always found them satisfactory. Some plants, notably heathers and camellias, are started in a simple mix of equal parts sharp sand and peat (or peat substitute). Carnations and pinks and some other plants are best started in pure sharp sand alone. Sand is a very important ingredient for all cuttings.

Insert the cuttings round the edge, and nearly touching it and nearly touching each other. The one time that most plants like to be crowded together is when they are cuttings. Plant very firmly, pressing the soil about the stems hard down with the fingers, except when using a proprietary compost. Intimate contact of the basal wound with the soil is essential. Water thoroughly by immersion of the pots, and after putting them under glass give an occasional syringe of water in hot weather. For cuttings, many old hands prefer clay pots to plastic ones.

If only one potful is needed, push two bent wires into it and pop a polythene bag over them, secured by a rubber band below the rim of the pot; this is the 'Wisley pot'.

Transplant the cuttings as soon as they have rooted well, either into other pots separately, or into a nursery bed or into permanent quarters.

Hardwood cuttings are less susceptible to death from excessive transpiration, especially those taken when leafless and dormant. Therefore, if a frame cannot be spared for the long lease they require, they can be inserted in the open ground outdoors, provided the site is a shady one, a bed on the north side of a wall or hedge being best. Make a narrow V-shaped trench of the depth required by the length of the cutting by waggling the spade to and fro, sprinkle sand in the bottom of it, put the cuttings in vertically and with their leaves almost touching each other, return the soil, tread down very firmly, and water thoroughly. Such cuttings, inserted in the autumn, may be expected to root the following spring or summer, but top growth often starts first, so do not disturb them too soon. This is the method for roses.

ROOT CUTTINGS

The roots of several herbaceous plants, if cut into small lengths, will grow into new specimens. Examples are phlox, gaillardia, mullein, anchusa, oriental poppy, romneya, horseradish, and seakale.

Lift the plant, or expose a portion only of its roots, between November and April. Cut up a root into pieces 1–3 in. long (some plants longer). Cut the lower end diagonally and the top square, for identification (sketch, page 56). Plant vertically 2 or 3 in. apart in a blend of sand and peat and a little loam, square-cut end uppermost, and cover with not more than an inch of sand or sandy soil. Thin cuttings, such as phlox, may be planted

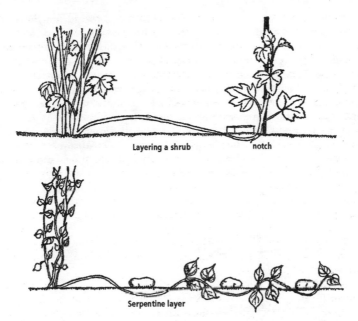

Layering a shrub   notch

Serpentine layer

Layering.

horizontally. Plant in deep seed-boxes, pots or a frame; if in boxes or pots, cover with glass as for seed. Water moderately until shoots appear, then more liberally before transplanting into a nursery bed.

LEAF CUTTINGS

A few plants can be propagated this way, including ramonda and fibrous-rooted begonias such as 'Rex' and 'Gloire de Lorraine'. In some the leaf is detached complete with stalk, and the stalk inserted in a compost of moist sand and leafmould. In others, as in the begonias, the veins of the leaf are nicked at several points and the leaf laid flat on the compost, weighted with a pebble or two. A moist, close frame or greenhouse is necessary.

LAYERS

A layer is much the same thing as a cutting, except that the shoot is not first detached from its parent. Layering is the favourite means of increasing carnations, and the special method appropriate to them is dealt with in the chapter on that subject.

Many shrubs are also so increased, such as rhododendron, winter jasmine, hydrangea, and some fruits.

Choose a well-grown young shoot that has not flowered, low down on the shady side of the plant and on its circumference. Make a small slanting cut or a notch in the back on the underside of the shoot, press it down into the soil, making sure that the soil gets well inside the lips of the wound and adding some sharp sand to the soil at that point. Cover that portion of the stem with an inch or two of soil and weight it down with a stone (better than pegging). Stake the growing end of the shoot to induce upright growth. Water. Late summer is the usual time. It is often necessary to build up a small mound or low wall of soil to receive the layer conveniently, and root formation can be assisted by treating the wound with a root hormone as for cuttings. When the layer has rooted well, of which new top growth will be the first indication, sever it from its parent, and move it to its new quarters when convenient.

DIVISION

This is the easiest of all methods of increasing stock. It is applicable to a great many herbaceous plants and to others whose habit is to extend themselves from the centre outwards, forming a dense and often matted 'clump', such as Michaelmas daisy, golden rod, helenium, polyanthus etc.

Lift the whole clump and drive two garden forks, back to back, through the centre. Levering the forks against each other, gently tease the clump into two, and further sub-divide if necessary. On tough and obstinate roots use a knife. Small plants can be gently pulled apart with the fingers.

The younger shoots round the perimeter of the plant are the best for new stock, and in old clumps the centre should be discarded altogether.

7

PRUNING

Outside the ranks of the expert, few garden operations are so misunderstood as pruning. Most of all, apparently, by our local authorities. The mutilation they allow to the trees in our streets and the shrubs in our parks is one of their several forms of vandalism. Another villain, whom I have already indicted, is the jobbing gardener who has had no technical training. One result is that every year our private gardens suffer enormous losses in apple crops alone.

It is notoriously difficult to explain detailed pruning in writing, and practical demonstration by an old hand is by far the best sort of tutorship. However, pruning is not a mystery, nor is it based on unreasoned rules of thumb, and the way begins to open up as soon as it is realised that pruning is based chiefly on intelligent observation of the natural habits and behaviour of a plant. This is the path I hope to point out, starting with the basic maxim of Shakespeare's sage old gardener:

> Superfluous branches
> We lop away, that bearing boughs may live.
> — The Gardener in Shakespeare's *Richard II*

Why we prune

The purposes of pruning are to maintain, increase, or prolong the vitality of a plant, or to keep it in bounds, or to direct its energy to a special purpose. Thus, in a young tree, the first task is to build up a sound and well-shaped framework, but when it is well-grown we shall have a different purpose. In the apple we shall seek, as a rule, to induce new fruiting spurs rather than new branches; in a rose we may want a large shrub with many small flowers or we may want it to produce a few large exhibition blooms, and we can prune it for either purpose accordingly. In a hedge we shall want a dense barrier shrouded to the ground.

The most elementary pruning is the 'dead-heading' of border flowers, by which we remove spent blooms in order to induce new ones, and this is a form of pruning that should be constantly going on. No plant should be allowed to go to seed unless it is grown specially for its fruits or berries or unless we specially want to gather seed, provided, of course, that the plant is not so big as to make the removal of all seed-pods unreasonable. We are also unconsciously pruning when we cut flowers for the house, and the canons of pruning should be observed when we do so. Similarly we are

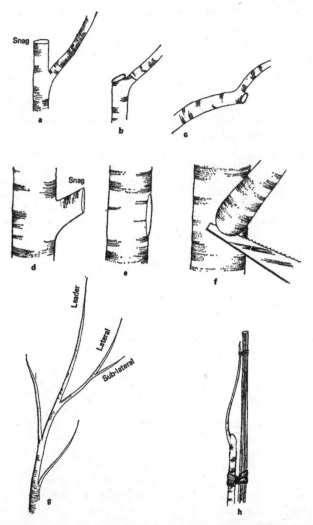

Pruning: **a**, *leave no snag – cut immediately beyond selected shoot (or bud) as in* **b** *or* **c** *according to habit of plant;* **d** *and* **e**, *wrong and right methods of lopping the branch of a tree;* **f**, *on any thickish branch, make a slight upward cut with the saw from below first;* **g**, *illustrates pruning terms;* **h**, *training in a new or 'replacement' leader by tying a new shoot to a cane.*

pruning when we disbud roses and chrysanthemums, and when we 'pinch out' the growing tip of a seedling snapdragon or wallflower. However, what we are really concerned with in this chapter are hard-wooded plants – trees, shrubs, roses, fruits, climbers, while hedges of course are a subject to themselves.

This brings us to the really important topic of a plant's habits and behaviour. It is fundamental to note whether a plant blooms or fruits on:

(a) 'new wood', i.e. whether it sends out a new branch or shoot and produces flower on that shoot all in the same season; or
(b) 'old wood', i.e. a branch that grows this year but does not bear flower till next year, or even later.

This is the foundation of most pruning.

Broadly speaking, we may say that trees and shrubs that bloom in the spring or before midsummer do so on old wood developed the previous season, and those that bloom after midsummer do so on new wood. Thus forsythia blooms on old wood in early spring and its summer energies are devoted to developing the wood for next year. On the other hand, buddleia (the sorts with purple plumes) blooms in August on new wood that has been developing since the spring of the same year.

Other plants, again, may flower on both old and young wood, such as some of the clematis. Gooseberries fruit on both one-year-old wood and two-year-old wood.

When to prune

This follows fairly logically upon what has been said before. In general terms, the period for pruning is when the plant has completed one cycle of growth and is about to start another. Thus a raspberry and a Rambler rose of the 'Dorothy Perkins' type bloom and fruit on one-year-old wood, so soon after they have completed their purpose the old canes are cut right down to the ground, to direct maximum vigour into the new wood, which has been shooting up at the same time and on which next year's crop will appear.

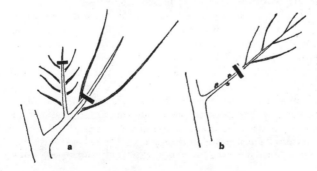

Pruning: **a,** *pruning a spent flowering shoot lightly results in several short new shoots — hard pruning gives two or more long, strong ones (e.g. forsythia);* **b,** *illustrates the phrase: 'prune old flowered wood to three buds of its base' (e.g. broom).*

So in general we may say that trees and shrubs that bloom before midsummer, as forsythia, the flowering quinces, winter jasmine, kerria, some ceanothus, are pruned immediately they have finished blooming, in order that all the summer's vigour will be directed into the new growth for next year. Plants at the other end of the time-scale, blooming after midsummer, are pruned in winter dormancy, often at the end of February, as with buddleja, other ceanothus, hydrangea and hypericum.

On plants that bloom on both old and new wood, the gardener encourages whichever he prefers for early or late blooms, or he adopts a middle course, always remembering the principle of encouraging the newer wood. Thus on bush roses we take advantage of their happy habit of constantly throwing up new wood by pruning out the old as soon as it has done its task. On plants cultivated for their fruits or berries, such as the apple and the cotoneaster, we naturally do not prune after flowering, but leave the task till winter dormancy, if any pruning at all is necessary.

There are a few special cases.

Evergreen trees and shrubs of all sorts, including conifers, are pruned, if at all, in late April. Normally, however, no pruning is necessary, except for shaping, restriction or the removal of decadent branches. Evergreens that are in bloom or bud at that time, such as rhododendrons, are pruned, if necessary, immediately after flowering.

Certain trees 'bleed' if pruned while the sap is rising. They include birch, walnut and liquidambar. Prune these late in August or autumn if necessary. Flowering cherries should be pruned in earliest June.

Vines also 'bleed' profusely and must be pruned before Christmas.

How to prune

The old axiom of 'spare the knife and spoil the tree' is not always true except as demonstrated by the experienced hand. The beginner should therefore go easy with the knife until he has felt his way. There are a few basic ordinances that must be obeyed, but beyond these it is a mistake to be dogmatic. One man may want to produce a different result from his neighbour, as with roses. General principles are therefore best, and the intelligent man will soon find how to apply them. In the chapters on roses, flowering shrubs, and fruit will be found specific injunctions where they are necessary, and many indeed, amount to emphatic commandments. The most difficult of all common subjects are the apple and the pear.

Taking first the specific precepts which must be observed in every sort of pruning:

First, if in doubt about pruning, don't.

Always and invariably cut out dead, diseased, and feeble, spindly growths.

Cut back into clean, healthy wood that shows no discoloration or scar.

Remove spent flowers and seed-pods immediately after flowering, if practicable, except on hydrangeas and on plants grown for their berries or fruit.

Where branches cross each other keep the one that will most help in making a shapely plant, and cut out the other or part of it; this applies more especially to roses and fruit trees, and one wouldn't be so fussy on a dense bush such as a barberry.

Use only sharp tools, and make clean, smooth cuts; never *break* the branch of a hard-wooded plant (except cobs and filberts).

Cut always just above a new bud (or 'eye') or flush with the junction of another limb; leave no 'snag' or stub. Choose an eye pointing in the direction in which you want the new shoot to grow – usually an eye pointing outwards.

Always make either a sloping or a vertical cut, never a horizontal one on which moisture can lie.

Treat all large cuts – certainly anything more than ½ in. diameter – with a proprietary wound-healer.

That is as far as one may dogmatise unequivocally. We have next to deal with the awkward problems of which wood should be pruned out? and how hard should it be pruned?

First, build up a shapely form and one suited to the purpose, whether it be a cordon apple, or a pyracantha hugging the wall, or a rounded, bushy lilac clothed to the ground.

Next, stimulate, year by year, the maximum display of flowers, fruit or berry, by the encouragement of new wood at the expense of the old. In some instances nearly all the old wood is eliminated yearly – or even more often on bush roses. Here again we differentiate somewhat between early- and late-flowering shrubs.

On *early-flowering* shrubs shorten the spent flowering stems as soon as bloom is over to a point where a strong young shoot is sprouting. Forsythia is an example. On *F. suspensa* you may cut to within 2 in. or so of the base of the spent shoot yearly but on other forsythias it is perhaps safer to treat only a proportion of the shoots so drastically each year, and lightly shorten the remainder. Occasionally cut older stems and boughs harder back still, so as to encourage new growth from low down.

On *late-flowering* shrubs remove altogether any old stem not carrying much new growth and lightly shorten others. Most of these need hard treatment, and some should be cut down nearly to the ground, such as David's buddleja (the big purple-plumed one), and ceanothus 'Gloire de Versailles'.

These are good general guides for use when in doubt, but no more. Quite a number of deciduous bushes, in addition to evergreens and trees, need not be pruned at all, as will be seen from Chapter 15.

Old and neglected bushes must quite certainly have drastic treatment, applying the above principles in more severe degree, the main aim being to get rid of old unproductive spindle-shanks.

Terms used in pruning

Eye. A young growth bud. Before it waxes fat, is often identifiable as a pin-head with a little curved wrinkle above, rather like an upper eyelid. Flower-buds are, of course, much more obvious.

Leader. A growth by which a stem or branch extends itself along its own axis or line of advance.

Lateral. A shoot springing sideways from any main branch.

Snag. A superfluous stump resulting from a cut not having been made far enough back.

Others are included in the chapter on fruit.

Pruning tools and their use

Secateurs. Don't buy cheap rubbish. Treat yourself to a Rolcut, a Wilkinson, or a Felco. The action in use is a squeeze; never twist or wrench secateurs.

A pruning knife, of shape according to fancy.

A pruning saw. Various kinds available; avoid double-edged ones.

A tree-lopper, which is a two-handed pair of extra-strong secateurs; for thick shoots.

A 'long-arm', for severing high-up twigs.

All cuts with knife or secateur must be clean and smooth, without ragged edges. For any task too thick for secateurs the saw must be called in, and the rough surface it leaves pared smooth with the knife.

For branches of large trees a carpenter's handsaw may be necessary. To prevent the under-surface of the limb splitting as the saw is about to come through, first make a short upward cut with the saw from the under-surface, then saw downwards in the same plane (sketch, page 64).

Keep all pruning tools clean and sharp. If lacking the skill yourself, send them to a specialist for sharpening.

8

PATHS AND TERRACES

Paths can make or mar a garden. They have a strong tendency to dominate the scene, and they have therefore to be considered as objects of adornment as well as of utility. The best policy is to have as few as possible. This rather curt chapter will deal only with their construction, and I am thinking chiefly of paths, but terraces are constructed in the same way.

There is quite a wide choice of materials, from cheap cinders for kitchen garden paths to expensive 'dressed stone' of rectangular pattern. Surroundings and usage, as well as your pocket, will determine your choice. Where traffic is light, nothing is more acceptable than grass, but for heavy usage, especially where wheelbarrows are to travel frequently, something more durable is necessary. One of the most charming treatments across grass, and quite enough for foot traffic only, is by means of 'stepping stones', which are simply slabs of paving, rectangular or 'crazy', embedded in the turf at intervals of one easy pace. The surface of the stones should lie a shade below the turf level, so that a mower can run over them without harm.

An inexpensive alternative to the use of stone is to cut out some outlines in the turf to a depth of 2½ in., lift the sods, wet the soil below, pour in concrete and level off smoothly a little below the grass level.

Foundations. Where slabs of stone or concrete are the order, I have found that it is totally unnecessary to lay down the heavy foundation of hard core so often prescribed by technical gentlemen. Sometimes I merely dump the slabs straight down on the soil (making sure that it is level), but usually I lay them on a bed of builder's soft sand. This seats them comfortably and makes levelling easier. Paths of this sort easily take the weight of man and barrow or a light roller. Solidity is much improved, however, by filling the gaps between stones and bricks with concrete, using a mix of four parts sand to one of cement.

A foundation of hard core is necessary only for: (a) gravel and asphalt; (b) heavy traffic (cars); (c) terraces; (d) soft ground over a high water table. Where such is needed the drill is this:

Remove the fertile top soil and stack it somewhere for future use. Drive in levelling pegs at intervals, and use a spirit-level laid on a rigid board at all stages. Make the bottom of the trench a trifle narrower than the top. Line the sides of the trench with brick, metal sheets, wooden boards well treated with preservative or 2 in. concrete walls – an essential first step.

Now lay a course of 'hard core' – broken brick or clinker – 4 in. deep all along the trench. Provided it runs the right way, this course of hard core, besides its purpose as a foundation, may often serve as a drainage channel, and side drains can be fed into it. For this purpose it is further improved by laying small field drains along the side, especially under gravel paths.

Rectangular paving. 'Dressed' rectangular paving stones make the hand-somest (and most expensive) of all paths and terraces, and their formality is softened if the slabs are of different sizes. Old pavement-stones from the streets can occasionally be obtained. Lay them on a bed of sand and joint them in cement, leaving a few gaps for paving plants if you like.

Crazy paving is apt sometimes to become not merely crazy, but lunatic. So also is the gardener, when confronted with several tons of stone jigsaw puzzle. But in the right situation it has a charm of its own. Lay them in the same manner as rectangular slabs, the cement jointing being important, leaving gaps for paving plants, which look most attractive in crazy. Set aside all stones with straight edges for the sides of the path, and put the largest stones in the centre at intervals of one stride.

For quantities, reckon one ton of

ᐁ 'old York' slabs, 2 in. thick, per 8 sq. yds.; (extravagant)

ᐁ 'quarried York', 1½ in. thick, per 12 sq. yds.;

ᐁ broken concrete (non-slip) per 10 sq. yds.

I refrain from quoting prices, as they vary in different parts of the country and each year cost more. Broken concrete is the cheapest.

Brick. Weathered red bricks are delightful for the quiet by-ways, being better suited to the narrow track than to the broad sweep. Bed them well in sand as for paving-stones, but lime-mortar may be used in lieu of cement for jointing. The bricks must be hard-baked, and those rejected by the brickworks as over-baked are admirable. They can be laid in a variety of patterns, edgewise or on the flat, and can look awfully well in a mixed design with square paving. A square yard needs 32 bricks of pre-metrication size if laid flat, 48 if laid on edge.

Gravel is much the best treatment for a broad drive, but requires some skill in the making. For a drive that may have to take the weight of a car, make the foundation a full 8 in. deep.

Spread a good 2 in. of the gravel on the hard core in a moist but not sodden condition. Rake repeatedly to get an even surface without pockets or corrugations, but with a very slight camber – 1 in. in 3 ft. is enough. Water slightly and roll thoroughly. Rake again to correct inevitable flaws, and continue rolling and raking till you are satisfied. Then treat the surface with a waterproof bituminous dressing and finish with a sprinkling of fine chippings or pea gravel.

When making good an old gravel path break up the old surface all over to a depth of an inch with a pick, to ensure that the new gravel binds with the old.

Cobbles are very agreeable to the eye, but are not kind to high-heeled shoes. They are best employed for varying a pattern of stone, brick, or concrete slabs, or for the guttering of a path. They have to be bedded in a good 2 in. of concrete. Get the 'hen's egg' size and reckon nearly 2 cwt. per square yard.

Asphalt. For utility uses only, such as in the kitchen garden, where it is efficient but ugly. On a sound bed of hard core only 1 in. is necessary. Tamp it down well and give it a distinct camber, or it will be wrecked by the freezing of surface pools.

Concrete in its solid and amorphous form is also an abomination except for severely utility purposes. It can, however, be perfectly acceptable made up in separate blocks with a little skill and artistry to imitate square or crazy paving. It can also be given a textured surface and its crudity can be softened by patterns of brick or cobbles.

Supposing that the path to be made is 3 ft. wide: select a flat piece of ground and construct a frame of 2 in. thick timbers, 2½ in. broad, on edge parallel to each other 3 ft. apart, and of any convenient length. Fix it rigidly to the ground with pegs. Between the trough so made spread sand to a depth of at least ½ in., levelling with a spirit-level.

Having mixed the concrete, pour it into the trough to a depth of 2 in. Level the surface with a straight-edge board which will fully span the outside frame, first using a sawing motion, then an easy up-and-down dabbing motion.

An hour or two later cut the concrete into slabs of the desired size and shape with a cement trowel, being sure to cut right through the underlying bed of sand.

Leave the slabs where they are for four or five days to set hard. When dry, number the slabs with chalk or pencil, and carry them off in the right order to where they are designed to lie.

If rectangular paving is desired, fit narrow strips of timber across the frame before pouring in the mixture.

The same method can be adapted for making small slabs in imitation of stone for building pergolas, or other small 'rock' works.

To mix concrete. For a solid path in the kitchen garden, garage washdown, etc., a good general-purpose mix is four parts shingle, two sand and one cement. Insist on fresh cement.

For smooth surfacing and for jointing between stones and bricks, use four of sand to one of cement.

To mix, use a flat, clean surface, spread the sand in a roughly flat heap and lay the cement atop. Thoroughly mix them together with a shovel, till the whole is of an even colour without streaks. Now spread the shingle or chippings, if required, and again mix the whole evenly.

Scrape out a rough hollow in the centre of the heap and pour in a little water through a rose. Mix the whole together with a shovel very thoroughly and intimately, stopping every now and then to add a little more water. Use no more water than is necessary to form a paste of the consistency of a very stiff porridge.

Concrete can be tinted if desired by adding a very small pinch of one of the recognised pigments, such as Venetian Red; this is often useful for the jointing between stones or bricks.

Edgings. Plants in the kitchen garden or along the edge of flower-beds need some form of kerb to prevent the soil from constantly spilling over on to the path. The kerb can be made from bricks, thick tarred planks, concrete, or imitation stone walling. Another very good material, strong and of good appearance, but irregular in size, is old granite sett from city streets, if they can be obtained.

Whatever is used, the surface should be level, not jagged – as one often sees with bricks set slantwise. Bricks really need laying two deep and setting in cement or mortar. Planking should be thick, buried to two-thirds of its breadth and braced with stout pegs. A concrete edging should be 2 in. thick (using the pure sand-and-cement mix mentioned above) and laid to a depth of 3 or 4 in. below ground. It can be laid *in situ* by putting down a light timber 'shuttering' or frame on the spot, kept in place by pegs, and pouring the mix into the trough so made.

Weeds in paths are considered on page 43.

9

THE SMALL GREENHOUSE AND OTHER GLASSWORKS

GENERAL MANAGEMENT AND USES

A 'Bit of Glass' is a tremendous asset in any garden and of course for all 'serious' gardening is a necessity. A greenhouse, garden frame, a few cloches, even a glass porch over a doorway enables the range of one's efforts to be extended and cheapened. But it must be recognised at once that without some degree of heating the possibilities are extremely limited. We classify greenhouses into 'hot houses' (which are outside my brief), 'cool' ones, and cold ones. The cool house must be capable of sustaining 40°F in the coldest weather as the barest minimum, and 45°F gives a much wider scope. The snag about the entirely unheated house is not only that it admits frost, but also that it admits excessive dampness, particularly fog, at a time of year when damp is most injurious. Thus any form of heating which will keep out frost and damp immediately multiplies the dividends of a greenhouse.

Many people do this quite successfully with special types of oil-heaters which are readily available, and that was how I started myself many years ago. It sufficed to keep alive some things in pots and boxes that would otherwise have succumbed to frost and damp and enabled nurselings to steal a march of a few weeks upon the outside weather. But the ideal thing for the busy amateur is electrical heating. Units can be bought for use in the tiniest structure, and a thermostat is a further blessing. In a small place the expense is not outrageous and certainly less, I would say, than the cost of seedlings and plants, particularly as it enables you to raise flowers for the dwelling-house at a season when the florist's productions are pretty extravagant. Thus with the introduction of only sufficient heat to constitute a 'cool' house the prospect immediately begins to open up.

The tubular form of heater is usually the most convenient, connected direct to the mains. The loading is about 60 watts per foot, and for a small house a pair suffices if the total loading is about 700 watts. Fit it with a waterproof thermostat of the rod type in the coldest part of the house. Thermostats may safely be set a good 5° below the temperatures culturally advised.

The amount of heat necessary is much influenced by the siting of the greenhouse. For general purposes a span or ridged-type house (which is the best) would have the ridge running north and south, though for some

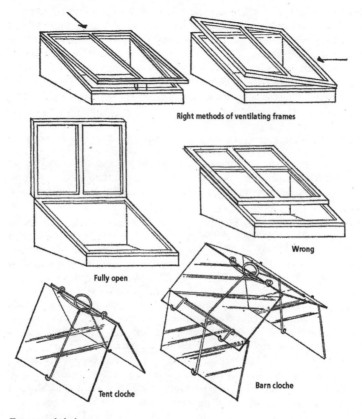

Right methods of ventilating frames

Wrong

Fully open

Tent cloche

Barn cloche

Frames and cloches.

uses east-to-west is preferred. The lean-to type and the garden frame should if possible be on a wall facing south for general purposes. Old-fashioned wood-frame structures (especially if you can run to hardwood) are better all-round than the modern metal ones, though the metal ones save painting, and the whole thing must shut up tight and close for fumigation and the exclusion of draughts and drips. Best of all for general purposes, but the most expensive, are those erected on low brick walls, for brick retains heat longer than glass. Avoid sliding doors if you can; they stick. Hinged ventilators in both roof and sides are essential. Automatic ventilators in the roof, operated by the sun's warmth, are a great blessing and cost only a little extra; for general use set them at the bottom extremity, so that they open at the lowest temperature. Louvred vents in the sides are good. Fix a rainwater tank (with overflow) inside the house, fed from guttering under the eaves, and cover the tank with a light wooden lid.

Inside the structure there can be a narrow border of good loam at ground level, in which to grow tomatoes, chrysanthemums, a climber or two or what you will. Most people, however, prefer a raised wooden staging, on which plants are grown in pots. What is less known is the great value of wide, shallow metal trays filled with pebbles and kept moist – a far better practice than the open wooden slats of a staging. Some sort of contrivance close up to the roof for accommodating seed-boxes is a necessity. A wire-netting grill over lean-to structures will break the fall of snow from the roof of the dwelling house.

The cheapest sort of glasshouse today is the 'Dutch light' type, with an aluminium framework and large sheets of glass right down to the ground. These are good for some uses, but are not good all-purpose structures, being subject to excessive fluctuations of heat and cold. But whatever sort of glass structure is used, there are certain basic ordinances to be obeyed, not all of which are susceptible of precise definition.

First, and above all, is cleanliness. Glass structures are terrible breeding-houses for both insect pests and fungal diseases. The whole structure must be washed down and scrubbed inside at least once a year, and fumigations will be necessary from time to time. Pots and boxes, and the crocks used in them, must also be clean. No dirt or rubbish should be allowed to accumulate and all dead or dying foliage should be removed.

Next is ventilation, and this is very much a question of experience and judgement. Broadly speaking, the first rule is to ventilate very freely, especially from the ventilators in the roof. A free circulation of fresh air, but without draughts, should always be encouraged. At high noon in summer everything will be open, on cold winter nights everything will be shut, and between those two extremes one cannot prescribe beyond the reminder that the things to be excluded are frost, draughts and excessive winter dampness.

Humidity is a factor closely related to ventilation. In winter the general rule is to keep the atmosphere and the plants on the dry side. The colder the weather the less the watering. Water plants only sufficiently to prevent them from flagging, and turn on the heat when the air becomes raw and moisture-laden. In high summer the rule is the very reverse – sprinkle the floor, walls and staging with water each morning, syringe the foliage, and look over all pots and boxes to ensure that the plants do not suffer from excessive transpi-ration. The standard test with clay pots (it does not work on plastic ones) is to tap it with knuckle or small wooden mallet, and if the pot rings hollow, water is needed. To overdo greenhouse watering, however, invites disease while too dry a house invites insect pests.

It seems odd that we should erect a glasshouse to catch the sun, but then be obliged to keep it out, but so it is when the sun becomes too powerful for a good many plants, such as tomatoes, grapes, begonias and gloxinias. So some sort of shading must be provided, whether by a special paint on

the roof to give a cloud effect, or by blinds or, more cheaply, but less conveniently, by a close-mesh nylon netting.

These elementary rules show that a greenhouse is by no means a thing
that can take care of itself. Let us face the fact that it needs a great deal of
attention. The house that, say, in autumn needs to have but one light
opened before master leaves for the office, may need to have everything
fully opened by noon, but shut up again a good hour before sundown to
retain warmth. For these emergencies one must call up the feminine
reserves or install an all-automatic house, in which the heating, ventilation,
watering, and screening are all done as by a fairy wand (and at a fancy
price).

In small places another problem is what *not* to grow. There is at first a
natural impulse to get in everything the place will hold – a grape-vine,
tomatoes, seedlings, flowering plants, bulbs, and so on. But with only one
house it can't be done. One of the earliest lessons to be learnt is that one
must select; for plants vary greatly in their needs, especially in temperature
and humidity. A vine, once it has started into leaf, virtually shuts the door
to any other lodgers, for its foliage casts all into shade; begonias, however,
will accept these conditions, and in the vine's dormancy early seedlings and
bulbs in pots will be welcome visitors. In a small place a vine is not really
economical and tomatoes are much more profitable and less trouble. After
these, chrysanthemums will handsomely increase the greenhouse dividends, especially if there is enough heat to keep out the frost. After them
in turn – and here a trifle of heat is essential – one can enjoy freesias,
cinerarias, azaleas, cyclamen, and so on.

Greenhouses or glazed porches that open off a living-room often
challenge the gardener's skill for adorning a naked prospect. Provided that
the glass does not perversely face a cold quarter, the gardener can meet this
challenge, even without heat, from at least early March to late November
with a programme starting with bulbs, going on with those hardy and half-
hardy annuals that take kindly to pots, and ending with chrysanthemums;
and he could include one or two near-hardy climbers such as the lively
blue plumbago, and, of course, a climbing rose or two. An entirely utilitarian
programme in an unheated house would be confined to tomatoes in
summer, the starting of dahlia, begonia and potato tubers, and the germination of hardy and some half-hardy seeds a little earlier than they would
outdoors but a little later than with heat.

WHAT TO GROW

Here is a very short list of plants for the decoration of small greenhouses,
cold or warmed.

Annuals
Many of the hardy and half-hardy ones do well. A normal spring sowing
gives early summer display, but many can with great success be sown in

August–September to give a show in spring. After germination, prick-on into small pots and then pot-on to larger ones, the 5 in. pot being suitable for the majority.

Pride of place is won by the butterfly flower, schizanthus. Its nickname aptly describes its dainty beauty. Get a packet of mixed colours from a first-class seedsman, of a tall or dwarf strain. Sow in August or September, and again in January if you like. No heat needed. Keep them close up to the light while young, and pot on as necessary. Pinch out the tips after first potting, and feed with liquid manure.

Other good and easy annuals (see more fully in Part 2) are:

Clarkia (one of the best), sow in March for June blooming, or in August for May blooming, sowing two or three seeds direct into small pots (not seed-boxes) and moving the best on to 5 in. pots; godetia, similar treatment; the cornflower 'Jubilee Gem'; the trumpeting salpiglossis; antirrhinum (sow in August or March); the beautiful little annual delphinium 'Blue Butterfly'; forget-me-not; bartonia; nicotiana; petunia.

Bulbs

Most of the popular bulbs do excellently in pots, particularly hyacinths, daffodils, tulips of all sorts, bulbous irises, crocuses, begonia (in summer keep a rather damp atmosphere, and screen from fiercest sun), the harlequin-coloured tigridia and gladiolus. All these are easy and straightforward. Many lilies are also easy enough, particularly *Lilium regale*.

Those who can take the chill off their greenhouses, however, should make **freesias** their very first pick among bulbs. Their lovely clustered trumpets, so richly scented, can now be had in a range of sparkling colours, and they last wonderfully in a vase as well as in the greenhouse. For a succession of bloom, pot up a few at a time from August to October, putting about six in a 5 in. pot. Just cover the corms. Put them outdoors for two months, preferably in a cold frame, keeping them just moist, and covering them only if frost threatens. Then take them into the greenhouse. A temperature of about 10°C (50°F) suits them. They need a little light staking.

Other good bulbs for our purposes, given a modicum of warmth, are:

Clivia. Scarlet, lilyform, scented flowers in big clusters, of easy culture, blooming in spring. Plant in March in good soil. Ease off the water in October and start again in February. They like being pot-bound, but can be increased by division.

Lachenalia. Elegant spires of drooping temple bells in yellow or orange, of easy culture. Raise as freesias. For pots or hanging baskets.

Scarborough lily (*Cyrtanthus elatus*, syn. *Valotta purpurea*). Showy scarlet trumpets in late summer. Of easy culture; needing very little heat. Pot the bulbs in March, one to a 5 in. pot. Water stingily till growth begins, then fairly freely. Give them sun. After flowering almost stop watering from November to March. Very nice room plants.

Climbers

The greenhouse, if large enough, has a wide choice of handsome climbers, which are best grown in the greenhouse border rather than in pots. **Roses** come high on the list, two of the best being the grand old fragrant yellow 'Maréchal Niel' and the chaste white 'Niphetos', the latter now rather difficult to get. Where there is enough artificial warmth to maintain a winter minimum of 5°C (40°F) however, preference even over roses might be claimed for the beautiful *Lapageria rosea*, which, when trained up between the rafters, enriches the scene with chains of festive red bells. It needs shade and an acid soil. Water it very freely from April to September and syringe daily.

Next I would put *Plumbago auriculata*, which throws out Cambridge-blue flowers in trusses like those of phlox. Easy and decorative, and all the better for just a little winter warmth. Water and syringe daily throughout summer, and prune in March.

For smaller greenhouses, with the minimum of heat, the following few climbers offer themselves. The first three are very easily raised from seed sown in early spring and are so nearly hardy that, outdoors, they are treated as half-hardy annuals, though in fact perennials. All need something on which to attach themselves.

Eccremocarpus scaber. Sprays of jolly orange tubes from lacy foliage. Grows 10 ft. in a season. Survives mild winters outdoors.

Cobaea scandens. Large, wide-mouthed bells that start white, turn mauve and deepen to purple. Sow the seeds on edge. Easily grows 15 ft. in a season.

Thunbergia alata. One of the plants called black-eyed Susan. Very easy. Showy daisy-form flowers of orange or lemon with black central disc. Only about 5 ft.

Hoya. Tightly packed clusters, like pink snowballs, of small, waxen florets, borne on slim and flexible twining stems, amenable to being twisted about anyhow at your will. Looks tender, but isn't.

General

Astilbe. The feathery plumes of the astilbes are delightful in greenhouse pots (Chapter II).

Azalea. Pot into 5 or 6 in. pots in September in acid soil, peat, and leaf-mould, firmly rammed. Stand in rain-water up to soil level till soaked and rest them in cool shade for ten days. Then house them, raising the heat gradually to 15°C (60°F) or more. Syringe the foliage daily and keep the soil moist. Next May, sink the pots outdoors in shade and keep them moist.

Bleeding heart (*Dicentra spectabilis*). This graceful hardy perennial (*see* Chapter II) can be lodged in 6 in. pots to flower early. Heat is not essential, but of course brings it out earlier still.

Broom. The pretty little bush, animated for many weeks with golden pea-flowers, usually called *Genista canariensis*, is of the easiest culture and needs no heat. Grown cold, it blooms in April. From June to September stand it outdoors in the sun and keep it watered. Multiply by cuttings in spring or autumn, and when established pinch out to get bushy growth.

Busy Lizzie (*Impatiens*). Popular, free-blooming plants of the easiest culture where a winter temperature of a good 10°C (50°F) can be maintained, but 20°C (70°F) is needed to raise them from seed. Water liberally in summer, meanly in winter. Full sun. Can be planted outdoors June 1st. Trim back old plants in February and repot. Easily multiplied by spring or summer cuttings in sandy soil in some warmth or even in a jug of water.

Cineraria (*Pericallis*). With enough warmth to maintain a winter minimum of 5°C (40°F), these beautiful daisy-form flowers of many colours are not difficult to raise. There are large-flowered sorts, the small, starry stellatas, and good intermediates. The law and the prophets on cineraria culture is this: at all stages keep them *cool* and well ventilated, never over-water them, never bury the plant's tiny crown when transplanting. For a spring display, sow *very thinly* in boxes in a frame under a north wall in late July. Prick off into deeper boxes, move on singly into 3 in. pots, and finally into 6 in. pots. Never close the frame entirely except for a day or two after transplanting. Move into the greenhouse early in October. Continue ventilating as freely as weather allows, but from now onwards be very stingy with the water. Kill the leaf-mining maggot with a pin, and spray with derris against greenfly.

For a winter display, seed must be sown indoors in April in a temperature of 13°C (55°F) or more.

Fuchsias of the less hardy sorts are perfectly easy, given just enough warmth to keep out frost. The dwarfer ones are the more suitable, and the pendulous varieties are as charming on the greenhouse bench as they are in hanging baskets.

Heliotrope or cherry pie. Definite heat is needed for propagation, but if plants are bought the adults will be safe during winter with a minimum temperature of 5°C (40°F). Those that have been planted outdoors (which is done the first week of June) must be brought inside at the end of September, put into the smallest pots that will take their roots, and pruned fairly hard.

Marguerite. In the unheated place *Argyranthemum* cultivars are very useful for summer decoration. Will last for some years, growing bigger and bigger. Multiply by cuttings of young non-flowering shoots in spring or late August in a propagating frame.

Pelargonium. Soi-disant 'geranium'. The main types for the non-expert are the zonal-leaved pelargoniums (which are those commonly seen in bedding-out schemes), the extra large Irenes, the daintier Ivy-leaved pelargonium, which is a trailer or semi-climber, very decorative for tumbling down over the front of a pot, a window-box, or a hanging basket, and the charming Miniatures. All have an uncommonly long season of bloom if dead-headed.

In the greenhouse give pelargoniums the amplest ventilation in spring and summer; in the winter a temperature of 5.5°C (42°F) is desirable. Those grown outdoors must be brought in by the end of September. Nodal cuttings taken in August strike very easily in a gritty compost in greenhouse or frame or even in a shady spot outdoors in sandy soil. Move them separately into 3½ in. pots in March, and when these are full of root move on into 5 in. pots. Still keep the compost rather lean and gritty.

Cuttings may also be taken in spring for rooting in the greenhouse. These can be induced to flower in the winter by continually picking off the flower-buds as they appear. Stand them outdoors in a frame from June to September. There are quantities of named varieties to choose from and the initiate cannot do better than start with the established successes, such as 'Gustav Emich', 'Festivum Maximum' or one of the Irenes.

Outdoors, the only point to make is that pelargoniums should have a rather poor, gritty soil and, preferably, full sun.

The superb Regal pelargoniums, with their flared colours, need rather more skill, but not much more warmth. The main thing is to pinch out the growing shoot at about five leaves and repeat the operation on the four new shoots that result. Also trim back the spent flower-heads to a point of new growth. Water fairly freely and feed with a general fertiliser when in full growth.

If you can maintain a temperature of about 20°C (70°F) either in the greenhouse or, say, on the kitchen window-sill, you can now grow pelargoniums from seed, then pot-on in the usual way, for planting out in the first week of June. Good Series are Sprinter and Multibloom.

Primula. Of the winter-flowering greenhouse types, *P. sinesis* is the loveliest, *malacoides* is the easiest; *obconica* and the golden *kewensis* are also charming. *Malacoides* and *kewensis* need only just enough warmth to expel frost. All are treated as annuals.

A temperature of about 15°C (60°F) is needed for the usual March sowing, but *malacoides* can be sown in May or June with no trouble. Prick off the seedlings when they have three leaves into pans or trays, then into 2½ in. pots, and finally into 5 in. pots. Plant the crowns very shallow, so that water does not lodge in them. Keep in the greenhouse or frame all summer, but shade them from hot sun. Water moderately in summer and very sparingly in winter. After flowering the plants must be discarded.

THE FRAME

The greenhouse is by no means essential in a garden, but the frame, or at least the cloche, is. Its uses are manifold – to raise early seed, especially for the kitchen garden, for cuttings, for hardening-off non-hardy plants and for over-wintering them, for growing late and early lettuces, and so on. Indeed, one frame alone is by no means enough except in the smallest places.

Frames with brick or concrete sides are best, but wooden ones are acceptable, and the portable wooden Dutch frame has a special value. For cuttings a shady place is needed, but for general purposes the site should be in full sun, and better still if sheltered from the north by a wall, fence, or hedge. Have it close to the greenhouse if you can. It can be fitted with electric soil-heating cables for special uses, and indeed in every way can be treated as a small greenhouse. Thus by keeping it sprayed inside one can create that close atmosphere neeeded for softwood cuttings. Perfect control of watering, of ventilation, and of shading from hot sun when necessary is given by the frame.

Normally, as in the greenhouse, the fullest ventilation should be given at all times, according to the weather. This is done by lifting (*not* sliding) the lid, either to its fullest extent in fine weather, or propped open a mere inch or two, and of course completely closed on frosty days and nights. Open it always in a direction away from the wind. For really tough winters, thick sacking should be spread over the top.

Seedlings in pots or boxes should be kept as close up to the light as possible, by propping them on bricks or inverted flower-pots.

By making up a special bed of soil, out-of-season vegetables can be grown in the frame, such as lettuces, carrots, and radishes. Winter violets may also be indulged in, lifting the plants from their outdoor quarters in September, and filling up the frame with soil so that the plants are close up to the light.

CLOCHES

These are a real treasure to the small gardener. Their crowning uses are in the kitchen garden — to bring on early vegetables, to continue the growth of late ones into autumn, to over-winter lettuces for early spring maturity, to bring on early strawberries, late tomatoes, and haricot beans when summer is over, and so on. They have, of course, similar uses in the flower garden, and, like the frame, are valuable for providing some closeness of atmosphere for cuttings.

The cheapest type of glass cloche (but today polythene cloches are cheaper still) is the 'tent' form, which is adequate for raising seed and for plants such as lettuces when small, but it will soon be found that the larger 'barn' type is wanted. One may reckon that cloches allow you in spring to steal about three weeks' march on nature. They are grand for early lettuces, peas and French beans. Their use is simplicity itself, but a few tips will save buying experience.

In cold weather block up the ends of the 'runs' of cloches with sheets of ordinary glass. Do likewise for even single cloches when used for cuttings.

If the soil is too wet for sowing, put the cloches in position ten days ahead to dry off the surface.

Keep them clean, so that light is not obscured. When not in use, stack them in nests on their ends.

Watering is the obvious problem, since the cloche keeps off rain. The answer is to dig the soil fairly deep, work in plenty of granulated peat into the top spit, and decayed organic matter down below, and to wet the soil thoroughly a day or so before sowing or planting if at all on the dry side. Thereafter, the rain shed by the cloche and percolating through the soil laterally will give enough moisture in a normal season. If not, one can put on the hose for prolonged spells without moving the glass, but in persistent drought it will, of course, be necessary to move them all.

In prolonged warm weather lift a cloche or two here and there for extra ventilation. Discard the cloches when the power of the sun waxes strong in full summer.

Glass cloches, though they have their inconveniences, are easily broken and are not now cheap, are far better all-round than plastic ones, except for short-term use, but the plastic continuous 'tunnel' cloches for small plants are much favoured by market gardeners.

SOIL HEATING

Inexpensive, low-voltage electrical equipments are valuable for heating soil in either the greenhouse or the frame. Their great value is that they stimulate growth by providing mild 'bottom heat'. Their uses are wide. They can warm the soil in a small propagating box for cuttings or for seeds of half-hardy and of tender plants (tomatoes, aubergines, zinnias, morning glories, snapdragons, petunias, etc.). The box can be home-made if you have the know-how or, at some cost, it can be factory-made. Stand it on the greenhouse bench, not in full sun.

The whole bench may also be equipped with heating cables, laid in 3 in. or so of seed or cuttings compost, according to purpose. They can also be laid in a border inside the greenhouse, to bring on early tomatoes, or in the soil of a frame for early lettuces or what-you-will, but in frames some heating of the air as well as of the soil will probably be needed.

These soil-warming equipments use a negligible amount of current. They require a transformer, of course, but no thermostat, for, since the temperature of soil changes so gradually, ordinary hand-switches and occasional observation of the temperature with a thermometer in the soil are sufficient. You may have to switch on overnight only. In a heated house a 100-watt transformer does for a bench of about 24 sq. ft., or 15–20 sq. ft. in an unheated one. Temperatures should be kept from 13–15°C (55–60°F).

PART TWO: FLOWERS

Now we emerge. From the earth to the fruits thereof. 'The folded leaf is wooed from out the bud', and we arrive in such a jocund company as makes even a modern poet sometimes gay.

I have picked the company with some care. It is not helpful to the initiate seeking positive guidance to offer him a multitude of choices. Worthy plants, and worthy plants alone, are admitted here, few of them difficult in appropriate soils and circumstances. Study the catalogues critically, even sceptically. Avoid the cheap-jack and the 'bargain lot', and cock a suspicious eye at over-effusive blurbs. Facts are what you want. Does it tolerate lime? Will it stand shade? How big does it grow? Is it hardy? And so on.

It is an old saying that the apprentice starts gardening with annuals, journeys on to herbaceous plants, and when he has reached the status of master-gardener turns to flowering trees and shrubs; unless he is lured into those crevices where the pygmy sirens of the rock garden dwell. Don't tread that path. Begin with shrubs and little trees, which are easy and permanent and make a backcloth for whatever else you like to show upon your stage. Lay out an herbaceous or mixed border, rose-beds, a carnation bed (separate, please), and use your annuals for filling, for the 'odd spot', or for little bedding schemes; not all annuals are easy by any means.

Finally, *label your plants durably*, especially shrubs, roses, and clematis; it is vital for the purpose of pruning, which is one of the secrets of successful gardening.

In the appendices will be found some classifications of plants to suit various conditions and soils.

10

ANNUALS AND BIENNIALS

BEDDING

In this chapter I shall deal with: hardy annuals (h.a.), half-hardy annuals (h.h.a.), and hardy biennials (h.b.), and shall include those gay favourites which, though they are not botanically within those classes, are culturally treated as though they were, such as antirrhinums and wallflowers.

Though repetition is a literary sin, I shall for emphasis say again that if you really look for that 'crowded holiday of scent and bloom' that the annual and biennial can give you, you must give them good cultivation just as much as you would to their longer-lived brethren. There are only a few exceptions. The popular notion that you have only to sprinkle a few seeds about the place to get a 'riot of colour' is entirely mistaken. Give them, therefore, ground that is well drained, deeply dug, and reasonably fed with organic foods. Most of them want plenty of sun, and I implore you not to crowd them too closely together. The result of such treatment will be bonny plants full of blossom, instead of the scraggy starvelings so often seen. Among annuals this is especially true of clarkia, larkspur, and chrysan-themums, which when grown in deeply dug and well manured soil will astonish people who have never treated them that way.

Plants that branch naturally, such as wallflowers and antirrhinums, should be pinched out when a few inches high to induce shrubbiness, but those of a different habit, such as larkspur and stock, should be left alone. When in doubt, refrain. Most plants in these classes need staking at a very early stage with twiggy sticks. Pick off all dead blossom persistently to encourage further blooming, though some sorts, such as stocks, make no second effort.

As a rule, annuals and biennials look best in bold splashes and can be used to fill up blanks in the border or partnered with spring bulbs, or used as edgings. Foxgloves and evening primroses are entirely right among shrubs, and Canterbury bell takes her place with dignity and grace in the herbaceous border.

The term 'F$_1$ hybrid' will be met in the better catalogues. These are first-generation hybrids raised afresh every year by controlled cross-pollination, as they do not themselves produce true-to-type seed. They cost a bit more than other seed but are very good value.

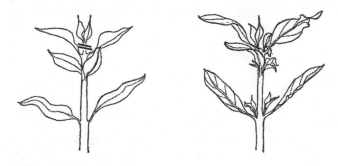

'Stopping' or 'pinching' some young plants (e.g. antirrhinum) makes them sprout more vigorously.

Hardy annuals

The best results come from sowing direct into the plants' permanent quarters. If beds are occupied at sowing time, many can be raised in seed-boxes, using a John Innes Seed Compost or a soil-less one, but some that we shall note do not transplant well. Peat pots can help here; sow in the pot and transplant complete with pot.

For sowing in the open, dig the bed well in advance, allow the soil to settle, and prepare a fine seed-bed by treading and raking. The usual time for sowing is late March, if weather permits, but any time up to the end of April will suit; if delayed longer many will have but a short season of bloom. For the reasons already given in Chapter 6, sowing 'at stations' is better than broadcasting.

The hardiest of the annuals can also be grown as biennials, sown in later summer (about mid-August) to over-winter and provide early bloom for next year.

For those who would like a ready-made selection of hardy annuals, I should say that the pick of them is: sweet pea (in a class by itself), larkspur, godetia, love-in-a-mist, the rose mallow, clarkia and the rudbeckia 'Rustic Dwarfs'. But there are some excellent ones that are little known, are just as delightful, and that can give a gay diversity to our gardens; of such are the annual delphinium 'Blue Butterfly', the gentian-blue *Phacelia campanularia*, and the golden bartonia.

Half-hardy annuals

These must generally be raised in gentle heat in March, sometimes earlier, or they will mature too late: otherwise they must be got as seedlings from a nursery at the end of May, and this is what the beginner is best advised to do.

To raise your own, sow in boxes or pans and prick off into other boxes, using the same composts as before. Before being planted in their permanent quarters they must be 'hardened off', which means accustoming them to the colder outdoor conditions by degrees. The process consists in opening up the greenhouse or frame gradually more and more according to the weather, shutting off the heat about the end of March if the season is normal, and finally leaving the plants outdoors altogether for about ten days before planting. Hardening-off should not be hurried, and any risk of frost must be avoided, especially at night.

The earliest safe time for planting out half-hardy subjects is the first week of June – 'the first week-end after the Derby' was the rule that my old gardener taught me, though I must say that in the South nowadays one takes a week or two's licence and risk. The use of cloches is a great help, and plants can be got out into permanent quarters some three weeks earlier beneath their shelter.

Biennials

These provide some of our bravest flowers and are pretty easy. Sow some time in June, or a bit later in the South, in well-prepared nursery beds. Sow thinly in drills. As soon as the plants are big enough to handle, prick off into good soil in a reserve bed in straight lines at distances appropriate to the size of the mature plant – say 4 in. for wallflowers, and 9 in. for Canterbury bells. They will be ready to go into their permanent quarters in early autumn.

BEDDING

To bed out means to fill a flower-bed with plants already well advanced in growth, and often actually in flower. Characteristically, such plants are the semi-hard or tender ones that have to live under glass till June. Most famous of the bedders, I suppose, is the pelargonium (or 'geranium'), often in dual marriage with the calceolaria and lobelia, though they marry even more gladly nowadays with petunias, antirrhinums, and marigolds. Without your own warm greenhouse, you must get pelargoniums from a nursery, and so you must the beautiful heliotrope (cherry pie), the spirited busy Lizzie and verbena. The jocund begonia, which you will find dealt with in the chapter on bulbs, you can raise yourself as a rule.

Flowers from this chapter that make splendid summer bedding schemes, according to one's taste, are antirrhinum, zinnia, Drummond's phlox, nemesia, ageratum, petunia, and stock. The glaring scarlet salvia should be used to complement other colours, not used as the 'main orna-ment'. All can be bedded out from the seed-boxes into which they were pricked out, but if you can get them grown-on into pots, they will unfurl their banners all the sooner.

There are also spring bedding schemes, which are planted out in autumn. Bulbs usually take first place. There is still nothing more lovely for spring bedding than the old marriage of the pink tulip 'Clara Butt' with the azure of forget-me-not. Wallflowers, Brompton stocks, polyanthus, and auriculas also make very fine spring bedding.

THE BEST ANNUALS AND BIENNIALS

The following list of varieties contains a small selection only of the more meritorious. The more difficult sorts, the very fleeting, and the less interesting are omitted. Named varieties are far too numerous to quote in this chapter, especially as nurseries have the annoying habit of calling a variety 'So-and-So's Perfection', or something of the sort. I have assumed that the best-known kinds need no description.

Ageratum houstonianum (h.h.a.). One of the best pygmy edging or carpeting plants, embellished with toy powder-puffs in varying shades of blue or mauve. Get an F_1 hybrid or a variety such as 'Blue Chip' or 'Blue Mink'. Spacing 6 in.

Alyssum (*Lobularia maritima,* h.a.). Familiar little cushions, usually white, used for edging or carpeting; the lilac forms are also attractive. Almost hardy and can be raised direct outdoors under cloches in April. Happy in poor soils and tolerate partial shade. 'Wonderland' is a spectacular red. The yellow alyssum is something quite different; *see Aurinia saxatilis,* Chapter 12.

Antirrhinum. A perennial, but best treated as h.h.a. The 'intermediate' varieties are the most usually grown, but there are several other types, from dwarfs to giants, with confusing fancy names. You may have dense ones with little resemblance to a snapdragon and others with tubular flowers like a penstemon. All flower best and are hardiest when planted out in a rather lean, stony soil.

The beginner should get a box or two of seedlings from a nursery, plant out 9 in. apart in a sunny bed in the first week of June, stake with twigs at once, and nip off the tips after a week. Antirrhinums are very subject to the rust disease.

The non-beginner who has glass and a little heat can raise snapdragons from seed sown in January or February, guarding against the damping-off disease, to which they are very liable, with Cheshunt Compound. Early and good results can be got by sowing under glass in October and moving on gradually into small pots, before hardening off, and some may go into 5 in. pots to flower in the greenhouse. If so minded, you can also propagate them easily by heel or nodal cuttings of firm young shoots, stuck in sandy soil in pots in a close frame in late summer.

By persistent dead-heading, antirrhinums can be induced to flower continuously till autumn. They love rocks and brick walls, and will often last for years in old brickwork. Whichever style you like – dwarf, medium, or tall – I would go for one of the F_1 hybrids or the rust-resistant strains if that disease is prevalent in your area.

Unfortunately the best new strains are rarely obtainable from local nurseries as growing seedlings.

Aster (h.h.a.). These justly popular China asters are not really aster at all, but *Callistephus* and are not to be confused with the true *Aster*, which is the Michaelmas daisy and its brethren. The China asters are very decorative, extremely flowerful, and fine for cutting. Treatment is as for antirrhinums, but, if raising from seed oneself, do not sow before mid-March. Seedlings are very subject to the damping-off disease. Destroy any plants seen to wilt after being planted out.

One is often confused with the variety of types under fancy group-names in catalogues. Personally, I prefer the charming single-flowered varieties which are like coloured marguerites and about 15 in. high. Others, ranging from ankle-high to thigh-high, are often hardly to be distinguished from chrysanthemums. They go by such names as 'Ostrich Plume', 'Princess', 'Duchess', 'Californian Giants' and so on.

Bartonia (*Mentzelia lindleyis*, h.a.). An easy summer annual with large golden buttercup-like flowers that should be more grown. Very gay. Sow *in situ* and thin to 10 in. Height 15 in.

Calceolaria. Pot-bellied little things of mixed breeding, once the high kick of fashion for bedding or greenhouse. Half-hardy. Best buy a box of seedlings and plant out early June, in sun or part-shade or sow the dust-like seed in January, merely pressing it into the soil. *C. integrifolia* 'Sunshine' is brilliant and expensive. Other breeds can be sown about June to flower in the greenhouse next spring. *C. integrifolia* is a 4 ft. shrub for a warm wall outdoors.

Calendula. *See* Marigold.

California poppy (*Eschscholzia*, pronounced Esholtzia, h.a.). One of the easiest and most colourful, with festive trumpets of orange, gold, red, pink. Likes warm, dry conditions. Height 9 in. Sow in situ, and thin to 7 in. Keep spent blooms removed. Does best in poor stony soil. Seeds itself profusely.

Candytuft (*Iberis*, h.a./h.b.). Easy and familiar. Usually white, sometimes pale mauve. The usual form is the dwarf, but you may care for the tall, hyacinthine spires of the varieties of *I. amara* (syn. *I. coronaria*), for which nurserymen have their own pet names. Sow *in situ*, and thin to 8 in. *See also under* Rock Gardens.

Canterbury bell (h.b.). Members of the *Campanula* genus (for example, *C. medium*) and one of our grandest old garden favourites. Very easy to raise. Some have a bell only, others a ring of coloured sepals which give them the name 'cup and saucer'. 3 ft. high in white, pink, blue, or mauve, and very broad and bushy. Excellent in part-shade.

Chrysanthemum (h.a./h.b.). The annual *Ismelia carinata* is very spectacular and distinctive, beautifully marked by rings or zones of contrasting colours in the petals. It varies in height from 18 in. to 3 ft. Deep and generous soil treatment is essential. Sow *in situ*, and space the big ones at 15 in. at least. Must be staked. For the perennial chrysanthemums, *see* Chapter 18.

Clarkia (h.a./h.b.). Deep and generous soil treatment is necessary for the brilliant results obtainable from this lovely annual (*C. unguiculata*, syn. *C.*

elegans) with its spires of frilled blossoms in many colours, instead of the poor stunted things usually seen. A first choice that richly rewards good treatment. Sow *in situ* (will not transplant) and thin to 10 in. Succeeds in partial shade. Stake very early. A good pot plant for the greenhouse.

Convolvulus. Some of these are weeds, but the so-called *C. tricolor* has produced some first-rate varieties, of which 'Royal Ensign' is particularly fine in its colours of rich royal-blue and gold. A hardy annual, it is a foot high and one of the best.

Cornflower (*Centaurea cyanus*, h.a.). The pink and mauve shades are nearly as lovely as the traditional blue. A beautiful dwarf one, among the best of annuals, is 'Jubilee Gem', which measures a foot. Avoid the very tall sorts. Fine for cutting. Sow *in situ*.

Cosmos, or **Cosmea** (h.h.a.). Graceful daisy-form flowers and thin ferny foliage. Some go to 3 ft. and others are dwarf. *C. bipinnatus* Sensation Series, mixed, is excellent for cutting.

Delphinium. The annual delphinium named *D. grandiflorum* 'Blue Butter-fly', as distinct from larkspur, is an outstanding annual, producing deep blue flowers in great abundance, and making a compact bushy plant 1 ft. high. Excellent also in pots in the cold greenhouse. Though treated as an annual, since it flowers from seed the first year, it is actually perennial, and may be kept to give its bounty another year.

Dimorphotheca (h.a.). South African daisies, usually in brilliant yellows, that close up at night. Easy, showy, and quick, 9 in. *D. sinuata* 'Tetra Goliath' is outstanding. Must have full sun and a light, rather dry soil. Sow *in situ* and thin to 8 in.

Evening primrose (*Oenothera biennis*, h.b.). The biennial sort is a 3 ft. bush studded with gay blossoms of primrose hue, fleeting but successional, opening late afternoon. Excellent among shrubs, tolerating partial shade as well as full sun. Space at 18 in. in groups of three or more. *See* next chapter for the perennial species.

Flax (*Linum*). There are several species of flax, perennial and otherwise. Of the hardy annuals, one that is quite outstanding is *L. grandiflorum* 'Rubrum'. Its slender, filigree foliage is crowned with brilliant rose-scarlet clusters of satin trumpets, individually fleeting, but following each other in rapid succession in July and August. A foot high, it is as easy as possible. Sow *very sparsely* and thin to 8 in.

Forget-me-not (*Myosotis alpestris* and *M. sylvatica* hybrids, treated as h.b.). These easy old favourites prefer moist places, are lovely in shrubberies, and are a beautiful groundwork for tall tulips. One or two old plants heeled-in in a moist corner will seed abundantly.

Foxglove (*Digitalis*, h.b.). The modern hybrids, now in a wide range of colours, have great beauty. *D. purpurea* Sutton's Excelsior Group, which carry their flowers all round the stem and pointing a little upwards, are very distinctive. Valuable for prospering in shade, even dense shade beneath trees. Final spacing 18 in. Foxy Group is a pretty dwarf in various colours.

Godetia (*Clarkia amoena*, h.a./h.b.). One of the half-dozen best, forming a bushy pyramid enlivened with sparkling porcelain cups in many colours. Succeds almost anywhere, including shade, if the soil is well dug. Heights vary from 8 in. to 3 ft. Sow *in situ*, and thin to 6 in. for the dwarfs and 1 ft. for the tall ones. Good grown as a biennial. 'Kelvedon Glory' and 'Sybil Sherwood' are two beauties of 15 in.

Kochia (*Bassia scoparia*, h.h.a., pronounced Kokia). Shapely little bushes just like dwarf cypress in appearance, grown essentially for their foliage, which is a tender green in summer and fiery red in autumn. Good for the poor man's rock garden and for formal, rather prim effects. Can be raised under glass without heat early April. Don't call it burning bush which may also mean dittany.

Larkspur (*Consolida*, h.a./h.b.). If the sweet pea is the queen of annuals, the larkspur, or annual delphinium, is certainly the princess royal, but to attain her full 4–5 ft. (1.2–1.5 m.) of glory she must have deep and generous soil treatment, like clarkia. A very top choice. Get the double-flowered form in mixed colours and sow *in situ*, thinning to 1 ft.; don't transplant. Excels as a biennial.

Lavatera. *See* Mallow.

Lobelia (*L.erinus*, h.h.a.). The ever-popular little edging plant with multitudes of tiny flowers of vivid blue. One of the best places for it is at the feet of standard roses. The white-eyed 'Mrs. Clibran' is a charmer. 'Rosamond' is claret-red and 'Sapphire' is for window-boxes, slopes, walls etc. Spacing 5 in.

Love-in-a-mist (*Nigella damascena*, h.a./h.b.). Of these well-loved old cottage flowers, with their blue cockades, half-veiled in slender foliage, the variety 'Miss Jekyll' is quite the best. A thing of delicate grace and beautiful form and atmosphere. Sow *in situ* and space to 18 in.

Love-lies-bleeding (*Amaranthus caudatus*, treat as h.h.a.). This is the amaranth, or flower gentle, so loved of our ancestors. It has long, dropping trails, like catkins, of deep crimson or some other colour, most effective when dotted among other plants, rather than massed. It needs sun and a poor, gritty soil and looks well tumbling down a bank. 30 in. There are also erect cultivars grown for their brilliant foliage, such as *A. tricolor* 'Illumination'.

Mallow, or rose mallow (*Lavatera trimestris*, h.a.). One of the biggest annuals, making a bushy plant nearly 4 ft. high, with blooms like a single hollyhock. Easily the best varieties are 'Tanagra' and 'Loveliness'. Sow *in situ* and thin to 2 ft. An exceptionally good seaside plant, resisting salt, filtering the wind and, in spite of its height, needs no staking.

Marigolds. The familiar pot marigold (so-called because its dried petals are used to flavour soups and stews) is *Calendula officinalis*. A kindergarten plant, it does well anywhere, including poor soils. Sow the large seeds 5 in. apart and thin to 10 in.; the thinnings will transplant. There are orange and lemon shades, and the variety 'Radio' has attractive quilled petals. Among

the many double-flowered varieties, Fiesta Gitana Series, mixed, has won
many prizes.

The African marigold (*Tagetes erecta*) has stiff stems from 15 in. to 3 ft.,
topped with bold orange or lemon orbs whose brassy splendour shows at
its best only when the soil has been well cultivated and in hot, dryish places
in full sun. 'First Lady' and 'Orange Jubilee' are striking.

The dwarf French marigold (*Tagetes patula*) usually has crimson or
chocolate showily mingled with its gold. Gay, flowerful and easy. The single
'Naughty Marietta' is jolly.

Both the Frenchman and the African are h.h.a. New varieties of both
are constantly coming out in bewildering profusion, and they have been
much inter-married, as in 'Seven Star'. The brisk little plant usually sold as
Tagetes in the market is *T. tenuifolia* var. *pumila* (syn. *T. signata pumila*) and in
mild districts can be grown as h.a.

Space the tall ones at 1 ft. and the smaller ones at 8 in. They are really
Mexican, not French or African. Keep all marigolds dead-headed and they
will bloom a long time.

Morning glory. The best loved of these twining plants, displaying
brilliantly coloured bugles, is *Ipomoea rubrocoerulea* 'Heavenly Blue'. Normal
h.h.a. treatment. There are also striped and pink varieties.

Nasturtium (h.a.). Has stolen this name from the water-cress, as it was
apparently introduced here as Indian cress, its spicy leaves being good in a
salad. Legally it is *Tropaeolum majus*. It does best in poor soils. Try Tip Top
Series. Sow the big seeds 6 in. apart, 1 ft. for the trailers or 'climbers', which
are excellent for tumbling down a bank of poor, stony soil. The seeds,
gathered young, can be used as capers.

Nemesia (h.h.a.). These showy little bedding plants of many colours are not
easy to grow well, and the poor specimens often seen are usually the result
of their having been left crowded too long in the seed-box. They dislike a
check and, after germination, must be moved along quickly, into small pots
if necessary, before planting out. Better still, use peat pots. They like things
moist, cool and peaty at all stages.

Nemophila (h.a./h.b.) is a pretty little annual, alive with a multitude of
small, azure, white-eyed flowers for many weeks after midsummer. It grows
only 6 in. high. Sow *in situ* in a sunny place in any good garden soil. Thin
to 5 in. Carnival is one good strain.

Nicotiana (the flowering tobacco, h.h.a.). The 1–3 ft. stems carry a number
of blossoms having long, tubular necks and wide-open faces that embalm the
evening air with their fragrance. Very decorative and easy and very welcome
under a sitting-room window. 'Lime Green' is a delightful variety and
'Crimson Rock' is a dwarf red.

Pansies, or heartsease, are a sort of viola, but usually treated as hardy biennials, sown in June, pricked off into a shady nursery bed and planted out in
early autumn in sun or partial shade in a fairly rich soil. Keep them dead-
headed and they will bloom for months. Most have an almost black splash

in the centre of the blossom, others have clean faces. Varieties abound, each nurseryman having his own pets. The notable Roggli Giants Series have very large blossoms. Gay Jesters Series and Clear Crystals Series are thronged with clean faces in many colours. Winter-flowering strains give cheer to those months.

Petunia (treat as h.h.a.). This popular flower has erupted into all manner of varieties and colours, small or large, flamboyant or tender, single or monstrously double. Choose at your will from the catalogues. Delay sowing till March and give the same quick-moving treatment as for nemesias. Excellent for any use, including window-boxes and hanging baskets.

Phacelia (h.a./h.b.). A charming little 8 in. plant of special value for its brilliant and rare gentian blue and for its long season of flowering. Sow in full sun *in situ* in mid-April and thin to 6 in. for July blooming. Order *P. campanularia*.

Phlox. The annual type is *P. drummondii* (h.h.a.), 1 ft. only, adorned with large trusses of bloom in delicious colours. A pearl among annuals, but it is useless to expect good results without thorough digging and really generous soil treatment and plenty of sun. Move into small pots about the end of April before planting out in June.

Poppy (*Papaver*) Finest of all is the Iceland poppy, *P. nudicaule*, which illumines the border or the vase with jaunty flowers of orange and lemon or of pastel pinks and apricot. A delightful adornment in any garden. Needs full sun, a soil containing plenty of leafmould or peat, and plenty of moisture. Best treated as h.b., though really a perennial.

Of the annual poppies, the two main sorts are the popular Shirley poppy (*P. rhoeas* Shirley Group) 2 ft. and the opium poppy (*P. somniferum*) with grey leaves, 3 ft., both in many colours. The former can be had in either single or double forms, and in delicate pastel shades or flaunting reds. The opium poppies are mostly very large doubles, some of them looking like carnations. Sow both *in situ* (will not transplant well) in gritty soil and full sun and thin to 1 ft. apart. Keep dead blooms rigorously cut down. Unfortunately their foliage becomes an eyesore after flowering.

All sorts have very fine seed, which should be merely dusted over. *See* Chapter II for the Oriental poppy.

Rudbeckia. Of the annual forms of the gloriosa daisy, far the best is Rustic Dwarfs Group, which adorns the bed with very large daisies in rich tones of chestnut, yellow, flame and mahogany. They make compact plants of up to 20 in. Treat as h.h.a. or h.b.

Salpiglossis sinuata (h.h.a.). Graceful plants 2 ft. high with trumpets of various colours delicately veined. Good for an unheated greenhouse, but quite suitable also for outdoors if sheltered from wind, well staked, and given plenty of sun. Rather short-lived.

Salvia. The 15 in. plant of vivid pillar-box red, used for summer bedding, is *S. splendens* (h.h.a.). The seed has to be raised in a temperature of 66°F, so those without this facility must buy the plants and put them out the first week in June. If you can raise them yourself, prick them out first into small pots and then into 4 in. ones. There are pink and violet varieties as well as the usual flamboyant scarlet. The true annual, hardy salvia is *S. horminum*, known of old as annual clary, its diverse colours displayed in its bracts, not its flowers, as in poinsettias. *See* Chapter II for the perennial salvias.

Stock (*Matthiola incana*). One of the garden's prime favourites. Of the rather confusing classification with fancy names given in catalogues, first choice for Southern gardens is the popular ten-week stock. Is a h.h.a., but may be raised under glass without heat in mid-April. Guard against damping-off. Plant out 10 in. apart. Do not pinch out the tips, and do not discard the smaller seedlings, which often turn out the best. The desired double-flowered ones can be identified in the seedling stage by their noticeably paler foliage.

East Lothian stocks are the ones to have in the North, particularly Scotland, where they prosper with hyacinthine splendour from the end of July onwards. Sow in heat in February, or treat as biennials and sow outdoors in late July.

Brompton stocks are treated as hardy biennials. They bloom in the spring at the same time as wallflowers, which they certainly equal and perhaps surpass in beauty, charm, and fragrance. Raise them in exactly the same way as wallflowers, but plant out 15 in. apart. In cold and damp districts they may not stand the winter outdoors.

Beauty of Nice stocks are for heated greenhouses only. Virginia stock (*Malcolmia maritima*) is an easy 6 in. annual for edgings and crannies. Night-scented stock (*Matthiola longipetala* subsp. *bicornis*) is a dwarf of insignificant appearance but glorious perfume, exhaled as evening approaches. Sprinkle the seed under the sitting-room window, or in a window-box, mixed with more showy things.

Sunflower (h.a.). All the *Helianthus* are sunflowers, but the one popularly so called (*H. annuus*) is the giant with rubicund face nodding over the cottage wall. It needs well-dug soil and full sun to attain full stature. Sow a seed or two every few feet in April and thin to one at each station. If the seeds are wanted for parrots or chickens, cut off the flower-head as soon as the seeds begin to loosen in September and dry it off indoors in a sunny window. *See also under Helianthus* in Chapter II.

Sweet pea (*Lathyrus odoratus*, h.a.). There are two methods of raising this queen of all annuals. The first is for ordinary garden decoration, and the other is for getting specially fine blooms on long stems for the vase or for exhibition. For either purpose, note especially – first, that the sweet pea demands full sun, and secondly, that it is a gross feeder, rooting very deeply, and needs large quantities of animal or vegetable organic food. For garden decoration grow them in clumps about 4 ft. wide in a mixed border or, if wanted mainly for cutting, in straight lines in the kitchen garden. Unless the soil is in very good heart already, bastard-trench it according to the

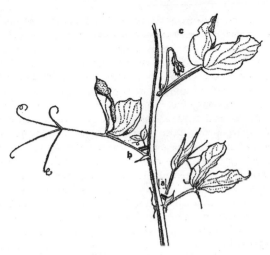

Sweet peas. When growing for big blooms, remove leafy axillary shoots a and b, but not the young flowering stem c. Take care to distinguish between the two.

precept of Chapter 5, fortifying it with all the organic riches you possess. The area of prepared ground should extend some 9 in. beyond the sowing stations.

In early April sow the seeds 1 in. deep and 3 in. apart. Soak the tough-skinned black ones in water for 24 hours beforehand. If mice are feared, dip all seeds in paraffin and roll them in red lead. Take anti-slug precautions. Plant bushy pea-sticks, 5 ft. high, thickly and deeply.

After the seedlings have shown their second pair of leaves nip out the tips of the growing shoots. When they show their first buds, give them a liquid feed. Pick the blooms early, go on picking and remove all spent blooms. Water the plot liberally and *regularly,* or the buds may drop before opening.

The gardener can also get pretty results by sowing seeds casually among other plants, especially other climbers, such as roses, clematis and wisteria.

As this book is not intended for exhibitors, I shall touch only very lightly on the method of growing for that purpose, that is to say, with multiple blooms on long, straight stems.

Carry out the full trenching operation, a good three spits deep. Raise the seedlings in pots in the autumn and plant them out in April, 9 in. apart, or sow direct in the ground early that month. Erect a phalanx of canes, 7 ft. tall, braced together with wires, one cane per plant. Keep each plant restrained to one single stem only, plucking out all sideshoots. Tie each stem to its cane every foot or so. When the plants reach the tops of their canes, take them all down (very tricky), lead them along to a cane 7 ft. further on, and start again. A boring business.

Of the many strains of sweet pea, the usual one is the Spencer strain, with waved and frilly petals. Those that have scent are found chiefly in the lavender and the pastel shades. The Galaxy Series is nearly as good for garden purposes, very vigorous and multi-flowered but less refined. The American Knee-Hi Series grows waist-high in Britain. For rich scent and old-world charm, go for old Grandifloras or for the wild *Lathyrus odoratus* 'Matucana' or *L.o.* 'Cupani'.

Sweet sultan (*Amberboa moschata,* syn. *Centaurea moschata*). Pretty feathery mops are borne on 18 in. stems from July onwards. An old-time favourite, but China asters are usually preferred.

Sweet William (h.b.). This fine old favourite is a member of the carnation and pink genus (*Dianthus*). The bicolour form called auricula-eyed is specially attractive to most people; and there is a dwarf variety. Sweet William stops blooming at an awkward time of year, and something should be grown-on in pots, such as dwarf dahlias, ready to follow it in July. Space at 10 in.

Tagetes. *See under* Marigolds.

Wallflower (*Erysimum,* h.b.). There are two popular sorts – the scented wallflower in many colours blooming in early spring (*E. cheiri*), and the slightly later Siberian wallflower, which is a glowing orange ball of fire (*E.* × *marshallii,* syn. *E.* × *allionii*), immensely vivid and warm. Both easy to raise from a normal June sowing. 'Stop' them when about 4 in. high. The Siberian blooms right on till mid-June, and when it is over presents the same problems of succession as Sweet William. The pretty mauve *E. linifolium* is good for edging and stone work. *See also under* Rock Gardens.

Zinnia (h.h.a.). Either you rave about zinnias or you consider them stiff and artificial. To do it justice, *Z. grandiflora* needs a hot summer and generous cultivation. This is another plant that rebels at being checked in youth; don't buy boxed seedlings from a garden shop. Sow in April in a greenhouse with or without heat, and prick them out into pots, or sow direct outdoors in permanent stations under cloches. Space at 15 in., having fed the soil really well organically. Give copious draughts of water during growth. Quantities of new varieties of all sorts and sizes appear nearly every year.

II

HERBACEOUS AND MIXED BORDERS

THE USE AND MISUSE OF BORDER PLANTS

The herbaceous border has long been one of the glories of the British garden, and although in large places there is a tendency to supplant it by flowering shrubs because of the labour involved, it is likely to hold its place in the smaller gardens, in some form or other, for a very long time to come. For the border is relatively inexpensive to stock, especially if the plants are grown from seed, as many of the best can easily be grown if one has the patience to wait a year, using annuals in their place meantime. Those not easily raised from seed, such as Michaelmas daisies and phloxes, can generally be multiplied from stem or root cuttings, and others by division, so that from a few initial plants a wealth of stock can soon be built up if desired.

In the small garden herbaceous plants have many uses besides their employment in herbaceous or mixed borders; they may adorn many odd corners, or occupy small beds, and some mingle happily with shrubs. Conversely, there are some *not* at their best in the heterogeneous company of the border, such as violas and lilies-of-the-valley. Others again, being essentially flowers for cutting and not very showy in the border, can with advantage be grown in straight rows in the kitchen garden, such as pyrethrum and scabious. But it is with the 'border', not necessarily entirely herbaceous, that I shall be specially concerned in this introduction.

Borders can be of many shapes and sizes – straight or curved, broad or narrow. They can face in any direction, but the south-facing border is the easiest, and the north-facing one requires a special technique in the choice of plants. As a backing for the border, nothing is better than a bank of shrubs, but there is seldom room enough in a small place. Stone or brick walls are excellent, giving shelter for the less hardy things and allowing the employment of wall plants, but of course a border can quite well be out in the open, though shelter from stiff winds is to be desired.

In siting the border, try to have it running directly or obliquely away from the main windows of the house, so that one looks or walks down its length in perspective. A border should not be looked at full in the face, for there are always seasonal gaps. Island beds, to which much publicity has been given, are a flop in small gardens.

Borders should never be directly overhung by large trees, but some slanting shade for part of the day will be appreciated by some inhabitants, such as phlox and lupin.

As the plants are to stay in their home for some years, it is common sense to prepare their beds thoroughly. Having made sure of good drainage – the first essential – dig the ground a good two spits deep, incorporating manure or other organic food at all levels and bonemeal in the top one. A few plants, however, dislike manure. The work should be done several weeks before planting. In general, herbaceous plants can be put out any time from November to March if the ground is not frostbound or saturated, but on cold, heavy clays spring is best. Moreover, there are a few plants that should always be planted in spring only, including scabious, gaillardia, pyrethrum, *Aster amellus* and *A.* x *frikartii,* and some others mentioned in the notes that follow.

In the after-care of the border, there are some important considerations. First, do *not* dig over the plot in autumn; it tears up roots and disturbs or damages precious things such as lilies or other bulbs and alstroemerias. Much more important, having got rid of weeds, is to mulch it in spring with manure or, in default, with a deep bed of leaves in autumn underlaid with fertiliser.

Other after-care measures are the staking of any kinds of plants liable to flop as they attain full height, and the removal of spent blooms. A great many herbaceous plants will go on and on if dead-headed, particularly anything that has the form and shape of a daisy.

About every third or fourth year the border, having become overgrown, will need sorting out. Leave alone the plants that resent disturbance – alstroemerias, delphiniums, Japanese anemones, lilies and other plants named in these notes; but lift all other herbaceous plants, divide them and replant. In big borders a portion can be done annually. If an annual top-dressing has been given, re-manuring will not be necessary.

The use of lime will depend on the condition of the soil and the nature of its inhabitants. The lupin does not care for much lime, but gypsophila and iris do. The general run of herbaceous plants, however, seem indifferent to all but extreme conditions.

The soil may have been well and truly made ready according to Cocker, but the border may still be a failure if it is not well laid-out. Composition, or design, is the touchstone. It requires, first, a little elementary knowledge of the characteristics of each plant – its height, spread, colour, season of flowering, and foliage – most of which can be got from any good catalogue, but it also requires something less easily taught – an eye. Variations in height, blends, or contrasts in colour, a bold handling of shapes and forms, a sympathetic grouping of different leaf textures, the counterpoint of light and shade – these are the things that make a border beautiful. I have room for only one or two guiding precepts, but I must emphasise from the first that, just like any other artistic composition, it has got to be worked out with care, indeed loving care, on paper beforehand. There is no other way, and the best paper to use is the large-squared paper of a child's arithmetic book (not graph paper).

Formality is to be avoided like the plague. The hand of man must be in no shape evident. No straight lines, no regimented gradations from the dwarf in front to the giant at the back, no plants dotted singly here and there, save one or two of the more high-pitched colours. Everything must seem as though 'painted o'er with nature's hand, not art's' – and nature sheds her seeds in drifts and clusters. If you possess only three phloxes, put them all together. While obviously 7-ft. plants must not be right in front, nor miniatures right at the back, let a promontory of helenium or campanula thrust out towards the front, and a drift of penstemon sweep back towards the centre. Let the clusters be irregular in form – some roughly circular, some elongated, some sweeping away at an angle, and so on.

On colour composition one can in this small compass speak only in general terms. In the small garden a communism of colours must be accepted. Plants adjacent to one another should harmonise rather than contrast, with the more vivid colours used just here and there for 'accent' notes, as in music. The red *Lychnis chalcedonica* is ideal for such a purpose. Orange and bronze shades are sometimes difficult to fix, and jar discordantly against a delicate blue. Generally speaking, however, the mixed colours of nature do make happy marriages (witness the fuchsia), and much that is written on this subject is rather arty and affected. No colour scheme, however, is entirely balanced without a few touches of white here and there, and nothing has a greater charm for this purpose than the white campanulas. A few plants of silver-grey foliage – such as cotton lavender, the silvery artemisias, rose campion (*Lychnis coronaria*) and the dwarf yarrows (*Achillea*) also make melodious variations of the theme.

In small places grace and strength are given to the garden if the herbaceous border is made into a 'mixed' one by inviting into it two other classes – bulbous plants, and the smaller flowering shrubs. Of the former, lilies add a note of distinction and dahlias are valuable for filling blanks left by early flowering plants. Of shrubs, there is one lovely little shrub with chaste pale blue florets just like those of a plumbago and with a slender airy habit that I would never do without again. Unfortunately its only name is *Ceratostigma willmottianum*. Other small shrubs particularly suitable for a mixed border are *Brachyglottis* (Dunedin Group) 'Sunshine', potentillas, hypericums, fuchsias, some spiraeas, Floribunda roses, the dwarfish varieties of philadelphus, with helianthemums for the front edge.

Depth is a great boon in a border – more important than length. Those who can spare 12 ft. or more are fortunate, and anything less than about 8 ft. creates problems in composition. For narrow borders or strips there are but two choices – be satisfied with a collection that will give you a full blaze for a short period, or have only a limited number of subjects and cluster them boldly. By way of example, the awkward 3 ft. strip is admirably furnished by using only lupins for early summer, followed by phlox for mid-season, succeeded by medium dahlias.

A border about 5 ft. wide, if of reasonable length, could comfortably accommodate an arrangement of lupins, *Achillea filipendulina* 'Gold Plate', purple salvia, phlox or bergamot, liatris, Michaelmas daisy, campanula and a few delphiniums, together with pinks, camomile, flax, erigeron, cranesbill, and stonecrop at or near the front. And if you are habitually on holiday in August, you can cut out all flowers that bloom at that season.

A SELECTION OF PERENNIALS

The following is a short selection only of the more meritorious and easily grown perennials. Among them are some unhackneyed plants of great merit that make a border 'something different' and that I specially commend to beginners. These are the *Alstroemeria ligtu* hybrids, echinacea, the queenly romneya, liatris, dittany, the modern agapanthus, bleeding heart, the eryngiums, *Aster × frikartii*, heuchera, and the delightful *Chrysanthemum zawadskii* (syn. *C. rubellum*).

This list contains flowers suitable for all sorts of conditions – wet soils and dry soils, sun and shade. Oddly, not all herbaceous plants are suited to the borders, such as lily-of-the-valley and meconopsis, but have their special uses elsewhere. The classifications in the appendices may be a help.
Achillea. The yarrow or milfoil genus provides some tiresome weeds, but also some excellent garden flowers. The finest is *A. filipendulina* 'Gold Plate', an outstanding border plant, vigorous and easy, carrying on its erect 5 ft. stems bold and striking golden platters, 7 in. across, which are of great service in giving diversity of form and feature to the border, and which gleam above the foliage for many weeks. 'Coronation Gold', the handsome, silver-leaved 'Moonshine' and *Aclypeolata*, are fine for middle distance planting. 'Cerise Queen' is a gay version for the front of the border but rather invasive. Increase all by division. *See also under* Rock Gardens.
Agapanthus. Copious sheaves of strap-like leaves from which arise thick rods surmounted by large orbs of numerous bluebells. The Headbourne hybrids are quite hardy. Heights vary from 18 in. to 4 ft. (40 cm. to 1.2 m.) and colours from violet to white. For lean, sandy, gravelly or chalky soils only. No manure on any account, but buckets of water in summer. Excellent in tubs.
Alstroemeria, sometimes called Peruvian lily. The brilliant and rampant orange species so familiar everywhere (*A. aurea*) has been displaced by the *A. ligtu* hybrids, which, with their sparkling pink shades, have a butterfly brilliance that makes them one of the loveliest things yet introduced. But they require full sun, a deeply dug soil enriched with organic matter and a situation on the dry side. The fleshy roots resent disturbance, and so should not be more than a year old when bought. Plant them vertically, bud end

uppermost, 6 in. deep in August or September. Easier still is to grow them from seed. Put three seeds in a 5 in. pot, and when well sprouted, plant out the whole ball of soil without disturbance. Weed carefully by hand only.

Anchusa. Bushy plants (of short life) for the back of the border enamelled with little brilliant blue flowers like forget-me-nots, 4–5 ft. Valuable for infusing the blue influence in May and June before the delphiniums, and for being drought-hardy, but take up a lot of room and leave bare gaps after midsummer. 'Opal' and 'Loddon Royalist' are fine varieties.

Anemone. Of this versatile and beautiful family two are of special value. One is the familiar Japanese anemone (miscalled *A. japonica*), with slender 3 ft. stems and chaste salvers of white, pink or mauve in late summer and autumn. It is of special merit for succeeding in the shade, even moderately dense shade, where the white and pale pink forms gracefully lighten up the gloom. A slow starter but then fearfully invasive. *Plant in spring.*

Quite different is our lovely native Pasque flower, *Pulsatilla vulgaris* (syn. *Anemone pulsatilla*) ('shaking in the wind'). In April it lifts up purple emblems, enriched with golden stamens, on 10 in. stems, the whole draped with a soft, silken down. This plant is a chalkdweller, so likes sun and a dry situation. *See* Chapters 12 and 13 for other anemones.

Aster. Among the perennial asters the most important race is the large and splendid class of Michaelmas daisies, ranging from 6 ft. giants to 6 in. pygmies. There is a wealth of choice, and new varieties appear every year with larger and larger blooms, but some of the old guard, such as *A. novi-belgii* 'Beechwood Challenger' and *A. novae-angliae* 'Harrington's Pink', still hold their own. Trim back the tops of all the Micks with shears in late April to promote bushiness and be prepared to spray against mildew.

Some of the smaller perennial asters, though less well known, equal or surpass the big Michaelmas daisies and are admirable for small gardens. I specially recommend:

A. x *frikartii*, a 3 ft. hybrid, is a joyful profusion of large, brilliant blue florets around a bright orange eye. It flowers for three months from July and is one of the finest perennials we have. The variety called 'Wunder von Stäfa' is inferior to *A.* x *frikartii* 'Mönch'.

The gay *A. amellus* clan, has big, deep-golden discs, about 2 ft. high, of great charm and longevity, especially the pink 'Sonia' and the violet 'King George'. Plant in spring, not autumn.

A. yunnanensis 'Napsbury', 2 ft., is a glowing heliotrope with golden disc that has the distinction of starting as early as June.

x *Solidaster luteus* is a cross between a Michaelmas daisy and a goldenrod. Often listed as *A.* x *hybridus*, it is thronged with a busy swarm of tiny gold stars in July and August.

All these asters are increased by division, which should be done about every three years, selecting the outside shoots.

Astilbe. This is a gay genus with feathery plumes in brilliant and in pastel colours 1–4 ft. high, often mistaken for spiraeas. They prefer a moist and partially shaded position near water, but succeed well elsewhere provided the soil is not very dry. *A.* x *arendsii* 'Fanal' is an old favourite in dazzling red. *A.* x *arendsii* 'Bressingham Beauty' and *A.* x *arendsii* 'Venus' (3 ft.) are pink. *A. chinensis* var. *taquetti* 'Superba' throws up purple plumes of 4 ft., and there are some charming dwarfs. Excellent also in pots in the greenhouse. Easily multiplied from its own seed immediately it is ripe, or by careful division in early spring.

Bergamot (*Monarda* hybrids). An old-world plant with aromatic leaves and curiously wrought flowers of bold design and audacious colour. Blooms prodigiously. The dazzling 'Cambridge Scarlet' is the best known, but 'Croftway Pink' is also desirable, and there is now a whole new range in claret, violet, ruby and other shades. A splendid substitute where phloxes fail. Needs moist soil. Top-dress each spring with fine soil and bonemeal. Sometimes short-lived.

Bleeding heart or Lucy Locket (*Dicentra*). From graceful, arching wands are suspended strings of pink jewels in the shape of a broken heart. It has an air of wistful elegance, and it likes a rich soil and ample moisture to prolong its rather short display in July. Also an easy pot-plant for the cold greenhouse. *D. spectabilis*, 18 in., is the one to have. Guard against slugs and quilt it with leaves in winter. Gently pull out its outer petals and you will see why it is also called lady in the bath.

Camomile (*Anthemis*). Old-world favourites with yellow daisies, esteemed for blooming from midsummer right into autumn and fine for cutting. The best variety is 'Beauty of Grallagh' of 2½ ft., but the species *A. sanctijohannis*, which is St Ivan's camomile and shorter, is also a very merry fellow. *See also under* Rock Gardens.

Campanula. No border is perfectly harmonious without the music of the harebells. They rise in airy steeples hung with bells of cool, clear blue or white, giving lightness and grace to their surroundings. They thrive not only in the sun, but also in dense shade, where the white varieties are particularly welcome. Out of a large family the first pick is the blue *C. persicifolia* ('peach leaved'), and second comes the white *C.p.* 'Snowdrift'. Other fine ones are *C. lactiflora* 'Prichard's Variety' and *C. latifolia* 'Brantwood'. All about 3 ft. Increase by division. *See also* the chapter on rock gardens.

Carnation. *See* Chapter 18.

Catananche. Abundant flowers very like cornflowers, and much longer-lasting. Wants sun and succeeds in very dry soils. The flowers are semi-'everlasting'. Get *C. caerula* 'Major', June to September, 2 ft. Multiply by seed or by root cuttings 1½–2 in. long.

Catmint (*Nepeta*). This grey-leaved favourite with lavender flowers should have a sunny position and does best in dry, poor soils. Plant in spring, not autumn. Do not cut down dead growth till spring. For general use the ordinary hybrid *N.* x *faassenii* (often wrongly listed as *N. mussinii*) suffices. Multiply by division in spring.

Christmas rose (*Helleborus niger*) and **Lenten rose** (*H.* × *hybridus*). The elegant but expensive woodland hellebores have large white or plum chalices, which in turn enrich the scene from November till April. They revel in chalk. Plant where they will hide the naked legs of deciduous shrubs. Excellent pot-plants for the cold greenhouse.

Chrysanthemum. *See* Chapter 18.

Columbine (*Aquilegia*). Few flowers are more charming than these dainty wing-footed ballerinas dancing on slender stems. Easily grown from seed sown in June, and a packet of 'mixed long-spurred hybrids' will delight anyone. They succeed in partial shade as in sun.

Cranesbill. The true geranium, as distinct from the summer-bedding pelargonium that has pinched its name, is a decorative hardy perennial making a leafy, spreading bush, bearing multitudes of dainty chalices in sun or shade and good for woodland also. Remove spent blooms for a continuous show. Best of the lot is *G. himalayense* 'Gravetye', pale blue. Other good ones are the pink *endressii*, the rose *G.* × *riversleaianum* 'Russell Prichard' and *G. psilostemon*, a richly barbaric magenta. Several of the rock-garden cranesbills, which are probably the most attractive, can also embellish the edge of the border. *See* Chapter 12.

Delphinium. Those who want to see the queen of the border in her full measure of stately beauty must give her better treatment than the common herd. Good drainage, a soil deeply dug and well enriched with organic food, a place in the sun and plenty of elbow room are her due. She prefers a fairly heavy loam, not too acid; very light, sandy soils are unpropitious, otherwise there is no difficulty about her upbringing.

The gorgeous named varieties of the catalogues are expensive, but it is a fact that equally good results can sometimes be got from seed of really good firms, such as Blackmore and Langdon.

The American Giant Pacifics and Sutton's dwarf Blue Fountains Group are also excellent from seed.

In spring sow 2 in. apart in boxes or pans in a cool, shady position. Not in a greenhouse. Transplant when ready into a nursery bed in semi-shade about 9 in. apart. 'Cool, moist, and shady' is the rule until planting into permanent quarters, which is normally in early autumn. Then put them in the sun 2 ft. apart. *Cut out any flower-spikes that form the first year.*

Next spring, before the plants are 6 in. high, thin out the young shoots, allowing not more than one or two the first year, three the second and five or six thereafter. Cut cleanly at the base with a sharp knife. This is the secret of long, strong spikes. Then feed well with a liquid fertiliser (I use Maxicrop) and mulch yearly with manure.

Staking is a serious problem. The gales and heavy rain squalls of June can play havoc with the opulent spires. Plant 4 ft. canes firmly when the plants are about 2 ft. high, one cane per spike. Tie the plants round first when a foot high and a second time just below the flower-spike. I and other people tie each spike separately (but loosely), to a cane.

When flowering is over, cut down each stem just below the bottom of the flower-spike and leave the foliage to die down in the natural way; *don't encourage a second blooming by cutting them right down on the ground.* To mask the blank that there will be after blooming, have planted in front of them something that will grow up and flower after them, such as phlox, salvia or dahlias. In winter scrape away the soil from around the crown of the plant and cover it thickly with very sharp sand as a basic protection against slugs, which play the very devil with delphiniums. *See under* Slugs, page 265.

You can multiply your favourite varieties by taking cuttings in earliest spring when the young shoots are about 3 in. high. Remove some soil and, with a very sharp knife, slice off these growths with a thin sliver of the crown attached. Take none with hollow stems. Insert them in *very* sandy soil in pots or boxes in a close and shaded frame, taking care to observe all the rules for softwood cuttings. In a month they should have roots an inch long; transplant them then into 4 in. pots. Plant them in their permanent stations in May.

Regrettably, I cannot spare space to list named varieties, but do specially commend the 'short' ones, notably 'Blue Tit', Blue Jade Group and 'Page Boy'.

The Belladonna delphinium is a less regal kind, growing only to 3 ft. and more loosely built.

See also under Annuals (p. 90).

Dianthus. *See* Chapter 18.

Dittany, or fraxinella (*Dictamnus*). A fine old-timer. Aromatic and distinctive, it has 2 ft. racemes of mauve-pink (*D. albus* var. *purpureus*) or white (*D. albus*) in June and July, and will tolerate partial shade. Its peculiarity is that it gives off a volatile gas which will ignite when a match is put just below a bloom on a warm, still evening with no harm to the plant; hence it has been called burning bush but so is Kochia. Dislikes disturbance, but easily raised from seed.

Doronicum (leopard's bane). Large golden daisies of the easiest culture, opening in April, which I like to call spring sunflowers. *D.* x *excelsum* 'Harpur Crewe' (syn. *D. plantagineum* 'Excelsum') grows impressively to 3 ft.; 'Miss Mason' is nearly 2 ft. and 'Frühlingspracht' (Spring Beauty) is a little shorter still with doubled flowers.

Echinacea. Includes one or two splendid varieties sometimes catalogued under Rudbeckia. 'Magnus' is a fine 4 ft. variety like a small crimson sunflower. The rosy-red Bressingham hybrids are shorter. August and September. Increase by division.

Erigeron. Another ideal 2 ft. plant for the small (or big) border, resembling a large-flowered Michaelmas daisy of low stature, and having a long season of bloom throughout summer. There are several new ones, but I prefer the old, such as 'Quakeress' and 'Foersters Liebling'. Division.

Eryngium sp. Distinctive and very attractive plants with bristly teazle heads and spiny foliage, esteemed for their all-over metallic sheen and for the diversity of form they give to a border. For a start, take *E. alpinum*, *E.* x *oliverianum*, and *E. variifolium*, the last steely blue all over. Avoid rich feeding.

Evening primrose (*Oenothera*). The perennial sorts, too little seen, are mostly 18 in. plants spangled with red buds opening to bold golden cups from June till August. The best is *O. macrocarpa* (syn. *O. missouriensis*) low, spreading, with very large, luminous flowers of pale primrose. *O. fruticosa* 'Fyrverkeri' is a brilliant 18 in. In contrast to the biennial sorts, they need full sun and stay open all day.

Gaillardia. Those who want good results from these fiery splendours, especially for cutting, must observe three rules – give them a rich soil; keep them staked from an early stage with bushy pea-sticks; cut spent blooms down to the base of the stalk. Fine varieties are 'Mandarin' and 'Wirral Flame'. Plant in spring, not autumn. Increase by seed, division or winter root cuttings.

Geranium. *See* (p. 103) Cranesbill *and Pelargonium* (p. 79).

Geum (avens). Not as good as the rather similar *Potentilla*, but, for those who want it, the best are 'Fire Opal', 18 in., and the shorter orange *G. coccineum* 'Werner Arends', both excellent flowers for the front of the border. For very wet places get 'Leonard's Variety' of the water avens (*G. rivale*).

Gypsophila. Beautiful for its border effects as for its cutting value. It relishes lime. The best is still 'Bristol Fairy'; 'Rosenschleier' (syn. 'Rosy Veil') and 'Pink Star' are good too. Dig the ground deeply, for their tap-roots go far. Increase is difficult, but can be made by taking sturdy basal shoots with a heel in July, inserting them in sandy soil under close, moist conditions.

Helenium. Provided you have no prejudice against bronzy shades, helenium will give great satisfaction for its showiness, ease of culture, and long season of bloom. It has yellow, bronze, or mahogany daisy-form flowers, grows to 3 ft. high, and should be planted in clusters of three or more 18 in. apart and in full sun. 'Moerheim Beauty', 'Butterpat', 'Bruno', and 'Wyndley' are fine sorts. Increase by division.

Helianthus. The perennial sunflowers are coarse, floppy and usually fearfully invasive. If you must have one, make it 'Capenoch Star' or 'Loddon Gold', 5 ft.

Heuchera. These have graceful sprays of dainty brilliance, rather like London Pride, in brilliant reds and pinks, and are delightful for the front of the border and for cutting in June and July. 'Scintillation' and 'Red Spangles' will do you well. x *Heucherella alba* 'Bridget Bloom' is a pretty pink hybrid of 8 in. Division.

Hollyhock (*Alcea*). This fine old fellow is best treated as a biennial, and is easy to raise from seed sown in June. It also seeds generously, and always looks best in the odd corners and crannies that it selects for itself.

Hosta. Much prized by flower-arrangers for their big, ribbed, and beautifully tailored leaves, the hostas also have elegant, lilyform flowers, often scented. Usually they are planted in partial shade. A first picking would include *H. crispula*, with leaves broadly margined white, *H. undulata*, having wavy leaves streaked with cream, the bold, cream-edged *H. undulata* var. *albomarginata*, and *H. sieboldiana* var. *glauca*, with large, crinkled, blue-green leaves.

Iris. See Chapter 18.

Liatris. The monstrous name of *L. pycnostachya* ('densely clustered') obscures one of the most useful but little known characters of the border stage. It flourishes 3 ft. truncheons densely wreathed with rosy-purple tassels, needs no staking, and blooms all July and August. An acquisition and good for cutting. Another fine one is *L. spicata* 'Kobold'. Liatris needs sun, a well-drained and deeply dug soil, and a good share of rain. Increase by offsets from its corm-like base, or by seed as soon as it ripens.

Lily-of-the-valley (*Convallaria majalis*). Not suitable for the mixed border and should be planted in partial shade. It is essential that the soil be deeply and richly cultivated, its particular requirement being leafmould, with which also it should be mulched every March. Plant the 'crowns' 6 in. apart in autumn, covered with one inch of fine soil. When overcrowded lift and divide. Also easily grown in pots.

Loosestrife, purple (*Lythrum salicaria*). The purple loosestrife is a gay and easy plant with tall 4 ft. steeples thronged with small blooms. It prefers a moist situation with some shade, but also does well elsewhere. The carmine variety 'The Beacon,' the roseate 'Brightness' and the shorter 'Robert' are excellent. Division.

Lupin. The cultivation of the splendid named varieties of the Russell lupins (from *Lupinus polyphyllus*) has tended to decline, but many good varieties are still available. However, the Russells come very easily from seed, often with excellent results, and good seed strains are to be had. Hurst's Lulu Series gives short plants in several colours. Sow in June a few inches apart in an open nursery bed in partial shade and transplant in autumn. Those that you like (whether named varieties or from seed) are easily perpetuated from cuttings in the same way as described for delphiniums.

As the lupin has long, fleshy tap-roots, deep digging in good soil is necessary, but avoid a limy soil and give them *no manure*. Partial shade is acceptable.

For convenience the tree lupin (*L. arboreus*) may be mentioned here. This is an excellent, bushy, fast-growing evergreen, 5 ft. high, densely covered with scented yellow blooms in June. Good at the seaside, easy from seed sown in pots, but shortlived.

Lychnis. From this large and versatile genus I shall pick three only, all of which give individuality to a border scheme.

L. chalcedonica is a bold, erect grenadier, 4 ft. tall, terminating in an orb of scarlet. One of the few things best dotted about singly or in small clusters, when they look like guardsmen in the park. No other plant is so good for this purpose. Excellent in wet soil.

A fine little fellow with a long name and sticky stems is *L. viscaria* 'Splendens Plena'. Rather like a rosy-purple stock, 15 in. high. It flowers from June right through till September and grows anywhere.

L. flos-jovis is the delightful old 'flower of Jove' or pink campion, with florets in charming little clusters like those of a phlox, 1 ft. high, set off by silver-grey, velvety leaves.

Michaelmas daisy. *See Aster.*

Monarda. *See* Bergamot.

Monkshood (*Aconitum*). Bushy plants with the form and habit of delphinium, but less showy; their blossoms are hooded like a monk's cowl. One of the best shade plants. The best is the blue–and–white *A.* x *cammarum* 'Bicolo'; most others rather sombre.

Mullein, or Aaron's rod (*Verbascum*). A grand old family with some progeny that are quite first-class, and easily within the dozen best for border work. They have the habit of the hollyhock, throughout June and July. *V. olympicum* reaches to 7 ft. The *V. phoeniceum* hybrids are but 3 ft. and in between are the handsome 'Gainsborough' and 'Pink Domino'. *V. bombyciferum* is a curiosity, thickly coated in down, like cotton-wool, but it is not perennial.

Pansy. *See* Chapter 10.

Penstemon. The popular hybrids of this good border plant display carillons of long, tubular bells that are borne for long periods on erect stems. They are fairly hardy and are very satisfying in full sun and light soils, but they need to be raised afresh every year or two, for they quickly exhaust themselves by exuberance of flowering. You can buy named varieties if you like, but they are easy to raise from seed – in a packet of mixed colours – sown about July under glass and pricked off into boxes in a cold frame. You can also sow in February. In either case, plant out in April. Those that take your fancy can be multiplied by heel or nodal cuttings of young, basal, unflowered shoots taken in August and planted in a close frame. Of the named varieties, the most reliably hardy are 'Schoenholzeri' and 'Andenken an Friedrich Hahn' (syn. *P.* 'Garnet').

Peony. Another lovely, but expensive, family whose beauty is all too fleeting. They pay us a three-weeks visit in May or June and are gone. They will flourish in sun or shade, some in dense shade, but need deep digging with plenty of organic food, including bonemeal. O.K. in lime. It is essential to plant them with their crowns not more than 2 in. below the surface. Plant firmly. Once in the ground they should be left undisturbed. Top-dress each early spring, but on no account allow animal manure or chemical fertiliser to touch the crown. The mixed border is not really the place for them, but if put there they should be at middle distance behind some later-blooming plant.

There is a host of very lovely varieties, many scented, and for a start you are recommended to 'Lady Alexandra Duff' (white with crimson markings) and 'Sarah Bernhardt' (pink).

The tree peonies, which are shrubs, are scarcely beginner's plants, unless it be the 7 ft. yellow *Paeonia delavayi* var. *ludlowii*.

Persicaria. In a family that contains several weeds and rampant growers, there is one to be welcomed for a shady corner – the bell-flowered *P. campanulata*. From a full, rounded bush, it throws up clustered trusses of little bells branching from wiry stems 3 ft. high in summer. *See also* Chapter 12.

Phlox. The border one is *P. paniculata*, with big trusses of bloom in a handsome range of colours from July onwards. To do well they need a rich soil with plenty of moisture, and they enjoy a little shade. It is, moreover, very important to plant them rather deeply, burying the crown an inch or so. Feed and mulch well early in May. In soils where phlox is distorted and withered with eelworm, use bergamot instead. There are a hundred varieties to choose from; 'Norah Leigh', the cream-leaved one popular with arrangers, is a plant of very uncertain behaviour.

Phlox is increased by root cuttings in winter, or by firm young stem cuttings in April. *See also under* Annuals *and* Rock Gardens.

Pinks. *See* Chapter 18. In contrast to carnations, many are useful and valuable in the border.

Poppy. The Oriental poppy (*Papaver orientale*) flowers in barbaric splendour in late spring, but is a grizzly mess afterwards. The Iceland poppy (Chapter 10) far excels it.

Potentilla. Gay flowers of buttercup form with strawberry-like leaves, happy even in a dry soil. Best of the lot is 'Monsieur Rouillard', but 'Etna' and 'Gibson's Scarlet' are good too. All about 18 in. Increase by division. *See also under* Shrubs *and* Rock Gardens.

Primula. A large and versatile tribe. It includes the primrose, the cowslip, the auricula, the hybrid polyanthus, and innumerable other hybrids, besides many species that are known simply as *Primula* So-and-so. Some come from waterside haunts, others dwell in the mountains or the woods. A great many are for the expert only, especially the genuine species. None, easy or difficult, are really plants for the formal border, but they are admirable for small beds, odd places, among shrubs or skirting a path. For those purposes the easiest are those beloved by gardeners for so many centuries – the polyanthus, the coloured primroses and Keats's vestal flower, the chaste auricula. They have wide variations of colour, and leading nurseries cherish their own 'strains'. The hybrids of *P. juliae*, such as 'Wanda', are deservedly popular in their shades of claret, ruby, and rose.

Give all these sorts a soil that does not dry out, and behead them when they finish flowering. Increase by division in July. They are also easy, but not true nor quick, from seed, sown preferably under glass about March in cool and shady conditions.

Almost as easy as these popular hybrids, if the soil is moist, is *P. denticulata*, which, on an erect stem, holds aloft an orb of lilac. So also are the charming little *P. frondosa*, *P. munroi* (syn. *P. involucrata*), and 'Micia Visser-de Geer' (syn. *P. rosea* 'Delight'). In a waterside garden, or very moist soil, if you are not a complete novice, you must certainly grow also the beautiful Candelabra primulas, such as *P. japonica* and *P. pulverulenta* whose stems are ringed with tier upon tier of floral circlets. *See also* Chapters 9 and 12.

Pyrethrum (*Tanacetum cocoineum*). These florist's favourites, like coloured marguerites, are one of the most desirable of cut flowers, but a bit 'thin' and short-lived for the herbaceous border. I grow them in the kitchen garden in straight lines for cutting only. They need generous soil treatment and don't do their best till well established. 'Eileen May Robinson', 'James Kelway' and 'Evenglow' are very good varieties.

Red-hot poker (*Kniphofia*, usually pronounced Niphofe-ia). These flaming red or yellow torches need sun and really good drainage but a rich, moisture-holding soil. Plenty of summer rain is welcome, but winter damp fatal. They are splendid seaside plants, resisting salt spray and high wind with equanimity. The six footers take up too much room for small gardens, but there are some excellent hybrids of short stature, of which none is better than *K. galpinii*. Of the taller ones, pick 'Royal Standard'. All need careful placing to abate their flamboyance, and one of the best homes for the autumn varieties is among Michaelmas daisies, with which they make a splendid marriage of form and colour. Plant in spring, not autumn.

Romneya. The Californian treepoppy is a splendid, queenly plant, half-shrub, half-herbaceous. It makes a bush of 6 ft stature bearing very large, immaculate, silky white 'poppies' adorned with a boss of golden anthers from July to September. Hardy enough in all but the coldest counties. It multiplies itself generously by underground runners, and thrives even on poor soils, given ample sun and a fairly dry situation. The sort usually quoted is *R. coulteri*, but *R. coulteri* var. *trichocalyx* is virtually the same. The secret of success is to cut the plant right down almost to the ground either in early spring or in late autumn. Increase by winter root cutting 2½ in. long.

Rudbeckia. Daisies, usually yellow with protruding black discs. Most are commonplace and coarse, but *R. fulgida* var. *sullivantii* 'Goldsturm', *R. fulgida* var. *deamii* and the double *R. laciniata* 'Goldquelle' are cheerful and well-behaved. A moist soil is needed. *See also under* Annuals.

Salvia. The sages provide us with one or two of our most splendid border plants, and are one of the first essentials in any herbaceous scheme, though curiously neglected in smaller gardens. First choice is *Salvia* x *superba*, a grand 3 ft. bush that throws up sheaves of erect stems, needing no staking and crowded with small, dark-blue flowers with purple-red bracts, which give soft colour for months and blend happily with the grey-green foliage.

Its smaller brethren *S. nemorosa* 'Lubecca' and *S.* x *sylvestris* 'Mainacht' grow only 18 in. Another splendid one is *S. pratensis* Haematodes Group, luxuriant with lavender spikes; short-lived and grown from seed. For the scarlet bedding salvia, *see* Chapter 10.

Scabious. Like pyrethrum, scabious is essentially a flower for cutting rather than for the border. It is sparse in bloom, but successive. A creature of chalk soils, it is an ardent lime-lover. Plant in spring, not autumn. The outstanding variety is *Scabiosa caucasica* 'Clive Greaves', but *S. caucasica* 'Miss Wilmott' is a lovely white. Increase by division, or grow from seed.

Schizostylis. Pretty flowers of gladiolus form, specially welcome for blooming in the drear days of late autumn; need a warm spot in the shelter of a sunny wall. Plant 3 in. deep in April. Water well in summer. The pink 'Mrs Hegarty' blooms in November and 'Viscountess Byng' (which should be cloched) in December.

Shasta daisy. *See Leucanthemum* x *superbum,* Chapter 18.

Solidaster. Included under *Aster.*

Spiraea. The name given to a large family that included many shrubs, the herbaceous sorts known by their frothing plumes. The names of the herbaceous species have been fearfully confused by the diktats of botanists, who have thrust some of them into the tents of the genus *Filipendula.* I accordingly choose:

- *S. aruncus,* the goat's-beard. Massive creamy plumes, 4 ft. June. Now *Aruncus dioicus.*
- *Filipendula rubra* 'Venusta Magnifica'. Deep cream plumes, 6 ft. June–September.
- *Filipendula palmata.* Foaming crimson, 3 ft. July–August.
- *Filipendula vulgaris* 'Multiplex', the dropwort. Gracefully nodding feathers, 18 in; the only one to like a dry wicket.

Our old meadow-sweet is now *Filipendula ulmaria.* Choose 'Variegata' or the all-gold 'Aurea'. Decapitate the proletarian flowers.

For the shrubby spiraeas, *see* Chapter 15.

Statice (pronounced *stat-*issy), now re-named *Limonium*, but popularly called sea-lavender, because one species grows close to the sea. A fine border plant, its large panicles borne on rigid 15 in. stems in late summer. If cut just before full bloom and hung up under cover upside-down for a week or two, some kinds will last indoors (without water) all the winter. *L. platyphyllum* 'Violetta' is an outstanding one. No staking. Full sun. Plant in spring.

Stonecrop (*Sedum*). Most of these we grow in the rock garden, but *S. spectabile*, to be seen in most gardens, is a showy and easy one for the border, with large pink platters, in September and October, and fleshy, pale-green leaves, 15 in. The lax 'Ruby Glow' and the big 'Herbstfrende' (Autumn Joy) are more spectacular.

Rarer and more distinguished is a slightly taller one called *S. telephium* subsp. *maximum* 'Atropurpureum', whose foliage is the colour of mahogany, with flowers of a bronzed cream; it strikes an impressive note in a mixed border, especially when stationed next to a grey-leaved plant, but it needs a place in warm sun. *See also* next chapter.

Trollius, or globe flower. Giant orange or lemon 'buttercups' of great merit, flowering in May and after, repeating the performance in July. They prefer moist soils. Most are about 2 ft. *T.* x *cultorum* 'Orange Globe' and 'Goldquelle' are splendid. Increase by division.

Veronica (speedwell). Of the herbaceous breed, the typical habit is an erect, tightly packed spire of blue. I like the 18 in., rose-pink *V. spicata* 'Barcarolle', the 30 in., royal-blue *V. subsessilis*, and *V. spicata* 'Minuet', a pretty pink-and silver, 15 in. Increase by division. *See also* next chapter. For the shrubs once called veronicas, *see Hebe*.

Viola. In this lovely family are included the violet, the little violetta and the pansy (*see* Chapter 10). What are, in the garden, specifically termed 'violas' are compact and tufted little plants of a neater habit than pansies and more perennial, often with a little yellow eye. Besides the named varieties, leading seedsmen have their own special strains, some of pure colour, others with rays like cats' whiskers.

Violas like a rather moist soil or partial shade, and in dry weather need lots of water. They are overpowered in the herbaceous border, and are better by themselves or at the feet of standard roses or companioned by other creatures of modest stature. Easily raised from seed in June and pricked off into a cool and fairly shady seed-bed. Those that one likes are readily increased by nodal cuttings in July.

Of named varieties, the old favourite 'Maggie Mott' is still one of the best. 'Pickering Blue', 'W. H. Woodgate', 'Barbara' and 'Irish Molly' are all bonny. *See also under* Rock Gardens.

The common sweet violet is *V. odorata*, of which there are several named hybrids in diverse colours. Violettas are charming little hybrids.

Viscaria. Shown under *Lychnis*.

SECOND ELEVEN

To conclude, here are some good second choices, for which I have not been able to afford much room.

Baptisia australis. A good substitute for lupins where the soil is limy. Strong, 4 ft. plants with blue pea-flowers. Not for wet places.

Coreopsis. Of the several species of this popular yellow daisy form plant, the best is *C. verticillata,* a dainty plant with fine foliage, 18 in. The much advertised *C. grandiflora* 'Badengold' is apt to bloom disappointingly in good soils

Daylily (*Hemerocallis*). Those who like this useful old stager should try some of the new colours instead of the familiar yellow or bronze. Especially good for moist situations and, contrary to a popular fallacy, very good in full sun.

Dierama pulcherrimum (angels' fishing rods), 4 ft. long, that swing to the lightest wind, bearing pendant blossoms in August. Sun or partial shade.

Foxtail lily (*Eremurus*). Elegant ladies of hyacinthine appearance and 6 ft. stature or more. Expensive and not a beginner's plant. If tempted, start with the Shelford or Highdown hybrids. Handle the queer, brittle roots very carefully, plant on a slight mound, just covered. Beware slugs.

Goldenrod (*Solidago*). Popular and awfully easy, but too apt to become a weed. 'Golden Falls' is a better sort and the dwarfs are good.

Linum narbonense. Among the perennial flaxes, the enchanting 'Heavenly Blue' is a pretty plant near the front of the border.

Lobelia cardinalis **hybrids.** Quite different from the little bedding plants, the herbaceous species and hybrids rise to 2½ ft. in spires of curiously wrought flowers in brilliant colours. Wet soil, full sun. Protect against slugs.

Lysimachia clethroides is one of the loosestrifes. Slender leaves topped by tiny, tightly packed flowers in clusters that bend over like a goose's head. Moist soil. 1 ft.

L. punctata is an erect, 18 in. cottager, its spires crowded with open, yellow flowers in July.

L. nummularis is the creeping Jenny, very invasive and best in its golden cultivar 'Aurea'.

Marsh marigold or kingcup (*Caltha palustris*). Golden lamps usually seen at the waterside, but good in any moist soil. Not really marigolds, but buttercups. Most people prefer the double 'Flore Pleno'.

Meadow rue (*Thalictrum*). The best of these, *T. delavayi* 'Hewitt's Double', is a beautiful 5 ft. plant with clouds of mauve thistledown, but it is not easy or cheap. A moist, peaty soil is needed.

Physostegia virginiana. The cultivar 'Vivid' is an admirable and easy autumn plant for the front of the border. Small roseate flowers on rigid stems. Called the 'obedient plant' because the tubular flowers will amusingly stay in whatever direction you push them.

Pulmonaria (lungwort). Familiar little 8 in. plants that have both blue and pink flowers in clusters in early spring. The usual one is *P. saccharata* (spotted dog or soldiers and sailors), but the gentian-blue *P. angustifolia* is much better. Shade or sun. Easy.

Sanguisorba obtusa. Tufts just like pink bottle-brushes from bushy mounds of decorative, compound leaves in late summer. 2½ ft.

Solomon's seal (*Polygonatum multiflorum*). Arching, 3 ft. stems and ivory, tubular flowers dangling in early summer; valuable for thriving in deep shade under trees.

Stokesia laevis. Elegantly chiselled blossoms like large, pale-blue cornflowers, standing above strap-like leaves in late summer.

Valerian (*Centranthus ruber*). The deep-red forms of this familiar wild flower, of which Sir Winston Churchill was fond, are excellent for dry, stony places and rough banks.

12

ROCK GARDENS AND STONEWORKS

THE LURE AND THE HAZARD

I have already warned you about rock gardening. If you allow this particular siren to ensnare you, you are likely to be her slave for life. But it is a benevolent captivity, and if your friends think you have got life a little out of focus through rhapsodising over some pygmy darling of one-inch stature, you may console yourself that you have a deeper vision.

Few branches of gardening reach a higher degree of specialisation, and the beginner must naturally start on simple lines, but they should be the right ones. A rock garden which is well conceived, well built, and well stocked with carefully chosen plants will be a joy for many years; wrongly done, it will be an eyesore, a source of constant trouble, and the jest of those who know. You are warned that to do the job thus is not cheap, though the first cost is the last except for occasional replacement of plants. Good stone is heavy and expensive, and a ton does not go far (nor do the plants at first sight!). You could, of course, start with a wee garden of a few square yards and add to it yearly, but my first advice, however large or small your intentions, is that, if you are not prepared to do the job properly, don't do it at all. Nothing is more dismal to contemplate than the lumps of clinkered bricks or broken concrete that masquerade as 'rockeries'. A rock *garden*, properly conceived, should represent a natural outcrop or other formation of rock, seemingly unmolested by the hand of man, though more *soigné* than nature in the rough.

Fortunately, however, there are several ways of employing rocks, and growing flowers among them, which do not constitute true rock gardens, and we can enjoy many of the lovely creations of cliff- and mountain-side in settings which do not profess to simulate natural scenery and are frankly the artificial work of man. In particular there is the so-called 'dry wall', which can be employed in many forms. It can be a retaining wall supporting a terrace or a formal sunk garden or the edge of a raised flower-bed; or it may be a stone facing to an awkward bank, draped with plants that thrive in a dry, hot environment; or it may be just a wall for its own sake and purpose employed instead of a hedge or fence. There is also the more restricted medium of the pavement, into the crannies of which we may insinuate prostrate plants that suffer being trodden on. All these are intended to simulate nature's encroachment and man's neglect. Again, there are little edgings of flat stone that are employed for neatness here and there, ornamental steps, and so on. Moreover, several rock plants can, of course, be most effectively used on the edge of a mixed border.

THE ROCK GARDEN PROPER

In our true rock garden any fault in concealing the hand of man and in simulating an extract from nature is a measure of artistic failure. It is difficult to prescribe in print just what this implies except in general terms,

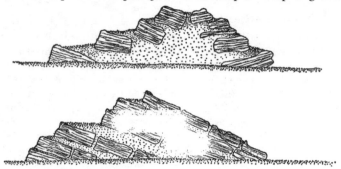

Top: *sectional view of a simple, naturalistic rock garden suitable for a small place; drainage not shown.* Bottom: *profile of another simple scheme.*

for a little art may adapt the most unlikely place convincingly – even within the unpromising wooden palings of a suburban villa. Taste and judgement must be our guides, but a few general suggestions may be given. Obviously the middle of a lawn is an unnatural place in which to suffer rocks to erupt, and on any flat site there is always a danger of incongruity. But the *end* of a lawn – yes, with the grass gradually merging into a low and scattered outcrop.

The shape and design of the rock formation must be informal, irregular, and loose, but not an unplanned jumble. The outline may be compounded of bays or jutting promontories. Its size, and its height in particular, should be in proportion to the garden as a whole. Advantage should be taken of any unevenness of ground there may be, and a naturally sloping bank or depression is a great opportunity for a naturalistic design. Unless something specialised is intended, the rock garden should be in full sun for the greater part of the day, and not under trees, but if part of it can have a north aspect, with a little shade from its own rocks, a greater range of plants can be introduced.

Types of rock
The rock should be all of the same type and of a porous nature. Quarried sandstone and limestone are best; a hard, impermeable stone such as granite is not sympathetic. Excellent stone comes from Cumberland,

Westmorland, Derbyshire, Yorkshire, and the West Country, such as the attractive Cheddar stone. Limestone should be avoided where it is specially desired to grow lime-hating plants. The stones should be of varying sizes, and in small places flattish ones are best. What is particularly important is that the striations or graining of the stone should all run one way, as they do in nature, and in like manner, when the stones are built into the new garden, they should all lie more or less in the same plane, stratum by stratum. If proposing to build the rock garden oneself, it is quite essential to go to the nursery or stone merchant's and select the stone personally.

Building the rock garden

The first essential is good drainage. This above all. What is most wanted is protection from damp, not frost. If natural drainage does not exist, dig out about 18 in. of soil (preserving the top spit), lay in a bed of broken brick or clinkers, and dig a channel to a soakaway or to some other outlet if there is one. On top of this drainage lay a mat of close-set turves upside-down.

In any case, remove the top spit from the selected site and keep it on one side. Using this top spit as base (if it is good enough), prepare a soil mixture of two parts of this loam with two parts of leafmould or granulated peat and one part of sharp sand; for lime-loving plants incorporate with it liberal handfuls of small limestone chippings or of mortar rubble, but of sandstone for lime-haters. Soil for rock plants should contain plenty of grit and not be too rich; but, while draining off excessive rain, should be capable of retaining sufficient moisture through the agency of the peat or mould.

Assuming the rock garden to be a raised one, work from the bottom upwards over the whole expanse, placing the rocks layer by layer. The function of the rock is to provide the plants with a *cool root-run*. In general, about one-third or so of each rock should be buried. The rock should *emerge* from the soil, not appear to have been dumped on top of it, and there should be an impression that a mass of solid rock lies hidden below surface. Tilt all the pieces slightly backwards and their noses just a little upwards, but always preserve the graining parallel, for one rock standing erect or otherwise out of plane will spoil the whole picture. No should the

'Here lies poor Fido'

The wrong sort of rockery — the 'Dog's Grave' type.

pieces slope generally to the front, or both rain and soil will be washed away. Don't put a big rock on top of a small one.

Bed the rock in firmly, ramming the earth well down with a pick helve or something of the sort. There must be no chance of the soil being washed out by rain. *Fill every cranny and crevice*, and make sure that there are some vertical crevices for plants that like that sort of home. The pockets of soil between rocks should vary in size from a few square inches to broad 3 ft. expanses.

If it is intended to grow lime-hating plants, such as dwarf rhododendrons or the lovely lithospermum, then either the whole of the soil mixture may be made from lime-free constituents or selected pockets may be so filled, but in such a plan avoid limestone rocks, and have your lime-haters in peat-beds, on the top storey of the garden. Lime-loving plants on the other hand, such as pinks, stonecrops, gypsophila, and house leeks, should have big handfuls of small limestone chips or old mortar rubble mixed into their pockets; chippings, or fine, clear gravel in lieu, should also be thickly strewn on top of the soil right up the collar of each plant.

Planting

Good nurseries send out most of their rock-garden stock in pots, and therefore they can be planted at any time of the year when the weather is suitable. Those not sold in pots are usually best planted in early spring unless that is their flowering time. First-class nurseries will not send their stuff except at the right time. Normal planting rules apply – well spread-out roots, firm planting, ample watering-in, especially of shrubs. Think out the planting plan carefully with due regard to the ultimate spread of the plants (often considerable), their habit, the colour scheme and season of blooming. Try to ensure that there is colour in the rock garden from early spring to late autumn, while for winter *Erica carnea* will do you proud.

Plants that have to go into crevices between rocks, whether horizontal or vertical, should be planted while the rock garden is being built, but few of us are clever enough to plan so exactly.

DRY WALLS AND BANKS

A dry wall is one which is made without cement or mortar. For this purpose one orders 'walling stone', of which there are several good sorts, such as York or Somerset walling, the cream tints being effective for several uses. All should be fairly flat, and they should not be too dissimilar in size. Bricks, especially dark, matured ones, can quite well be mixed with them informally.

In building the wall, a layer of prepared soil should be laid between each course of stones. The stones must be properly 'bonded' – those of one course overlapping the junction of two stones of the course below it.

When building a free-standing wall, as distinct from the retaining face of a flower-bed, build it with two faces, and fill the space between – about a foot – with rammed earth of the same blend as for the rock garden. Finish, if you like, with a narrow ribbon bed at the top of the wall, except in wet and cold districts, where the wall should be topped with coping-stone, to prevent the lower courses being shattered by frost after heavy rains. Unless the wall is a very low one, give a slight backward tilt – or 'batter' as architects call it – to each course of stones, so that the top is a little narrower than the base. If much more than about 2 ft. high, put in extra-long stones as 'ties' at intervals of about 8 ft. horizontally and 18 in. vertically. Such a wall should also have a strong foundation of fairly large stones just below ground level.

Both sides of the wall (if two-sided), and the top, can be studded with plants, but if the wall runs east and west then the north face should receive shade-tolerating sorts, and all should be plants which tolerate a good deal

Top: *front view of a dry wall; the circles show the right places to stow plants and the crosses wrong ones.* Middle left: *sectional view of a dry wall, showing slight backward slope and tie-stone;* right: *wrong way to house a plant; roots trapped in a stone prison.* Bottom: *two methods of finishing off the top of a dry wall.*

of dryness. Put in the plants as you build the wall, preferably at the bottom of a junction between two stones. At the bottom of the wall put the least choice, such as aubrieta and persicaria, at the top the daintier ones and those most capable of standing drought, such as dwarf brooms, stonecrop, potentilla and thyme.

MORAINE AND SCREE

These are specially stony conditions prepared for plants from high mountains. A scree is a raised bed with more stone and grit than soil, having very sharp drainage. A moraine has a controlled water supply underground (usually a pipe drilled with a few small holes) and a scree has not. These refinements are best deferred until one is no longer an apprentice.

WHAT TO PLANT

I am purposely keeping this list very short, and restricted to the simple things. It is a mistake to advise the beginner to attempt any *recherché* or difficult plants. He who becomes an enthusiast is often dissatisfied with his first rock garden and pulls it down to build something more ambitious, incorporating a moraine or scree and perhaps a little running water and pools as well. Then is the time for the specialist's plants – for *Daphne petraea*, the wayward androsace, the pretty soldanella, the Asiatic primulas and anything called a 'specialist's treasure'.

The purist says that a rock garden should be inhabited only by those plants that grow among rocks in nature. I am not preaching purism, but one should be wary about recruiting outside the accepted rock tribes. Again, taste, discretion, and the length of one's purse must rule. Obviously only small plants should be chosen, and if expense is at first an obstacle one can in the first year or two fill up with small annuals from seed. *Phacelia campanularia*, so like a gentian, is very appropriate. Others acceptable are the pretty little leptosiphon, the pimpernel (*Anagallis*), annual candytuft, kochia (which looks exactly like a dwarf cypress), forget-me-not (very like a true rock-garden plant), alyssum, and that pleasing little nuisance *Limnanthes douglasii*. Other suitable ones are auriculas, dwarf ageratum, portulaca (for mild districts and dry sites), mesembryanthemum (likewise) and dwarf snapdragons.

Apart from this rather unorthodox company, there are, broadly speaking, three groups of plant for the rock garden – small shrublets and dwarf conifers, bulbs of miniature size, and the general run of soft-wooded plants, some evergreen and some deciduous. Many of the little bulbs, endearing and tempting though they are, are generally expensive for the display they give, and can be omitted till another year's budget. But the mountain anemones are inexpensive and far too lovely to omit, and other small inexpensive bulbs can go in, such as the dwarf forms of iris, daffodil and allium.

I am afraid that in this chapter it is inevitable that in many instances I should use longish botanical names again, if you are to be certain of getting the right things – and many haven't got any other names.

Next shrubs. The following is a short selection of the best and easiest, further details being given in the chapter on shrubs:

Helianthemum. Easy and good; beginner's first choice.

Conifers. Two or three should be included for their 'atmosphere'. Start with the toy sentinel juniper (*J. communis* 'Compressa'), the Irish yew (*Taxus baccata* 'Standishii') and the golden *Chamaecyparis lawsoniana* 'Minima Aurea'. These must be neighboured by something prostrate or creeping, or their effect will be spoilt. Plant them about mid-way up the rocks, not on top.

Brooms. The prostrate Kew broom (*Cytisus* x *kewensis*), spangled with pale gold, and the prolific ardoinii of deeper hue; put these drought-resisting plants high up, to fall in cascades.

***Daphne cneorum* 'Eximia',** and other dwarf daphnes.

Ericas in great variety, especially the pygmies and those that glorify the winter (Chapter 18).

Euryops acraeus (syn. *E. evansii*). A beautiful shrublet, brilliantly silvered, with bright yellow daisies in early summer. Full sun and gritty, quick-draining soil.

Hypericum. The dwarf brethren of the favourite rose of Sharon with her cheerful golden bowls. Choose between *H. coris, H. olympicum* and the prostrate *H. empetrifolium* subsp. *tortuosum*.

***Hebe* 'Youngii'** (syn. *H.* 'Carl Teschner'). A dense shrublet, violet-flowered, wide-spreading.

Lilac. The dwarf form, true lilac in colour and fragrance, is something quite new to most people. There is a bother about its name, but you must ask either for *Syringa pubescens* subsp. *microphylla* or for *S. meyeri* 'Palibin'. For the larger rock garden.

Rhododendron. Three excellent ones, among many others, are the mauve *impeditum*, the dark-red 'Carmen', and the rosy-mauve *calostrotum* subsp. *keleticum*.

Roses. There are many dwarf forms appropriate for the rock garden.

We come now to the soft-wooded plants, and for the apprentice's assistance I shall group these into first and second choices; and it may be a help if I say at the outset that if I were asked to pick a First Eleven for him this would be it:

Campanula – a great many all on a par, but I would choose the lovely *C. cochlearifolia* var. *pallida* 'Miranda'.

***Phlox* 'Vivid'.**

Aubrieta – variety according to one's colour fancy.

Thyme – the red prostrate *Thymus* Coccineus Group.

Any dwarf Pink. ***Potentilla* x *tonguei*.**

Geranium (Cranesbill) – the rose-pink dwarf *G. sanguineum* var. *striatum* (syn. *G. sanguinecum* var. *lancastriense*).

Saxifraga – one could easily pick an eleven from this large and versatile breed alone; let us choose the pretty pink hybrid *S.* x *anglica* 'Cranbourne'.

Auricula hybrids.

Sedum cauticola, for autumn.

I have said that we would keep to the fairly easy things, but it will be noted that in the following lists I have included gentians and lithospermum, which not everyone would call easy. However, the apprentice often succeeds with them where the master gardener fails, and they are so very lovely that it would be a pity not to try; but do treat them conscientiously.

Most of these plants will flower for very long periods, or make a second blooming, if the spent flowers are removed; those that make close and dense growth you must firmly trim back with shears, such as aubrieta, candytuft, soapwort, viola, arenaria, alyssum, rock phlox, thyme, and the mossy saxifrages.

Here, then, is my little catalogue. The figures included below are the normal height and spread in inches.

Aethionema is a toy shrub like a celestial candytuft with roseate crowns for full sun and a gritty, limy, briskly drained soil. Excels in a dry wall. Not for cold counties. 'Warley Rose' is a gem of a plant but *A. grandiflorum* seems rather easier.

Anemone. Specially suitable for a partially shaded site are the Apennine anemone (*A. apennina*) and *A. blanda* 'Atrocoerulea'. *See* chapter on bulbs.

Arabis. The grey-leaved, white-flowered *A. alpina* subsp. *caucasica* or rock-cress, is a kindergarten plant, found everywhere and very invasive. Far more decorative is a compact little carpeter enriched with creamy-gold leaves, which staggers under the name *A. ferdinandi-coburgi* 'Aureovariegata'. Very easy and pleasing. Space at one foot.

Arenaria. Two easy ones. *A. montana* is a very pretty, ground-hugging plant covered with gleaming white moons at midsummer, 4 × 20 in. *A. balearica* is a minute creeper that closely hugs the rocks, shining with a myriad of tiny white stars, spreading widely. Both easy to grow from seed but infuriating to prick out.

Aubrieta. Everyone knows these. Raise them from seed (very easy) or buy a named variety of the colour you like. 4 × 20. The golden-leaved 'Aureovariegata' is delightful.

Campanula. The prostrate rock harebells, crowded with their jaunty little bells in mauve, blue, or white, rising from a close green carpet, are quite essential. The best to start with are the following species, all of which have several varieties with fancy names. Avoid *C. poscharskyana*, a ruthless invader.

The demure *C. cochlearifolia*, which wanders here and there in an engaging and harmless manner; especially the silver-blue variety *C. c.* 'Miss Willmott' and *C. c.* var. *pallida* 'Miranda'.

C. portenschlagiana, very rampant, but good for a dry wall or as a ground-cover among shrubs.

C. garganica. Radiating stems with blue, starry flowers over kidney-shaped leaves in June–August. 4 in. Sun or part-shade. A favourite variety is 'W. H. Paine'.

Hybrids of the very large-flowered Carpathian harebell *C. carpatica*, especially the cool sparkling white *C. c. f. alba* 'Weisse Clips'; cut it back hard and it will bloom again. Excellent for a dry wall, for crevices, for steps, and for the front of the herbaceous border. Easy from seed.

All these harebells will tolerate some shade, but prefer sun, and they are the mainstay of the rock garden in the summer months with prolonged and brilliant displays. Increase by division. Avoid the difficult ones, such as *C. alpestris*.

Cranesbill (true geranium). Before reaching this stage of the book, the reader will, I hope, know what a geranium really is. It gives us some nice rock plants, as easy as pie, with delicately cut leaves and gaily coloured cups. First choice is *G. sanguineum* var. *striatum* (syn. *G. s.* var. *lancastriense*) a warm rose-pink cranesbill from the Isle of Walney in Cumbria. The Dalmatian cranesbill, *G. dalmaticum*, has low hummocks and *vin rosé* cups. A saucy crimson fellow with black eye is called *G. subcaulescens* and his sister *G.* (Cinereum Group) 'Ballerina' is a gentle lilac, long in bloom. Increase all by division.

Gentian (*Gentiana*). The queen of the rock garden, with her sensational fanfares of blue trumpets, shares with the Madonna lily and the *Daphne cneorum* a secret not yet discovered by the horticulturist – why it will grow like a weed in one garden, as the Chinese sort does in Scotland, while next door, with all the care in the world, it never blooms at all. Three points are to be noted – first, that gentians need a rather richer soil than most rock plants, so incorporate some old cow manure or well-rotted compost; secondly, that dry conditions are inimical, so, while being well-drained, the soil must be able to retain moisture; and thirdly, that some gentians like or tolerate lime, while to others it is poison.

The beginner might start with *Gentiana septemfida*, not the very choicest but very good and very easy, 8 in., summer. Of the more famous sorts, the gentianella (*G. acaulis*) and the star gentian (*G. verna*) both like lime, are a vivid deep blue, like the sun, and flower in the spring. The glorious gentianella is notoriously wayward and coy in the south and east. The star gentian grows wild in some counties, but turns shy when brought into the cultivated gardens. It seems to demand a moist, gritty, peaty, or leaf-mouldy soil in full sun, with frequent water. The best variety is *angulosa*.

Opposed to these in every way is a cluster of gems that are lighter blue, flower in the autumn, and hate lime. The best and probably most wooable are *G. sino-ornata* and the ethereal *G. farreri* and their lovely offspring *G.* × *macaulayi*. Feed these on lime-free loam, granulated peat, and sharp sand in equal parts. Top-dress after flowering. They should be grown in shade or partial shade, and do well facing north.

Geranium. *See* Cranesbill.

Gypsophila. The prostrate and trailing forms are easy and delightful for the rock garden, especially in dry situations and in a dry wall. They relish lime. I specially like *G. cerastioides*, and *G. repens* 'Fratensis'.

House leek (*Sempervivum*). Great favourite of odd charm and special usefulness for bare rock ledges, crevices of dry walls, and roofs. Needs practically no depth of soil but best started on a 1 in. spread of fairly rich soil. Must not get waterlogged. Readily increased by removal of baby offsets once they have rooted. Start with any variety of the 'cobweb' house leeks (*S. arachnoideum*).

Iris. In addition to specialists' sorts, those suitable for the rock garden are *I. histrioides* 'Major' and *I. reticulata*. *See* Chapter 18.

Lithodora diffusa. The prostrate species is a pearl of the rock garden. The little flowers are a vivid gentian-blue, and indeed resemble pygmy gentians, crowding the ground over a square yard. But it hates lime, and wants a peat-and-loam soil with maximum sun, and good drainage. *L. d.* 'Grace Ward' is of rare loveliness, but *L. d.* 'Heavenly Blue' is nearly as good. *Lithodora* is another jewel that may cheat the expert and reward the novice. 6 × 24 in. May–June. Increase by cuttings in sand in summer.

Omphalodes. Very like forget-me-not. *O. cappadocica* is excellent and easy for shady spots, flowering in early summer and again in autumn. 8 × 15. *O. verna* is blue-eyed Mary, lovely as a child but soon a menacing invader. Don't attempt *O. luciliae*, which is a 'specialist's treasure'.

Phlox. The prostrate species are quite indispensable. The most popular are the named varieties of *P. subulata*, which are dense, matted plants, with small, moss-like leaves, and smothered in late spring and early summer with lovely little phlox blooms in red, pink, mauve, or white. Have a mixed bag, which would include the startling crimson *P. s.* 'Temiskaming' and the lilac *P. s.* 'Lilacina' and the pink *P. s.* 'Betty'. The varieties of *P. douglasii*, such as *P. d.* 'Boothman's Variety', make dense hummocks and want a hot spot. *P. stolonifera* 'Blue Ridge' is a gem, but must have things cool, shady and lime-free; plant in spring.

Pinks. The rock-garden species and varieties are among the most enchanting of the great *Dianthus* genus. Give them the same general treatment as recommended in Chapter 18 – full sun, plenty of lime-stone chips or old mortar rubble, and (most important of all) a pocket of soil where they will have really good drainage. Many prosper exceedingly on a dry wall. Trim them back after first flowering, and many will go on all summer. Plant in September. Here are a few of the best and easiest for a start.

The Cheddar pink (*D. caesius*). Glowing rose-pink, 6 in., good anywhere in the sun, including crevices and dry walls, one of the dozen best rock plants; but go to a reliable nursery and get a good form or variety. The hybrid arvensis is a pretty 3 in. replica of it.

The maiden pink (*D. deltoides*), a first-class trailing sort with ruby flowers, grand also for the dry wall; again insist on a good variety, such as *D. d.* 'Leuchtfunk'.

Of the hybrids (which I dare say will most catch the beginner's fancy) first choices are: 'Pike's Pink', 'Grenadier', 'Inchmery', 'Little Jock' and his hybrids, 'La Bourboule'; and the Allwoodii Alpinus Group, of which I have raised some charmers from seed; so can you. Refer to Chapter 18.

Persicaria. Provides us with some tiresome 'knot-weeds'; but two useful ones, serving as low, dense, wide-spreading ground-cover (but decidedly invasive), are *P. affinis* 'Donald Lowndes', handsome in bronze and pink, 9 in., and the old, shorter *P. vaccinifolia*, suitable for covering dry walls and banks.

Potentilla. A most obliging breed, hallmarked by its strawberry-like leaves, but some are difficult, others too invasive. Easy ones are *P.* x *tonguei*, a fine trailing or tumbling plant starred with orange discs, the rather similar 'Roxanne' and *P. neumanniana* (syn. *P. verna*) which spreads neatly in tight, ground-hugging, green-gold mats.

Primula. This great and wonderful genus, of extraordinary diversity, includes many gems that are true rock plants and many others that may be admitted. However, take care to avoid those that are of difficult culture, those that belong to the greenhouse, and those that dwell in the riverside and marsh, such as *P. japonica* and *P. florindae* (unless of course your garden gives these conditions). Most primulas, however, do demand ample moisture, with cool and partly shaded positions. As a mere introduction to this large subject I suggest a start with:

The auriculas, most economically got by ordering a batch of mixed seedlings, but being careful to avoid the difficult show auriculas. Easy from seed.

The popular dwarf named 'Wanda' in wine red, and other hybrids of *P. juliae*, which are really small coloured primroses.

Any hybrid primrose of low stature, but not the robust polyanthus.

Of the natural species, the pretty little *P. frondosa*, *P. rosea* 'Micia Visser-de Geer' and the drumstick primula, *P. denticulata*.

Saxifrage. Another enormous and widely diverse family, with innumerable hybrids. Many rank as 'specialist's treasures'. All must have a moisture-retaining content in the soil, but drainage is of first importance. The easiest are London pride (*S.* x *urbium*) (not suitable for rock gardens) and the mossy sorts. The main groups or sections for us are:

Silver or encrusted saxifrages. Showy plumes or sprays of blossom from 2 in. to 3 ft. spring from rosettes of richly silvered leaves which betray their love of lime. Summer flowering. Need full sun and gritty, stony soil, and look well in vertical crevices and dry walls. Varieties of *S. aizoon*, *S. cochlearis*, and *S. cotyledon* are all good. The hybrid 'Kathleen Pinsent' is another delight. Eschew 'Tumbling Waters' unless it has two or more offsets; each lasts only a year.

Cushion or Kabschia saxifrages. The neat and compact cushions of tiny foliage are animated with multitudes of lovely Dresden-china miniatures. Early spring flowering. Extra gritty soil, fast drainage, and partial shade. Suggested first choices are *S.* x *elisabethae*, 'Carmen', *S.* x *anglica* 'Cranbourne' and *S.* x *irvingii* 'Jenkinsiae'.

Mossy saxifrages. Soft, moss-like foliage, fast-growing, flowering April to June. Kindergarten plants for *shady* places. Get a mixed bag in red, pink, and white. Most are about 4 in. Trim back sharply after flowering. Scraps transplant easily.

Soapwort (*Saponaria*). The trailing *S. ocymoides* grows anywhere and spreads rapidly with a multitude of pretty little pink flowers through June and July; a good beginner's sort. 4 × 30 in. Easy from seed.

Stonecrop (*Sedum*). We have reviewed these fleshy-leaved plants in the previous chapter. For rocky places of all sorts we can have:

∾ *S. cauticola*, beautiful semi-trailing plant, purplish foliage, dense crimson flowers, spreading and enriching September and October.

∾ *S. spathulifolium*, especially 'Cape Blanco', prostrate, spreading, brilliant gold flowers from foliage dusted with talcum powder; grand for dry walls, steps, and the chinks of pavements.

Thyme (*Thymus*). To omit the creeping *T. serpyllum*, from any garden, is almost unthinkable. Tightly hugging the ground, it spreads out close-woven little mats in brilliant colours – *T.* Coccineus Group (red), *T. serpyllum* 'Annie Hall' (flesh pink), *T. serpyllum* 'Pink Chintz', and others. For the rock garden, the dry wall and especially the pavement. It likes being trodden on, when it gives out its aromatic fragrance. *T.* 'Doone Valley' is a welcome newcomer splashed with gold.

Two little shrubby thymes, not for treading on, are to be noted. People disagree about their names, but if you ask simply for *T.* x *citriodorus* 'Silver Queen' you will get a pretty shrublet tinted with pewter, or for *T. pulegioides* 'Goldentime', the 'golden thyme' (when you will get a gilded one).

Veronica (speedwell). The rock-garden species of this versatile family are mostly dense trailers or prostrate shrubs. Easy, colourful and hardy are the varieties of *V. prostrata* (or *rupestris*), especially the golden-leaved 'Trehane'.

Viola. Only the smaller and daintier sorts should be used, such as 'Ardross Gem' and the violettas. The trailer *V. gracilis* is pretty but short-lived.

SOME SECOND CHOICES

Achillea. The dwarf breed of the big border yarrow are effective and flowerful. Some are weed-like, but a very good one is the sulphur *A.* x *lewisii* 'King Edward'.

Aurinia saxatilis. Familiar lusty plants of golden splendour often seen associated with aubrieta. Showy but not choice and too rumbustious for small

rock gardens. The lemon-yellow 'Citrina' and the small, double, long-lasting 'Flore Pleno' are better. Prune it hard, or it wears out very quickly.
Candytuft (*Iberis*). The dwarf variety of the evergreen, white-crowned candytuft (*I. sempervirens*) is called 'Weisser Zwerg' and is a very good little 6 in. plant for many uses, not least as a pygmy hedge. Trim it back fairly hard after flowering. Snowflake goes to 9 in. and spreads widely.
Chrysogonum virginianum. Showy 8 in. plant, blazoned for months with deep gold stars. Easy in any soil.
Dryas octopetala. A flat evergreen carpet with foliage like tiny oak leaves, spangled with flowers like white anemones in June. Full sun. Delightful in a pavement. Is the mountain avens.
Erinus alpinus. Endearing, tiny-flowered plant that spreads and clings to rock surfaces like a vest to the body. Good for dry walls, too. Best-known is the carmine 'Doktor Hähnle', 3 in.
Frankenia thymifolia. Prostrate spreader with minute leaves and the prettiest little lilac stars. Nice for pavements.
Haberlea and the closely related **Ramonda**. Choice plants particularly valuable for the special task of filling vertical crevices on the shady side of the garden. Plant so that the leaves are nearly in the vertical plane, to shed off the rain, but put plenty of moisture-holding peat or leafmould at the roots when planting. Both throw up 6 in. clusters of charming flower of unusual form. Get *H. rhodopensis* and *R. myconi*.
Thrift (*Armeria*). Most people know this hardy maritime cliff-dweller with tufts of grass-like leaves, flowered with many pink globes. The crimson variety *A. maritima* 'Vindictive' is most recommended. 9 in. Early summer.
Wallflower (*Erysimum*). For the rock garden the one to have is *E. cheiri* 'Harpur Crewe', a bush densely robed in gold; April–June. 12 × 15 in. Increase by plucking off the young side-shoots for cuttings in summer.

ROCK GARDEN PATHS AND PAVINGS

Small walks, paths, or other places liable to be trodden on in and about the rockery often present a problem. If grass is used, the mower cannot get at them. But there are happier solutions than grass. One is to plant these places with camomile (*Chamaemelum nobile*), and the other is to plant with low creeping things. The creeping thymes, in different colours 8 in. apart, are the stand-by for this. Add to them the frankenia mentioned above; *Mentha requienii* for use in shade; a resistant little plant called *Leptinella squalida*, with tiny, fern-like leaves closely hugging the earth; and the prostrate New Zealand burr, *Acaena microphylla*. A carpet of this sort is both picturesque and economical – and the poorest soil will suit.

   The same plants can be used in paving-stones, together with such plants as *Dryas octopetala*, toadflax (*linaria*), dwarf thrift, *Veronica prostrata*, etc., for the places less trodden upon. Dwarf pinks also excel in pavements. One of the most engaging, especially for steps, is the little daisy *Erigeron karvinskianus*, which you can grow easily by scattering the seed where you like.

PLANTS FOR DRY WALLS

Aethionemas (not in severe districts).
Aurinia saxatilis (large walls only).
Arenaria montana.
Aubrietas.
Dwarf brooms (*Cytisus* and *Genista* species).
Campanulas, especially, *C. muralis.*
Pinks, any according to your fancy.
Perennial candytuft.
Erigeron karvinskianus.
Gypsophila cerastioides and *G. repens.*
Helianthemums.
House leeks.
Lithodora (if no lime).
Phlox subulata cultivars.
Persicaria vacciniifolia
Potentilla x *tonguei.*
Soapwort.
Saxifrages (mossy varieties on the shady side).
Stonecrops.
Thymes, creeping or shrubby.
Veronica prostrata.

13

BULBS AND THEIR KIND

BULBS IN GENERAL

Bulbs, corms, and tubers are all forms of swelling which different plants have evolved as devices for storing energy during their periods of dormancy, as electricity is stored in a battery. A quality of freshness and virginality dwells in them. They are easy to handle and to plant. If they come from a good nursery they are almost certain of success in their first year, but success in subsequent years depends on good cultivation.

This easy first success deludes many people into thinking that bulbs can take care of themselves in any sort of conditions; whereas the success of the plant this year is the result mainly of the good treatment it was given last year, and if it does not go on being well treated it will deteriorate.

In evolving their storage devices the bulbous families have exploited different parts or members. In the bulb proper, as in the narcissus or daffodil (and in the onion), the battery is a swelling of the leaf bases, which form a sheath round the embryo flower within, perfect and complete in all its parts. The corm, on the other hand, as in the crocus and gladiolus, is a swelling of the stem. Rhizomes can also sometimes be swollen, the most familiar example being the flag iris. The tuber may be a swollen underground branch, as in the potato, or a swollen root as in the dahlia and the popular breed of anemone.

Soil and situation

Except for many of the small bulbs, and all lilies other than Madonna, a habitation open and sunny is best.

As ever, good drainage is the first care; yet the top soil must be of a loam that will retain a certain amount of moisture. Anything in the nature of free water in the subsoil on the one hand, or of complete drying out on the other, may well be fatal.

Organic matter – compost, leafmould, hop manure, peat – provides these conditions. *But on no account use animal manures for bulbs* unless it is old and well rotted. Bonemeal is always excellent, and heavy soils may be lightened with sand. Most bulbs are tolerant of lime, but to certain lilies it is damaging. In a few instances, as in the wild tulips and irises, a somewhat harsh and stony soil is the rule.

Unimaginative planting can quite spoil the natural charm of the bulbous families. Hyacinths and tulips indeed look their bravest when dressed in ranks like regiments of light-opera soldiers. But the care-free beauty of all others abhors rigidity. Daffodils in straight lines are as ill-suited as ballet dancers in battle-dress. Informal drifts and clusters are their best formations. There is no better dodge for getting the right effect than the old one of taking a handful of stones, of size according to the bulb, tossing them down casually, and planting where they fall.

A special problem of planting is that, once the beauty of their blossom has passed away, too many bulbs become an array of unkempt foliage. Therefore, make a special point of planting these sorts – narcissus, tulip, muscari, hyacinth, gladiolus, etc – where their sere and drooping foliage is not an eyesore, e.g. in the middle or back (not the front) of an herbaceous border, where they will be covered by the on-coming foliage of other plants when they sink to rest; or among shrubs, where the smaller breeds in particular look well; or naturalised in grass; or in beds by themselves, where, if need be, they can be lifted and removed after flowering.

These, of course, are generalisations. You wouldn't plant tulips among shrubs, and rarely in grass. Nor is all bulb foliage disagreeable – anemones, for example, go excellently in the front edge of a sunny border. But there is one place where virtually all bulbous plants are absolutely barred – the formal rose bed. Not only will the bulb be completely out of its element, but also it will do the roses no good, and the dying foliage on the bare beds will be an eyesore. I allow them, however, in informal beds of the 'old' roses.

Sorts that go well among shrubs, especially deciduous shrubs, are snow-drops, muscari, crocus, fritillary, scilla, chionodoxa, the woodland anemones, cyclamen, winter aconite, and narcissus. They adorn the bare feet of the shrubs very charmingly in spring, and their foliage in decay is less objectionable.

Many of the small ones also go well in the rock garden, and there are some specially bred pygmies of elfin beauty and charm for this purpose.

Naturalising

Those best for naturalising are narcissus, snowdrop, crocus, fritillary and chionodoxa, but the smaller flowers should, of course, not be in tall and rampant grasses. The mower should on no account go over places where these bulbs lie till their foliage has died right down, so plant them in clus-ters or drifts convenient for manoeuvring the machine, preferably near the corners or edges of the lawn in small gardens.

Planting can be done with a special tool for naturalising; alternatively, lift a few slices of turf with a turfing-iron or spade, fold them back, dig and loosen the soil beneath, plant in the ordinary way, and replace the turf.

Planting

Take care always to plant bulbs at their correct depths. In the cultural notes that follow, 'plant 3 in. deep' means that there must be 3 in. of soil above the top of a bulb. In very light soil plant a bit deeper, in heavy soils not quite so deep. For most lilies a spade must be used, but generally a trowel is the best tool. Never use a dibber, except for planting a lot of very small bulbs; then use a blunt dibber, not a sharp one. There must be no air pocket beneath the bulb. In heavy soils seat the bulb on ½ in. of sharp sand.

The time for planting the great majority of bulbs is September–October. Start early. Daffodils are best put to bed in August, and snowdrops and autumn crocuses as early as July. Don't plant tulips, nor the turban ranunculi, however, before the end of October. Another group is planted in March–April, chiefly gladioli and the hybrid anemones.

After-care
When the flowers wither, nip off all seed-pods. Never, if avoidable, cut or damage the foliage. Leave it to die and wither completely. Do not tie them into knots, though they may be gently pushed to one side.

One of the menaces to bulbs is the enthusiastic autumn digger. I have said elsewhere that, once a bed is properly prepared and planted out, it should not be dug over – only hoed – until it becomes overcrowded. Avoid planting bulbs where you may have to dig.

Lifting
With few exceptions, bulbs are best left in the ground once planted, until they multiply sufficiently to need dividing and replanting. The chief exceptions are begonia, gladiolus, tulip, ranunculus, dahlia, but others can be lifted if necessary to make room for bedding plants, though this should never be done to lilies, amaryllis, crinum, or cyclamen. If avoidable, do not lift till the foliage has died right down or is touched by frost. Then dry the bulbs, etc., clean off the earth, separate, grade, and store in a place that is cool, dry, and airy, but frost-proof.

Although lifting is best done after complete withering of the foliage, it may nevertheless be done earlier to make room. In such an event, lift carefully and complete with roots and a ball of soil, and 'heel in' the plant in a reserve quarter in a trench deep enough to cover the bulb, water, and leave till the foliage has died; then treat as in the previous paragraph. This frequently has to be done to tulips, whose formal nature generally requires them to be put in a bed of their own, to be followed by a summer bedding-out of begonias, antirrhinums, etc.

Propagation
Many bulbous plants can be raised from seed without great difficulty but usually it is a long business. For the general run of the more popular bulbs and corms proper – daffodil, crocus, gladiolus – one's stock is more easily multiplied by detaching the young bodies that form at the base or side of the parent and planting them out separately, the smaller ones in a seed-bed. Hyacinths unfortunately are a subject for the expert only. Tubers are treated differently.

Many of the most endearing little ones, however, happily multiply themselves in the most natural manner if left to run to seed, forming ever-widening colonies. Among them are such jewels as: *Anemone blanda*, the hardy toy cyclamens, chionodoxa, scillas, snowdrops, and muscari.

BULBS INDOORS

A limited range of bulbous flowers can be grown indoors to enliven the grim days of January and February, by growing them either in pots in a normal compost or else in prepared fibre in undrained bowls. Only a few can be successfully reared in fibre, and when ordering it is as well to specify if bulbs are wanted for this special purpose. Hyacinths excel in this mode of life, and so do some daffodils. Several tulips, crocuses, and snowdrops also are good. Less usual and of rare charm are the dwarf irises, *I. histrioides* 'Major' and *I. reticulata*, which do particularly well in fibre or in a mixture of peat and sand. Many more grow bravely in ordinary soil in flower-pots, reared in unheated greenhouses or frames.

September is the right time to do all such planting. The methods of cultivation are much the same whether by pot or bowl. Use pots large enough to take at least three hyacinths or five tulips. Bowls must be non-porous, and circular ones are better than fancy shapes. Pack the bulbs as closely together in the receptacles as you like, provided they do not actually touch one another. There is no need at all to bury the bulb, all it needs being a firm seating, and it is therefore quite enough to insert it to only half its depth. Leave sufficient space between the level of the soil and the rim of the pot to permit watering. For bowls, the fibre should be thoroughly moist but not sodden, so that when squeezed in the hand moisture is not pressed out. If the fibre does not arrive in this condition from the shop or nursery, tie it up in sacking or similar porous material and suspend it with a weight in a cistern of water for at least a day.

Hyacinths planted in a bowl of fibre, with charcoal at the bottom.

The bulbs having been planted, they must now go into darkness for several weeks. The method of putting them in a dark cupboard or cellar should be adopted only by those who have no garden. They are much better outdoors. My own experience is that the best method is to bury them in sand, peat, or weathered ashes to a depth of a good 6 in. in a shady position, preferably under a north wall, and forget about them altogether, for six weeks at least. Then unearth and inspect, taking care not to damage any young shoots. Those that are well through by 1 in. or more can be taken out, and others put back to bed for a further short spell.

Whether the outdoor or the cupboard method is adopted, the bowls must next go into a place of semi-shade, but still quite cold, and then gradually moved up into full light. From then on give them utmost light and careful watering, seeing that the soil or fibre is nicely moist but never sodden. You can give them heat presently if you like for early results, but it should only be very gentle. Never hurry them; light is more important than heat. Bowls, of course, are normally brought into the dwelling-house, where they should go right into a good light window until they are in blossom. Keep them well away from any gas-fire or lamp, and out of any room with violently fluctuating day and night temperatures.

The bulbs that are in pots can also be brought into the house, provided they are stood in a receptacle to take water from the drainage hole; or they can go into a greenhouse, conservatory, frame, or glass porch as long as one likes. In the little conservatories attached to many small houses there is no better method of providing early spring cheer. The taller sorts will need staking as the flower-heads develop, and for heavy-headed hyacinths in bowls of fibre thinly split canes with sharp points, or rigid wires, should be thrust firmly into each bulb itself.

Bulbs grown in this artificial manner get pretty exhausted and are quite unfit for similar use again, but if, after drying off, they are planted among shrubs or in odd corners, they will provide a little quite cheerful bloom in subsequent years.

A SELECTION OF BULBOUS PLANTS

In the following list I have chosen those on which most people would like some guidance, together with a few of the less hackneyed things that are specially recommended. A few of the things I specially suggest, as 'something different' are: allium, the plumed grape hyacinth, species crocuses and tulips instead of the usual hybrids, nerine, belladonna lily, crinum, and especially the lovely rock and woodland types of anemone. Nor omit on any account one or more species of lily.

The general advice which has been given for soil preparation, planting, lifting, etc., will not be repeated save in special instances.

Allium. Though these are garlics, many varieties are virtually odourless and are of striking beauty, their rigid stems crowned with splendid orbs in many colours during May and June. Very suitable to the herbaceous border, to which they lend a note of distinction. Quite easy and inexpensive. Plant 3 in. deep in autumn and leave undisturbed till overcrowded, then lift and divide. Some good ones for a start are: *A. caeruleum,* sky-blue, 2 ft.; the delightful dwarf *A. oreophilum* and *A. karataviense,* both pink 6 in., and *A. cristophii,* with high orbs of lilac stars (2 ft.).

Anemone. In this sumptuous race there are many breeds. The most widely grown, sold in the shops by the million, are the flaunting hybrids of *A. coronaria* called Saint Bridgid Group and De Caen Group anemones.

They are rarely well grown. They need full sun, a well-dug soil, well-drained but moisture-holding, and liberally supplied with leafmould or peat, with bonemeal, and with sand if the soil is heavy. They like lime. Plant for preference in March, alternatively October, though other times of year will also suit if soil and weather allow. Plant little more than an inch deep, ensuring that the little scar left by the old leaf-stalks is uppermost; if in doubt, plant on edge. In light, warm soils they may be left alone, but in others it is best to lift and dry them off, when the foliage fades. Easily grown from seed sown very thinly in June in a sunny position and light soil ¼ in. deep, leaving them to flower in the seed-bed the first year.

Very like them, but better still, are the hybrids of the peacock anemone called *A.* x *fulgens* Saint Bavo Group. They have a crisp and brilliant beauty, and are just as easy, but a warm, sunny place is specially important. Grow these rather than the coronarias.

The lesser-known species anemones, however, have a chaste and porcelain beauty much more desirable than the holiday riotousness of the Saint Bridgids and their kind. Plant in September or October 2 in. deep. They may usually be left in the ground and some, such as *A. blanda*, rapidly colonise by seed. Some are difficult, but specially commended for ease and beauty are:

A. blanda 'Atrocaerulea' (late winter) with daisy-form rays of fragile and virginal blue − for sun or half shade in gritty, gravelly soil where water drains away well. Does well among the roots of shrubs and small trees.

A. nemorosa, especially *A. n.* 'Robinsoniana', whose silver-blue rays are adorned with golden anthers; a haunter of the woodland, requiring shade.

See also Chapters 11 and 12.

Begonia. In the forefront of tuberous plants, begonias are not hardy, and the more sophisticated ones, such as Rex Cultorum Group and Gloire de Lorraine, need heated houses. Of the popular outdoor sorts, the very large and sumptuous named varieties are plants priced for the enthusiast, but those unnamed and sold by colour are excellent. So are the 'multiflora' begonias, which are smaller but more riotous in flower and entirely suited to Everyman. The Pendula begonia is for hanging baskets and window-boxes.

Start the tuberous sorts in early March in some warmth (the kitchen will do if allowed) in seed-boxes in a blend of loam, sand, and leafmould or peat. Plant hollow side upwards, the tuber just covered. Keep moist. When rooted, pot into 4 in. pots and, when necessary, into 6 in. ones. Harden-off in May and plant out about June 1st.

After the first autumn frost dig them up with a ball of soil and pack them in boxes in a cool but frost-free place. Leave the foliage and stem to wither naturally, then store the tubers in clean, nearly dry sand.

B. semperflorens Cultorum Group is the gay little chap, only a few inches high, that makes a magical bedding display for months in red, pink, or white, with leathery leaves, often themselves coloured. Impervious to all weather, except frost. This is a fibrous-rooted begonia, not tuberous, so you must start afresh next year. The dust-fine seed needs heat, but nursery-grown plants can be put out about June 1st. Pot them up in autumn and they will go on blooming in the greenhouse in winter.

Belladonna lily (*Amaryllis belladonna*). Those who live in the South and have a really warm south wall should have a go at this enchanting flower. It opens its fanfares of fragrant pink trumpets in September, borne in clusters at the head of a 2 ft. stem, which shoots up from the bare earth after the foliage has died down (to reappear in winter). It must have a very warm, very sandy soil mixed with plenty of leafmould, and its foliage must be copiously watered in summer. Plant in June–July, 3 in. deep in the south-west, 5 in. deep elsewhere, and blanket it with leaves in winter.

Chionodoxa. One of the jewels of the bulb world, for which the translation Glory of the Snow is too high-sounding. In earliest spring it throws up blue starry flowers 4 in. high, looking their best in clusters or drifts. Plant 3 in. deep in autumn and leave undisturbed. *C. luciliae* has a sparkling white eye and *C. sardensis* is gentian blue. Also successful in bowls and in pots.

Crinum. Very beautiful, pink-and-white, swan-necked trumpets like lilies, 3 ft. high in summer. Treat like belladonna lilies though they are hardier and more reliable. *C.* x *powellii* is the safest. Plant so that the shoulder of the long bulb is 7 in. down.

Crocosmia. *See* Montbretia.

Crocus. Plant the corms of the popular garden hybrids 3 in. deep in early autumn in drifts and clusters, not as edgings. They naturalise beautifully in grass, and are attractive among trees and shrubs. Once planted, leave them alone until thick enough to need dividing.

Much more dainty and desirable than these big hybrids, to my mind, are the smaller species crocuses, and their variations, which flower not only in spring but also delight the heart in late autumn and the depths of winter. They must, however, have sunny positions and good drainage in a privileged bed, not in grass, and they are delightful in rock gardens. Some of the best are:

For autumn – *C. speciosus*, which forms drifts like pools of deep blue water; the fragrant *C. laevigatus*, with feathered lilac petals; and the bi-coloured *C. pulchellus* and *C. kotschyanus*.

For midwinter – the purple *C. imperati* and the little yellow *C. ancyrensis*.

For late winter – *C. chrysanthus*, especially the delightful varieties 'Snowbunting', in white, gold, and purple, 'E. A. Bowles', in gold and bronze, the unique 'Blue Pearl' and the easy *C. tommasinianus*, a charming silvery lavender.

The autumn and winter sorts should be planted in July, the spring ones in September. *See also* Meadow saffron, unfortunately styled autumn crocus in popular usage. Much more like a real crocus, and an autumn one at that, is the golden **Sternbergia lutea**. It looks exactly like a crocus, and is the colour of a buttercup, with the same enamelled sheen. It needs a hot, gritty, fast-drainage slope in baking sun. The leaves come after the flowers have died.

Cyclamen. The big, showy sorts that one gives and receives at Christmas are Persian cyclamens and subjects for the greenhouse. The hardy outdoor pygmies are altogether more lovely, having an exquisite, elfin beauty all their own. They are among the few things that really succeed under trees, and they can indeed be planted in the root-crannies near the bole. The loveliest and best are *C. hederifolium* (autumn), *C. purpurascens* (August), and *C. coum* (midwinter). There are others, too, for other seasons. Plant them only ½ in. deep and leave them severely alone, but mulch them with leaf-mould each winter. They associate miraculously with the daintier of the 'species' anemone. *C. purpurascens* wants complete shade, the others partial. These little cyclamen are not cheap, but they are easy, are likely to outlive you and me and spread quickly into ever-widening colonies through the helpful agency of the ant.

Daffodil. *See Narcissus.*

Dahlia. One of those flowers you either rave about or can't stand. There are quite a lot of dahliaphobes, but the dahlia has many virtues, for, although not hardy, it is easy to grow, virtually free of disease, prolific with its blooms if spent ones are persistently picked off, and it provides lasting cut flowers. Dahlias, which grow from tubers, not bulbs, are officially classified in numerous groups. Average gardeners not concerned with exhibition will probably be satisfied to know just the chief types.

Decoratives have a large number of broad overlapping petals, very solid and sometimes of huge size.

Cactus dahlias have rolled or quilled petals.

Collerettes, an outer ring of large petals and an inner ruff of small ones, showing the disc.

Anemone-flowered. Pin-cushion effect, the disc hidden.

Peony-flowered. Doubles, showing the disc.

Pompons are precisely spherical and formalised.

Ball. Larger style of Pompon, less formal.

Dwarf bedding of various sorts.

Single-flowered explain themselves.

When received from the nursery, dahlias are 'ex-pots'. Except in the mildest frost-free districts, they must not be planted out till the first week of June. The position should be in full sun, and the ground deeply dug and well enriched, for dahlias are gross feeders. The tall ones should be 3 ft. apart, ranging down to 12 in. for the dwarf bedders. All but the dwarfs must be well and firmly staked *before* planting, but stout 4 ft. canes, four to a plant, are quite enough. Pinch out the growing tip at 10 in. and, if large blooms are wanted, disbudding must be practised. Take precautions against earwigs and greenfly.

When the foliage is blackened by early frosts lift the tubers at once, cut the stalks down to within a few inches of the base, drain the water out of the hollow stems by standing them upside-down, dry, and store the tubers in a frost-proof place. Dry peat is a good storage material. In the milder counties some people leave the tubers in the ground all winter, but they take a risk in doing so every year.

Next spring there are the following choices of method of treatment of the old tubers: (a) Having a little heat, start the tubers into growth in February in boxes of soil in greenhouse or frame, take the new shoots as nodal cuttings and insert them in pots of sandy soil. (b) With unheated glass, start them in April, and before planting out in June, divide the cluster of tubers with a sharp knife, ensuring at least one shoot per tuber. (c) With no glass, plant the whole cluster outdoors early May with at least 3 in. of soil over it, allow only one or two shoots to develop, and protect them before June with cloches or with flower-pots at night.

Dahlias are easily raised from seed in the manner of half-hardy annuals, but only the dwarf bedders are really suitable.

To select varieties is difficult. New ones appear in quantity every year, and the darling of today is cast aside tomorrow, but I daresay that such established favourites as 'Doris Day', 'Gerrie Hoek', 'Glorie van Heemstede' and 'Klankstad Kerkrade' will hold their own for a few more years.

Erythronium. The nickname dog's tooth violet refers only to the shape of the bulb. These endearing little flowers are like pygmy, wide-mouthed lilies, 5–9 in. high, with diapered foliage, flowering March and April in many colours. As they hang their heads, plant them in some raised position, or you will miss their beauty. They need partial shade, and a cool, moisture-holding soil with peat or leafmould. E. dens-canis cultivars are the cheapest and easiest. Plant 3 in. deep in September.

Freesia. See Chapter 9.

Fritillary (*Fritillaria*). There are two very different types, both shy in their first season. One is the big crown imperial (F. imperialis), with a peculiar cluster of red or yellow bells hanging from underneath a tuft of leaves that terminates the erect 3 ft. spire. Plant them 5 in. deep in clusters of three or more.

Totally different and more dainty is the snake's head fritillary (F. meleagris). Its deep-mouthed bell, hung from a thread-like, 10-in stem, looks down demurely to its feet. The typical bloom is speckled like a snake's head, but the white variety is also charming. For damp beds or woodland or naturalising in shady grass. Plant 3 in. deep in early autumn and leave alone.

Galtonia. G. candicans is rather like a giant hyacinth, growing 4 ft. high, with quantities of large, white, drooping bells, loosely arrayed, over a long period in summer. Essentially a plant for the mixed border. Plant 6 in. deep in March.

Gladiolus. Most people are interested chiefly in the large and showy hybrids that bloom in late summer, but the smaller Butterfly and the Nanus cultivars also have charm, tending to daintiness rather than immensity. All must have full sun. A rich soil is not necessary, but gives more splendid results.

To my mind the gladiolus is essentially a flower to cut for the house, and not for the adornment of the pleasure garden, for when the blooms are over, the 'sword flowers' look like a shattered army. For house decoration, therefore, plant the corms in rows in the kitchen garden 4 in. deep and 6 in. apart, any time from March till May. Thus grown, lines of string or wire stretched between occasional stakes will be sufficient for their support, but in the pleasure garden each spike must have a separate cane.

When cutting, try to take the flower-stem only and *no leaves.*

The gladiolus not being fully hardy, the corms must, except in the mildest districts, be lifted in the autumn for storage. The expert tells us to do this six weeks after flowering is over. Cut the stem off an inch above the new corm, dry and clean the corms, break off the old shrunken one underneath and store in a cool but frost-free place, after dusting with flowers of sulphur. Before replanting next spring destroy any corms showing dark, shrunken, scabby patches. For the usual reason I must leave you to pick varieties from a standard catalogue.

Other and less common gladioli attract one's special attention for the mixed border. One is the wild *G. communis* subsp. *byzantinus,* rosy-purple, quite easy. The other is a most attractive hybrid called *G.* x *colvillii,* but these need a really warm spot in rich but gritty soil and a thick blanket of leaves or other litter for winter. They flower in June, 18 in. high. 'The Bride' heads one's list.

Gladioli are attacked by aphis and by the minute, sucking thrip, which shows itself in a silver or brown streaking or patching. Use a systemic insecticide.

Grape hyacinth. *See Muscari.*

Hyacinth. Besides being the finest of bowl plants, the hyacinth is very beautiful indeed outdoors, but nowadays its price discourages its use in large numbers. Plant 4 in. deep and 6 in. apart in a sunny and well-drained site in October, with a pinch of sand under each bulb. They are likely to need staking. Remove the spent flower-heads but leave the bulbs in the ground. Perhaps the most beautiful, for indoors or out, are: 'Myosotis' (azure), 'Gipsy Queen' (apricot), 'Ostara' (rich deep blue), 'Queen of the Blues', 'Lady Derby' (lovely flesh-pink, my own favourite), 'Jan Bos' (best red). If you want very early hyacinths indoors you must get the specially doctored prepared Christmas Hyacinth, available in a few varieties, or the loosely built Roman hyacinth.

Iris. *See* Chapter 18.

Ixia. Pretty stars in brilliant colours in June, 15 in. high, good for cutting. Plant 3 in. deep in October in a warm, sunny position, enveloping the bulb in sand. Do not lift in autumn, but protect against frost with a thick coverlet of leaves.

Lily (*Lilium*). The lily is a difficult subject to write about in small compass, for one man's experience is not the same as another's. Moreover, the needs of one species differ widely from those of another, but we may note at the outset these fundamentals :

- ∾ All lilies insist on good drainage, anything like waterlogging in the subsoil being fatal.
- ∾ They dislike gross manures, but rejoice in leafmould.
- ∾ All, except the Madonna lily, need basal shade.
- ∾ Some like or tolerate lime, but to others it is poison.

On no account buy lilies from a shop, unless you see that they are stored in damp peat, and never buy them as a 'cheap line'; but only from reputable growers. They are rarely if ever dormant, should be out of the ground the minimum possible time, and must not be allowed to dry up. Plant them immediately they arrive, or, if this is impossible, store them in damp peat. Never accept any bulbs that are lacking their basal roots.

Cultivation. Very sandy soils and very heavy clays are alike usually unpropitious, but most lilies are well suited by any good medium soil in good heart, provided the drainage is beyond doubt. Do not use newly manured beds. Except for Madonna, use a soil well cultivated in a previous year, but old leafmould has special value and so has sharp sand if the soil is heavy. Unless you are planting only the odd bulb or two, the best plan is to dig out the soil completely to a full spade's depth over all the area required and stir up your mixture in a wheelbarrow. When plotting the area allow 8 in. between bulbs.

Except for Madonna, plant where the roots and lower stems will be in shade, but the heads in sun or partial sun. Among low shrubs or in semi-woodland are ideal situations. Spread the roots out well on a little saddle of soil (as shown for irises on page 197) at the bottom of the hole. Encase each bulb in sharp sand against slugs.

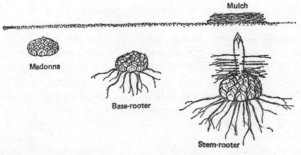

Mulch

Madonna

Base-rooter

Stem-rooter

Planting depths for lilies.

Depth of planting is *critically important*. It is vital to know that some lilies root only from the base of the bulb, but that others root also from the stem above the bulb; the latter, therefore, need deeper planting than the former. The best practice for the stem-rooters is to plant about 6 in. deep and to add a thick mulch of leaves on the surface annually with some fertiliser.

Once planted, do not disturb the bulbs until they become overcrowded. Label their positions, so that they are undamaged by digging or hoeing. When lifting becomes necessary, do so when the foliage has completely died down, and replant with the least possible delay.

Lilies can often do without staking, but I find it safest to support the taller sorts, particularly in windy places, or they will loll forward. I use light canes, but plant them well away from the new shoots when they sprout in spring. Stunted shoots may be caused by slugs attacking the underground stems.

Propagation. Several methods, fairly easy but slow. One method is to divide the bulbs and their babies when digging up. Another is to remove a few scales of the bulb, plant them right way up in pots or boxes in a mixture of leaf-soil (or peat) and sand, with the tips just showing. In a greenhouse or warm frame bulblets form in about six weeks. Transplant when established. Some lilies, such as tiger lily, *L. lancifolium*, form tiny bulbils in the axils of the leaves. Sow these in autumn in a JI compost, like seeds, lightly covered with soil.

Species and varieties. Like daffodils and dahlias, lilies have been put into pigeonholes accordingly to their shapes and demeanours. We need not go into these beyond remarking on the diversity of the lily's performances, which include trumpets, turkscaps (in which the petals roll fully back to form loose orbs), semi-reflexed like a half-peeled banana, cup-like and upward looking, level-gazing or contemplatively down-looking, sometimes arranged in pyramids, sometimes in spires. In addition to the natural species and named varieties, there are also hybrid 'strains', in which there are some slight variations. Omitting the more expensive enchantments, I select the following few as perhaps the best for a start.

Madonna lily (*L. candidum*). A fine old lady, albeit temperamental. She will often take kindly to the cottage plot, but spurn the lord's demesne. Madonna is specially fond of lime, and a plain, stony diet suits her best, though she often prospers in clay also. Unlike most other lilies, she demands a position in full sun from head to foot. *Be most particular* to plant her only 1 in. deep on light soils and only barely covered on heavy ones. Madonna is base-rooting, and has a cluster of sumptuous white trumpets borne at the summit of a 4 ft. stem. Plant in July or soon after.

L. regale. Perhaps the easiest and certainly one of the most beautiful; 4 ft. high with a large cluster of white trumpets. Ample shade for roots most important. Lime-tolerant. Stem-rooting. Depth 4 in. plus mulch. Easily grown from seed in sandy-peaty, soil in pots or even in the open.

L. regale 'Royal Gold' is a very fine yellow version.

L. henryi. Very easy. Densely crowded with orange turkscaps. Stem-rooting. Notably lime-loving. 7 ft.

L. x hollandicum. Very easy. Wide-open cups, looking upwards, 2½ ft. Stem-rooting, lime-tolerant.

L. martagon and its hybrids. Pyramids of small, half-reflexed blooms looking down. Base-rooting, lime-tolerant. The white *L. martagon* var. *album* is the best, others often muddy.

'Limelight.' Lovely, cool, shining lemon. Stem-rooting. 4 ft.

Mid-Century Series. A series with many colour variants. Grows anywhere that daffodils will. The favourite named varieties are the flame-coloured 'Enchantment', the yellow 'Destiny' and the crimson 'Paprika'. Stem-rooting. Lime-tolerant. Average 3 ft.

Olympic. Another easy Group. White or pink-tinted trumpets. Stem-rooting. 4 ft. Lime-tolerant.

Golden Splendor Group. 5 ft. pyramids of trumpets in yellow shades. Lime-tolerant.

'Green Dragon'. Large white trumpets, flushed chartreuse on the exterior. 3½ ft. 'Black Dragon' is flushed deep maroon, 6 ft. Stem-rooters.

Plenty more are available, many fit only for skilled or fortunate gardeners. Those who have an acid soil, deep in old leafmould, and very well drained should go for the varieties of the sumptuous *L. auratum* and *L. speciosum* or the hybrid Imperial Group in crimson or gold. Not cheap.

There is much disease among lilies. Dust the bulbs before planting with flowers of sulphur. Apply a systemic insecticide when in growth, against greenfly. Watch for small, brownish, watery markings on the leaves, which then turn brown and drop. This is botrytis; spray with a copper fungicide.

Meadow saffron or naked ladies (*Colchicum*). Misleadingly called autumn crocus. Not a crocus at all, and the autumn-flowering true crocuses are much more attractive. Meadow saffron has large, coarse leaves, poisonous to cattle. Plant 2 in. deep.

Montbretia. Colourful gladiolus-like flowers blooming July–September, which we are now expected to call *Crocosmia*. The fashionable species is *C. masoniorum*, which produces long, bending sprays of blazing orange in summer. Plant the corms preferably in March, 4 in. deep. I still have a strong affection for the old, less hardy 'His Majesty', scarlet and gold, 4 ft.

Muscari. The lovely toy grape hyacinth is available in several colours, of which *M. armeniacum* 'Heavenly Blue' is perhaps best, though the lighter-hued *M. armeniacum* 'Cantab' is also delightful. Plant 2–3 in. deep in autumn in any good soil in the sun and leave undisturbed. They multiply readily and spread. Easy and charming, but the foliage is untidy. Excellent for bowls in fibre.

Less well known is the rather taller plumed grape hyacinth (*M. comosum* 'Plumosum'), embellished with a plume of blue feathers; very decorative and distinctive.

Narcissus (daffodil). Daffodil is simply the English vernacular for narcissus, whether the trumpet be long or short. Daffs have been segregated by the RHS into several pigeonholes, according to their floral forms. Ignoring the various subdivisions, these are:

ᴕ Division 1. Large trumpets.

ᴕ Division 2. Large cups or short trumpets.

ᴕ Division 3. Small cups.

ᴕ Division 4. Doubles – horrible abortions.

ᴕ Division 5. Triandrus. Clusters of small, nodding flowers, for porous, gritty soil.

ᴕ Division 6. Cyclamineus. Delightful, pensive flowers with swept-back perianths. For damp soil.

ᴕ Division 7. Jonquils.

ᴕ Division 8. Tazetta. Having multi-flowered stems.

ᴕ Division 9. Poeticus. Flat flowers with a small, bright-eyed central disc.

Culture. Plant in August or earliest September if possible, but later plantings will do. Cover the bulb with soil 1½ times as deep as the length of the bulb. Place them where their dying foliage will be concealed in summer – the middle or back of a mixed border (not the edge), the shrub garden or naturalised in grass. Leave them undisturbed until over-crowding requires them to be lifted and divided, which is done in July.

Certain maladies can afflict daffodils. The worst is eelworm, for which the amateur has no cure except to dig up and burn the bulbs; look out for any stunted, distorted or withered growths. A colony of 'blind' shoots, having no flower-stems, suggests the depredation of the narcissus fly, usually a result of the bulbs being too near the surface and needing to be planted deeper.

Varieties. Among the less expensive sorts, the following are well-tried standard varieties :

ᴕ Division 1. Among the yellows – 'Kingscourt', 'Golden Harvest', 'Rembrandt' (early), 'Rijnveld's Early Sensation' and 'Binkie'. Among the lovely all-white daffodils – 'Mount Hood' and 'Beersheba'.

There is now an exquisite range with pink or apricot trumpets, but at present the only one of modest price is 'Mrs R. O. Backhouse', which I greatly enjoy, but you may not.

ᴕ Division 2. 'Kilworth', 'Fortune', 'Carlton', 'Carbineer', 'Camelot' and 'Passionale'.

ᴕ Division 3. 'La Riante' and 'Segovia'.

'Actaea' is a splendid and vigorous Poeticus; and 'Geranium' inaptly names one of the best Tazettas.

Miniatures. Some of the easiest and most endearing are: *N. minor*, most reliable of the tiny trumpet daffodils; *N. triandrus* var. *triandrus*, 7 in.; the cyclamen-flowered daffodil (*N. cyclamineus*) with swept-back perianth,

6 in., and the hoop-petticoat daffodil (*N. bulbocodium*), 6 in., like a little bugle with virtually no perianth. Some charming hybrid miniature Division 1 trumpets are 'Little Beauty' and 'Little Gem'.

Absolutely top-class hybrids have come from the parental influence of *N. cyclamineus*, especially 'February Gold', 1 ft., 'Charity May', 'Beryl' and 'Bartley' to which the earlier-flowering 'Peeping Tom' is very similar. 12–15 in. All are excellent in bowls or pots.

Nerine. Autumn has no more radiant flowers than *N. bowdenii*. Its short, thick stems are crowned with a rapturous cluster of sparkling, pink, star-like florets, but it must have a really warm spot, preferably against a south-facing wall. Like several other South Africans, in our summer it shows us only a sheaf of strap-like leaves, which die down to reveal the flowers in their naked beauty in late September. Plant the bulb with the tip of its long neck only just below soil level in November or March. Shy for the first year.

Ranunculus. The tuberous forms of the garden buttercup, 9 in. high, glowing in a galaxy of colours in May and June, are splendid for cutting. They need heaps of sun and a well-drained soil with ample leafmould or peat. Plant claw downwards, 2 in. deep, the turban types in November, and the French and Persian types in March. Lift and store in July, being sure they are dry.

Scilla. This includes the little blue Siberian squill, an enchanting midget. The variety to get is *S. siberica* 'Spring Beauty'. Plant it in autumn among bushes or in borders 2 in. deep and leave it alone. It spreads rapidly until the earth looks as though it had been sprinkled with sapphires.

Snowdrop (*Galanthus*). The world provides many lovely snowdrops, but you cannot do better than stick to the common British one, *G. nivalis*, or its double cultivar 'Flore Pleno'. Naturalise it in short grass, or drop it among bushes and trees. Plant very early, 3 in. deep. Leave it alone to increase naturally; in fact, it transplants best when actually in bloom or in full leaf. Other fine ones, large-flowered, and fitted best for special places, are *G. elwesii* and *plicatum*. All these are of sound constitution and easy culture, but the autumn snowdrops should be left to the expert. If you want snowdrops in autumn, then plant the equally charming **snowflake** (*Leucojum*), of which there are also several kinds, very like a real snowdrop but larger. *L. autumnale* is an exquisite 5 in. plant with pale pink bells, and there are charming ones for other seasons, such as *L. aestivum*, which is called the summer snowflake or Loddon lily and is tipped green, and of which 'Gravetye' is a good cultivar but is too tall at 2 ft. It prospers in deep shade. For spring there is the 9 in. *L. vernum* which succeeds in the poorest soils.

Tulip. *General culture.* Choose a site in full sun and very well drained. Plant the first week of November (never earlier than late October), 4 in. deep. The best effect usually is from formal, geometrical patterns.

Tulips may be attacked by the 'fire' disease, shown by a scorching of the leaf edges. To discourage it, lift and store the bulbs, every year after the foliage has died down (or heel in earlier with a ball of soil if the ground is needed), and do not plant tulips in the same bed year after year. Should the disease appear, no tulips must be grown for at least four years.

Species and varieties. All sorts of forms of the tulip have been evolved in centuries of hybridisation, but none is more beautiful that some of the original wild species. They eclipse the popular hybrids in brilliance and in colour and grace of deportment, but not all are easy. Of these wildlings (which often have several variations) these are recommended:

The water-lily tulip (*T. kaufmanniana*), a tulip of lovely form and glittering colour combinations, with many variations on the theme of primrose-carmine-cream, about 7 in. high. Excellent and early in bowls. Now has several varieties which are not cheap.

∾ *T. linifolia* Batalinii Group. A 6 in. charmer in primrose.

∾ *T. tarda.* Starry gold-and-white miniature.

∾ *T. fosteriana.* Enormous bloom of dazzling oriental scarlet on a 15 in. stem; 'Madame Lefeber' is a fine hybrid.

∾ *T. eichleri*, another scarlet dazzler, 10 in.

∾ *T. praestans* 'Fusilier'. Two or more scarlet blooms on each stem; 6 in. Some multi-flowered ones are also to be found among the tall hybrids.

∾ Viridiflora Group: Stunning concoctions of green and other colours, as in 'Artist', 'China Town' and 'Spring Green'.

∾ Greigii Group: Dazzlers with broad leaves striped chocolate or maroon. *Popular hybrids.* These fall into several Groups. There is no point in singling out varieties, and one cannot do better than order a mixed bag of '100 bulbs in 10 varieties'. The very tall sorts – Darwin, Cottage, Lily-flowered, Rembrandt and Triumph – are apt to be beheaded by high winds, so are best avoided in exposed places. The following are the main groups:

Single Earlies: Bloom with the daffodils in April in a wonderful range of colours on short stems, usually about 1 ft.

Double Earlies: Solid peony-like blooms in lovely colours, very long-lasting; short stems. Excellent for bowls or pots.

Parrots: Fantastic in design with fretted edges and splendid colourings.

Darwins: The well-known tall, single tulips of May with ramrod stems and flowers of severe and formal elegance.

Cottage tulips: Similar to Darwins, but a trifle less formal. May.

Lily-flowered tulips: Tall, elegant, with the tips of the petals flared outwards. May.

Triumphs: Mid-season single tulips including the Darwins.

Rembrandts: Streaked and feathered in diverse colours.

Many tulips do well in pots or bowls indoors. Among the early singles, well-tried ones are 'Apricot Beauty' and fragrant 'Generaal de Wet'. Among the early doubles – 'Peach Blossom', 'Monte Carlo' and 'Oranje Nassau'.

Most of the Darwins and similar tall breeds succeed in pots (rather than bowls); start with 'Maureen' and 'Queen of Night'.

Winter aconite (*Eranthis hyemalis*). Only an inch or two high, is like a buttercup with a green ruff round its neck. January and February. Plant in shrublands 2 in. deep in early autumn and leave alone. Shy at first. *E. hyemalis* Tubergenii Group is considered by some people as superior to the more usual species.

14

ROSES

I have no doubt that in any Gallup poll of garden favourites the 'Queen of flowers all' would easily head the list. Like Cleopatra, 'Age cannot wither her, nor custom stale Her infinite variety'. It is not surprising, therefore, that for hundreds of years eager hybridists, both amateur and professional, have been busy breeding or selecting new forms, encouraging special virtues and eliminating weaknesses, but occasionally sacrificing something, as, for example, luxuriance of foliage.

The main efforts of more recent hybridists have been directed to giving us the highly decorative roses now so popular – large, full of glowing colours, with buds of shapely elegance, reflexed petals, and often highly fragrant. They are commonly grown in beds in the forms of 'dwarf bushes' and little standard trees, and for our convenience I propose to group these together as 'bedding roses'. The rose, however, shows her variety not only in form and colour but also in habit and purpose, and we must begin by being clear about these things.

THE SHAPES AND FORMS OF ROSES

Bush or **dwarf** roses are the form commonly seen everywhere in formal beds. They are bushes in name only, for their foliage is very sparse, and they are not to be confused with 'shrub' roses, which in the language of the fancy means something else.

Standards have little erect tree-stems about 4 ft. high budded at the top with the same variety of rose as the dwarfs. They look delightful on either side of a path as a little avenue. There are also half-standards. A weeping standard is budded with the flexible Rambler rose types, drooping to the ground.

Ramblers are roses which, like 'Dorothy Perkins' and other Wichurana varieties, produce long flexible canes; they are best used to clothe pergola, arch, or trellis, but *not* walls. Most have one short and very vivid season of bloom and are then over. They are declining in popularity and giving way to the modern hybrid climbers which bloom at least twice or even continuously.

Climbers are commonly confused with Ramblers, but there are sharp differences. Climbers are either long-caned 'sports' that have sprung from the dwarf bedding types of rose (e.g. 'Climbing Madame Butterfly'), or else they are developments from the wild species of rose or are crosses with the Rambler types. These grow as a rule less rampantly and less flexibly than the Ramblers, but are larger in flower and some of them bloom intermittently throughout the summer. They are also less liable to mildew. The climbing sports have exactly the same flowers as their dwarf parents. Neither of these classes are really 'climbers', having no apparatus for clinging except their thorns. They look best on walls, pergolas, or isolated pillars, rather than on arches or trellis; some are called 'pillar' roses and show their full glory best that way. Unfortunately some nurseries mix the climbers and Ramblers together in their catalogues.

Shrubs. This term includes (*a*) the wild species (*see* next page) and (*h*) several exciting modern hybrids, some of which bloom 'perpetually' all summer; they grow very large and, like the species, are not suited to formal rose beds.

THE BREEDS OF ROSES

A rough idea of the classification of roses by breeding is a practical necessity. The parentage of many, however, is so complicated that often even experts disagree. All we need do as practical gardeners is to group them together for purposes of treatment and use.

First there are the familiar large-flowered **dwarf bedders**. The great majority are called Hybrid Teas (H.T.), but a few Hybrid Perpetuals (H.P.) are still with us. These all have the same use, and for gardening purposes differ only in their vigour and thus in spacing and pruning.

Floribundas are characterised by densely clustered heads of blossom. For our purposes there are two groups. One is the low, dwarf bedding form formerly called Polyantha roses, with massed trusses of little pompons. The second is the result of a happy marriage between Polyanthas and H.T.s and are called Floribundas. They are very showy and ideal bedding plants. Many have large blossoms like the H.T.s, but few have scent so far. We shall see many more of these large-flowered Floribundas, for they make splendid garden roses.

Wichurana roses and their hybrids. These have given us the greater number of our extra-vigorous popular Ramblers, such as 'Dorothy Perkins'.

Other types of climber, mostly hybrids, have been referred to in the previous section.

Species. A term loosely applied to the true species, or wild roses, and their progeny. They are easy of culture, need little pruning, and often flourish on poor soils. They vary greatly in style, habit, and size. Many bloom for a short season only, and others may be too big for small places. Some, however, such as the Rugosa roses, have a very long season and are ideal for any garden.

146 ♦ THE SMALL GARDEN

Old roses. These are what I call the poets' roses, dominant from early times till about the middle of the nineteenth century. They lack the high-pointed centre of H.T. and are massed with petals in rounded outline, often gorgeously scented. Purple shades mingle with their pinks and whites. They include the Gallicas, Centifolias, Albas, Damasks and Bourbons. Some have floppy stems and most flower once only in the season.

Rose stocks. This is a convenient place to say that all hybrids are normally propagated by budding the cultivated 'scion' on to a root 'stock'. The quality of this root stock is of the greatest importance to the buyer. His safeguard is to go only to a rose *grower* with a good reputation. Rugosa is one good stock, especially for standards, recognisable by its thickly prickled stem, and there are other reliable ones.

CULTIVATION

Because the rose is one of our most willing and gallant triers, and will do well in so many soils, some ancient misconceptions still linger.

For example, it was for long a prevalent notion that roses demanded clay and that they needed lime. Neither idea is true. Certainly they will put up a good show under these conditions, but what they really like best is a medium loam a trifle on the acid side – one that is well drained, well aerated, and easily worked, but which will retain moisture and not dry out quickly in hot spells, as sandy soils do. What they will not stand is water-logging or very acid peats. As for lime, they like best a pH reading of about 6.5. Lime should therefore be given only if there are indications of strong acidity or sourness, or if there is a *physical* need to crumble down a stubborn and sticky clay.

Situation is almost as important as soil. Except for the sorts grown on walls, roses hate being shut in. They are fresh-air fiends, and demand an open situation where the air and the breezes can circulate freely. They also demand sun, and must on no account whatever be directly under trees, but they do not dislike slanting or oblique shade at midday, especially those of the yellow and orange shades.

If possible, do not plant roses where other roses have long grown. Soils become 'rose-sick'. If unavoidable, import some fresh top soil from elsewhere in the garden or from outside.

Prepare the soil well before planting – a month ahead if possible. Bastard trench it. Invigorate both spits with organic matter. In the absence of animal manure, use old turves, roughly chopped up and turned upside-down. In the top spit compost is excellent, so is hop manure. Then let the bed settle.

If animal manure is used, it must be kept fairly well down, and 2 in. of fine soil should come on top of it, for it is deadly to allow the roots of roses to come in actual contact with animal manure.

Just before planting prepare a special planting mixture made up of fine, crumbly soil, peat, and bonemeal, with a little sand added if the soil is heavy. You can make a quantity in a barrow or mix the materials in each planting hole.

PLANTING

October–November is the best time, but any time up to March will do provided the soil is neither frost-nipped nor saturated. Container-grown roses from a garden centre can be planted at any time in theory, but unseasonable planting means that you cannot properly spread out the over-crowded roots.

If you cannot plant when the nurseryman's package arrives, follow the guide-lines set out at the end of Chapter 5. Any plants with withered stems should be sent back to the nursery with a shirty letter, but you could try reviving them by immersion in water for 24 hours.

When ready to plant look over the roots. Cut out any coarse growth in the nature of a tap-root and trim back damaged shoots with secateurs. Those that are inconveniently long can be cut back; ten inches is ample. Should the roots be very dry, make a stiffish mud puddle and swill the roots in it.

Prepare a hole about 15 in. in diameter and about half that depth, according to the need of each plant. If the roots are disposed all in one direction, as they often are today, make the hole fan-shaped. Spread a 2 in. layer of the planting mixture in the bottom. Put in the plant, roots properly disposed. Cover with another 2 in. of the mixture and tread down firmly. Top up with the original soil. *Make sure that the crowns of bush roses are covered by not more than 1 in.* and the roots of standards some 3 or 4 in., according to the soil-mark.

Standards and half-standards need firm staking. Plant the stake, 1 ft deep, before planting the rose. Tie stake and rose-stem together, at the top and lower down, with a piece of felt, sacking, or other soft material

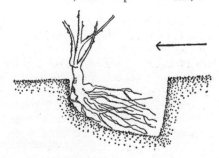

Fan-planting a rose bush. Roots well spread out in a fan-shaped hole. Arrow shows direction of prevailing wind.

between stake and stem to prevent chafing. Climbers and Ramblers also need tying to some form of support. Planting distances are:

∞ Bushes: for H.T.s and Floribundas a good 18 in., but some need more; dwarf forms 15 in.

∞ Standards: 3 ft.

∞ Climbers and Ramblers: an absolute minimum of 7 ft.

∞ Species and shrubs: according to ultimate spread.

AFTER-CARE

Pruning and spraying are prime needs in the after-care of the rose, and I deal with these separately.

Keep the weeds down, a job admirably done by the modern weed inhibitors mentioned in the section on weeds in Chapter 5.

On H.T.s and H.P.s, if fine blooms are wanted, pinch out all the small buds that often form below the central one for a distance of 5 in. or so; this is 'disbudding', as shown for chrysanthemums in Chapter 18. Any lower buds can be left to develop. Do not disbud other types of roses.

Behead all spent flowers, cutting back to a promising new eye, or growth bud, in the axil of a leaf. In Floribundas this means the whole truss of flowers; no funking.

In July, in order to maintain virility after the first flush of bloom, treat the rose to a chemical tonic fertiliser, of which there are several proprietary brands.

In autumn gather up and burn all fallen rose leaves, for they may carry fungal infections, and then mulch thickly with oak or beech leaves if you can. Birds and winds will scatter the leaves, a nuisance that you must put up with.

Next spring top-dress with animal manure or with peat plus a fertiliser.

PRUNING

Chapter 7 dealt with pruning generally, and the application of those principles to roses is not difficult, the main question being the degree of severity to apply to different sorts. One may attempt to lay down precise and dogmatic rules, especially for exhibitors, but the general run of people need some simple general rules at first, and here again 'group treatment' is an answer.

The problem is immensely simplified by an understanding of the natural habits of the rose. In a state of nature the rose is constantly throwing up new growth. Into these new shoots it gradually directs its sap, and the older growths become starved out. What the pruner does, therefore, is to hasten the rejection of the old wood before it becomes useless and to encourage the plant's instinct for producing ever fresh young shoots;

especially does he encourage those from the base of the plant, though in some types new growth does not come readily from the base but sprouts from some point high or low on the main stem.

That is the sum and substance of pruning in principle, and intelligent observation will point the way. The important things to know are: Does the particular rose bloom on new shoots of this year's growth, or on old wood grown in a previous year? Does it bloom on main stems or on laterals? What is its degree of vigour?

For example, 'Dorothy Perkins', the familiar Wichurana rambler, flowers on 'wood' or shoots that grew last year, but 'Climbing Ophelia' flowers on laterals and sub-laterals as well as sending up occasional new wood. And, among the bedders, the tremendous vigour of 'Hugh Dickson' means light pruning, while the little 'Allgold' may be cut back hard. Thus, while it is important to keep roses durably labelled, observation of habit and vigour will be sufficient guide if identities are lost.

Bearing this in mind, and the general principles of Chapter 7, we can write down certain guiding precepts, some general and some particular.

General precepts

For all except China roses of whatever nature. Prune harder in the first year than in subsequent years. Prune spring-planted trees harder than autumn-planted; standards harder than bushes; weak varieties and thin shoots harder than vigorous varieties and strong shoots.

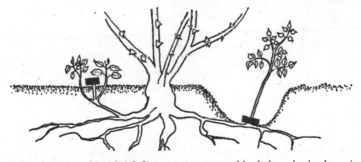

Suckers (rose or anything else): left, wrong: cut at ground level, the sucker breaks again, more strongly; right, plucked out (not cut) at the point of origin.

Root out all suckers at their point of origin. A sucker is a shoot from the root stock appearing below the point of union – from below ground in a bush, but in a standard either from below ground or from the main stem. It is recognisable by the foliage being quite different from that of the cultivated scion. If coming from below ground, scrape away the soil, find the point of origin and smartly pluck it out; don't *cut*. Be careful of recognition in Ramblers and climbers which also sprout from the ground legitimately; and bear in mind that any growth from the ground in a 'species'

rose may be true to type and should not be cut out, the Scotch rose, which
suckers freely, being an example (if on its own roots). So also for roses
grown from cuttings yourself.

For all bedding types (H.T.s and H.P.s, Floribundas, etc., whether dwarfs or
standards). Except on very sprawling types, cut always down to an outward-
pointing eye, and keep the centre of the plant open, seeking to build up a
cup-shaped structure; for floribundas this is of less importance. When two
shoots cross, cut one back below the point of crossing.

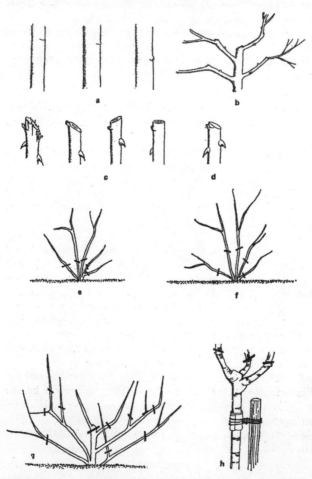

Pruning roses: **a**, *typical rose 'eyes';* **b**, *prune to an outward-pointing bud;* **c**, *wrong pruning
– jagged, below the eye, wrong way, too flat;* **d**, *just right;* **e** *to* **g**, *pruning a weak-growing
rose, one of moderate vigour and a vigorous one;* **h**, *hard-pruning of a first-year standard.*

When midsummer blooming is over, cut back to some strong outward eye for the next display. Observe pruning rules when cutting for the house. Weeping standards are pruned as Ramblers.

Time for pruning. A much debated matter. The old rule was the last week of March in the South for bedding types, ten days later in the North. Most people, however, have come round to the view that you follow the rule for any deciduous shrub: prune in winter dormancy. This sounds sense. I start after Christmas and reckon to finish by February. Do not, of course, prune during a hard frost and if your young buds are frizzled up after pruning you must cut back again.

Ramblers: soon after flowering, when the new shoots are growing strongly.

Climbers: Shorten flowered laterals after flowering, and prune the whole in winter.

Particular precepts
This concerns the *degree* of pruning for different types. Dogmatism here is out of place, but the following notes will be a good guide for general garden display.

Bedding types (*other than Floribunda*). In the first winter or spring cut down to a bud about 4 in. from the ground, lower still on weak shoots. In subsequent years prune to about five eyes on strong basal shoots; and to three or less on weaker basal shoots, on strong laterals, and on plants of very dwarf growth. On H.P.s and some very vigorous H.T.s prune less severely, e.g. 'Peace', 'Perfecta', 'Prima Ballerina'.

Bush Floribundas. First season, cut down to about 5 in. from the ground. In after years, for normal usages, shorten the best stems by about a half, and remove the remainder. Alternatively, you can get a brilliant mass effect with the pompon types by cutting right down to within 3 or 4 in. of the ground annually. Conversely, the Floribundas can by light pruning be built into charming low hedges, though some wood must always be removed each year. Varieties of great vigour are pruned much more lightly, but 'The Queen Elizabeth' should be cut back to about 18 in. every year.

Species roses. No pruning, other than occasional removal of exhausted old wood, or such trimming as is needed to keep a good shape.

Ramblers and climbers. Here classifications are not clear-cut and the boundaries of breeding indistinct. Habit of growth must therefore be our guide, and the following formula is intended to simplify the problem on the basis of intelligent observation.

Cut out old-flowered wood in proportion to the degree to which new wood is produced. Thus:

(a) for every new cane springing right from the ground or near it, cut out the whole of an old cane, provided that the plant as a whole does not thus become too poorly furnished; if, for example, there is only one old cane and one new one, treat the old one as in (*c*) below.

(b) When new growth sprouts not from the base but from somewhere on an old cane, cut the old cane down to the strongest of the new shoots, and cut back the laterals on the remaining old wood by about two-thirds.

(c) If there are no new canes at all, cut back the old laterals as above, and slightly shorten the tip.

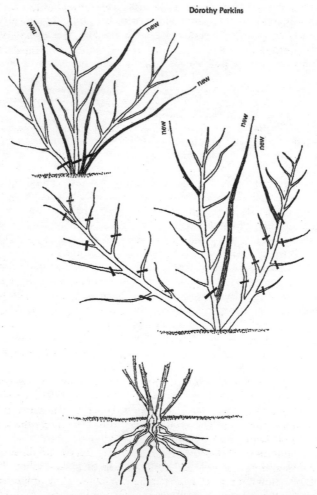

Dorothy Perkins

Top: *pruning a Rambler of 'Dorothy Perkins' family; cut all old flowered canes to the ground in autumn (unless no new canes). Middle: on other Ramblers and climbers generally, prune according to the vigour of new wood; on old wood that is retained shorten laterals. Bottom: a dwarf bush rose correctly planted.*

Easiest of all is the 'Dorothy Perkins' group of Ramblers, characterised by their *lax, flexible canes* (cf. Climbers). These behave exactly like raspberries and loganberries. Long new canes sprout from the base every year, and they flower the following year. Therefore, we cut *all* the old canes down to the ground every year after flowering.

By the same token, you amputate Dorothy's family in the year of planting to 15 in. of the ground (or to within five buds of the crown on weeping standards), expecting *no bloom the first summer*. This is a cardinal injunction and you mustn't funk it. On other groups, especially the climbing sports, you need not cut back in the year of planting, bar any weak or damaged shoots.

One or two special cases remain to be dealt with:

∽ 'Gloire de Dijon'. Treat as a climbing H.T. sport.
∽ 'Mermaid'. Do not prune at all the first spring, and very little afterwards, except for removal of decadent old wood.
∽ 'Albertine', though a Wichurana cross, is best treated as a stiff-stemmed climber.

THE ROSE'S ENEMIES

In Part Four I have dealt with the gardener's enemies in general, and only a little amplification is necessary here.

Let us briefly catalogue the insect pests first. Commonest is the greenfly that in its myriads sucks the sap from young shoots, and the spittle-bug that likewise sucks away under the shelter of his slimy foam. The slugworm delicately chisels out the skeleton of a leaf, the sawfly grub rolls up the leaf like a paper-spill and the leaf-cutting bee scollops out neat half-moons on the edges of the blade. The caterpillars of the tortrix moths burrow into the heart of a young bud, and the rose chafer consumes the blossom itself.

Several of these can be dealt with by insecticides such as pyrethrins (including pyrethrum itself), rotenone (derris) and insecticidal soap (fatty acids).

There remain the more difficult fungal diseases. Mildew appears as a grey powdering of the foliage; blackspot is shown by black or purple-brown patches; 'rust' is a rusty speckling; and 'leaf scorch' starts as small yellow patches, later turning brown and dropping out, giving the leaf the appearance of having been peppered by shot.

The commonest of these are blackspot and mildew. The former, very conspicuous and ugly, is very stubborn and can be a slow killer. To deal with these, systemic fungicides containing myclobutanil or propiconazole are available. Penconazole is not systemic but works partly by hindering production of spores. For organic gardeners, sulphur will control powdery mildew.

PROPAGATION OF ROSES

The propagation of roses by budding and grafting is great fun and not particularly difficult, but the easiest way for amateurs to increase their own supplies (of certain sorts) is by cuttings. Experience and opinion on this subject varies a good deal, but it is generally agreed that ramblers are easy and that the H.T.s with any yellow in them are not.

Autumn is the time. Take 'trimmed heel' cuttings (*see* Chapter 6) from firm, ripe wood of the current season's growth, or nodal cuttings from low down on the same wood. If longer than about 10 in. cut them down to that length or less, shortening from the top of the shoot, not the base. Cut out all eyes on the lower half, and treat the cuttings with a rooting hormone. Insert to nearly half their depth in V-shaped trenches, the bottoms of which are lined with an inch of sharp sand, in a shady place, not directly under trees. Tread firmly and water well if the ground is at all dry. By the following autumn the young plants will be ready to go into their permanent stations.

You are not likely to get 100 per cent 'strikes', especially in heavy clays, so take more than you need. Roses grown this way have the advantage that there is no 'brier' to throw up suckers, and any growth from below ground can be left alone, or transplanted.

LAYOUT AND DISPLAY

It is an axiom of the purists that roses should never lie in the same bed as other flowers. This may be too severe a morality in the confines of a small garden, but any bed-mates you give them must be chosen with care. Noting rumbustious. Ideal companions are violas and lobelias, and a fringe of pinks round the margins of the bed is also charming.

As compared with the shrub species, the bedding roses are creatures of the drawing-room. They demand formal beds, rather prim, and they demand especially a carpet of green grass round about them. The lawn is the perfect setting for the rose. Let the situation always be open – not shut in by walls, trees or high hedges.

VARIETIES TO CHOOSE

From the enormous Who's Who of roses there are at least three or four dozen that merit the term 'outstanding', and it is difficult enough to make up one's own mind which twelve roses one most likes personally. Squadrons of new ones are paraded before us every year, but it is only once every five or six years that anything appears which is really better than its predecessor. So what I have done in the following lists is to pick a few that seem likely to hold their own for the next few years, omitting varieties better left to the exhibitor, those that behave badly in rain, those that are particularly subject to disease, and any that have other faults. You must get their descriptions from the better catalogues.

Avoid all new roses until they have been tested in commerce and do not swallow all the guff about 'each new-hatched, unfledged' darling. Most of them fall by the wayside after a few years. This caveat does not apply, however, to 'Silver Jubilee', a rapturous pink issued in 1977, raised by Cockers of Aberdeen and named by The Queen herself.
H.T.s. Most of the following have scent:

- 'Wendy Cussons' (every virtue)
- 'Piccadilly' (best, bicolour)
- 'Prima Ballerina' (great vigour, erect)
- 'Ernest H. Morse'
- 'Blessings'
- 'Alec's Red'
- 'Peer Gynt'

'Pascali' (best white)
'Grandpa Dickson'
'Whisky Mac'
'King's Ransome'
'Pink Favourite'
'Mischief'
'Rose Gaujard' (vigorous)
'Peace' (great vigour)
'Super Star' (tall and slim)

Floribundas. A fast-expanding class, getting more and more of the H.T. element in them, sometimes to the detriment of their continuity of bloom.

- 'Evelyn Fison'
- 'Allgold'
- 'Paprika'
- 'Pink Parfait'
- 'Orange Sensation'
- 'Dearest'
- 'Elizabeth of Glamis'

'Lilli Marlene'
'Rob Roy' (strong)
'News' (burgundy)
'City of Leeds'
'Iceberg' (white, strong)
'Southampton' (resists disease)

I exclude 'The Queen Elizabeth' because, on account of its great vigour, I count it a shrub rose.

Several pretty dwarf Floribundas (not to be confused with the Miniatures) have been developed. Those that I have found to be most reliable against disease are the red 'Marlena' and the yellow 'Kim'.

Climbers. The climbing sports, which burst out into one magnificent display at midsummer, are tending to give way to the modern hybrid climbers that bloom more or less repeatedly, but 'Climbing Madame Butterfly', 'Climbing Shot Silk', 'Climbing Madame Edouard Herriot' and many more gracefully perpetuate the memories of some beautiful H.T.s of yesterday. Of their modern rivals, impressive garden pictures are painted by such as 'Handel', 'Danse du Feu', 'Pink Perpétué', 'Leverkusen', 'Compassion', 'Maigold' and 'Schoolgirl'. Other and older climbers of the highest order are 'Allen Chandler', 'Mermaid', 'Madame Alfred Carrière' (all of great vigour) and the century-old 'Gloire de Dijon'.

Ramblers. For pergola, arch, or trellis, but preferably not for walls: 'Albertine' (the best), 'Paul's Scarlet Climber', 'American Pillar', 'Thelma', 'New Dawn' (continuously in flower, very thorny), 'François Juranville', 'Crimson Shower' for late effect, 'Dorothy Perkins'.

Pillar roses or short climbers. 'Golden Showers', 'Aloha', 'Zéphirine Drouhin' (bad for mildew), all flowering 'perpetually', and 'White Cockade' nearly so.

Polyantha Pompons. 'The Fairy' (outstanding, wide-spreading, makes a fine standard), 'Ellen Poulsen', 'Yvonne Rabier'.

Miniatures. 'Baby Masquerade' (best all-rounder), 'Starina', 'New Penny'. 'Cécile Brünner' gives us the most beautiful miniature H.T. bloom, but the plant is no miniature.

Species and their hybrids. Those I specially recommend are:

R. xanthina 'Canary Bird'. Gleaming yellow, single flowers, quite large, on a dense mound of fine foliage, 7 ft. high. May-flowering only.

R. primula. Grown specially for its beautiful dense foliage that embalms the air. Buttercup-like flowers in May. 6 ft.

R. ecae. Long sprays of small yellow flowers on a slim and elegant plant. May-flowering only.

R. moyesii. A rose of lyric beauty in dusky, antique red, and a crop of handsome bottle-shaped hips in autumn. June-flowering only. It will grow to 10 ft., has naked legs and so should go at the back of a border.

Hybrid Musks. Wonderful roses for any garden. Very vigorous, very prolific, throwing out great bouquets of small, scented pastel-tinted flowers. Cut the flower clusters back to a strong eye for succession of bloom. Prune out old growth occasionally. Good hedgers. 'Penelope', 'Cornelia', and 'Felicia' will do for a start.

Rugosa roses. These splendid roses are densely bushy with thick, dark-green foliage to the ground. 6 ft. × 6 ft. Fine varieties are the purple 'Roseraie de l'Haÿ', 'Fru Dagmar Hastrup', 'Sarah van Fleet' (big and fiercely thorned), and 'Blanche Double de Coubert'. Fine for hedging.

Scotch or Burnet Brier (*R. spinosissima*). Very sturdy, vigorous, spiny, suckering freely. Strong, impregnable 5 ft. hedges. The variety 'Stanwell Perpetual' is particularly good, fragrant and ever-blooming. The modern hybrids 'Frühlingsgold' and 'Frühlingsmorgen' are tall, ethereally beautiful, flowering in spring only.

Bourbon roses. Of an old-world, drawing-room loveliness, richly scented. 'Madame Pierre Oger' is an ever-blooming shell-pink, erect in habit. 'Madame Isaac Pereire' is tall and sumptuous.

Modern Shrub roses. All but one of the following flower continuously or in successional bursts: 'Chinatown' (rich yellow, 6 ft.), 'Golden Wings' (pale yellow, 5 ft.), 'Fritz Nobis' (salmon-pink, scented, summer only, 7 ft. plus), 'Nevada' (one of the loveliest in creation, wide-flung ostrich plumes, white) and its pink sport 'Marguerite Hilling'.

Note. Readers who would like to pursue the matter further may care to read my *Roses for Small Gardens*. The Royal National Rose Society, whose beautiful garden is near St. Albans, is a treasury of rose knowledge, and is open free to all its members and, on payment, to anyone.

15

FLOWERING SHRUBS AND SMALL TREES

Trees and shrubs are dominant elements, and their shapes, textures, and manners immensely influence the general atmosphere and character of a garden. There are tall slim trees, plump round ones, light and airy ones, those with dark green leaves, others with silvery or purple leaves, and so on. Outline and skyline and architectural effect are critical factors, and variety and contrast must therefore be sought in making one's selections of trees and shrubs, whether they are to be used as backgrounds or screens, or planted as conspicuous 'specimens'.

But I would particularly draw attention to the immense usefulness in the small garden of that form of tree known as 'fastigiate' – that is to say, slim, erect and close-pressed, in the fashion of the Lombardy poplar. They take the minimum ground space and do not overhang and enshadow the soil. There are several of these among small trees, and one can often get a fastigiate form of a tree normally known only as a standard or as a bush. The best-known of the smaller sorts is the flowering cherry 'Amanogawa', but fastigiate forms are also to be found in the crab apple, the hawthorn and the koelreuteria. More obviously, we can use the slim, steeple-like conifers, such as *Chamaecyparis lawsoniana* 'Fletcheri' and *C. lawsoniana* 'Ellwoodii'.

Another very desirable form of small tree for providing variety of form and outline is the 'weeping' shape. Here again there are several, including weeping cherries, a weeping almond, a nice weeping crab apple (*Malus* x *gloriosa* 'Oekonomierat Echtermeyer'), all looking like great umbrellas mantled in pink or white and splendidly decorative. Another fine one is the *Cotoneaster* 'Hybridus Pendulus', its drooping wands festooned in berries. Of no floral value, but of decorative form, are the little weeping birch and the Camperdown elm, beloved of children.

Other forms to consider when making a plan are trees or shrubs grown specially for their beauty of foliage, such as the exquisite little Japanese maples for slightly shady places, the copper or purple forms of crab apple and others, the very solid forms of the barberries, and, of course, there should always be a proportion of evergreens.

All these considerations imply that, when thinking of a planting of trees and shrubs, planning is essential. Plot it out on squared paper, according to the *ultimate* height and spread of the plants, and plotting out the skyline as well. Catalogues of the best nurseries usually give some clue.

If your catalogue does not give the spread as well as height, you may for general purposes take the spread as being three-quarters of the height, but of course there are exceptions. Do not at any cost crowd the plants, and if your plan shows great gaps, as it will do, you can for the first two or three years fill up with other plants. The choicer trees and shrubs are best planted in selected and separate positions as 'specimens', on a lawn or elsewhere.

A problem that is felt by many people who live in houses very close together is that of forming some screen from neighbours' overlooking windows or to mask off some unsightly prospect. If speed be the prime object, the things to have are Leyland cypress (especially the exciting new golden Leyland 'Castlewellan') or *Thuja plicata*, which are dense, fast-growing conifers. Eucalyptus and birch also grow very fast.

Planting follows normal rules, as described in Chapter 5. Generally, the best time is about early November. But, if the weather is open and the soil not sodden, any time up till March will do. In cold areas and at the seaside evergreens should wait until the middle of April.

Pruning is dealt with in general terms in Chapter 7, and more specifically where necessary in the cultural notes on each plant. Remember especially not to prune trees, evergreens or berried shrubs, except as stated in Chapter 7, and to prune deciduous bushes according to their season of flowering. Note those that should not be pruned at all except for the removal of dead or feeble wood.

In this chapter I shall not give an alphabetical list of plants, but will deal with a choice of trees and shrubs in groups, as this is a greater help to the reader in making selections.

SMALL TREES

None of these necessarily demands any pruning except the removal of dead, weakly, or misplaced shoots.

First comes that wonderful group which comprises the ornamental fruit trees − flowering cherries, almonds, and so on, all belonging to the genus **Prunus.** They are among the loveliest things in the world, their mantles of massed pink or white blossom being nature's nearly most perfect work. All are of easy culture, given a sunny, uncrowded position, good drainage and a reasonably rich soil. Their glory is enhanced when they stand with their feet among daffodils. They are obtainable in the forms of standard, half-standard, or forking close to the ground in the manner of a bush, and it will be a long time before they take up all the space I quote for them. Do any pruning that may be essential about 1st June (no other time).

First the cherries, of which I have already mentioned the columnar 'Amanogawa'. The hybrid P. 'Spire' is rather broader. Of other forms, first in popular favour comes 'Kanzan', luxuriantly smothered (for ten days only) in deep cyclamen-pink on upward-shooting branches convenient for the side of a road or path. More tenderly beautiful (and my own favourite) is 'Shōgetsu', from whose more level branches dangle the prettiest blush-pink ballet skirts. Then there are the glorious, queenly-white 'Taihaku' and the unique, less-known 'Ukon', crowded with its almost untrue green-gold treasures. All will reach 25 ft. or more. For really small gardens 'Okame' is ideal.

Smaller still, and more of a bush, is the Fuji cherry (*Prunus incisa*), a perfect small-garden tree in flesh-pink that may reach 9 ft.

In the weeping forms, which make alluring, wide-spreading crinolines, there are several. One of the most popular, 8 ft. wide, is 'Kiku-shidare-zakura'. Just as pretty are the several forms of *P.* x *pendula*, especially 'Pendula Rosea', the rosebud cherry.

For winter there is that great pink-starred treasure *P.* x *subhirtella* 'Autumnalis Rosea'.

Of other small prunuses, the following are all very desirable. There is an awful mix-up of names, which I have tried to simplify without being too unorthodox.

Flowering apricot *P. mume*. Very early, sweet and breath-taking in February or early March.

Apricot-plum hybrid. *P.* x *blireana* is a splendour of pink flowers among bronze leaves.

Almond. What all the world has called *P. amygdalus* is now *P. dulcis*; the most rewarding of its varieties is the double-flowered 'Roseoplena'. Spray against the peach leaf-curl disease (*see* chapter on fruit).

Peach. The lovely *P. persica* 'Clara Meyer', double-flowered, is a great favourite. April. Spray against the peach leaf-curl disease.

Purple plum. Larger and of rather richer colouring than the apricot is *P. cerasifera* 'Pissardii'.

Next among the flowering ornamental fruits are the **crab apples** (*Malus*). The first ones to go for here are the glorious blush-pink *M. floribunda*, the small, picturesque *M. hupehensis*, the magnificent *M.* x *moerlandsii* 'Profusion' with copper-red leaves and rosy blossoms, and the unique *M. tschonoskii*, of erect, almost pyramidal carriage and dazzling autumn foliage. 'John Downie' and *M.* x *zumi* 'Golden Hornet' have fine fruits.

Magnolia. With its gleaming waxen goblets or bowls, the magnolia is certainly the queen of flowering trees and shrubs. Some become too big for small gardens and others produce no blossom until many years old. Their roots are brittle and grow close to the surface, so you must plant them with care, fairly firmly but not roughly; so also must you weed their immediate root area by hand only and allow no competition. Spring planting is safest.

The favourite species is *M.* x *soulangeana*, especially its wine-red variety 'Lennei'. Close competitors are the lilac hybrid *M.* x *loebneri* 'Leonard Messel', the long-flowering *M. sieboldii*, with nodding cups, and the similar

M. wilsonii. All these are small trees and flower when young. The first and fourth are safe in lime. The very small star *M. stellata* is seen in many gardens, but its petals are ragged; its pink form 'Rosea' is much prettier.

A far bigger tree is the noble evergreen *M. grandiflora.* If you have space for it, get the varieties 'Goliath' or 'Exmouth'.

Laburnums, Tennyson's 'dropping-walls of fire', need no introduction. For our purposes we need look no further than the handsome hybrid, *L.* × *watereri* 'Vossii'. A fountain of gold, it produces few seed-pods, so is far less poisonous than other laburnums.

Koelreuteria paniculata I have already mentioned. Mantled in golden blossom in late summer, it is normally a broad, bushy tree.

The **hawthorn** (*Crataegus*) is easy and excellent for small gardens. The most striking of all is *C. laevigata* 'Paul's Scarlet', a tree of vivid splendour. The French *C.* × *lavalleei* is a fine hybrid with white flowers in prodigal abundance, followed by orange haws. The picturesque cockspur thorn, *C. crus-galli*, is much bigger (35 ft.), flat-topped and fiercely thorned unless you get the smaller *C. crus-galli* var. *pyracanthifolia.*

For any garden that can accommodate a tree 30 ft. high and 20 ft. in breadth a first-rate tenant is ***Catalpa bignonioides.*** Extra-good in town gardens, it is fast-growing, has large, handsome leaves, and in July bears trusses of blossom rather like those of the horse chestnut. The golden-leaved *C. bignonioides* 'Aurea' is a little dwarfer and very handsome.

Two choice little trees are provided by the **dogwood** genus (*Cornus*). The first is *C. kousa*, which in May is thronged with brilliant ivory bracts beautifully chiselled, 20 ft; a beautiful creation and the best of the tree dogwoods fully reliable in Britain. The second is the Cornelian 'cherry', *C. mas*, whose naked boughs are encrusted with tiny, pale gold florets in the chill of February, followed by large, garnet, edible berries. But it is a dull thing after flowering and you must get the much more attractive and smaller *C. mas* 'Variegata', the leaves of which are edged with white.

The berried **rowan** or mountain ash (*Sorbus aucuparia*) is a familiar, extremely hardy favourite everywhere. For small gardens one of the very best is the elegant little Chinese species *S. vilmorinii*, with luxuriant, ferny foliage and rose-red berries that turn pink. Rarely more than 18 ft. high. Slightly larger but no less elegant is *S. hupehensis*, with blue-tinted leaves and glistening white fruits. Another sorbus is *S. aria*, which is the whitebeam and of which 'Lutescens' is a literally shining example.

The ***Gleditsia***, which is one of the trees that the Americans curiously call a 'locust', provides one outstanding specimen for us. In short terms, this is *G. triacanthos* 'Sunburst', a sovereign choice for a quarter-acre garden, highly ornamental, airy and loose-limbed. The small, pinnate leaves are sheathed in gold, slowly turning a light, olivine green, but always gold-tipped, the branches drooping at the tips. Prune, if necessary, at the end of summer, or it will bleed.

The exquisite Japanese **maples** (*Acer*), though not flowering trees, have a rare elegance of form and habit. There are purple-, green- and silvery-hued varieties. My favourite, with its delicately sculptured, almost fern-like foliage, answering to every breath of wind, is *A. palmatum* var. *dissectum*, especially the deep purple Dissectum Atropurpureum Group. Each tree has its own individuality; you generally see them only about 7 ft. high, but some are low, gnarled, spreading bushes. Give them a position protected from east winds.

We can have nothing to do here with the big maples, but a few of their smaller brethren fit handsomely into small gardens. I choose three only:

A. griseum, the paper-bark maple, in which the old bark peels back amusingly to reveal the brilliant cinnamon of the new bark beneath. An elegant tree with trifoliate leaves.

A. negundo 'Variegatum'. Very decorative leaves broadly margined cream. Extra hardy.

A. shirasawanum 'Aureum'. Beautiful golden leaves of rounded outline but toothed as though trimmed with pinking shears.

In many a garden today we see the golden-leaved *Robinia pseudoacacia* 'Frisia'. Too often it is grafted high by the nurseryman and looks like a bush stuck on the top of a pole. You should demand a 'feathered' or low-grafted tree and train it with a central stem, removing, if you wish, some of the lower branches flush with the stem in early autumn.

FLOWERING SHRUBS, MOSTLY DECIDUOUS

Reasons of space oblige me to be highly selective and to omit many attractive things that the reader will no doubt welcome later on. I can do little more than introduce the subject. Don't forget the shrub types of rose, dealt with in the chapter on that genus.

The **barberry** (*Berberis*) is a large, handsome, and generous family. They give us flower in spring and berry in autumn. There are both evergreen and deciduous species, several make splendid hedges, and they normally need no pruning. They need a good, loamy soil that does not dry out too quickly, and in severe districts some of the evergreens are not fully hardy. A particularly beautiful one, of recent introduction, is the pink-leaved *B. thunbergii* 'Rose Glow'. Otherwise, my first choice is for the evergreen and hardy *B.* x *stenophylla*, which is adorned with gracefully arching cascades of deep gold that make a glittering display in May. *B.* x *stenophylla* also has some fine semi-dwarf varieties ideal for small gardens, including the golden 'Gracilis', the ruddy *B. coccinna* and the pink 'Corallina Compacta' – all about 4 ft.

Almost as good as *B.* x *stenophylla* is Darwin's barberry (*B. darwinii*), a noble 8 ft. bush, with leaves like tiny hollies and ablaze with orange flowers in April. The hybrid *B.* x *lologensis*, a child of *darwinii*, is also a fine evergreen of modest size.

The deciduous barberries are generally hardier but of less interest, except for the big hybrid B. x ottawensis f. purpurea, which is magnificent. B. wilsoniae and B. thunbergii are also very good. There are some excellent dwarf and prostrate barberries, particularly B. thunbergii 'Atropurpurea Nana', 2 ft. high and a bit wider, very dense and very good indeed.

Akin to the barberry is the **Mahonia**. The best of the fully hardy sorts (excluding the hybrids) is M. japonica, which has long, luxuriant, primrose tassels, strongly scented, borne on the crests of very long, pinnate leaves, each leaflet like a holly. A great success in full shade, as elsewhere, and welcome for its winter flowers. To 6 ft. The dwarfer M. aquifolium is a good ground-cover beneath trees, where it will form a dense thicket.

Buddleja to most people means the large bush that throws out long plumes, usually in August. This is David's buddleja, B. davidii. The right treatment is to cut it fearlessly down every February, even to within a foot of the ground, when it will throw up finer wands; otherwise it deteriorates. A much better one is the smaller, grey-leaved, lavender-flowered B. 'Lochinch', of 5 ft.

Even more desirable is the Chinese B. alternifolia. It is adorned with slender arching wands thronged with soft mauve lilac-seeming florets in midsummer, and as a small standard tree (reaching about 12 ft.) it is a delightful decoration in any garden. It prefers a rather dry situation. Cut out a proportion of the old flowered wood immediately after blooming, otherwise it becomes very untidy especially when grown as a bush. If you want it as a standard, grow it from seed (very easy), and keep it to a single stem until it reaches 5–6 ft.

The buddleja with clusters of round orange flowers is B. globosa; cut it back lightly after flowering. Propagate all sorts by cuttings of firm young shoots in October; or seed sown under glass in early spring will flower in autumn.

The **Ceanothus** is one of our very finest large blue shrubs, profusely garnished with little tuffets in various hues. Some are evergreen, these being very good for dry soils, some flower before midsummer and others after. Few if any are completely hardy in the coldest counties, and they are therefore usually grown on a south wall, for which purpose they are beyond praise. Selection is awfully difficult. Of the early varieties the loveliest is C. cuneatus var. rigidus, dark blue dusted with gold, dwarfish, but it is for mild counties only; elsewhere use C. dentatus. Of the late sorts, 'Autumnal Blue' or 'Burkwoodii'. My own favourite is 'Delight'. For colder places, C. thyrsiflorus is the hardiest, but it is ultra-vigorous. All these are evergreen and delightful furniture for a wall. Prune the early-flowering sorts after flowering, the late ones in April.

Deciduous ceanothus are hardier and make lovely open-ground bushes in mild districts, the best being C. x delileanus 'Gloire de Versailles' in powder-blue, and the rich, deep C. x delileanus 'Topaze'. Cut these back very hard in April. Ceanothus species grow quite easily and quickly from seed.

Another lovely blue shrub, ideal for small gardens in all but the severer districts, labours under the burdensome name **Ceratostigma willmottianum**. Rarely exceeding 3 ft., it rejoices the late summer and autumn with trusses of vivid azure flowers like those of the plumbago, and it is an ideal shrub for mixing in the herbaceous border. Give it full sun and cut it down almost to the ground every April.

There is small doubt, however, about the hardiness of the **Cotoneaster**, a fine genus of berried shrubs, some evergreen and some deciduous. The most familiar is the herring-bone cotoneaster (*C. horizontalis*), so often seen growing fanwise against a wall. Of the big fellows *C. frigidus* 'Cornubia' is outstanding, a magnificent evergreen (or nearly so), weighed down by the enormous burden of its red fruits; it may reach 20 ft. and is too big for the smallest places. *C. salicifolius* 'Rothschildianus' and the similar *C. salicifolius* 'Exburyensis' are yellow-berried, evergreen, not quite so big but almost as good. *C. lacteus* is a rounded evergreen of handsome bearing, attaining 10 ft., a noble shrub. *C. franchetii*, semi-evergreen, is full of grace, distinguished by its grey-green leaves, orange fruits and slightly languorous bearing.

The cotoneaster also provides some useful dwarfs and creepy-crawlers, notably *C. dammeri*, *C. adpressus* and the hybrid, wide-spreading *C. salicifolius* 'Herbstfeuer' (Autumn Fire), all excellent for ground-cover. Something a bit different is 'Hybridus Pendulus', which is very decorative when grafted on a 6 ft. stem to form a pretty little weeping tree.

Cotoneasters make splendid hedges. The one usually recommended is the erect, semi-deciduous *C. simonsii*, but the variable evergreen hybrid *C.* x *watereri* is probably better.

Nothing is more gay, colourful, and easy to cultivate than the **brooms**, a name which embraces three genera – *Cytisus, Genista* and *Spartium*. They will flourish not only in normal conditions, but also in dry, parched and poor soils. The dwarf or prostrate ones are first-rate on the upper slopes of a rock garden. In most gardens, unhappily, brooms are allowed to get top-heavy, lop-sided, and bare at the base, through lack of pruning. The *vital* thing is to cut back the flowered branch to within an inch or two of its point of origin immediately flowering is over. See sketch b, page 65.

Named varieties of *Cytisus*, such as 'Lena' and 'Burkwoodii', are numerous and colourful, but short-lived. One of the nicest is the hybrid *C.* x *praecox*, a 4 ft. cascade of pale sulphur in April, of which there are several clones in other shades. Of totally different character, with trifoliate, silken leaves is the big, shrubby July-flowering *C. battandieri*, the scented pineapple broom, 10 ft; this does produce a new basal shoot. Best on a warm wall.

The loveliest of all brooms, however, is the golden May-flowering *Genista lydia*, especially when tumbling over a terrace, but the grey-green *G. cinerea*, of 10 ft., is also beautiful after midsummer. All brooms resent root disturbance. They seed very easily, but sowing should be in pots.

In contrast to the broom, the fragrant and delectable **Daphne** should never be pruned at all. Some members of this lovely genus are difficult, but no garden should be without the favourite old *D. mezereum*, so easy of culture and so inspiring in the grim days of February with her wreathed wands of perfumed mauve. In a good loamy soil she grows up to 4 ft. Let some seed ripen and fall – they are easy and good. Of the other evergreen species, the most wooable are *D. tangutica* and *D. retusa*, with lustrous foliage and scented, rosy-purple flowers, growing slowly to 3 ft. *D. cneorum* 'Eximia' is enchanting in rocks but fickle. *D. odora* 'Aureomarginata' is gorgeous. All daphnes need sun, a rich, humusy soil, limy or acid, and sharp drainage.

Forsythia must be one of the first choices in every garden. Its golden bells, strung along flexible wands, are one of the glories of the early spring, and it will succeed in shade almost as well as in sun, and in town as well as country. The one that takes the cake is *F.* x *intermedia* 'Lynwood Variety', with large flowers all along the branch, but the older *F.* x *intermedia* 'Spectabilis' is also very good. The drooping species, *F. suspensa*, is excellent for garnishing a north wall in deep shade. Prune forsythias by cutting the spent flowering branches hard to a strong young shoot at their bases, treating one-third or a half of the bush like this each year. Multiply by cuttings of well-ripened young growth in autumn outdoors.

Only a few **fuchsias** are hardy, but in those mild parts of the southwest and west and in Ireland they are among the chief joys of the countryside in summer. The most beautiful are those with coloured foliage – *F. magellanica* var. *gracilis* 'Variegata' and *F. m.* 'Versicolor', both pretty hardy. Of the named varieties, 'Madame Cornélissen', 'Chillerton Beauty' and 'Dollar Princess' are the most reliably hardy. The big 'Riccartonii' is also hardy and is the one used for hedging in the West Country. Cut all fuchsias, except 'Riccartonii', down to the ground in April. The more tender ones bought from a nursery must not be planted before June, but are then very easily increased by July cuttings and overwintered in a greenhouse.

Of the relatively few shrubs that bloom in late summer, the Syrian **Hibiscus syriacus** is one of the best. Totally different from the flamboyant creatures of high-temperature romance, they have blooms very like those of the hollyhock, borne on stiff, erect stems reaching to 9 ft. Often dormant and leafless in the first year, they will reward patience. The outstanding variety is 'Oiseau Bleu' (Blue Bird), a very fine plant. Give them full sun, and no pruning.

Hydrangeas must be differentiated, for our simple purposes, into three main groups. One is the breed with sumptuous, semi-spherical trusses of bloom in August and September, so widely grown in pots and embellishing hotel lounges. These are one of the branches of *H. macrophylla* and are usually known as the Hortensias or mopheads. Some of the best of them are 'Maréchal Foch', 'Ami Pasquier', 'Altona', 'Hamburg', 'Générale Vicomtesse de Vibraye' (usually shortened to 'Vibraye'), and the white 'Madame Emile Mouillère'.

Another group, less opulent, more refined, are often called Lacecaps, having a circlet of brilliant, sterile florets besieging a bevy of more demure fertile ones. 'Mariesii Perfecta' (syn. 'Blue Wave'), and the very pretty 'Mariesii Lilacina' are first choices and 'Lanarth White' is a charming dwarf. *H. villosa* is valuable for doing well on chalk.

The blue tints so often admired in all these hydrangeas may sometimes occur naturally or may be obtained by using a blueing compound. However, you can't blue them on a soil containing much lime, nor, apparently, in an acid soil if it is of peat. What seems best is a lime-free turf loam. Even then not all varieties will succeed; no whites will. But if you have the right soil all the other varieties I have mentioned should blue magnificently, and if you haven't, they will still be very fine indeed in their reds and deep pinks.

Our third group of hydrangeas comprises the hardier forms, completely, different in character. The most opulent is *H. paniculata* 'Grandiflora', a showman's piece with enormous conical trusses of cream turning to pale pink (cut back to about five buds on each branch in March). There is also the climbing hydrangea, noted elsewhere.

The mopheads and the Lacecaps need copious draughts of water, with mulchings of leaves. They enjoy a west aspect and a little noonday shade, and are first-rate on north walls also. They are best unpruned, except for getting rid of dead or spindly shoots. For increase, cuttings (of side-shoots or tips) root with ease. For blueing, the amateur is best advised to use a proprietary blueing powder. The popular idea that old iron does the trick is fallacious; it may be good for the health of a sickly plant, but does not turn the flowers blue. What does this is sulphate of aluminium.

The **Hypericum** is known to most people as providing the useful evergreen dwarf rose of sharon or St John's wort (*H. calycinum*) with its golden salvers and gold boss of stamens, so valuable for flourishing under trees. It does even better, however, in the sun, and is a grand little plant for carpeting an awkward bank. Trim it back *hard* with shears early March. The excellent larger bush, *H.* 'Hidcote', produces the same golden flowers on rounded bushes some 5 ft. high in great abundance from July onwards; of the easiest culture and very showy. An Everyman's bush. Cut the old flowered branches thigh-high in March. A real little charmer has Joseph's coat leaves in pale-green, pink and cream. This is *H.* x *moserianum* 'Tricolor'. Cut it hard back in March.

Lilac is one of everybody's flowers. Its right botanical name is *Syringa,* and the white, perfumed bush often so miscalled is not a syringa at all. Given a good, loamy soil, acid or limy, and an open position in the sun, lilac is of the easiest culture, but too often it is allowed to grow into a dowdy, straggly bush with naked legs. Newly planted stock should be cut back boldly to make them bushy, for new growth comes from the tips of the shoots only. Cut out all weak and straggly growth, and always remove dead seed-pods as soon as flowering is over. Look out for suckers and wrench them out.

A few of the finest lilacs are: 'Katherine Havemeyer', lavender-mauve; 'Masséna', 'Andenken an Ludwig Späth' (syn. 'Souvenir de Louis Spaeth') and 'Charles Joly', all variations on the theme of purple; and 'Madame Lemoine', double white. Young hybrid plants are not always true to colour at first. A lovely and unusual little species for small spaces is the white Persian lilac, Syringa x persica 'Alba'. The Preston hybrids, such as S. x josiflexa 'Bellicent' and S. x prestoniae 'Elinor', are splendid but rather large. See Chapter 12 for the dwarf lilac.

Potentillas are most useful little shrubs anywhere in the garden, decorated continuously all summer with flowers like those of the strawberry, usually in gold. They need full sun. Most are cultivars of P. fruticosa. All are good, but you won't do better than the 3 ft., large-flowered 'Elizabeth', or, for a shortie, the silvery-leaved 'Beesii'. In 'Sunset' and 'Tangerine' there is a red tint. 'Red Ace' is usually a good deep orange. All make good low hedges. No pruning. Easy from cuttings. See Index for other potentillas.

Another easy one, the **Philadelphus**, so often erroneously called syringa, is one of our best summer bushes, clothed in a glittering white mantle of spicy fragrance, but not very glamorous after flowering. If you want to call it by a fancy name call it mock-orange, but don't call it syringa, or the nurseryman will send you a lilac. Given sun, philadelphus succeeds in almost any soil. Of the larger ones, 'Virginal', 'Beauclerk' and 'Belle Etoile' are prime choices. 'Sybille' is a pretty 5-footer. 'Manteau d'Hermine' and S. microphyllus are delightful dwarfs. Cut flowered shoots hard back to strong new buds after flowering.

There are few greater glories of the winter and early spring than the Japanese flowering **quince**, oddly known in general speech as 'japonica', regardless of species. The quinces make wonderful bushes aflame with colour, usually in red, but also in pink and in white. Their fruits make good quince jelly.

There is a maddening confusion of names among the Japanese quinces, which, after several vicissitudes, are now called Chaenomeles. The larger ones, often grown on walls, are variations of either C. speciosa or their hybrid C. x superba. Some good ones are 'Knap Hill Scarlet' (slow at first), 'Moerloosei', 'Falconnet Charlet' and C. x superba 'Pink Lady'. These may go to 10 ft. or so, but the blood-red C. speciosa 'Simonii', one of the most brilliant shrubs in the garden, is a 2-footer of superlative quality. C. x superba 'Rowallane', bright red, goes to 3½ ft., spreading. Another brilliant dwarf, in orange-scarlet, is C. japonica 'Sargentii', which grows to about 3 ft., but spreads very widely by suckering branches to about 10 ft. if allowed; first class.

Wall-trained quinces, for maximum flower, should be induced to form spurs, as in cordon apples, by pruning the laterals in both summer and winter.

A very variable genus is the **Spiraea**, most of which are robed in shining white. The tiny stars of S. thunbergii enliven March, then comes

'Arguta', the bridal wreath, aptly festooned, and in May the big S. x *vanhouttei* delights us. For damp soils, S. x *pseudosalicifolia* 'Triumphans' is most useful with bold, upright plumes of deep rose in July. Quite different is S. *japonica* 'Goldflame', a happy dwarf clad in glowing orange and lemon leaves, but dull flowers in July, a great improvement on S. *japonica* 'Anthony Waterer'. Cut the old flowered branches back *hard* to new young growth, summer varieties in March, early varieties immediately after flowering.

Another large and versatile genus that includes both summer- and winter-flowering varieties, evergreens and deciduous, is the **Viburnum**. The gem of them all in my opinion is one which has the unique and striking habit of branching horizontally in tiers, and these tiers are smothered as with heavy snow in May. It is *V. plicatum* f. *tomentosum* 'Mariesii', and it is a wonderful picture isolated as a specimen plant, or first-class for hiding an untidy fence. 9 ft. × 12 ft. *V. plicatum* f. *tomentosum* 'Lanarth' is similar but of stronger growth.

Characteristic of other viburnums is their habit of throwing out handfuls of China-white bloom like snowballs, often sweetly scented and pink-tinted. *V.* x *bodnantense*, replacing the old *V. farreri*, embalms the air in mid-winter and in spring come the 9 ft. *V. burkwoodii* and the 5 ft. *V.* x *juddii* (a much finer shrub ultimately than *V. carlesii*). All these are fragrant. The popular laurustinus (*V. tinus*) also blooms in winter, is densely ever-green, good in towns, and a fine plant much misused; it has an improved cultivar in the pink-tinted 'Eve Price'.

In summer come the several varieties of the guelder rose, *V. opulus*, which usually have white lacecaps followed by glistening white berries. The finest florally is the snowball *V. opulus* 'Sterile', but it bears no fruits.

The **Weigela** has some species and cultivars that are excellent and easy small-garden bushes with their pink or red trumpets in June. Tidy, shapely, easy to grow, generally reaching about 7 ft., they are greatly improved if the spent flowering branches or laterals are cut back neatly to their point of origin. Do not touch the young shoots. Best of these is *W.* 'Florida Variegata', with cream-edged leaves and pink flowers. Next come the deep rose *W. styriaca* and the bright red hybrid 'Bristol Ruby', both about 7 ft. and both first-class plants for all gardens.

WINTER-FLOWERING SHRUBS

Among shrubs and small trees there is quite an array that braves the frosts and some of these I have already mentioned in the previous sections – the winter-flowering cherry and other sorts of prunus, *Daphne mezereum*, the Cornelian cherry (*Cornus mas*), the mahonias, and some of the viburnums. Others, having borne flower in the spring or summer, will gladden the winter with bright berries, such as holly, barberry, pyracantha, and cotoneaster. Some of the best – jasmine and honeysuckles – are climbers or wall plants, and will be dealt with in that chapter.

In addition, there is one shrub that stands out as a winter decoration. It is the **witch hazel**, a thing of piquant and captivating charm. You must ask for *Hamamelis mollis*, which is the best. From Christmas till well into February it bears on its naked branches ingenious little twisted frills of spun gold – a merry bush that should be the haunt of elves. But you must allow for it an ultimate 12 ft. or more of breadth and as much height. Its sprays are marvellous in a vase. It needs, however, an acid soil.

Almost as attractive is wintersweet, the fragrant *Chimonanthus fragrans*, but it takes some years to do itself justice, and is otherwise rather dowdy.

In addition wonderful winter displays are provided by some of the ericas, and these are dealt with in Chapter 18.

SHRUBS FOR LIME-FREE SOILS

Most of the trees and shrubs mentioned in the previous sections of this chapter will succeed perfectly well on acid soils, but there are several important shrubs that will prosper in no other. Probably the best soil for most of these is a lime-free loam; failing that, a mixture of loam with ample peat or leafmould. After planting, and every autumn, they should be mulched with oak or beech leaves.

With a few exceptions, all these plants prefer, but do not always insist upon, some degree of shade. The ideal is the 'high' shade, or dappled shade, of thin woodland. Plant firmly, using plenty of peat. No pruning, except careful removal of spent flowers.

First and above all, the **rhododendron**. Some will succeed in full sun, chiefly those one calls the 'hardy hybrids'. Be careful to plant very shallow. The only pruning normally necessary is to snap off spent flowers and seed-pods after blooming; this is important and should be done carefully to avoid damaging the new growth that is starting immediately below the truss of pods.

There are varieties in almost every colour except true blue, and in every size from prostrate rock-garden pygmies to great bushes 15 ft. high and more. Many of the glorious hybrids with 'fancy' cultivar names are expensive and too big for small places, and azaleas may take their places. As there are over 2500 rhododendrons listed, it is pretty tricky to give selec-

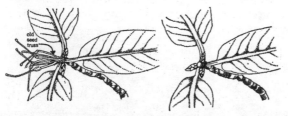

Dead-heading a rhododendron. Left, snap off the truss of seed-pods at the arrow immediately above the tiny new buds. Right, the seed-truss removed, showing three new buds.

tions, and the best plan is to consult a good nurseryman, specifying colours and heights preferred. Three very good starters for small gardens are Blue Tit Group, Blue Diamond Group, and the red 'Elizabeth'. *R. impeditum* and 'Carmen' are splendid dwarfs. For medium height, three of the best are Bow Bells Group, 'Doncaster', and 'Britannia'. For those who do want suggestions for the best larger varieties, the following is a primary guide. 'Pink Pearl' and its offspring (e.g., 'Professor Hugo de Vries' and 'Souvenir de Doctor S. Endtz', 'Scandinavia', 'Purple Splendour', 'Susan', 'David', *R. orbiculare*, 'May Day', 'Betty Wormald' 'Fabia', 'Sappho', 'Goldsworth Orange', 'Bagshot Ruby', and the widely grown 'Cynthia'. *See also under Rock Gardens.*

Azaleas are a sort of rhododendron, equally showy, generally smaller, often perfumed, often more tolerant of dry conditions. They fall into two groups – evergreen and deciduous. The evergreens are dwarfs, the deciduous much taller and broader. The dwarfs are dominated by the Kurume azaleas, of which the first choices are: 'Hinomayo' (sumptuous pink), 'Hinode-giri' (crimson), 'Beni-giri' (scarlet), 'Esmeralda' (soft pink) and the dazzling 'Hatsugiri'. Other splendid dwarfs are 'Vuyk's Rosyred' and 'Vuyk's Scarlet'. 'Palestrina' is a superlative white, somewhat larger.

The deciduous azaleas grow in a wide range of superb colours. The ones to go for are the brilliant race known as the Knap Hill hybrids and the wonderful Exbury azaleas, hardy, vigorous and splendid, as in the exquisite 'Silver Slipper' and 'Cecile.' As these finish the Ghent hybrids, or 'honeysuckle azaleas' come on. They have small, tubular flowers, often sweetly scented, have a graceful habit, are amazingly flowerful and extra hardy. The inexpensive wilding *Azalea pontica* (*Rhododendron luteum*) is one of the best of the lot and makes a fine hedge. The azaleas you buy in a pot in the winter are not hardy and can be grown outdoors only in favoured places.

Closely similar to the rhodo is the **Kalmia** but it has bunches of dainty pink cups instead of the rhodo's big throats. The usual one is *K. latifolia*. Very flowerful and attractive. Plant in sun, *not* shade as often advised.

Camellias, I am glad to say, are growing rapidly in popularity, for they are much hardier than was formerly supposed and their serene blossoms, enamelling their dense masses of dark-green, polished foliage, are one of the greatest joys of early spring, and sometimes of winter, too. Most are happy in full sun or in partial shade, will do well in neutral as in acid soils, provided it is a rich one. Mulch them heartily with oak or beech leaves every autumn and, to promote the development of flower-buds, treat them to 1 oz. per square yard of sulphate of potash in earliest September. Bud-drops may be caused by sudden physiological changes, so make sure at least that they have *regular* watering, by heaven or by hose, especially in late summer, but that their toes are not waterlogged. In the colder counties they had better not have an easterly exposure, where a sudden thaw after a sharp frost may burst their buds.

The two dominant species are *C. japonica* and the splendid hybrid *C.* x *williamsii*, of which there are now numerous varieties. From among these two breeds I suggest that you begin with *C.* x *williamsii* 'Donation' (very first choice), *C. japonica* 'Adolphe Audusson', 'Elegans', 'Lady Vansittart', 'Gloire de Nantes', the single white 'Alba Simplex' and the *C. reticulata* hybrid, 'Leonard Messel'. Western counties may grow the big *C. reticulata* cultivars, of which 'Captain Rawes' is the doyen.

One of the great glories of the lime-free garden is the **Pieris**, of which there are several species and cultivars, grown mainly for their beautiful foliage but, in favoured places, adorned also by enchanting sprays of flowers like lilies-of-the-valley. Grandest of all are those that throw cockades of brilliant red leaves in spring, as in the hybrid 'Forest Flame' and in *P. formosa* var. *forrestii* 'Wakehurst'. They make big shrubs of 12 ft. high and wide after several years. Of great beauty, but slower and smaller is *P. japonica* 'Variegata', whose young foliage is pink, turning to a soft green edged with cream. More conspicuous for floral effect is *P. japonica* Taiwanensis Group, an 8 ft. mound of dark green showered with erect trusses of lilies-of-the-valley in April; happy in full sun.

Pernettyas (*Gaultheria mucronata*) are valuable for making dense, evergreen thickets, 4 ft. high, smothered with a fuzz of cream flowers in spring, followed by large, gleaming berries, like marbles, in divers colours. Being nearly unisexual, you should have one male to every four or five females. 'Bell's Seedling', however, is bisexual, with dark-red marbles.

Witch hazel. *See* Winter-flowering shrubs.

EVERGREENS

Of whatever size, every garden should contain a proportion of evergreens, both as a solace to the eye in the skeletal bleakness of winter and because the handsome dense foliage that many of them carry provides a backdrop and a foil for the coloured drama of summer. Except lavender and rosemary, normally none needs any pruning.

Evergreen forms of some genera have been named in earlier sections of this chapter, such as those of the barberry, hypericum, ceanothus, daphne, and viburnum, and nearly all those in the section on lime-free soils are also evergreen; so, of course, are conifers. Others again, such as pyracantha, are in the small garden more conveniently grown on walls or as hedges, and are therefore dealt with elsewhere.

The most handsome in this section, when properly grown, is the **holly** (*Ilex aquifolium*). Besides its use as a hedge, it can be grown as a tree or a bush, and in small gardens the bush form is best, when it should be clothed to the ground. Most people like the variegated forms, with golden or silver edgings. The important thing about holly is to ensure that the chosen variety is bisexual or that males and females are associated; thus 'Golden King' (female!) is pollinated by 'Silver Queen' (male!). So (and not otherwise) will you have berries.

One variety that combines many virtues is 'J.C. van Tol', bisexual, almost thornless, the leaves olive green; to boot, it has a gilt-edged variant, 'Golden van Tol'. A few hollies have yellow berries instead of red.

Challenging it closely is the glittering *Elaeagnus pungens* 'Maculata'. This handsome shrub is densely clothed with leaves heavily splashed with daffodil, its golden beauty most appreciated in winter. It will reach 12 ft. high and wide, prospers in sun or shade, in chalk or loam. What more could one ask? Flowers? No. If any dark-green shoots appear and do not turn yellow, cut them out at the point of origin.

The *Escallonia* is another handsome fellow, with small, glossy leaves, and sprays of pink or red bells. Not entirely hardy everywhere, but particularly valuable at the seaside, the gloss of its leaves resisting spray and wind. Also fine inland where the climate is not severe. Their best employment is as informal hedges, but they do grow very wide. Plenty of good varieties: e.g., for small gardens the pink 'Donard'; for seaside hedges, *E. rubra* var. *macrantha* or *E. rubra* 'Crimson Spire'.

Evergreen *trees* for the small garden are rare, and therefore there is particular value in the handsome *Arbutus*. Sometimes called the strawberry tree, it carries, at one and the same time in autumn and early winter, clusters of pretty white or pink flowers like lily-of-the-valley and of small red fruits vaguely resembling the strawberry. Prefers a peaty soil, but does well almost anywhere. Forks low down like a shrub and slowly makes about 20 ft. × 15 ft. The most reliable is *A. unedo*.

In mild districts a small shrub of great value in the little garden is the *Cistus* or rock rose. The cistus makes a wonderful show in June with colourful blossoms that have the texture of tissue paper, but the leaden foliage is not attractive in winter. It thrives on dry, poor soils, does not fear drought and wants no feeding or pruning, but must have all the sun it can get. Outstanding in popular favour (but not mine) is the little 3 ft. *C.* × *argenteus* 'Silver Pink'. The best all-rounder is *C.* × *purpureus*, 4 ft. with rose-pink petals splashed dark red at the base. The beautiful and fairly hard *C.* × *cyprius* grows to 6 ft., with white flowers, splashed crimson, its young shoots coated with a fragrant gum.

Hebe is the name that should now be used for the shrubby plants formerly included in the genus *Veronica* (now reserved for the herbaceous species). Hebes are small, evergreen shrubs, most of them hardy only for the seaside and other mild districts. I suggest 'Midsummer Beauty' and 'Autumn Glory', shrubs about 3 ft. high with lavender or violet spikes. No pruning. *H. pinguifolia* 'Pagei' is a low, pearly-leaved shrublet, useful for ground-cover.

Very different from all these are the **lavender** and the **rosemary,** both too well known to need description. What is not so well known is that these are made or marred by their pruning. The vital thing is to trim them over immediately after flowering. Rosemaries are difficult to keep tidy when they age.

Of lavenders, easily the most popular sort is *Lavandula angustifolia* 'Hidcote', a dwarf of 15 in. The larger *L. angustifolia* 'Twickel Purple' has long spikes spraying out fanwise for 2 ft. or so. Propagate by firm cuttings in late September.

The usual rosemary is *Rosmarinus officinalis*, of which most people choose the one known as 'Miss Jessopp's Upright'.

DWARF AND CARPETING SHRUBS

For convenience of garden arrangement and planning I have put these separately. They are suitable not only for the front of the shrub garden, but also for the herbaceous border and many for the rock garden.

Probably the most useful of all is the **Helianthemum**, the sun rose. The helianthemum is far hardier than the cistus, is only a few inches high, but spreads very broadly and rapidly, and is thronged for several weeks from late May onwards with a crowd of delicate flowers the size of a florin in red, pink, yellow, or white. Very easy, but it must have full sun and a dry soil, and will indeed flourish on parched, ill-nourished stony soil. After flowering, trim it hard back with shears to keep it compact and flowerful. You may buy named varieties, but they come very easily from seed, and a packet will give you dozens, though the colours will not be predictable. Use them anywhere, including the rockery and the dry wall. Propagation by cuttings in July is as easy as possible; take maturing young growth with or without a heel.

The cotton lavender, **Santolina,** is another easy and good dwarf shrub, whose silver foliage in the front of the herbaceous border is of special value as a foil to the prevailing colours. Evergreen, 18 in., with cheap little golden flowers that should be beheaded. Needs sun, but does well on poor soils. The most popular one was known for long as *S. incana*, but now you ought to use the horrible mouthful *S. chamaecyparissus*; there is a good green version called *S. rosmarinifolia* subsp. *rosmarinifolia*. For good results trim back the previous season's growth pretty hard in March. Both these make excellent little dwarf hedges planted 9 in. or so apart, but an even dwarfer effect is got with the Lilliputian *S. chamaecyparissus* var. *nana*, which makes a charming 9 in. edging, highly 'frosted'.

Brachyglottis (Dunedin Group) 'Sunshine' is another silver-grey but much bigger shrub and one of the very best, low-growing but spreading widely, with brassy daisies. Cut down the flower stem early and cut back the whole plant each April to keep it compact and it becomes one of the dozen best shrubs. Very easy from summer cuttings. *Senecio cineraria* is the right name for the dwarf silver-plated shrub that was once called *Cineraria maritima*.

Then there are 'carpeting' plants for covering rough places or growing under trees. The **rose of Sharon** is one of the most useful of these, and in shady, lime-free soils the partridge berry, *Gaultheria procumbens*, is dense and good-looking.

The **periwinkle** (*Vinca*) is a useful trailing plant, with pretty blue flowers, for the like purpose. *V. minor* is better than *V. major* and *V. minor* 'La Grave' is better still.

More beautiful than any of these, however, are the dwarf forms of larger shrubs, such as rhododendrons, daphne, broom, barberry, and the dwarf conifers. Heathers (Chapter 18) also are among the most beautiful of dwarf shrubs, and I have mentioned the silver euryops in Chapter 12.

SECOND ELEVEN

Reasons of space and a desire not to confuse the beginner with an embarrassment of choice have induced me to restrict the above selections. Here, however, are a few very brief notes on some others:

Caryopteris x *clandonensis*. A pretty powder-blue shrub for the same uses and season as ceratostigma.

Choisya ternata. An easy evergreen with fragrant 'orange blossoms' for the milder counties; 6 ft.

Deutzia. The usual *D. scabra* is a tall shrub densely covered with white blossom at high summer, too apt to become leggy and scrawny. The dwarfer hybrids *D.* x *rosea* 'Carminea' and *D.* x *elegantissima*, however, are charming small bushes, the first in soft pink to 4 ft., the other rose-purple to 5 ft. Cut back the spent shoots hard after flowering.

Flowering currant (*Ribes sanguineum*). Easy in any conditions, including shade and town gardens. The best is the blood-red 'King Edward VII'. March–April.

Halimium. Low, spreading, grey-green shrubs, almost hardy, enamelled with buttercup-form flowers. The usual one is *H. lasianthum*, maroon-eyed. Very nice. 2 ft. x 4 ft.

Indigofera heterantha. A pretty bush, with rose-purple pea-blooms, blooming all summer. Cut to the ground each April. 4 ft.

Kerria. Easy and very common shrub. Sparse foliage, yellow blooms. Most people prefer the double variety. Sun or shade. Cut old flowered stems hard back to new shoots in June.

Rhus. This includes the familiar stag's horn sumac (*R. typhina*), a bold-foliage shrub with fiery autumn hues; and the smoke plant with dense feathery masses, purple or tawny, and brilliant autumn hues, now called *Cotinus coggygria*. Particularly good varieties are *C. c.* Rubrifolius Group and 'Notcutt's Variety'.

Kolkwitzia amabilis. A beautiful, arching shrub clustered with small pink bells in June. 7 ft.

CONIFERS

A sprinkling of conifers is important in garden design, and several are suitable in small places, but they rarely succeed in towns. The statuesque columnar shapes are particularly good, and those with golden, silver-blue, or other tints diversify the scene very elegantly. There are also many dwarf and pygmy conifers which lend character to the rock garden, or add a finishing touch of formality to terraces or steps. Forgive the unavoidable long names.

Lawson cypress (*Chamaecyparis lawsoniana*, with the Ch pronounced as K) provides some of our best garden cultivars, and of them I choose first 'Columnaris'. Slim, erect, tall, tapering, with blue foliage, it is the ideal small 'specimen' tree. Of similar habit, but much shorter, are 'Fletcheri' and 'Ellwoodii', both ideal for small places. Lawson cypress also gives us several slim, gold-tinted trees, such as 'Lutea', 'Stewartii' and 'Lanei', all ultimately tall, but using little ground space.

Other selected conifers are:

Leyland cypress (× *Cupressocyparis leylandii*). A galloper at 3 ft. per year. Fine for screens and hedges. There is an exciting new golden variety called 'Castlewellan'.

Chamaecyparis obtusa **'Crippsii'**. A golden splendour, with loosely spraying branches, not stiff or compressed.

Chamaecyparis pisifera **'Plumosa'**. A handsome, broadly conical tree, 30 ft. × 12 ft., with fine feathery foliage; again there is a slower, golden variety, 'Plumosa Aurea'.

Cupressus arizonica **'Conica'**. Like the slim Italian cypresses, soaring to 40 ft. or more.

Juniperus communis **'Hibernica'**, the slender Irish juniper. Makes a dense pillar 10 ft. high by only 2 ft. When aged needs to be tied round.

Taxus is the yew, and the most suitable form for small places are the columnar Irish yew, *T. baccata* 'Fastigiata', and its golden variant, Fastigiata Aurea Group. Both grow in time to 16 ft. or more.

Thuja. A bright-green feathery spire, very fast indeed. Used mostly for making quick screens. The best for this is the glossy green *T. plicata*. 'Zebrina' has a golden tint, but is slower.

Among the many really dwarf conifers for the rock garden it is difficult to make recommendations. It is essential really to visit the nursery and pick those of a shape and habit you like best in consultation with the nurseryman. There are little columnar ones, and globular sorts and others prostrate and spreading. Of the erect, conical sorts, I offer:

Chamaecyparis lawsoniana **'Minima Aurea'**. Greeny-gold. Fine.

C. pisifera **'Plumosa Aurea Nana Compacta'**. Feathery soft yellow.

C. p. **'Boulevard'**. Steely-blue. Part shade.
Thuja occidentalis **'Rheingold.'** Gingery-gold.
Juniperus communis **'Compressa'**. Tiny Noah's Ark tree.
The gold ones want full sun. 'Boulevard' may reach 10 ft. in time.

The very opposite effect is obtained with *Juniperus communis* 'Hornibrookii'. This grows only 12 in. high, but will spread 5 ft. over the ground and mould itself to its shape. So also will the larger Sabine juniper, *J. sabina* 'Tamariscifolia'; dense and shapely, it will measure about 3 ft. × 8 ft. Both of those, apart from their natural grace, can also be employed as utility plants to cover an awkward spot.

Another good form for contrast is the 'obtuse' or rounded form, as in the delightful *C. obtusa* **'Nana'**, of which there are several variations. The miniature Scotch fir, *Pinus sylvestris* **'Watereri'** is another gem for rocks. And, besides the cypress and the juniper, there are some excellent toy spruces, yews, and thujas.

When planting conifers, water the soil and foliage copiously. In dry spells wet foliage and roots daily until established.

16

CLIMBING AND WALL PLANTS

To grow a creeper over a house is something of an insult to an architect. Unfortunately not many of our houses have been designed by architects, and even so it is a regrettable fact that too many are improved by being hidden. How many of our dwellings owe their only claim to grace or mellowness to the soft shroud of the Virginia creeper!

But even if our house has beauty enough to stand before the world naked and unashamed, there is generally something else that is better hidden – an old fence, an out-house, a tree-stump. And if still there is nothing of the sort, then we should deliberately create an excuse – pergola, arch, or trellis – for giving admittance to some of the loveliest plants in the catalogue.

The general word 'climber' is ambiguous, and we can divide the field roughly into three. There are the clingers, such as ivy, Virginia creeper and the climbing hydrangea, which cling to their host as it were with claws; these need merely to be planted at the foot of a wall, and away they go by themselves. Then there are the twiners and ramblers, such as clematis and honeysuckle, which need some visible means of support in the shape of a trellis, arch, or a host-shrub. Finally there is a wide range of bushes which are adaptable to being planted against a wall, and will, either naturally or by inducement, grow up and along the wall or fence or whatnot; this last class includes some of our very finest wall plants, such as the rose, ceanothus, flowering quince, and pyracantha. Not counted among these is a yet further range of plants which, by reason of some tenderness in their constitution, benefit from the protection which a wall provides against wind and frost.

Thus, in choosing 'climbers' for particular places and tasks, we have to consider both habit and vigour. The clingers require a large wall-face of brick, stone or concrete not too much broken up by windows. The twiners are generally of lesser vigour, and, being provided with a suitable host, are appropriately draped over doorways or arches or trellis screens. A third, and most important, factor is aspect. While almost anything will grow on a south-facing wall or fence, those that will grow well on a north wall are limited, and are of particular value, for a north wall has too often a colourless and gloomy visage. The following choice of the better flowering and berried climbers and wall plants for various aspects may be of help.

South wall: almost anything except plants that hate full sun, e.g. camellias, clematis unless the roots are shaded, and honeysuckle unless the ground is damp. The best wall for campsis, passion flower, and ceanothus.

West wall: an ideal wall, good especially for clematis, honeysuckle and camellia.

North wall: provided the wall is not overhung by trees, the following will all do well, though usually better still on other walls: morello cherry, pyracantha, cotoneaster, climbing hydrangea, clematis, winter jasmine, forsythia, camellia, and some roses.

East wall: as for the north wall, except camellias and clematis.

Some wall plants will prosper in any aspect, however, such as the flowering: quince, celastrus, pyracantha, winter jasmine, and forsythia. Before going on to consider the merits and use of individual plants, there are one or two special points I would like to make.

The footings of a brick, stone, or concrete wall are usually very dry and littered with builders' rubble; therefore set your plant in the ground a good 12 in. away. Prepare the site with the same cultural care as you would for an open-ground bush.

Wooden-pale fencings are seldom objects of beauty, but they make excellent stations for the third class of plant I have mentioned. Make full use of fences, and plant them with pyracantha, quince, jasmine, fruit of various kinds, and so on. Their stature can be raised, if desired, by topping the fence with trellis-work.

Whatever artificial host you provide for the twiners, make sure that it is strong, permanent, sufficient in extent, and sightly; a honeysuckle or clematis that is flopping all over the place in a tangled mass, held up to a nail by a piece of string, is not a thing of beauty. If against a wall, such support can be provided either by a strong wooden trellis, or by wires held away from the wall by galvanised 'wall-eyes' driven into the wall or by one of the new square-mesh wires, which are excellent and easy to fix.

Before deciding on any climbers or creepers, consider the use of fruit trees as discussed in Chapter 20. They are both economical of space and decorative – on a south wall the pear or nectarine, on a north one the morello cherry and the fan-trained redcurrant, on fences the berried fruits on canes or as cordons. For arches and arbours there are the hardy vines, which have every delight.

Now for the clinging plants, of which there are only a few. The **ivy** (*Hedera*) offers us some handsome sorts, particularly those with variegated leaves, and they will thrive in shade. For an awkward corner under the deep shade of trees, for covering old tree-stumps, or for carpeting rough ground, ivy is excellent. The most impressive is the large-leaved, grey-and-white Canary ivy *H. canariensis* 'Gloire de Marengo', and for a gold-leaved one there are the charming *H. helix* 'Oro di Bogliasco' (syn. *H. h.* 'Goldheart') and the Persian ivy in its yellow cultivar (*H. colchica* 'Dentata Variegata'). Many others have small leaves, prettily tinted.

As a covering for large walls **Parthenocissus** is not easy to surpass. The finest is the true Virginia creeper, the five-leafletted, *P. quinquefolia*, gloriously coloured in autumn and as magnificent when climbing a decadent tree as when clothing a house.

Far less stereotyped, and worthy of much wider use, are two handsome flowering creepers. One is *Campsis radicans*, hardy in most parts of Britain given a warm south wall, with 3 in. orange trumpets in late summer and large pinnate leaves, highly decorative but deciduous. It needs a hearty loam and will climb 20 ft. The secret with it, as with wisteria, is to prune back the young laterals in winter, as on a vine, to two eyes. *See* the sketch on page 225 in the passage on grapes. Needs a warm August to flower well; cool nights make the buds drop.

The other is the climbing *Hydrangea anomala* subsp. *petiolaris,* which can climb to the tops of trees. Quite hardy, it has bold, handsome leaves and large flat corymbs of white blossom, arranged similarly to the lacecap shrubs. Deciduous, turning pale gold in autumn. Any aspect, but less good on the north than elsewhere. Rather similar to it is another useful one cumbrously named *Schizophragma hydrangeoides,* its flower clusters draped with large, white bracts like fluttering handkerchieves.

We turn now from these few clingers to those plants that mount by means of twining tendrils, leaf-stalks, or stems.

Vitis is the vine, and it gives us a few fine foliage climbers in addition to those dedicated to Bacchus. Grandmaster of them all is *V. coignetiae*, which has enormous vigour (it will climb a tall tree) and very large, handsome leaves that in autumn flame with tints of ruby and cornelian. A top choice for expansive walls and for outbuildings. There are splendid colours also in some of the varieties of the grape-vine (*V. vinifera*). Thus *V. v.* 'Purpurea' has handsome purple leaves, and the hybrid 'Brant' has leaves that become ensanguined in autumn with crimson and orange. They are excellent for quick screens on trellises or for embracing an arbour.

Noblest of all climbers, however, is the *Wisteria,* with its sumptuous trusses of cascading lilac blossoms. Its tremendous vigour is rather too much for the very small house. It will prosper in any reasonable soil and on any wall except the north one, but likes the south best. Easily trained where you want it to go – straight up the house with branches between each storey; or kept low along a balcony, terrace, or fence, and marvellous on a pergola. Can also be grown with great effect in the open garden as a standard tree or bush trained umbrella-wise, or as you will. The usual and best species is *W. sinensis.* After training it as you want, summer-prune the young shoots or laterals at the end of June to within about five leaves of their point of origin, and in winter cut back again to about three buds. Neglected old wisterias may need to have a few older shoots judiciously cut out in winter. You can cut back as hard as you like.

Queen to the wisteria is the **clematis**, and she is so important a lady that I have given her a section to herself in Chapter 18. **Roses**, which do not come comfortably within any of these classifications, are dealt with in Chapter 14.

Another popular twiner is the **honeysuckle** or woodbine (*Lonicera*). The usual ones are the Early Dutch and Late Dutch, which are quite nice, but a better one for general use is the hybrid *L.* x *americana*. This has scented, purple-and-rose flowers and is nearly evergreen. For utilitarian purposes – to cover an outhouse or form a quick, dense screen – there is the evergreen, fast-growing *L. japonica*, in one of two cultivars: 'Halliana', with biscuit flowers, or 'Aureoreticulata', with leaves patterned in a network of yellow. Far more splendid visually, but lacking scent, are *L. tragophylla* and *L.* x *tellmanniana*, sumptuous plants with opulent clusters of golden trumpets.

All honeysuckles, especially the better sorts, should have their roots in *moist shade*. They excel on trellises, screens, climbing up trees, and on sunless walls.

Many people think that the **passion flower** (*Passiflora*) is tender, but it comfortably rides English winters, especially if given the shelter of a south wall. Its intricate, exotic blooms, exquisitely chiselled, are so attractive that space should certainly be found for it if possible. Its passport to success is a poor, stony, gravelly soil or a severely restricted root area. Order *P. caerulea* and give it a small-mesh wire grid as host. Early in March cut back secondary growth to within two or three buds of their base.

Another useful one worthy of wider use is *Solanum crispum*, animated with dainty mauve flowers like those of the potato, and blooming all summer; it is a long-flowering scrambler for an arch or trellis, on which it makes a dense screen, in the milder counties. Not on a wall. The white *S. laxum* is delicate.

A twiner of quite a different order is *Fallopia baldschuanica,* a very rampant and express-speed climber common in early autumn, with its smother of big feathery bunches of ivory flowers. Very effective and attractive when properly used. Reserve it for utility tasks such as covering up unsightly sheds. Grows anywhere. Cut it back as hard as you wish in spring. Sometimes called the 'Russian vine'.

Here we leave the real climbers and meet the **jasmine** (*Jasminum*), which often climbs by twining stems but, if for a wall, must be tied up to it. No British garden is complete without the winter jasmine, whose golden bells on green, leafless stems bring cheer when little else of colour enlivens the dark days. Plant it where you can see it at close quarters from a living-room window, and order *J. nudiflorum*. It flourishes even on a north wall, and its only failing is in scent. After flowering cut back the flowered shoots to two or three new buds.

The summer jasmine (*J. officinale*), however, is full of the loveliest perfume and its flowers are white among pretty, pinnate leaves. It wants a south or west aspect. Don't prune except for any necessary thinning out after flowering.

Jasmines need training out and tying up carefully for good effect. They are increased with great ease by simply weighting a shoot down to the surface of the ground, when it will take root as a layer. Still greater splendours are *J. mesnyi* and *J. polyanthum*, but they are fit for the warm, western counties only.

We come now to those plants which naturally are open-ground shrubs, but which, by being planted close to a wall, can be induced to assume an ascending habit. They provide some of our very finest wall plants. Descriptions of most of them have been given in Chapter 15. First choices for a small place would be:

Ceanothus. Use almost any of the evergreen ones. South or west aspect. Up to 20 ft. high and 15 ft. wide. 'Autumnal Blue' and 'Delight' are strongly tipped.

Flowering quince (*Chaenomeles*). Any aspect, including partial shade. Outstanding.

Pyracantha. This is a handsome, evergreen, fast-growing race of berried and thorny shrubs which I have left to this chapter because in small gardens it is employed essentially as a wall plant or a hedge, in which roles it is beyond praise. Entirely hardy, immune to drought (but not the fire-blight disease), it will flourish even on a bitter north wall. Choose between *P. atalantioides*, *P. rogersiana* and the orange-fruited *P. coccinea* 'Lalandei'; both the first two have yellow-fruited variants. In spring all break out into a froth of cream flowers.

Cotoneaster horizontalis. Suitable for any wall (*see* page 163)

Euonymus fortunei var. **radicans.** Very handy where a short climber is needed. If planted near a wall it behaves just like ivy, clinging to its host securely. The varieties with colourful leaves are exceedingly attractive, such as 'Silver Queen' and 'Variegatus'. Any aspect. Also excellent for ground cover.

For the first three pruning is important, not only for the usual reasons but also to train them in the way in which they should go, and to make them hug the wall instead of growing outwards as rounded shrubs. Laterals should be led along horizontally in the manner of an espalier or fan-trained fruit tree. Those that flower before midsummer on wood grown the previous summer should have the outward-growing wood cut back to two or three buds of their base after flowering. Pyracantha should have its laterals shortened in this manner in summer, and again in March, to produce 'fruiting spurs', like apples.

Many other shrubs look fine on walls, without materially changing their rounded or bushy habit. On a lime-free soil camellias are an exquisite adornment, but remember that many are liable to sunstroke on south or east walls. For larger houses *Magnolia grandiflora* is sumptuous. On really warm, sunny walls you may enjoy several beautiful shrubs on the borderline of hardiness, such as *Coronilla valentina,* the various abutilons, the myrtles, and the choice little *Hebe hulkeana*. Many others more tender still are at the command of those who live in the favoured West.

17

HEDGES AND EDGES

In this chapter we shall consider briefly the various sorts of plant barriers and screens that may be needed in the small garden – boundary hedges, hedges between one part of the garden and another (such as the masking-off of the vegetable garden or the enclosure of a rose-garden), together with dwarf screens to flank a drive or footpath and low edgings for various purposes.

Unless one specifically wants a decorative, open type of screen, as might be provided by certain sorts of roses, the first essentials of a hedge are that it should be thick, dense, as tall as you want it, and clothed right down to the ground with foliage.

> As thick as is a castle wall,
> That whoso list without to stand or go,
> Though he would all day pryen to and fro,
> He should not see if there were any wight
> Within or no.

Even in Chaucer's day they thought so. A straggly, moth-eaten hedge with shameless naked legs is an abomination in men's eyes and a failure in its twin tasks of acting both as a mask and a barrier. To enable it to do its job properly and to look comely into the bargain, we must bring it up properly from its earliest days, for to cure an adult hedge that has gone wrong is as difficult as to reform an old lag.

The formula for its early training is: sound preparation of the ground (this above all), proper spacing of the plants and strict pruning (in most cases) so that the youngsters will throw out strong side branches immediately above the level of the soil.

Hedge cultivation differs from that of other plantings chiefly in the fact that the plants are set very closely together. It follows that the preparation of the ground must be particularly thorough. The trench should be at least 2 ft. wide for a single row. The soil should be broken up a full 2 ft. down, it must be well-drained and it must be generously fed with some sort of organic manure – dung, compost, hops, old turves, etc. – and well dressed in the top spit with bonemeal. This bottom feeding, besides improving the hedge, will encourage its roots to go deep down, and will thus allow other crops to be grown much nearer to the hedge than is otherwise possible.

The proper spacing of hedge-plants is important. A single row is usually quite sufficient. Spacing is influenced by which side you back in the speed v. cost contest. Close spacing (within limits) will generally provide a barrier more quickly but means more plants. When a hedge is planted close to a fence, it should be at least 18 in. away from it.

Plant according to the rules applying to any other tree or shrub. If the situation is a windy one, or if the plants are of large size or very bushy, they must be firmly staked until the roots have taken good hold. If the weather is on the dry side, water thoroughly.

Pruning

Bushy growth must be encouraged from the start, but the methods and degree of pruning will depend on the subject. The general rule to remember is that in the first year or two *frequent* pruning is even more important than hard pruning, and that the fast-growing species, such as privet, lonicera and Lawson cypress, need harder and more frequent cuttings than the slow ones, such as yew and holly. Broad-leaved plants, such as laurel, should never be clipped with the shears; trim them with secateurs.

Hedges of flowering plants require slightly different treatment, and here one should follow what has been said in Chapter 15 of flowering shrubs when used in their normal setting – that is to say, according to their habit of flowering.

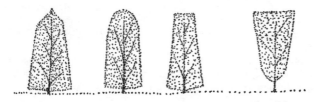

Hedges in cross-section. Three good shapes – and a bad one.

In all cases the ultimate shape of the hedge should be borne in mind from the beginning; and here there is one governing rule – that all tall hedges should be narrower at the top than at the bottom. Moreover, except for strong trees such as holly and yew, they should not be cut square at the top, specially in districts liable to heavy snow; the top should instead be either rounded or else in the form of a pointed ridge, the latter being particularly necessary for anything of weak or lax wood. This, of course, need not apply to dwarf hedges or to open screens of roses, etc.

After-care

The hedge having been established, the chief need is obviously clipping or pruning according to the nature of the plant. People without a really straight eye haven't a hope of maintaining a hedge that needs close-clipping and should employ an experienced professional. In any case, the beginner should not make his first attempt without using a garden line and a few lathes as guides. The standard time for clipping non-flowering evergreens is about 1st August.

It is too often forgotten that established hedges need food as much as other plants, perhaps more so. Therefore give a generous top-dressing of manure or leafmould or a feed of a fertiliser every few years, and a feed of bonemeal as often as you like.

WHAT TO PLANT

The list below, short though it is, shows what a wide choice there is. I would make a special plea, particularly as internal hedges, for certain of the flowering and berried shrubs that lend themselves to this treatment. A floral hedge in full bloom is a picture not to be forgotten. Unfortunately few nurseries offer these as hedge-plants at low prices, but one can usually get a special quotation for a quantity.

Boundary hedges

In many situations floral hedges can be used with beautiful effect for boundary hedges also, but more often boundaries demand something solid and uncompromising.

Yew and holly are undoubtedly the best. Properly grown, they make a solid wall many feet high, through which only a mouse can infiltrate. But they have the objection in these impatient days of being very slow – about seven years is the time that small holly and yew plants take to make a full-grown hedge, and if you can afford to wait it is well worth doing so.

For a really fast job, Leyland cypress takes the cake and its new golden cultivar 'Castlewellan' is stunning.

A very strong contender for first place, however, is the pyracantha, especially its species *P. rogersiana*. It is evergreen, dense, quite fast, and will give us both blossom in spring and berry in autumn. Darwin's barberry (*Berberis darwinii*) and *B. × stenophylla* are also fine. The latter, with its arching cascades of gold, glittering and fragrant, is a model of picturesque and informal grace, but in town or suburban gardens abutting on to a pavement Darwin's species is more suitable. Barberries are slow, however, and these two may ultimately spread 8 ft. wide.

Similar in character to pyracanthas are the cotoneasters. They are very suitable for small gardens, taking up little lateral space, and enlivened by their loads of red berries late in the year and often all winter; the cotoneaster is not, however, fully evergreen, and is in danger from the fireblight disease (Chapter 23). Escallonias, so decorative with their glossy foliage and red, pink or white flowers, are excellent for the seaside in the west and south, resistant to salt and wind.

Another handsome and similar pair are the beech, either green or copper, and the hornbeam. The beech delights in chalky lands or other lime conditions, and on cold, heavy soils the hornbeam is to be preferred.

Their handsome russet-brown leaves, clinging all winter, make them as good as evergreens. Two of the best and cheapest.

It is the fashion among some people to disdain the privet as 'suburban' or bourgeois, and no doubt it is overdone. The real pity is that it is too often badly grown or wrongly trimmed. But the truth is that for the small garden there is nothing which so well fills the bill for speed, cheapness, ease of handling, and adaptability to nearly all conditions, including partial shade. When really well cultivated, clothed to the ground, and with rounded crown, or ridged like a roof, it is very satisfying. Privet, however, demands to be really well-tailored by frequent clipping, and thus looks best in spruce, rather formalised surroundings. The biggest objection to privet is that it is a hungry brute, and nothing will grow satisfactorily close to it.

Then there are hedges for special soils and situations – flowering ones at that. Thus for mild climates there are bountiful fuchsias; for tough, wind-bitten places the double-flowered gorse; and for heathlike or lime-free soils there are the taller sorts of ericas.

At the seaside, with its violent, salt-laden winter gales, special selections must be made, but fortunately there are several good candidates.

Internal hedges

Here we have an even wider choice, and there is a special opportunity for gay floral hedges; the need may be for a 6 ft. hedge or for only a dwarf one.

For fairly open screens, we have roses of many sorts, especially 'New Dawn', the forsythia, flowering quinces, fuchsia and the tree heathers. For little, low hedges there are the charming *Spiraea thunbergii*, the spicy dwarf philadelphuses and the shrubby potentillas. For really miniature hedges, we can use the lavender, the cotton lavender and the 9 in. aromatic thymes (*Thymus* x *citriodorus* and *T. richardii* subsp. *nitidus*).

LIST OF HEDGING PLANTS

The figures *in brackets* denote the heights to be expected in good cultiva-tion after five years. Note the differentiations between 'prune', 'clip', and 'shear'.

Barberry. Choose *B.* x *stenophylla* or *B. darwinii* (5 ft.). Spacing 2 ft. For a 4-footer, *B. verruculosa*. For a dwarf, *B. thunbergii* 'Atropurpurea Nana'. Space 15 in. Prune after flowering.

Beech (4 ft. 6 in.). Space 21 in. Shear sides hardish in August (some gardeners prefer February), but leave the leading shoots alone until desired height is reached.

Cotoneaster. Choose *C. simonii* or *C.* x *watereri* (5 ft. plus). Space 21 in. Trim after flowering.

Cypress. Out of the many, choose Leyland (x *cypress xypans leylandii*) (8 ft.), especially its beautiful golden cultivar 'Castlewellan'. Space 30 in. Leave tips until 1 ft. more than desired height, then cut off the top foot next year. Can grow very tall indeed.

Escallonia. Choose *E. rubra* 'Crimson Spire', *E. r.* 'Ingramii' or *E. r.* var. *macrantha*, but any will do. Excellent at seaside (average 4 ft. 6 in.). Space 24–30 in. Trim after flowering.

Euonymus. Essentially a seaside hedger, with tough, polished leaves resistant to sea-salt and wind. Not for the coldest counties. The most decorative is *E. japonicus* 'Ovatus Aureus', with leaves broadly edged cream. Space a good 2 ft.

Forsythia x intermedia 'Spectabilis' (5 ft.). Space 2 ft. Prune after flower.

Fuchsia 'Riccartonii' (4 ft.) Space 2 ft. Shear March.

Holly (3 ft.). Space 18 in. Prune or clip in August.

Hornbeam. As for beech.

Laurel is a term loosely applied to several genera. (*a*) *Aucuba*, with large, polished leaves. (*b*) Cherry-laurel (*Prunus laurocerasus*, best cv. 'Otto Luyken'). (*c*) Portugal laurel, small, dark leaves (*Prunus lusitanicus*). All 5 ft. plus, except the smaller 'Otto Luyken'. Space 4 ft. Prune August.

Lavender 'Hidcote' (15 in.). Space 1 ft. Clip after flower.

Lonicera nitida, the shrubby honeysuckle (5 ft.). Out of favour but very nice if well treated. Shear closely July and August. Space 15 in.

Myrobalan or cherry plum (*Prunus cerasifera*). Good utility hedge (4 ft. 6 in.). The purple 'Pissardii' is superior but dear. Space 2 ft. Shear early June.

Privet (4 ft.). Space 15 in. Shear early June, mid-July and late August.

Prunus x cistena. Brilliant red-leaved shrub for fairly heavy soils, most impressive when kept down to 3 ft. Space 21 in. Shear after flower.

Pyracantha. One of the very best. Use *P. rogersiana* or *P.* 'Watereri' (4 ft. 6 in.). Tough. Space 2 ft. Clip sides only till desired height, after flower and in June and August. If plants on arrival from nursery are more than 2 ft. high, cut down to that.

Quickthorn (*Crataegus monogyna* and *C. laevigata*). Cheap, fast, dense if well treated (5 ft.). Space 15 in. Shear as for privet.

Spiraea thunbergii (4 ft.). Space 18 in. Shear after flowering. Very pretty and unusual.

Tamarisk. For the seaside. Pretty, feathery, pink plumes in May. Use *T. gallica* (8 ft.). Cut down by two-thirds after flower.

Yew (*Taxus baccata*) (4 ft.). Space 21 in. Shear sides only in May and April till desired height.

RENOVATING OLD HEDGES

The renovation of shabby old hedges that have become bare-legged, straggly and of moth-eaten appearance often demands the ruthless use of knife and saw and hearty feeding.

The following will serve as a general guide for the surgical operations, which should be carried out on deciduous types during late dormancy – say late February. On evergreens late March is usually considered the best time.

Cut down very hard, to about 3 ft. 6 in. off the ground in bad cases: beech, hornbeam, privet, yew, holly, lonicera.

Cut laterals and sub-laterals hard with secateurs after flowering: quinces, cotoneasters, prunus varieties. Treat late-blooming floral sorts the same way late February.

Cut fuchsia down to 1 ft. off the ground.

Ragged old conifer hedges call for some expertise. Lacking it, scrap the lot and start again. The same applies to neglected lavenders, rosemary and brooms.

Before the amputation, mulch heavily with manure or lightly fork in an all-purpose fertiliser.

18

SOME SPECIALITIES

In this chapter I deal specially with a few favourites which for one reason or another are not conveniently dealt with elsewhere. Note that all, except the heathers, are more or less lime-lovers.

CARNATIONS AND PINKS

The great and lovely genus *Dianthus* includes carnations, pinks, sweet William and many plants that have no fancy or popular names, but are simply *Dianthus* so-and-so. The last-named include many ravishing rock-garden pinks. The branches of this ancient family with its poetic memories of 'Coronations', 'Sops-in-wine', and 'Gilly-flowers', cross-breed readily, and there are many hybrids. There are also annual carnations and pinks, while sweet William and the jaunty Indian and Japanese pinks, so-called, are biennials. In this chapter I shall deal with the perennial carnations and pinks that can be grown outdoors in the mixed border or in a border by themselves.

A characteristic of *Dianthus* generally is that nearly all of them appreciate lime. Of the several forms available, limestone rock is the best, being natural to them. A mild acidity, however, is no bar.

Other things that this family likes are good drainage, the full beam of the sun, and plenty of grit. They hate: wet and undrained sites, acid peats, very stiff clay, and fresh animal manures. Also, better not give them the usual chemical fertilisers.

Border carnations
By this term is meant hardy carnations that can be grown outdoors instead of in a heated greenhouse. Be careful about this when ordering plants, for I have known the mistake to be made. The term does *not*, however, mean that the outdoor carnation should be grown in the *herbaceous* border. Only pressure of space justifies one growing them in a mixed border, for undoubtedly they look best in a bed of their own and made to their own requirements. These requirements can be set out quite simply.

As they demand good drainage, give them if possible a slightly raised bed in full sun. Incorporate into the soil, when digging, plenty of old turfy loam and a little bonemeal. Top-dress with limestone chippings or dust – in default, crushed chalk, old mortar rubble, or ordinary hydrated lime.

Set the young plants out 12 in. apart. Plant very firmly indeed, and plant shallow, not completely burying the ball of soil in which they are rooted nor drawing any soil up to the stem.

As they come on, some thinning of the buds is necessary, even if not growing for exhibition. Pinch out the small buds clustering just below the main terminal bud on each shoot. Of buds arising from lower down the stem, a few may be retained at your pleasure according to the strength of the plant. 'Stopping', or pinching out the main stem, should not be done with border varieties. Some neat staking is essential.

Propagation is by 'layering' – a fairly simple process. It is done from mid-July to early August, using non-flowering shoots. With a very sharp knife or razor-blade make a slit longitudinally up the middle of the stem from the underside, starting just below a node and passing through and beyond it – a cut of half an inch or so in all. Having reduced the soil to a fine tilth, remove all leaves from that portion of the stem which will be under-ground, and lay the stem down in the soil with the wound gaping and the tongue of the cut projecting downwards. Press in very gently, cover with half an inch of soil, and keep in position with a hooked peg, a special layering pin, or a stone. *See* sketch. Some sand at the point of layering helps. *Water.* Layers should root in seven to ten days if kept moist, and will be ready for severance from the parent plant in six weeks, but if the weather has been hot and dry, leave them longer; there is no hurry.

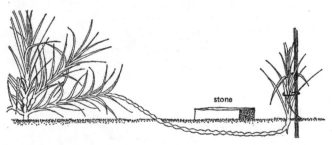

stone

Layering a carnation.

After severance from the parent, the layering may be left in the bed where it is if there is room, or it may be lifted and transplanted; October is best, but spring will do.

Varieties of border carnation are numberless, new ones constantly replacing the old, so there is no point in making suggestions. Leave the choice to a good nurseryman, stating the colour you like, but insist that all should have these qualities – a stiff, erect stem, a strong calyx that will not be burst by heavy blossom, and a long flowering period. Personally, I also insist on scent, except for the yellow varieties.

Good named varieties of carnation are expensive, but it is not difficult to grow from seed if you will be satisfied with a mixed bag. You can then increase the ones you like best by layering. Sow in a John Innes compost in March or April, and prick out early into prepared beds having plenty of sharp sand and limestone or fine mortar rubble if available. They should be bushy plants by September or October, ready for permanent quarters.

Cottage carnations may be described as small border carnations. Hardy, early, gay, and floriferous; no disbudding. **Picotees** are carnations with a piping of colour round the edge of the petal.

Pinks

These smaller members of the genus *Dianthus* are of great diversity, from tiny five petalled alpines to lusty hybrids very like small carnations. Nearly all are of great charm, and all but a few are of easy culture, a characteristic being an exceptionally long season of bloom if spent flowers are removed. They have not the formality of carnations, and can be freely used almost anywhere in the garden, given a sunny position, while many of the smaller breeds are enchanting in the rock garden or the dry wall (*see* Chapter 12). They are usually propagated by nodal cuttings rather than by layers.

Of the many wild species, the most important to us are the Cheddar pink (*D. gratianopolitanus*) and the maiden pink (*D. deltoides*), dealt with in the rock-gardening chapter, but for general uses we rely more on the wonderful range of hybrids, of which I give a small selection. I hope the reign of 'Mrs Sinkins' will soon be over. Though she has delighted several generations, she is a slovenly creature who always bursts her calyx, and there are many better ones.

For general garden use the Allwoodii pinks are outstanding. They grow about 9 in. high, in varying colours, needing just a little twiggy staking. Of the several named varieties, the most famous is 'Doris'. Others are 'Robin', 'London Poppet', 'Daphne' and so on.

Of the many other strains of pink, the following are all well proven:

- 'Pike's Pink'. A 6 in. beauty of neat habit.
- 'Grenadier.' Scarlet, 6 in., very reliable.
- 'Little Jock'. Pink with dark eye, 4 in.
- 'White Ladies'. Like a pure white carnation, far superior to 'Mrs Sinkins'. 10 in.
- 'La Bourboule'. Bright pink, 3 in.
- 'Dad's Favourite'. Double white with chocolate eye and ruby-red lacing, 10 in.
- 'Inchmery'. Double pale-pink, 9 in.

Like carnations, pinks also are easy to raise from seed, with varying results. A packet of seed of *D.* Allwoodii Alpinus Group has given me delightful surprises. Strains of annual pinks, such as *D. chinensis* Carpet Series and *D. chinensis* Magic Charms Series, are offered by seedsmen. The so-called Japanese pink, *D. chinensis* Heddewigii Group, is best treated as a half-hardy.

CLEMATIS

If wisteria is the king of climbers, clematis is certainly the queen. Yet she has no petals, for her beauty resides in the brilliance of her sepals and in the boss of stamens that they enfold. Wonderful in her range of colour, highly flowerful, modest in stature, adaptable to many uses, clematis is an ideal plant for the small garden, as for the large. But she does demand a little special treatment, neglect of which makes her appear a mere chorus-girl instead of the star she is. Clematis in her due season should be clothed with blossom almost from foot to crown, but too often she is a long, naked, spindle-shanked creature brandishing a tangled mop.

In nature the clematis grows in semi-woodland in lime-bearing soils, often above chalk, scrambling over bushes and up into branches of small trees. The bushes provide shade at ground level and an annual mulch of leaves over the roots. Let us apply these factors to her cultivated state.

Soil

Clematis seem to prosper in a wide variety of soils, from richly manured ones to brickrubble, but wisdom hints that you start them with plenty of good organic stuff. Least propitious is a lean porous sand.

Planting

October is best, but, the young plants being in pots, any time from September to May will do if weather and soil are right. Make a wide hole in the prepared site deep enough to plant the root crown 2 in. *below* the surface. Knock the plant out of the pot, squeeze the ball of soil gently to loosen the roots, spread the roots out well, work in some fine sifted soil and make firm.

The young stems are extremely fragile and brittle. Handle carefully and do not remove the cane to which they are tied. After planting protect the stems securely with a cage of twiggy sticks against damage by the hoe, the cat, and other enemies. Encircle the stem also with sharp sand or cinders against the slug.

The site

All clematis insist that their roots shall be shaded and cool, but their flowers in sunshine, or at least in full light. This is an order. The shade of a small bush – i.e. one on the south side of the clematis – is the usual thing, but a stone slab or a thick spread of loose stones will do as well. So also will the shade of a wall or fence; indeed, the Late Large-flowered, Viticella and Montana Groups will thrive nearly as well on a completely sunless north wall as elsewhere, provided it is not overhung by trees.

The host

Though clematis certainly look handsome clambering naturally up a large bush, there is a danger that, by the exuberance of their foliage, they will smother their host to its disadvantage. This is a point on which I have modified my opinion over the years. No tree of fine foliage or of special value should be so cloaked, but unimportant trees and those past their prime are given a new purpose in life, but one must bear in mind any pruning problems.

Thus, in the average small garden, artificial hosts are really best, notably those that absolve you of the bore of constant tying-in. Nothing is better than some form of inconspicuous wire netting. 'Twilweld' is almost invisible and black-coated chain-link fencing is also very good. Fix these to walls, arches, fences or (very impressive) wrap them loosely round a very tall pole among shrubs. Away goes the clematis on its own and you have nothing to do but watch it.

Pruning and after-care

Thousands of clematis are ruined by wrong pruning or no pruning. The methods vary according to the variety, so the detail is left till the next section, but for non-specialist purposes the thing is quite simple, provided you keep your plants really well labelled. Meanwhile the following few pruning rules apply to all:

- ❧ Cut all new plants right down to within 9 in. of the ground – and no shirking.
- ❧ Cut just above a node or joint, where a bud or twin buds appear.
- ❧ Cut out all dead, damaged and weakly shoots.
- ❧ Decapitate the fluffy seed-heads at once.
- ❧ Water abundantly.

The larger hybrid clematis are subject to a 'wilt disease', in which the whole plant, up to three years old, shrivels and dies. You have nevertheless little to fear if you have obeyed my injunction to plant deeply. Cut out the dying stems right to the ground at once and new stems should appear from below ground level.

Varieties

In my book *Climbing Plants for Walls and Gardens* I have gone into this and other matters in some detail, but the practical gardener not interested in the finer points will do well to disregard at first the old classifications – Viticella, Lanuginosa, etc. The simplest of all plans is to stick to the late-flowering species and varieties, i.e. those that flower after midsummer, which you prune simply by cutting them down, thigh-high every February. These include many splendours – 'Jackmanii Superba', 'Hagley Hybrid', 'Perle d'Azur', 'Gipsy Queen', 'Comtesse de Bouchaud', 'Ernest Markham' (optionally), and the delightful yellow species *C. tangutica* (the

Chinese lantern clematis) and *C. tibetana* subsp. *vernayi* (the lemon-peel clematis).

By sticking to these varieties, you avoid all pruning headaches, but you miss some others that elegantly adorn the garden earlier in the year. There are two breeds of these. The first are the spring-flowering species and their varieties. They include: Montana Group and its pink varieties, which will grow 30 ft. or more, *C. spooneri* and *C.* x *vedrariensis*, 20 ft., *C. macropetala* (the delightful ballet-skirt clematis), *C. alpina* in its several varieties, and the half-tender, tricky evergreen *C. armandii* (for warm places only).

These flower on shoots that have developed during the previous summer, so you prune *immediately after flowering* (say end of May). This also is easy enough if you have taken the trouble initially to train out the shoots to form a basic framework. All you do then is to shear back all the flowered shoots crisply near to the main framework. *C. armandii* is best left alone, and *C. macropetala* will come to little harm if you merely cut off the seed-heads. *C. montana* also is usually left alone to shoot heavenwards, but can be cut back hard whenever you like.

A third sort consists of the midsummer hybrids, which sometimes flower again in early autumn. These can become tangled up in the most awful 'bird's nests', especially if you follow some people's advice to 'leave them alone'. Again, if you start by fanning them well out, you may follow the rule of 'light pruning', cutting back each flowered shoot to some pair of strong buds. This you do *in February*. This group includes such great favourites as 'Lasurstern', 'Nelly Moser', 'Ville de Lyon', 'William Kennett', and 'Marie Boisselot'.

A clematis of great excellence but with no 'visible means of support' is *C.* x *durandii*, a glowing royal-blue star. Plant it at the foot of some loose, open shrub, cut it down knee-high every February and lead the young shoots up the branches of their hosts, which they will shoot up like a boy after apples.

The herbaceous border types of clematis we shall leave alone.

Propagation
Take down a strong shoot, shorten it to about 5 ft. and make layerings, just as with carnations. Two or three serpentine layers may be made from one shoot, but the best comes from a node near the tip.

CHRYSANTHEMUMS

Apart from the annual sort, dealt with in Chapter 10, there are a great many breeds and hybrids of chrysanthemum, some of which are not easily recognisable as such.

For practical garden purposes I pop them into two pigeonholes, which I call the country girls and the mandarins. The former are the hardy sorts that dwell in the herbaceous border all the year, and the latter are those large and imposing creatures which are cossetted and fussed over for the exhibition bench and the mayoral reception (at ratepayers' expense).

The country girls
These are all easy, agreeable and very good company for other plants.

Leucanthemum x superbum. This chrysanthemum relative is the Shasta daisy, King Edward's daisy, etc. Large, bold, white 'daisies' from July onwards. Hard as nails, treat it as an herbaceous perennial, lifting only to divide every few years. Plant in autumn or spring. No stopping or disbudding. Probably the best varieties are 'Everest', 'Wirral Supreme' and 'Wirral Pride', all about 3 ft.

C. zawadskii (syn. *C. rubellum*). Delightful, fragrant, single, daisy-form blooms in great profusion, about 2 ft. high. No stopping or disbudding. Early September onwards. Sometimes shy the first year. Its offspring, the Rubellum Group, include 'Clara Curtis', a radiant soft pink, and 'Jessie Cooper', a bold brick-red; they go well together.

Koreans. Hardy, stocky, easy and trouble-free. Prodigal of bloom but colours not good, to my mind. Pinch out when 2 or 3 in. high. No staking or disbudding. Leave undisturbed except in severe districts. There are also several dwarfs, very flowerful little chaps for the edge of the border.

'Denise' and 'Jante Wells', with their profusion of little golden rosettes, are much prized not only for edgings but also for autumn window-boxes in towns.

Pyrethrums (*Tanacetum coccineum,* Chapter 11) are also chrysanthemum relatives; so, too, are many other flowers, both wild and cultivated.

The mandarins
The most celestial of these reign in glass temples, but those that are called 'early-flowering' grow very well outdoors, where they bloom in August and September, attaining 5 ft. or more (sometimes much more). They develop large blooms and may be single or double. Give them a place in full sun in a fairly rich soil, but avoid fresh manure. Plant, firmly, in early May, 18 in. apart.

They are surface-rooting, so give them plenty of water in dry spells, and give them also an occasional tonic of a liquid manure or a 'foliar feed'. Watch for the wriggly tunnellings of the leaf-miner in the leaves. Burn infected leaves.

Particular attention must be given to the processes of stopping and disbudding. Very few varieties other than the singles are satisfactory if allowed to grow at will — they merely become lanky and top-heavy, with a mass of insignificant blooms. A compact and bushy shape is to be aimed at, with some decent-sized blooms, even if not of exhibition size. A simplified method is given later in the paragraph on stopping and disbudding.

In November, after the stems have been cut down to within a few inches of the ground, orthodox treatment is to lift the plants, and replant them, closely packed in soil, under a frame or in the greenhouse for the winter; in mild places, however, they survive perfectly well outside until the time comes for taking cuttings for next season. The practice of allowing them to grow into large clumps does not give best results; they deteriorate. See the later paragraph on propagation.

As in so many other fanciers' flowers, a choice of varieties today is liable to be out of date in a year or two. The National Chrysanthemum Society or a good specialist nursery will help you, but enquire about size, habit, 'stopping', etc.

In favoured districts October chrysanths can be grown outdoors, but normally anything that flowers from then onwards needs to be grown in a greenhouse. Commonly classified as 'mid-season' and 'lates', they include many decorative forms – incurved, reflexed, single and the striking Japanese mopheaded creations. For ordinary amateur purposes no heat is necessary unless and until frost or autumn fog actually penetrates inside the greenhouse.

The following is the course of treatment:

On receipt from the nursery, plant in 3 in. or 4 in. pots, using the John Innes potting mixture and planting very firmly with a rammer. As the roots fill the pots, move on into larger pots, coarsening the compost by adding more loam, preferably in the form of old turfy stuff or 'top spit'. Their final homes are 9 in. (22 cm.) pots, using the John Innes No. 3 Potting Compost or some equivalent. Keep the plants in full light and ventilate the greenhouse very freely. Water in moderation till the weather warms up.

Towards the end of May, the plants being then in their final pots, stand them outdoors, on ashes, stone or planks to prevent the entry of worms. Give them an open position in full sun, but protected from high winds. Keep the soil moist (the leaves will throw off much rain) and the foliage syringed in dry spells. As the roots begin to fill the pots, give weekly drinks of a special chrysanth fertiliser (e.g. Chempak) or a good general one, using weak doses at first.

In the last week of September bring the plants back into the greenhouse again, giving plenty of light and plenty of room between plants. Treat early against mildew, and fumigate the house against aphis. Ventilate very freely. Fix muslin below the top ventilators to minimise the entry of fog and damp. Close the lights at night when frost begins to threaten. Water the plants only when the soil seems to be drying up. Gradually raise the temperature to 10°C (50°F), but don't attempt to force.

After the plants have finished blooming cut them to within a few inches of the soil. Do not interfere with the young growth springing up from the base, which will be wanted for cuttings.

Stopping and disbudding
The secret of growing successful chrysanths, as distinct from shaggy and untidy growths of small blooms, lies in stopping or pinching and disbudding,

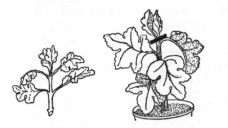

Chrysanthemums: left to right, *a prepared cutting, stopping, disbudding.*

which are separate processes. Stopping or pinching means nipping out the main stems in their early upward growth, and disbudding means the removal of excess flower-buds.

Apart from a specialised thing like the Cascade chrysanth, these processes are applied only to the large-flowered *double* sorts, i.e. the sorts grown in the greenhouse and the early flowering varieties grown outside in the border. Chrysanth fanciers have a weird jargon all their own, and if you want to grow fine blooms consult a specialist's book, but otherwise the following simple rule will serve well:

∾ 'Stop' the young shoots when about 5 in. high (earlyish in April).
∾ On indoor varieties, in mid-June, stop also the branches that result from the first pinching.
∾ As flower-buds develop, remove all those clustering round the major bud at the tip of each main stem, and remove also the buds appearing in the leaf-axils.

These processes will produce one good-sized bloom at the top of each stem. You can modify the process as you like – e.g. quite decorative cluster effects result from removing the lower axillary buds only. Don't disturb or stop the *single* varieties, but thin out any weak shoots.

Propagation
Ordinary division, or splitting up of old clumps, will suit for the Shasta daisy, Rubellums, Koreans, and dwarfs. The large-flowered sorts, outdoor and in, should be cultivated yearly from fresh cuttings for best results.

When flowering is over, cut the stems down to within a few inches of the soil, to encourage new basal growth. In unheated houses take cuttings in March. Shoots growing out of the old stems are of less value than the basal shoots springing from below ground. Cut these basal shoots just below soil level, trim them back with a sharp knife to a point immediately below a node or joint, remove the lower leaves, dip the cuttings in a nicotine insecticide, and insert them ¾ in. deep in boxes (better than pots) in a sandy compost. A close, damp atmosphere is not necessary provided they are watered fairly freely. When the cuttings have rooted, move them singly into small pots in a potting compost.

In selecting shoots for cutting, avoid both the lanky ones and the plump, sappy ones; take firm, short-jointed specimens about 3 in. high.

Outdoor varieties may be propagated by taking shoots from the old 'stools' with roots attached in March, and potting them up.

IRISES

This ancient and lordly race holds such sway in the hearts of gardeners that it has its own Society and its specialist nurseries. Irises of some sort bloom throughout the year, some with their feet bathed in water, others exulting in hot, dry soils. Almost all are beautiful, but many are too difficult for us unless we have just the right conditions and a good deal of expertise.

For our purposes we can divide the garden irises simply into four sorts – the slender bulbous irises, the splendid sun-loving bearded flags of martial carriage, the beardless waterside flags, and the little irises of winter.

Bearded flags. These are the stately creations, often more than a yard high, which grow in every garden and which originate in that great race of so-called German irises (since one of the ancestors in its mixed breeding was *I. germanica*). Their 'beards' are the hair-like growths on the drooping falls of the blossom. They are essentially lovers of the sun. Their special characteristic is that their rigid leaves rise from a thick, fleshy rhizome which is often mistaken by the apprentice for a bulb or root, but which is in fact a stem. Since it is a stem, it should not be buried, but should be planted flat (and firmly) on the surface and only barely covered with soil, its roots lying astride a little saddle or mound of soil roughly formed below ground with fingers or trowel. Deep or loose planting of this rhizome is the cause of many failures.

Flags are undoubtedly best grown in a border of their own, where, with their sword-like leaves, they suggest a squadron of bannered cavalry. What to do with the bed when flowering is over is sometimes a problem, for they are soon over, and nothing must be allowed to hinder the rhizomes from getting the sun-baking that they need. Thus they are very much separatists.

The bearded flags will grow well in any good soil, but they prefer it on the light side and are great lime-lovers. If lime is not already sufficiently present, add mortar rubble or broken chalk, though not all the pundits agree on this. If the soil is very light, thicken it up with well-rotted compost or leaves; if very heavy, lighten it with coarse sand. On all soils add bonemeal before planting, and again every February. In no case give animal manure. A slightly raised bed suits them particularly well.

The best time to plant is early in July, but autumn or early spring will do. After planting cut the leaves down to 9 in.; cut them down also on established plants at the end of August, not quite so hard. Remove seed-pods after flowering. Established beds should be broken up and divided every

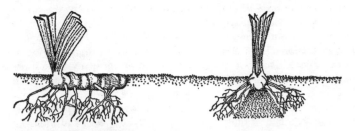

Planting flag irises. *On the right, end-on view showing roots astride a saddle.*

three years or so. Cut up the rhizomes into pieces about 2 in. long with ample root attached, and discard old and decaying portions. Do this in July.

For the usual reason I avoid giving varieties, though I should never forsake dear 'Jane Phillips' in her pale blue gown, quite an old lady now.

There are also some endearing little Dwarf Bearded irises. Two of the best are *I. pumila*, a plump little cherub squatting almost on the ground, and *I. lutescens* (syn. *I. chamaeiris*), a little taller. Each has varieties in divers colours.

The new race of intermediates may well be the answer to the gardener's prayer. Hybrids between the giants and the dwarfs, they flower freely from April to June.

Waterside flags. Apart from the heraldic flower-de-luce, we need notice only three of this group, differing mainly in the degree of their appetites for water. The first is the stunning *I. ensata* (syn. *I. kaempferi*), a goddess too exacting for most of us, for she likes her toes in acid soil that is wet in summer but dry in winter. The second is *I. laevigata*, a beautiful water iris in many colour forms, which grows with its rhizome just submerged, but is content with any very moist soil. Third is the common Siberian iris, *I. sibirica*, which prospers in any soil that does not dry out. It has many varieties in shades of blue but too small flowers for too much foliage.

The gladdon (*I. foetidissima*) is valued by arrangers for its sealing-wax seed. Moist soil in shade.

Bulbous irises. The best known are those which are popularly called Dutch, Spanish and English irises. Inexpensive, of easy culture and good for cutting, they have slender stems and petals that are more strap-like and less solid than the flags. They are in bloom from early June to mid-July, following each other. Plant in September, 3 in. deep, in any good soil. Leave them in the ground until overcrowded, then, after the foliage has died, lift, dry, divide and replant.

The English are the largest, with colours mostly in blue shades; they prefer to be near water. The sweet-scented Spanish I think the daintiest and most artistic, lovely varieties being *I. latifolia* 'Isabella', 'Queen of the Blues' and 'King of the Blues'. Of the Dutch, I think 'Wedgwood' the most attractive. It is lovely, too, in pots or bowls.

Winter irises. The little irises that 'warm the cold bosom of the hoary year' have a brave Cinderella charm. The largest, but still of only 1 ft. stature, is an Algerian of exquisite beauty in blue and gold, *I. unguicularis.* It blooms in succession all winter and should be picked for the house just as the buds show colour, when it will gladden the room for many a day. It has a rhizome and is best planted at the end of September. Flourishing only in austere living, it needs a light, dry, sun-parched, poor, stony, limy soil with a course of broken bricks or gravel 8 in. below for sharp drainage. If necessary, make a bed of this nature, built up. Take special and intensive measures against slugs, for whose piracy it is a favourite prey. Cut down the foliage early in June so that the sun can ripen it – heaps of sun and stones are its needs.

Then there are two lovely little bulbous ones. Best known is the violet-scented *I. reticulata* – the small

> Blue-netted iris, like a cry
> Starting the sloth of February

in Miss Sackville-West's words. I like best its hybrid 'Cantab' in Cambridge blue. But more beautiful is *I. histrioides* 'Major', a glowing ultramarine, a 3 in. darling that enchants the beholder for six weeks in January and February. Very easy in good soil in full sun and excellent in bowls. Avoid the disappointing yellow I. *danfordiae.*

HEATHERS

The flowers of the heathlands, which embrace the ericas, the calluna and the Irish daboecia, make delightful and trouble-free gardens. Indeed, they are perhaps the least troublesome of all plants, for, once well established, they carpet the ground and make life a poor look-out for weeds. They are perennial, mostly hardy, evergreen, bloom for astonishingly long periods, and need little attention beyond a light clipping once a year. There are varieties for every month in the year, those that bloom in winter being especially welcome. Nearly all are of low growth but some make splendid hedges.

The majority will not, however, tolerate a soil impregnated with lime. Be watchful about this. The few that succeed regardless of the lime content are among the best; but none will succeed with *chalk* too near the surface.

Unlike the great majority of plants, heathers are often chosen specifically for the beauty of their foliage, which puts to shame the floral efforts of many another plant. Apart from their many shades of green, they surprise and delight us in robes of orange, lemon, copper, gold, crimson and occasionally blue-grey. These must have full, all-day sun. Quite often the colour of the foliage changes with the seasons, as in *Calluna vulgaris* 'Sunset'. As a rule, however, those that have brilliant foliage are rather insipid in flower.

Heath plants favour a sunny, open situation, well away from large trees. They are very fond of old leaf-soil or peat, but any soil which is not too rich and has leafmould or peat in the top spit gives good results, provided the lime factor is borne in mind. The few that have special needs we shall notice as we go. Plant from October to March, according to flowering season. Work some peat into each root pocket, plant deeply, and press down very firmly. Stake the taller 'tree' heaths.

If the young plants are spaced out according to their ultimate spread (averaging about 18 in.), they will look fearfully 'thin on the ground'; so be a bit extravagant and plant at half their spread, thinning them out when they crowd each other. Afterwards your duties to them involve:

- ∾ watering at need;
- ∾ weeding (the chemical inhibitors being very appropriate) for the first three years, after which their own density protects them;
- ∾ cutting back the flower spikes when spent;
- ∾ combing out (with fingers or a soft rubber rake) fallen tree-leaves in autumn and winter, not the most enjoyable of jobs.

Propagation is usually easy enough from small cuttings, maybe only an inch long, put into a compost of peat and sharp sand, without necessarily removing the lower leaves. Bottom heat is a great help. The lings with grey foliage are usually difficult.

The floral year begins, and ends, with *Erica carnea*, the mountain heath, which defies the weather from Christmas to Easter. The little bushes spread out into low, dense carpets. Plant them very deeply and the branches will take root as layers, giving you new stock. Start with 'King George' (best all-rounder), 'Myretoun Ruby', 'Springwood White', 'Springwood Pink', 'Foxhollow' (brilliant gold in summer), and 'Pink Spangles'. For December there are 'Queen Mary', 'Winter Beauty' and others.

Overlapping the carneas is the robust hybrid *Erica* x *darleyensis*. Several very good clones, especially 'George Rendall', 'Arthur Johnson' (December–April), 'Silberschmelze' and the golden-leaved 'Jack H. Brummage', the majority becoming broad mounds 18 in. high. Extremely good value.

Following hard on the heels of these is another breed of robust growth, averaging about 2½ ft., conical in shape. This is *Erica erigena*. 'Irish Salmon' and 'Brightness' are splendid varieties for late spring. 'Superba' is indeed superb, growing to 5 ft.

All these so far will do splendidly in limy soils and in clay, but we now have to be a thought more careful as spring strides in and we meet the taller 'tree' heaths. *Erica arborea*, the largest of these, from the roots of which 'briar' pipes are made, is really too big for us. Possibly we might accommodate the Spanish heath, *E. australis*, but even this grows a good 7 ft. and bellies out with aldermanic pride; the rose-purple 'Riverslea' and the white 'Mr Robert' certainly catch the eye from April to June. These will stomach a little lime, but greater dangers are snow and wind, which break the branches.

We can all, however, very profitably find room for the narrower tree heath. *E. terminalis*, the Corsican heath, which becomes a slim 6 ft., is completely tolerant of lime and does not mind a heavy soil. 'Thelma Woolner' is a pretty rose-pink cultivar, in flower from midsummer right on till autumn.

June brings us three heathers of dwarf habit, which, to be seen at their best, need soils a little different from those that we have been considering so far. First of these is *E. cinerea*, the June bell-heather, which is at its best in a hot, dry, lime-free, sandy soil. In such conditions it blazes throughout summer in a rich range of colours, the peak period being July–August. 'C.D. Eason', 'Foxhollow Mahogany', 'Stephen Davis', 'Knap Hill Pink', 'Pink Ice', 'P.S. Patrick' and 'Pentreath' lead the field for brilliance of flower, and to them are added some very attractive cultivars with foliage of a more-or-less golden hue, notably 'Apricot Charm', 'Ann Berry', 'Golden Drop' and 'Windlebrooke'.

E. tetralix, the cross-leaved heath, starts at about the same time and often stretches right out into September. To get the best results here you must give them a place that is moist, cool and lime-free. The characteristics of *E. tetralix* are that (with one exception) it carries a cluster of little, drooping blossoms at the tips of erect stems and that the foliage is nearly always grey – a combination seen to charming effect in 'Hookstone Pink', now rivalled by 'Pink Star' (the only one so far that holds its blossoms erect instead of drooping). 'Con Underwood', crimson, is a long-established favourite of great merit.

E. ciliaris, the Dorset heath, has the same sort of flowering season. Its needs are a moist, sunny, lime-free position. A severe winter may damage it, but rarely kill it. The best-known varieties are 'Mrs C.H. Gill' and 'Corfe Castle'. They grow rather more strongly than *E. cinerea* and *E. tetralix*, often more than a foot high and wide.

August brings us the rich splendours of the Cornish heath, *E. vagans*. Usually growing about 18 in. high, they are a great success in heavy soils and will tolerate a mild dose of lime. Most of them will flower for a good ten weeks. Easily the leader, and one of the finest of all heathers, is the dusky pink 'Mrs D.F. Maxwell', but you would be charmed also by 'Saint Keverne', 'Diana Hornibrook' and the white 'Lyonesse'. Something of an oddity in this company is the gleaming golden dwarf 'Valerie Proudley'. It holds its colour all the year and makes a dense mass of about 10 in. high; very attractive.

Before we finish with the ericas, two hybrids are to be noted. One is the outstanding *E.* x *watsonii* 'Dawn', whose soft purple blossoms are borne virtually all summer, especially if spent ones are occasionally snipped off. Having dense foliage, it makes a very nice mini-hedge. The other and much newer hybrid to notice is *E.* x *stuartii* 'Irish Lemon'. Its foliage is bright lemon in spring, gradually turning green, with soft purple blossoms as in *E. tetralix*, one of its parents. 'Irish Orange' is its non-identical twin.

Amidst this great wealth of ericas, which have brought us very nearly back to the winter cheers of *E. carnea*, two other superlative breeds of heather have been challenging our attention. The first in point of time is the so-called Irish heath, *Daboecia cantabrica*. This is noted for its extra-large bells, dangling loosely on tall, slim spires. Most of them bloom non-stop from June to October. 'Atropurpurea', 2 ft. high, is the outstanding one, but an exciting new hybrid has been raised of which 'William Buchanan' is the pioneer.

The Irishmen are a small clan but the calluna is a vast one, although there is only the one species, *C. vulgaris*. This is the traditional 'heather' or ling. The flowering season is extensive and various, but the peak is August–September. Provided that they are kept well away from lime, the lings will prosper in any reasonably good soil and are even tolerant of some shades. There is particular merit in those cultivars that have tall, densely packed spires of blossom, as in 'H.E. Beale', 'Peter Sparkes', and 'Elsie Purnell', which may reach 2 ft., but quite as beautiful are the dwarfer sorts such as 'J.H. Hamilton' and 'County Wicklow'. It is in the lings, moreover, that one finds the most splendid manifestations of coloured foliage; as in 'Beoley Gold', 'Sunset', 'John F. Letts', 'Gold Haze', 'Robert Chapman', 'Joy Vanstone' and 'Golden Feather'. In 'Silver Queen' and a few others we find foliage that is not silver, but an agreeable blue-grey.

Be careful of the company that you choose for heathers. One thinks instinctively of dwarf conifers. The dwarfer rhododendrons and the variegated pieris are charming. The dwarf barberries and *Hebe armstrongii* are very good and less often seen. In limy soils heathers mingle well with the smaller brooms (*Cytisus* and *Genista*) and with the blue rue.

Of recent years heathers (and other plants) have been attacked in some parts of the country by a nasty soil-borne fungus imported from the Far East; it has an equally nasty name, *Phytophthora cinnamomi*.

19

THE LAWN

For generations it has been an accepted fact that the lawn is the foundation and the special characteristic of the British garden. But in our hurried life today there are difficulties. Per square yard of ground, the lawn, if it is to be only reasonably good and reasonably well-groomed, occupies more man-hours than any other part of the garden. Our fathers, and many enthusiasts still today, would go over every square yard, marked out by garden line, eradicating by hand those weeds not amenable to mass destruction. It is worth it, of course. But if economy of labour is really a major consideration, then have the maximum amount of ground under flowers, vegetables or fruit, as the French and others do.

The best conditions for a really good grass lawn are: good drainage, a rich top spit, a fairly acid soil and a situation not too overhung with trees. As a rule one wants also a level surface but, unless for games, this is by no means essential. A slight slope, or very gentle undulations, can be very attractive, provided the mower is able to do its job. After levelling, the ground is prepared either for sowing grass seed or for laying turves. Seeding is the slower but the cheaper and easier method, and on the whole the better.

LAWNS FROM SEED

On no account buy cheap seed; you will regret it. Avoid mixtures containing the ryegrasses unless you want only a rough job. Go to a good firm and state as exactly as you can your own circumstances and requirements. Get a mixture that has been treated with a bird repellent. There are grasses to meet all sorts of needs – mixtures for shade or half-shade, for the hard uses of the tennis-court or the softer uses of bowls, for hot, dry, sandy soils, for damp places and for smoky towns. You cannot, however, expect any grass to succeed under the dense gloom of a cedar or a big hungry beech.

Subject to the weather, the ideal time for sowing is the third week of August, but you must prepare the ground well in advance and leave it fallow, so that dormant weeds may germinate and be got rid of before sowing. The old rule was to prepare in spring. If circumstances prevent this course, then at least make certain to get the digging done a full month ahead of sowing, or you will be in trouble. In the south sowing can be delayed until nearly the end of September. Alternatively it may be done in late March.

If the ground has previously been well cultivated, dig one spit down only, but on new ground or in old neglected gardens where there may be a hard pan of soil below, break up the second spit with the fork. Dress the top spit well with whatever organic matter you can spare or afford and work in plenty of peat. Level off.

A week before sowing, having got rid of the weeds, apply a top-dressing of fertiliser; level with exactitude and work the soil into a seed-bed of fine tilth by treading and raking as described in Sowing outdoors, Chapter 6. All this must be done, of course, when the soil is neither sodden nor parched by drought.

When you come to sowing, the problem is to spread the seed evenly, and on large areas it is necessary to mark it out in strips or squares, and weigh out the seed proportionately. Use the broadcasting method, and sow half the seed working up and down the length of the area, and the other half broadwise. The normal rate is 1½ oz. per square yèd. (40 g. per sq. m.) if the seed is good and the condition right. Sowing completed, rake the ground lightly in one direction and then cross-rake, to cover the seed partially. Seed that has not been treated with bird repellent needs a defensive network of black thread on little sticks.

When the young grass is a good 2 in. high, give it a light rolling to firm the roots and next day a light mowing with the blades set high. Actually scything is best, if in these days of 'progress' you can find an exponent of that dying art.

FROM TURF

Turves may be laid at any season if the weather is not frosty or too dry. A one-spit digging is normally enough, but feed the top spit with a good fertiliser, work in some peat, level off and allow the ground to settle.

Having raked the surface of the soil to a tilth, fit the turves in to one another, not too tightly, bonding them so that the ends of those in one row overlap those in the previous row, as when laying bricks. Do not tread on the ground that you are going to turf. Instead, starting at one corner, lay the first row of turves while standing outside the area. Then put down some planks on this first row and stand on these planks to lay the second and subsequent rows. Fill any gaps between the sods with peat or fine soil, and correct any unevenness of surface by adding or taking away a little soil from underneath. Beat each turf down with a turf-hammer, which is a flat, heavy board, about 1 ft. square with a suitable handle. Water copiously if the job is done in dry weather.

After a week, give a light rolling, and mow with the blades set high.

AFTER-CARE

The major canons of lawn maintenance are: occasional good top-dressing, weeding, raking, spiking and minimum rolling. In rather more details the main requirements are as follows:

Mowing. Don't cut the grass too short. But cut frequently; twice a week when the grass is growing fast. Little and often is the rule of mowing. Change the direction of your mowing 'lanes' occasionally. Cut less frequently in long dry spells; if obliged to cut in drought, leave the hood off. Stop mowing when frosts begin, but in mild winter spells further occasional mowings may be beneficial. Except for a rough job or an awkward bank, stick to a cylinder mower, not a rotary; *see* Chapter 4.

Rolling. Except for special purposes and occasions, rolling is now a thing of the past; it compacts the soil. The roller of a good cylinder mowing machine is enough.

Watering. If any has to be done, it must be copious, and a sprinkler of some sort is essential; a mere wetting of the surface in very dry weather may do more harm than good.

Raking and spiking. Aeration of the soil and clearance of half-decayed matter are of great benefit. Any sweepings with besom or dragbrush, piercings with garden fork or spiker, or scarifying with spring-toothed rake are good, especially in autumn, and especially before applying any kind of top-dressing. Rake before the first mowing in spring also. In autumn sweep up fallen leaves.

Weeds. Nowadays lawn weeds are almost entirely controlled by chemicals, which 'select' between the fine leaves of grasses and the broader ones of weeds. Some are applied as liquids, others in granular or powder form; for the latter you will need a 'spreader', which you can usually hire from a local shop.

If infestation is bad use one of these 'hormone' weedkillers, based on the 2, 4-D or the MCPA formulas. Do not let the stuff drift on to adjacent flower-beds; do not use it on new-made lawns for at least a year; and do not use mowings of recently treated grass on the compost heap nor as a mulch on beds. Clovers and mosses are difficult to tackle and the nimble-minded chemist has concocted special poisons for each; all you have to do is to obey the orders that he gives on the package. Repeated use of these hormone weedkillers tends to have a depressant effect on grass.

Where the infestation is not bad, one combines a weedkiller with a fertiliser – a 'weed and feed' concoction – of which most manufacturers in this market have their own brews, such as Toplawn and Murphy Lawn Phostrogen Feed and Weed and others that I know not of. Dandelions and other tough guys succumb at once to Elliott's Touchweeder or to 'spot' treatment. The pretty little blue-eyed speedwell will yield to Iotox.

Feeding. A 'feed' without 'weed' is as necessary to hard-pressed lawns as is a tonic to a run-down man. While the prime needs are for sulphate of ammonia in spring and sulphate of potash in autumn, many other influences are needed also. Instead of a long and boring essay, it might help learner-gardeners if I set out the routine I try to follow in my own small garden (in Surrey clay).

Early April. Dress with lawn-sand, an old weed-and-feed of great merit. If I was allowed only one lawn dressing, this would be it. Good against moss. Apply when the soil is dry, but turn on the hose if no rain falls within 48 hours. Be not alarmed if the sand scorches the grass for a few days.

Mid-May. A weed-and-feed that attacks a wider range of weed such as those mentioned a few paragraphs above.

Late July. A tonic feed applied by watering-can, such as Phostrogen Soluble Lawn Food or Maxicrop; the last is most effective if given in several applications.

Late September. Apply an autumn lawn dressing.

The expert could easily pick holes in this programme, but I have found it a useful rule of thumb, subject to the weather.

LAWN AILMENTS

The pests of lawns are ants, worms, leatherjackets and bitches; occasionally moles.

For ants there are plenty of proprietary poisons. Ants can be very destructive. Act quickly before the young emerge on the wing.

Worm casts are very bad for the health of grass. Scatter them with a besom or broom before mowing. If there is a bad infestation treat the lawn in autumn with chlordane.

Leatherjackets are the fat, grey, legless, stumpy grubs of the daddy-long-legs. They cause irregular brown patches of dead grass, the roots of which they have eaten. Biological control with the nematode *Steinernema carpocapsae* is possible in summer.

Moles. Gas with special 'fuses' or employ the mole-trapper.

Bitches' urine. Try heavy drenchings with water.

Less easily diagnosed than attacks by pests are those caused by disease.

The commonest is the fusarium patch disease. Brown or reddish brown patches up to a foot in diameter, most prominent in autumn.

Corticium disease produces large, straw-coloured patches with tiny, red hairs on the dead grass, in late summer.

Dollar spot. Very small, light-brown patches. Not very common.

In all cases treat with lawn-sand in spring and an autumn lawn dressing. Spike the lawn well in autumn and/or spring.

PART THREE: FOOD

20

FRUIT

I'm afraid there is no doubt that fruit gets terribly neglected in most private gardens. Enormous crops are lost every year. The main reason is that people are vague about pruning and spraying. And yet, except on the apple and the pear, these are simple tasks.

If there is room, and in even a quarter of an acre there is, fruit is best grown apart. Alternatively, greater use should be made of walls and fences. Pears and certain cherries and other *Prunus* species do awfully well on house walls. The redcurrant makes a splendid fan, even on a north wall, and looks highly decorative. It is also quite delightful as a little standard tree, like a rose, and as such, ornamented with drooping red jewels, takes a worthy place in any flower border. The gooseberry can be easily trained as a cordon or espalier on a fence. Blackberries and logans can earn a dividend on a shady fence.

Whatever the circumstances, don't dot your fruits about the kitchen garden in a random manner; if they have to be put there, plant them in straight lines in a section to themselves and face the fact that, once they are well grown, very few vegetables will grow successfully beneath them. Problems of space are made easier by using cordons and other 'artificial' forms, and by employing special stocks for apples and pears that keep the tree very dwarf. Moreover, the tree fruits, especially cherries, are in themselves ornamental, and can serve both beauty and economy in the flower garden instead of occupying vegetable space. A bush or standard apple never looks better than in a cottage garden surrounded by annual flowers.

The general requirements stated in the following sections on soil, planting, etc., will not be repeated in the notes on the individual fruits unless need arises.

Definitions (additional to those in Chapter 7)

Tree fruits. Those which, in their natural habit, make thick-limbed structures – apples, pears, plums, cherries, etc.; the term used is irrespective of the tree's shape – whether standard, bush, cordon, etc.

Stone fruits. Those that have hard kernels – cherry, plum, peach, etc. – all species of the genus *Prunus*.

Bush fruits. Gooseberries, redcurrants, blackcurrants.

Cane fruits. Blackberries, raspberries and their hybrids.

To pinch. To prune with the finger-nails.

Secondary. A little shoot that sprouts as the result of summer pruning or pinching.

Wood or growth bud. A bud that will later grow into a branch; it is pointed and lies close to the parent branch.

Fruit bud. A plumper, rounder bud that will bear blossom and, later, fruit.

SITUATION AND SOIL

Contrary to popular belief, the hilltop or upper hillside is a better situation for fruit than the valley. The worst enemy of fruit is late frost after the blossom has formed, and although the hilltop may be swept by wind, it is the valley that holds the frost. In frosty bottoms the less hardy fruits, if attempted, should be trained on a warm wall. Shelter from the east wind is always desirable, as the pollinating insects funk it in very early spring.

Tree fruits should be planted in full sun, though the morello cherry is famous as a north-waller. The currants and berries will stand quite a lot of shade, but will fruit earlier in the sun.

The soil that most fruits like is medium loam, not too rich. They adapt themselves to most conditions, but thin, sandy loams of a pale hue and cheesy, unworked clays are unpropitious. All (bar the strawberry, which is in a class apart) tolerate lime, especially the *Prunus* species, which will thrive in chalky soils, though solid chalk less than 3 ft. from the surface creates difficulties. The really important thing is good drainage, though not the excessive drainage of solid gravel and sand. The general prescription for soil treatment is this:

Dig at least two spits deep. Except for bush and cane fruits, use no animal manure unless the soil is very poor: but incorporate plenty of chopped-up turves and bonemeal. Beds for tree fruits on walls should not be less than 3 ft. wide and 6 ft. long.

After the first year or two the main foods are potash (very important) and nitrogen. Give top-dressings of a manure or a balanced proprietary fruit fertiliser.

PLANTING

This is best done for nearly all fruits round about November 1st. Follow the general principles of Chapter 5, but with special emphasis on two ordinances – plant very firmly and plant shallow. All fruits, especially the canes, carry their roots near the surface and much spread out. Plant to the soil mark (except for blackcurrant), and be most careful on tree fruits not to bury the point where stock and scion were united, identifiable as a marked swelling a little above ground level. Remember to stake the larger ones firmly, inserting between tree and stake a pad of some soft material to prevent chafing of the bark. Trees to be trained on walls should be planted a good 9 in. or more out from the footings.

Planting distances naturally vary, and will be given under each fruit. I implore you not to plant them too close together.

Having planted, never put a spade or fork into the ground anywhere near the roots, which may extend well beyond the branches. Keep weeds down by one of the modern chemicals; if a hoe has to be used, merely skim the surface.

SHAPING

Space forbids any extensive description of how to train the various shapes of fruit tree, and the reader is referred for this and all other advice on fruit to the Royal Horticultural Society's excellent handbook *Fruit and Vegetable Gardening.* The artificial forms – cordon, espalier and fan – are to be highly commended for small gardens. They are *the* thing. Although apples and pears are the most usual models for these forms, the gooseberry and red-currant are equally amenable. The gooseberry as a cordon or as an espalier, and the redcurrant as a cordon, fan or standard are very economical of

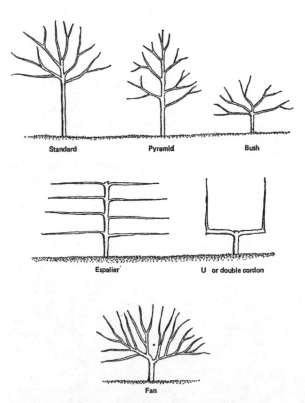

Fruit tree shapes.

space, are easy to look after and produce fruit of exhibition quality. The large, spreading fruit tree is quite out of place nowadays in small gardens.

The training of artificial forms is not difficult, but takes time. Therefore it is best to get them ready trained from a good nursery, but the process of further training will have to go on until the allotted space is filled. Fans of tree fruits need a really large wall. Espaliers and cordons don't need a wall, but an oblique cordon of apple or pear – the best job for those fruits – will go 15 ft. long if you like.

The business of shaping a natural form – standards and bushes – and the semi-natural form of a pyramid consists in principle of annually doubling the number of branches and in forming the desired shape. On apples, pears and redcurrants seek to build up a cup- or goblet-shaped framework, open in the centre. This does not apply, however, to black-currants or cane fruits, whose habit is quite different.

Do not allow any fruit to form on any plant from a nursery the first year (except strawberries). Pick off the blossom.

PRUNING

Pruning is the touchstone of successful fruit-growing, yet, as I have said, there is normally no difficulty about it except on the apple and the pear. Study the general principles in Chapter 7 before the particular directions under each fruit. The injunctions to cut out diseased and weakly twigs, and a branch that crosses another one, and so on, apply to everything. Note especially the fruits that bear on one-year-old branches and those that bear on older wood. This helps enormously in the approach to any pruning job; for, on all those breeds that fruit only or mainly on shoots grown last year, we want a constant supply of new wood, eliminating the old. Admirable examples of contrast between methods are the black- and the redcurrant, so unlike in all but their names. Sweet and sour cherries provide a similar contrast. The cane fruits are easy. So, as a rule, are the stone fruits, for, once the tree has been built up, you normally don't prune at all, unless it is grown on a wall; what has to be done on them should be done as much as possible in summer, to minimise the danger of disease.

Bear in mind that the effect of all pruning is to make the tree sprout afresh; so when the tree is young we prune hard in order to conjure up new branches, but when it is established, we normally prune more lightly in order to induce fruit. If a tree bears a poor crop in any season (other causes, such as lack of pollination, being allowed for), prune it lightly in the following winter; and in general terms remember the first rule of pruning – when in doubt, don't. As on the rose, lusty varieties, such as 'Bramley's Seedling', are pruned more lightly than others.

In fruit-growing there are several special methods of growth control. One is summer pruning. Though often a matter of high controversy, it certainly has to be practised on all the artificial forms, and is desirable also

'Pink bud' on apples or 'White bud' on pears, when the sepals of the calyx have opened, and the pink or white buds are disclosed but still unopened.

'Petal fall', when the petals are fully expanded and beginning to drop (the bee having then done its job).

Bud stages are important also in plums, cherries, blackcurrants and gooseberries.

In September, grease bands are tied round the trunks of all tree fruits to trap the wingless females of winter moths as they climb to deposit their eggs.

The paragraphs on spraying for each variety mention as a rule only the routine sprays and some special treatments. They are summaries only, and Part four should be studied for descriptions of each ailment and its antidote.

Birds are nowadays one of the grower's worst enemies. The only solution is netting and by far the best course is to enclose all fruit completely in a cage of small-mesh netting of some sort; on larger trees some dabs of grease on the branches are good bird scarers.

LABELLING

It should be evident from these notes that it is vital, especially on apples and pears, to keep the plants durably labelled.

BUYING FRUIT

Before going a line further let me implore you, Reader, to go to a specialist fruit nursery. Your little nursery round the corner *may* be knowledgeable on fruit, but you must be quite sure that he is before giving him your money. The snags are many and are often involved, as in the 'compatibility' of apples, pears and cherries. NEVER buy fruit trees from a shop or from the average garden centre that is not part of a nursery.

APPLE (*Malus domestica*)

The reader will already have gathered that the familiar apple, to grow *well* with sound and abundant fruit, is really a difficult subject. Not only is it liable to all sorts of ills, but varieties differ enormously from one another in their habits and their needs. Some fruit on spurs and others from the tips of branches, and so have to be pruned differently. Some are 'sulphur-shy', and thus need special spraying treatment. Many, such as Cox, are self-sterile and need a mate to pollinate them, a mate that must bloom at the same time. Indeed, even those rated as self-fertile need a mate for real fruitfulness. Others, again, succeed in one kind of soil, or in one county, but not in another.

However, the apple is pretty hardy. Moreover, many of the popular varieties (but by no means all) adapt themselves readily to being grown in one of the artificial forms, except the fan, that are such a blessing in small places. Grow cordons whenever you can, supporting them by a stout, enduring wire framework a good 6 ft. high, and tying them to 10 ft. bamboos fixed to the wire framework at the desired angle. Espaliers also must have support until fully built up. Vigorous varieties such as 'Bramley's Seedling' are not suited to these constricted shapes.

The root stock upon which apples have been grafted or budded is of paramount importance. One of the results of trials conducted by the East Malling Research Station over many years shows that certain stocks produce dwarf trees with great success. These stocks are designated Malling, or simply M, followed by a number. Thus M9 is a particularly dwarfing stock, also bringing apples into bearing exceptionally early. Certain varieties do better on one stock than on another, and the quality of the soil also affects choice of stock. The subject is technical, and the buyer should always consult his nurseryman.

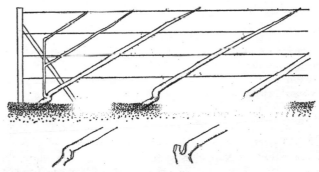

Top: *oblique cordon apples or pears (somewhat formalised).* Below: *when training new young oblique cordons, bend them over on the same side as the union of scion and stock, or there may be a broken romance.*

Few apples, if any, being wholly self-fertile, it is unprofitable to plant only one variety of apple. Whether the mate is a cooker or dessert variety doesn't matter.

Planting distances are: standards, 30 ft.; bushes 15 ft.; bushes on dwarfing stock, 10 ft.; cordons, 2½ ft., with 6 ft. between rows; espaliers, 12 ft.; dwarf pyramids, 4 ft., with 6 ft. between rows. All subject to variety and stock.

Be careful to pick apples at the right time. The early ones, such as 'Beauty of Bath', should be consumed as soon as ripe, for they will not keep. Others should be picked before they are ripe, and allowed to mature in store. The test for fitness to pick is whether the apple parts readily from the bough on being merely lifted up in the hand, or with only a just perceptible twist; but all should be gathered in by about mid-October. Handle them gently, to avoid bruising.

Store in a place that is cool, rather on the damp side, dark or partially so, ventilated, and having a temperature varying as little as possible. A well-ventilated and slightly damp cellar is ideal, a north-facing shed is good, a dry attic bad. Wrapping is desirable, but not essential for most varieties. Newspaper is quite satisfactory. Not tissue paper. Do not store any diseased, damaged, or bruised fruit, nor any stalkless ones.

Pruning

Apples fruit on wood that is two years old or more, except the tip-bearers.

Once the framework of the young tree has been built up, there are various courses open, according to the fruiting habit of the variety – whether spur-bearing or tip-bearing. It is really best to avoid tip-bearers, unless in the bush form on very dwarf stock (e.g. 'Bramley's Seedling' on M9). The best bet is the close-spurring variety grown as an oblique cordon – least space, least chance of going wrong in pruning, and easiest to get at.

Differences in variety and in stock, however, are by no means the only guide to correct pruning. Even with the same variety, what is right in my garden may be wrong in yours. All sorts of influences, including the soil, are at work. General principles, intelligent observation, trial and error must be our guides. On no account ever allow the hired hand to commit the crime of the 'annual haircut' which is all too common. However, with these reservations, the following will be a useful general guide.

Natural forms (bush and standard). Prune according to vigour and spurring habit. Thus:

(a) Those that bear fruit on short spurs: shorten laterals back to four buds in December, and shorten leaders by a half. E.g. 'Cox's Orange Pippin'.

(b) Those that bear on long spurs: shorten laterals to six buds and leaders by a half. E.g. 'Laxton's Superb'.

(c) Tip-bearers: thin out overcrowded and crossing laterals, especially in the centre of the tree, and lightly tip back strong laterals. E.g. 'Worcester Pearmain'.

On bushes and standards aim to keep an outline roughly cup-shaped. Learn to recognise early the difference between a fruit-bud and a growth bud.

If in doubt, or the variety is not known, try pruning different parts of the tree by each method, and observe results.

Artificial forms. Summer-prune laterals back to five strong leaves about 31st August, and in December cut further back to three buds – a little less severely on long spurrers.

Old neglected trees, bristling at the tip of each branch with tufts like witches' brooms, may need drastic doctoring. Whole branches may have to

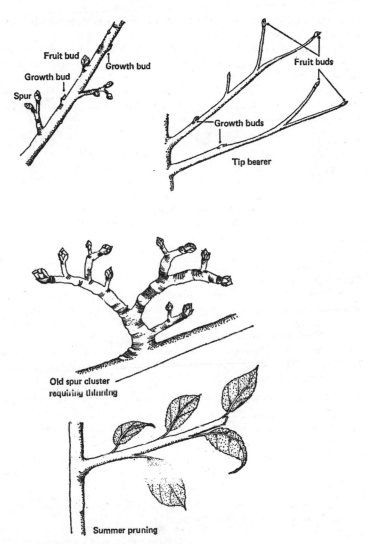

Apple and pear: buds, spurs, summer pruning.

be amputated and root-pruning performed. Leave the witches' brooms alone for a year, or tip them lightly, in the hope that fruit will form.

Good cultivation and pruning may actually result in overcropping. Fruit may be borne in such abundance that the tree's vitality is too heavily taxed. Then you must harden your heart, and, at whatever cost to your feelings, thin-out the fruit, using scissors. One cooking apple per six inches of branch, or a cluster of two for desserts, are the utmost limits. Thin when the fruitlets are the size of a walnut, eliminating first the 'king' fruit in the centre of a cluster. Allow for the 'June drop' when apples naturally cast off many of their young. A few varieties, moreover, such as 'Laxton's

Bud stages on apple and pear, important for spraying: 'mouse-ear', 'green cluster', 'pink bud' ('white bud' on pear).

Superb' and 'Miller's Seedling', are prone to 'biennial cropping', bearing heavily one year and resting the next.

Spraying etc.

Mancozeb or carbendazim against scab and mildew at green–cluster stage and again at pink bud. Pyrethrins against sawfly in early May (after blossom fall) and again a week later. The same against codlin moth in mid–June and three weeks later.

The imported fire–blight disease, carried by bees, is now savaging apples (and some related plants). Blossoms are blackened, leaves withered without falling, stems discoloured. Very dangerous. No cure. Cut out affected branches entire; maybe the whole tree will have to go.

Varieties to choose

Get rid of the idea that 'Cox's Orange Pippin', noble fruit though it is, is the only apple. Cox is not easy to grow unless the conditions are just right, is a failure in most parts of the North and Midlands, and is very disease-prone.

Apples are creatures of strong local patriotism. The best apple for Somerset may be one that the Yorkshireman has never heard of. So the first step to wisdom is to get local advice from the county horticultural adviser or other authority. Out of some 500 varieties, I have chosen, under the guidance of Mr. Harry Baker, Fruit Officer of the RHS, a mere handful of those most widely grown. All have a high excellence of flavour.

Several apples are equally good for dessert or cooking, including 'Charles Ross', 'Rival' (a good one), 'Blenheim Orange' and 'Wagener'. Economically, desserts are the things to grow rather than the cookers. Reasonable cookers can be readily got in the shops; good desserts are rare indeed. What greengrocer has ever heard of 'Orleans Reinette'?

All in these lists form their fruits on spurs and so are good for growing as cordons or espaliers, except for the three tip-bearers mentioned. The times for picking and the seasons of use are as for the south; in the north add a fortnight.

Desserts

'Discovery'. A very fine modern apple for early consumption. Non-keeping. Pick in August.

'Worcester Pearmain'. Pick as ripe for use Sept–Oct. Tip-bearer. Must be grown in bush form on M7 or MM 106.

'James Grieve'. Pick September for immediate use. First class. Mate for Cox. Rather prone to canker.

'Ellison's Orange'. Spicy aniseed flavour, which some dislike. Pick late Sept for immediate use. Very good in North and Midlands.

'Lord Lambourne'. Lovely apple and heavy cropper, but you emphatically must get it on EMLA stock to be sure it is virus-free. Pick late Sept. Keeps till Nov.

'Laxton's Fortune'. Pick Sept. Keeps till Nov. Scab-resistant. Good in the North.

'Sunset'. One of the very best. Pick 1st Oct for use till Dec. Very heavy cropper but fruit rather small unless thinned. Compact habit.

'Cox's Orange Pippin'. World-famous. Pick mid-Oct for Nov–Jan. For mild districts and good soil only. Disease-prone. Sulphur-shy. Give extra potash.

'Egremont Russet'. For those who like russets. Nutty flavour. Pick end Sept for Oct–Nov.

'Spartan'. Modern late-keeper (Nov–Jan). Mahogany-red fruits. Vinous flavour. Pick late Oct.

'Laxton's Superb'. Cox like flavour; good substitute for it in colder counties. Forms long spurs. Pick mid-Oct for Nov–Feb. Heavy but biennial cropper.

'Orleans Reinette'. Gorgeous flavour, rich and aromatic. Pick mid-Oct for Nov–Jan.

Cookers

'Arthur Turner'. Oct–Dec. Very reliable.

'Bramley's Seedling'. The most famous, but in small spaces must emphatically be grown only on M9 as a bush, being a tip- and spur-bearer. No good as a cordon. Pick mid-Oct for Nov–April.

'Lane's Prince Albert'. The tops. Pick Oct for Nov–April. Long spurs. Sulphur-shy.

'Crawley Beauty'. Very hardy and good. Pick mid-Oct for Dec–April.

'Grenadier'. Dwarfish and early (Aug–Sept). Excellent. Good pollinator for Bramley.

'Edward VII'. Hardy and scab-resistant. Pick Oct for Jan–April.

'Newton Wonder'. Famous sort, but must be grown in bush form on M26; tip-bearer; sulphur-shy. Pick mid-Oct for Nov–April.

'Wellington'. Hardy and stores well, extra good for baking, but disease prone. Long spurs. Pick mid-Oct for Dec–March.
'Encore'.Very good-flavoured late variety. Pick late Oct for Dec–April.

APRICOT (*Prunus armeniaca*)

In benign districts, free of frost pockets, apricots can be grown in the open as far north as Ayrshire, given a south-facing wall. Grow them as fans.They are self-fertile, so a lone tree can be grown, but, as the blossoms come out earlier than the average bee, hand-pollination with a camel-hair brush or something of the sort is usually necessary. Cultivate as for a fan-trained peach but prune as a fan-trained sweet cherry; they form spurs.

Varieties
'Moorpark' and 'New Large Early'.

BLACKBERRY (*Rubus fruticosus*)

Easy and delightful, but enormously improved if well fed. Dig in plenty of well-rotted organic matter, top-dress with bonemeal, and don't forget the potash.

Plant in autumn or winter at least 8 ft. apart, on a fence, wires, pillars, etc., to which the canes must be tied. They will succeed in shade but prefer sun. After planting cut the canes right down to within a foot of the ground.

Blackberries fruit best on one-year canes. After fruiting is over, cut the old canes right to the ground. As the new ones shoot up each year tie them in away from the old, so that the two don't get entangled, otherwise there will be the dickens of a mess. Handle the new shoots with care, as they are brittle – as well as prickly. Use gloves. After the old canes have been cut out, rearrange the new ones.

Multiply stock either by digging up suckers from around the base of the plant, or allow the tips of some shoots to droop to the ground and

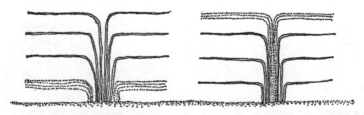

Two methods of training blackberries and loganberries to prevent a murderous entanglement; new shoots in dotted lines.

weight them down with a stone. The tip will take root. In February sever it from its parent and transplant where required.

Varieties

The old 'Parsley-leaved' blackberry (of which there is a thornless form) is still best: there are various hybrids – Boysenberry, Youngberry, etc. – but none are as good as the blackberry. 'Himalayan Giant' is very good, but the plant enormous.

BLACKCURRANT (*Ribes nigrum*)

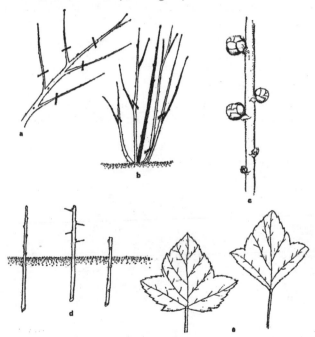

a, *branch of an established redcurrant; prune new laterals to two buds and shorten leader one-half; treat each branch the same.* **b**, *blackcurrant bush; preserve the new wood (black) and cut the old fruited shoots either to the ground or to a strong new shoot.* **c**, *'big bud' on a blackcurrant, with healthy buds below.* **d**, *bush-fruit cuttings – redcurrant, gooseberry, blackcurrant (lower buds not removed),* **e**, *'reversion' in blackcurrants: left, a healthy leaf; right, a diseased one.*

Another easy one. Plant 6 ft. apart. In contrast to the normal rule, bury the old soil mark about 3 in. deep. Cut all shoots down to 4 in. of the ground after planting.

Normally, blackcurrants are subject to two main afflictions. Commonest is 'big bud', a swelling caused by minute creatures; remove and burn them. The other is 'reversion', in which the normally broad leaf becomes narrow and pointed, lacking the basal lobes. Incurable. Cut out diseased canes or scrap the whole plant.

Pruning
The blackcurrant carries its fruit mainly on young branches grown last season. Just as on a climbing rose, some new shoots spring from the ground, others from half-way up an old shoot. Therefore, as soon as fruiting is over, prune the old fruited shoots back to a point where a *strong* new one has sprouted, and cut other old shoots down to the ground according to the number of new ones that have sprung from there; cut out all weak shoots.

Propagation
Take cuttings in mid-autumn from new wood grown that summer. Use the lower part of the shoot, cut just below a node, shorten it from the upper end to about 10 in. and plant firmly *without removing any buds*, and with only two buds above ground.

Varieties
'Boskoop Giant' (early), 'Seabrook's' (mid-season), 'Baldwin' (late), 'Jet' (very late).

CHERRY (*Prunus avium*)

With only one or two exceptions, cherries are all self-sterile. The exceptions are the 'sour' or cooking cherries (*Prunus cerasus*), most notably the famous 'Morello'. 'Morello' will pollinate many of the sweet or dessert cherries, but sweet cherries certainly must never be planted in one variety alone. The subject is involved and the nurseryman should be consulted, but whatever you choose the birds are likely to get the lot. You are warned.

The sweet cherries do best as standards, in which form they are very decorative but take up a lot of space. Several, however, do take kindly to being grown as fans on a large wall where they can be netted against birds. 'Morello' is famous for its enormous merit of flourishing on a north wall. Some skill is needed for wall training.

Pruning
As on other stone fruits, do no more pruning than is essential. Whatever may be necessary, as on wall fans, do in June, and June only. Sweet cherries fruit on wood two years old and more, and they spur readily. The 'Morello', however, bears on one-year-old branches. So –
Sweet cherries. As standards and bushes, normally no pruning. On walls – when laterals have made six leaves in summer, pinch back to three or four, and pinch out resultant secondaries. Should an old branch become worn out, train in a young one to replace it.
Sour cherries. Old wood must be replaced after fruiting. Prune as for fan-trained peaches. Do not pick 'Morello' cherries with their stalks; cut the stalks with scissors.

Sprays

Pyrethrins etc., against observed pests. Watch for silver leaf. Apply grease-bands in September.

Varieties

Desserts: 'Early Rivers' is the queen, but very large. Next, I would today have 'Waterloo' and 'Noir de Guben'. Between them all three will be pollinated.

CURRANTS. *See under* Blackcurrant and Redcurrant.

DAMSON. *See under* Plum.

FIG (*Ficus carica*)

Figs are not to be recommended for small gardens, but for those who have any already the following notes on pruning should correct the usual errors.

Figs fruit mainly on young branches grown last year – in fact the fruit begins to form the same year as the branch grows, and over-winters. After leaf-fall cut some of the old fruited wood right out and train in the strongest new shoots as annual replacements. In early summer pinch back to six leaves new side-shoots that are not wanted for replacement or for extension of the older shoots.

Root-pruning is equally important. Figs ought to be planted in concrete or brick pits about 3 ft. deep and 4 ft. square. If this has not been done, root-prune occasionally in October. Never give any manure. Figs need a harsh, stony diet, or they will run to leaf.

If you want to plant a fig, use 'Brown Turkey' as a fan on a warm wall.

GOOSEBERRY (*Ribes uva-crispa*)

The gooseberry fruits mainly on two-year-old branches and partly on those one-year-old. Otherwise it behaves very much like an apple. It forms little spurs fairly readily and submits willingly to being trained in any of the artificial forms. The cordon – single, double, or triple – is *the* way to grow them, stopping them when 6 ft. high or less.

Gooseberries do well in partial shade, but prefer sun. Like other bush fruits, they need a soil rich in animal or vegetable manure. Plant bushes and espaliers 5 ft. apart, single cordons 1 ft., doubles 2 ft. and triples 3 ft.

Pruning

On artificial forms summer-prune laterals, but not leaders, after five leaves have developed; winter-prune them to 2 in., and shorten each year's new leader growth by a half till full height is reached.

For the usual bush shape there is a choice of methods –

For fine fruit, treat each branch as a cordon, reducing leaders by a half in winter.

For general purposes, adopt this method. In winter thin out over-crowded and overlapping new shoots, especially in the centre. Of those retained, shorten strong ones by a half and others by a mere inch. Shorten leaders according to habit – on erect varieties reduce by a half to an outward-pointing eye, on drooping varieties cut at the top of the arch to an upward eye.

Propagation

After leaf-fall take shoots of the current season's growth. Shorten if necessary (from the tip end) to about 12 in. Remove all buds except three or four at the top. Plant very firmly about 8 in. deep. At the end of the first season lift and replant 12 in. apart. Ready for permanent quarters at the end of the second year, when shaping will be necessary.

Sprays

Tar-oil wash in winter. Spray with Mancozeb or carbendazim against mildew just before flowers open.

Varieties

Gooseberries have strong local associations, especially in the North. Do enquire accordingly, but 'Langley Gage', 'Howard's Lancer', 'Lancashire Lad', and 'Careless' are all good. Don't pick too soon; wait for them to sweeten.

Worcesterberry (*Ribes divaricatum*) looks like a blackcurrant but tastes like a gooseberry. Prune as for gooseberry.

GRAPE (*Vitis vinifera*)

This must be dealt with rather tersely, on the assumption that the reader has already had a year or two's general experience.

Soil

Dig three spits and mix in old turves in abundance, mortar rubble or small broken chalk and bonemeal. No manure unless the soil is very poor indeed. If drainage is suspect, lay in a 6 in. course of brick rubble covered with upside-down turves.

To save a season, it is best to get 'fruiting vines' – those which are ready to fruit next season if you were foolish enough to allow it. When planting, disentangle the roots and fan them out well, working in fine sifted soil.

Outdoors

In genial districts, on a warm sunny wall, a few varieties can be grown successfully. For the average amateur, probably the most reliable dessert grapes are 'Chasselas', 'Royal Muscadine', and 'Boskoop Glory'. The culture of grapes for Bacchanalian purposes is outside my brief and to a large extent outside my knowledge.

Training

For fruit, grow as a cordon or as a 'toasting fork'. For a cordon, cut the fruiting vine down to about 4 ft. the winter of planting, and it will probably reach the desired height the following summer. Stop it there. Perhaps a better practice is to allow only 3 ft. of growth a year (doing the cutting-back in early winter). Meanwhile summer-prune laterals at 12 in., and later winter-prune to two buds. For the gridiron style, cut rather lower and train out two laterals right and left for possibly 6 ft. Prune each as a cordon. Then allow laterals to form on these at about 3 ft. intervals and train them upwards, pruning each as a cordon.

Pruning

Induce spurs about every 12 in., rubbing out any buds that sprout between the spurs. Pinch new shoots from the spurs at two leaves beyond the bunches of blossom, and pinch secondaries at one leaf. If no blossom appears on a shoot, pinch at 2 ft. *After leaf-fall* cut back all laterals, whether fruited or not, to two buds, and next year allow only one of these buds to grow. Allow no fruit till the second season and then very little. Except for summer pinching, *never* cut vines after January 1st, or they bleed. If bleeding occurs treat with a styptic pencil or char with a red-hot iron.

As the fruit swells it must be thinned. Using the proper pointed scissors, snip off the berries *inside* the bunch while quite tiny – more severely towards the tip than at the shoulders. Do not touch the grapes by hand, but manoeuvre them with a stick.

Indoors

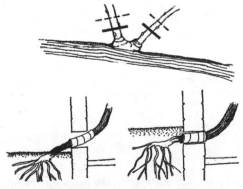

The grape. Top: *winter-prune to two buds (dotted lines); if both buds sprout next spring, trim back to one (thick lines)*. Bottom: *greenhouse vine with roots outside; two methods of planting – note different soil levels.*

The old 'Black Hamburg' (correctly 'Schiava Grossa'), its rival 'Muscat Hamburg' and 'Buckland Sweetwater' are tipped for an unheated or only slightly heated house.

The greenhouse must be properly equipped with wires beneath the glass. Plant the vine in a bed outside the house, leading it through a hole at ground level in the wall; heaven should then do the watering.

Plant indoor vines in March. Train and prune as for outdoors. Don't permit a dense mass of leafage. If only one vine is grown, train as a gridiron, making the initial amputation at such a height that, when the two laterals grow out, they will be above the level of the greenhouse's brickwork.

Winter treatment

At pruning time, or not later than 1st January, untie all the rods and let them droop down, suspended by strings, till they sprout in the spring, then re-hoist. This encourages the formation of new growth evenly along the rods. On old vines remove the loose bark by rubbing with the hand (not a knife) when the rods are bare in winter, to guard against mealybug, a white, waxy louse hidden beneath a white froth.

Humidity

Give maximum ventilation as the weather dictates, but shut up the house an hour before sunset except in very hot spells. When growth starts, syringe the foliage occasionally on warm days with rain-water from the tank inside the greenhouse until the blossoms appear. Then tap the rods daily to disperse pollen. After ten days renew the syringing, but stop again when the fruit begins to colour. Likewise slightly damp the floor and walls daily in the warm months, but only twice a week during flowering and after colouring. Don't overdo this inside wetting, or mildew will be invited. In dry periods drench the border where the vine is rooted. When the sun is at its most powerful some form of shading must be given.

In winter let in all the frost and ice you can (once any chrysanthemums are out of the way), but, where there is any heat, turn it on in February to induce growth till the sun warms up.

Sprays

Spray with mancozeb or carbendazim at the first sign of mildew. If the woolly patches of mealybug are seen, brush stiffly with methylated spirit.

GREENGAGE. *See under* Plum.

LOGANBERRY

Believed to be a cross between a blackberry and a raspberry. Cultivate as for the blackberry, including the spray programme.

Multiply stock by tip-rooting in summer. Transplant carefully, as the roots, like the young canes, are brittle.

NECTARINE (*Prunus persica* var. *nectarina*)

Is a variation on the theme of peach, and its cultivation is exactly the same. Smaller in size and smooth-skinned, it has the general appearance of a plum. Perhaps the most exquisite of all fruit. Slightly less hardy than the peach, it should be fan-trained on a warm wall.

Varieties

'Early Rivers' and 'Lord Napier', both maturing in August, are possibly the pick for all-round qualities.

PEACH (*Prunus persica*)

In all but the more austere parts of the country peaches can safely be grown out in the open, as bushes or standards, like apples, provided they are not in frost pockets. In less-favoured districts they must be fan-trained on a warm wall and protected with muslin at blossom time. Beware bullfinches.

It pays to buy a three-year-old tree on which the preliminary training has been done at the nursery; no pruning is then needed except to shorten old, exhausted branches in order to encourage new ones. The less pruning the better; when needed, do it in early June. Fruit is borne on wood of the previous season's growth. Allow for a spread of 15 ft.

Peaches like a fertile soil. Treat as advised in Situation and soil, early in this chapter, though nowadays there is less insistence on lime. Peaches are self-fertile.

As a fan. The process of building up the framework of the fan may go on for some years according to the size of the wall, but fruit-forming can be allowed concurrently. If your new plant is a three-year-old, a few 'fruiting shoots' can be allowed to grow that year for cropping next year. Part of the frame-building consists, of course, in the longitudinal extension of the main ribs as far as they will go.

The 'fruiting shoots' grow out of the main limbs. It is in the handling of these that people go wrong, yet the thing is not difficult. What happens is this:

The shoot will produce not only fruit but also some new growth-shoots or branches. You will want a new growth-shoot to replace the existing one next year, and you will want it from the base of the old. This is called the replacement shoot. So, just after the blossom has fallen, cut out all new shoots that are sprouting, except the basal one and also one near the tip a little beyond the last blossom. Allow the one near the tip to start and then pinch it beyond its fourth leaf, the purpose being to draw sap through the whole branch in order to ripen the fruit. When fruiting is over cut the whole of the old shoot back to the point where the replacement shoot begins. That is all there is to it.

In early years the tip shoot can be retained, and the whole member allowed to grow on to become part of the permanent framework. Shoots sprouting in awkward places can be stopped at two leaves.

Pruning wall-trained peach. **a**, *'Fruiting shoot', thinned to two fruits and 'stopped' beyond the last;* **b**, *sap-drawing shoot pinched at four leaves;* **c**, *shoots next to fruits pinched at two leaves;* **d**, *replacement shoot growing freely;* **e**, *fruiting shoot will be severed here after harvest;* **f**, *last year's fruiting shoot was cut here.*

The fruit also must be thinned. Allow no more than two peaches per shoot – one only on a short growth. Thin first to four per shoot when the size of a pea, and then to two when the size of a walnut.

Sprays
(*Very important*) spray against the leaf-curl disease with a copper product just before autumn leaf-fall and again in mid-February before the leaf-buds open; this is to deter the peach-leaf curl disease. Pyrethrins or derris against observed insect pests.

Varieties
Easily the best is 'Peregrine'; alternatively 'Rochester'.

PEAR (*Pyrus communis*)

Sister to the apple, the pear is a trifle less hardy. In the coldest counties, according to variety, it needs the protection of a wall, and the more *recherché* varieties are best on a wall in many districts.

Most pears readily and obediently adopt the spurring habit – a great blessing, allowing them to be shaped as espaliers and as single or multiple cordons. A few, however, are tip-bearers. Most are self-fertile or partially so, but the same care should be taken in the choice of varieties as with apples.

Special rooting stocks also are available. They are quince stocks, and the one usually most recommended now is that which is known as 'Quince A'. Some of the best varieties, however, known as 'incompatible', do not marry well with quince, and, taking two husbands as it were, have to be 'double worked'. The favourite 'William' is an example. Your safeguard is to avoid cheapjack nurseries.

Cultivation is in nearly all respects virtually the same as for the apple. On the spurring varieties summer-prune to five leaves near the end of July, and winter-prune further to 3 in. Do not summer-prune leaders on bushes and standards, and winter-prune according to vigour and habit – cut upright varieties such as 'Doyenné du Comice' by a third to outward buds, drooping varieties to upward buds, tip-bearers scarcely at all. Don't give any lime to pears unless the soil is definitely acid.

Storing
Trickier than apples, pears need an atmosphere slightly warmer and slightly drier. Handle very tenderly. Do not wrap. They must not touch each other. Examine from time to time, as they go 'sleepy' in the centre and rot rapidly.

Sprays
Against scab the simplest method is to spray with carbendazim or mancozeb in March at bud-burst (just before mouse-ear) repeating several times at 21 days interval. If caterpillars are seen use pyrethrins. Beware the fire-blight disease, to which pears are very susceptible; see under Apples.

Varieties
There is little point in growing a cooking pear, unless it be 'Catillac'; for bottling, the dessert varieties are superior. Of these, the following are prime choices:

'Doyenné du Comice', the queen of pears, large, sweet, melting, prolific, but not for cold places. Sulphur-shy. Pick early Oct.

'Conference'. Distinctive elongated shape. Prolific and hardy. Pick late Sept for Oct–Nov. Fine as a cordon. Very easy and beginner's first choice.

'Joséphine de Malines'. Delicious late pear. Pick Oct for Dec–Feb. Tip-bearing and best as a dwarf bush.

'Beurré Superfin'. Melting, sweet and aromatic. Pollinated by 'Conference'. Pick early Sept.

'Louise Bonne of Jersey'. Rich, melting, and exuberant. Pick late Sept for Oct. Easy but needs thinning.

'Williams's Bon Chrétien' (the so-called 'Bartlett' of America). Most widely known pear. Ready Sept; *pick when green*. Very disease-prone. Pollinator for 'Conference'.

'Jargonelle'. August. Dwarfish habit but heavy cropper.

'Winter Nelis'. Very late (Nov–Jan). Small, green fruits of very good flavour. Good pollinator for 'Doyenné du Comice'.

'Merton Pride'. Modern pear of excellent flavour for the south only. Sept–Oct.

'Gorham'. Hardy pear for the north for Sept use. Not a good keeper.

PLUM (*Prunus domestica*)

The plum is a very hardy fellow. The greengage is simply a celestial version of it, slightly less hardy, and (if you get the genuine article) vying with the nectarine as the most seductive of fruits. The damson and bullace (both *P. insititia*) and the sloe (*P. spinosa*) are closely related.

The standard and the bush are the usual forms, taking up much room; they *can* be grown as fans, but need a large wall and a bit of skill. There is much 'incompatibility' of stocks (*see under* Pears). There is a good semi–dwarfing stock known as 'Saint Julien A'. Plant at 15 ft. spacing.

Plums are often self-fertile, but it is best to consult the nurseryman. On the other hand, they flower so early that the bee often funks its job of pollination. If so, you must hand-pollinate.

Save as mentioned, planting distances are 30 ft. for standards, about 18 ft. for bushes, and the same for fans.

Pruning

The plum fruits on one- and two-year-old wood, spurring freely. As for peaches, the less pruning the better. It therefore pays to buy three-year-old trees, with the basic framework already built. What pruning may be necessary (e.g. crossing and rubbing branches) should be done in late May or after cropping and in dry weather (which reduces the risk of silver leaf).

Plums often over-crop heavily. Thin the fruit to about 3 in. apart, and prop up heavily laden boughs.

Sprays

Tar–oil in winter. Systemic insecticide against aphids and sawfly. If bacterial canker appears (*see* Chapter 23) apply Bordeaux mixture. Watch for silver leaf.

Varieties

'Reine Claude Vrai', the true original greengage, is most delicious of all, but very capricious in fruiting; best on a wall. A very good substitute is the more dependable 'Cambridge Gage'. Other choice ones are: 'Coe's Golden Drop', a jewel, but needs a wall in the North, self-sterile but mates with 'Victoria'; 'Early Transparent Gage', 'Imperial Gage' (syn. 'Denniston's Superb'), 'Transparent Gage', 'Jefferson'.

The best all-purpose plum – for cooking, bottling, or dessert – is 'Victoria'; self-fertile but disease-prone. Of cookers and jammers, 'Rivers's Early prolific' (syn. 'Early Rivers') and 'Pershore' (or 'Yellow Egg') are much better than the usual 'Czar'.

Likewise of damsons, the 'Prune Damson' (syn. 'Shropshire Prune') has a much better flavour than the more usual 'Merryweather Damson'.

RASPBERRY (*Rubus idaeus*)

Easy enough, but, like other cane fruits, immensely improved by enrichment of the soil with animal or vegetable manure. They do well in partial shade but prefer sun. Liberal watering and generous mulching (manure, leaves, etc.) greatly improve the crop and the quality. A neat and sturdy framework is needed for their support, one wire 2 ft. from the ground and another about 5 ft. Run the rows north–south if possible.

Plant 2 ft. apart, at least 6 ft. between rows. Cover the top roots by about 3 in. and cut the canes down to 9 in. when planting. They fruit only on canes of the previous season's growth. So the first year you will get no fruit, but a row of nice new canes to fruit next year.

Thereafter, as soon as fruiting is over, cut the old canes that have fruited, and any weakly new ones, down to the ground. If the new canes are very long, shorten to 5 ft. 6 in. in February. Autumn-fruiting varieties, if grown, are cut down in February.

Stock is readily multiplied by digging up a new cane with its roots in autumn. When hoeing, merely skim the surface.

Sprays

Derris at the first flush of pink on the fruits against the maggot of the raspberry beetle. A yellow mottling of leaves, which often curl downwards, suggests the 'mosaic' virus; burn all affected plants, complete with roots and suckers.

Varieties

Whatever the variety, it is absolutely essential to go to a specialist nursery and specify certified virus-free stock. I consider 'Lloyd George' to be quite the best; it fruits both summer and autumn. 'Malling Jewel', 'Malling Promise', and the old, late 'Norfolk Giant' are also good. For autumn 'Heritage' or 'Autumn Bliss'.

RED AND WHITECURRANT (Ribes rubrum)

Another easy one, either as a natural bush or in the artificial forms which I have mentioned and which I strongly commend. Fruits largely on two-year-old wood, and partly on one-year-old, and forms spurs readily. The whitecurrant is merely a colour variation of the red, often of finer flavour.

Cultivate, propagate, and space as for the gooseberry (not as for the blackcurrant). Whatever the shape, prune as for cordons, with summer pinching and winter cutting-back of spurring laterals. Leave leaders unpruned in summer but reduce by a half in winter. Keep the centre fairly open.

Sprays

Pyrethrins against summer aphis. Look out for coral spot, rust, and leaf spot.

Varieties

'Laxton's Number 1' is easily the best early red, and 'Red Lake' for later. 'Versailles Blanche' is a sweet and delicious white.

STRAWBERRY (*Fragaria* x *ananassa*)

Merely from the economic point of view, strawberries, like asparagus, are not worth growing in the very small place. For the limited amount of fruit they provide, all so quickly gobbled up, they take up a disproportionate amount of ground. They are best grown in the kitchen garden, taking their place in the vegetable rotation.

A slightly acid soil offers the best promise. A warm position in full sun and a rich humus content in the soil are essential. Good crops cannot be had without a heavy manurial dressing of some sort. In the top spit fork in Growmore or some other all-round fertiliser at 3 oz. per square yard.

Plant in July or August for preference; alternatively March, but if so allow no fruit to form that season. Space the plants 15 in. apart in rows of a good 2½ ft. apart. Take great care not to bury the crown of the plant, but to set it just level with the soil. Summer planting usually calls for ample watering. At the end of January work in sulphate of potash on both sides of the row at ½ oz. per square yard – an important need of strawberries.

As the fruits come on, lay down some barley or wheaten straw (not oats), to save them from soiling. This is better than polythene sheeting, which arrests circulation of air. Tuck the straw well in beneath the fruits. You must also net the bed, unless you want birds to have the lot. Arrange the nets, well off the ground, in a manner that will allow them to be easily thrown off and replaced.

Strawberries are preyed upon by many enemies. The worst are aphis, which carry virus diseases, and botrytis, a bad fungus. Against the first, spray with pyrethrins in April and afterwards as may appear necessary. Slugs can also be serious, so sprinkle some methiocarb pellets on the ground when laying the straw; this will also control the strawberry beetle.

Immediately after the berries have been gobbled up, set fire to the straw. Healthy new leaves will soon sprout. If for any reason firing is not practical, cut down the plants to 3 in. from the ground and remove their leaves with the straw for burning elsewhere.

Propagation

A strawberry plant is not much use after three years. To renew itself it throws out 'runners' that take root. Remove these until you are ready to make a new planting. Then allow only one rooting per runner, and only one or two runners per plant in the fruiting bed; but if a few plants are reserved specially for propagation, five runners may be rooted. There is no great merit in rooting the runners in pots in the ground. Let them root naturally, pegging them down with bent wires.

When rooted (in about six weeks) sever the young from their parents, lift a week later and plant in a new bed. They will fruit next year, and thus form one stage in the annual programme of renewal, which has a three-year cycle. Discard the three-year-olds, planning your space accordingly.

A strawberry runner has taken root.

Varieties

Once more, Reader, you run the risk of wasting your money if you fail to go to a specialist nursery, from whom you should be supplied with stock certified by the DEFRA Plant Health Propagation Scheme, for disease is rife among strawberries.

'Royal Sovereign' is still quite the best for flavour, but not a heavy cropper. It is prone to the usual ailments, but so are all. For a late variety, 'Cambridge Late Pine' is excellent. 'Cambridge Favourite' (resistant to mildew) and 'Redgauntlet' are heavy croppers, but of less distinguished flavour; the latter often gives a second crop in autumn and cloches will extend its season.

The so-called 'remontant' strawberries bear in irregular flushes from July till the frost, but never as heavily as the others. 'Aromel', 'Rhapsody' and 'Symphony' are good. They all want highly fertile and moisture-holding soil. Cropping deteriorates in the second year, so they are best renewed annually. Except in the milder counties, plant in spring. If a good crop is wanted in late summer, deflower the plants in late May.

Many people discern a delicate flavour in the little alpine strawberries (*F. vesca*), which fruit over a long season and have no runners. Grow them anywhere you like in the garden in partial shade. Choose 'Baron Solemacher'.

21

SIMPLE VEGETABLES AND HERBS

To grow good vegetables requires a higher standard of gardening and much more constant attention than is needed for acceptable flowers; but the economics of today, if not a natural predilection, impel many of us to grow them. A careful consideration of the space factor is first necessary.

If space is small, the kinds of vegetables which should have first priority – on economic grounds only and disregarding personal choice – are the easy salads of summer and the more difficult vegetables of winter that are often so expensive: celery, leeks, parsnips and winter greens generally.

Next in importance I would place those that ripen in summer but keep through the winter: onions, haricot beans, and such root crops as you care for. The long range of summer vegetables you will certainly grow if you have the room, particularly peas and beans, which are so delicious straight out of the garden, but generally they are an uneconomic crop for the room they take up. A row of peas, for example, is gone in no time, and the proper way to treat them is to grow them in succession – relatively small sowings at intervals of about three weeks, so that there is a continuous supply until autumn – for which you need a good deal of room.

The last things to be grown in the small garden, economically speaking, are potatoes. To sow enough for a family takes up a great deal of space. If a half-way course is decided on, then go in for early potatoes, but not main-croppers.

The average British housewife, I regret to say, is lamentably conservative in her choice of vegetables. She shies away from anything with which she is not familiar and is at the mercy of the farmer, who is not interested in the flavour of his crops but only in how many tons per acre they will yield.

So, whatever is the general plan, grow whenever you can those varieties which are a little out of the common rut. Flavour is the thing. All the varieties I suggest in the following notes are chosen, other things being equal, for the excellence of their table qualities. The mangetout, the golden waxpod bean, the calabrese broccoli, the flageolet bean, salsify, sweet corn, and the turnip grown especially for its top – these are the tasty things that make vegetable-growing worthwhile, and few of them are obtainable in the average shop.

For the same reason pick your marrows, beans, carrots, turnips and radishes, I urge you, while they are young and tender. Vegetables are for eating, not for pride of display. Look out also for some of the dwarf varieties I mention, such as the delicious dwarf French Brussels sprout, the dwarf broad bean, the dwarf lettuce; all these will save space.

GENERAL CULTIVATION

The prime secret of vegetable gardening is good digging, accompanied by the generous use of organic manure of some sort for those crops that need it; not all do, and the experienced gardener plans his digging and manuring to suit his crop rotations or sequences. Each year a part of the kitchen garden should be double-dug and dressed with rotted animal manure or an equivalent. The best time to do this is in November, but any time up to the end of February will do nearly as well. In years when plots are not due for manuring they are dug over one spit.

Lime can be important in vegetable gardens, except for potatoes. Again, by good planning, you do it to a part of the garden each year, preferably to plots intended for the cabbage tribe. Autumn liming is best on heavy soils, early spring on light ones, but you will remember that liming should be at least a month before or three months after manuring. Bear in mind that the amount of lime any soil may need depends on its acidity factor. Wherever I say in the following notes that lime must be applied, it is subject to the natural lime content of the soil and to the rotation you are following in your soil management.

Vegetables benefit greatly from chemical fertilisers also, and the amateur's best plan is to buy a good all-purpose fertiliser, such as Growmore, and follow directions. For all the usual vegetables give 1½ oz. of Growmore per square yard (50 gm. per sq. m.) two to three days before sowing. Well-preserved old soot from coal fires (not oil) and fresh wood ashes are also helpful, especially for the onion tribe.

The way in which a vegetable is started off in life affects its whole future. Be sure to sow only when the weather is suitable, and to reduce the seed-bed to a fine, loose, well-aerated tilth by raking and treading, whether the seed is sown direct into permanent quarters, as in onions, carrots, spinach, etc., or into the nursery seed-bed, as for cabbages, leeks, etc. Sow always in straight lines, running always north and south if possible. Sow very sparsely (except parsnips) and thin the seedlings as soon as you possibly can. Thinnings of cabbages, onions, lettuces, and others can be transplanted, but not those of root crops; these are commonly thinned first to half their final distances, and a second thinning follows.

When soils refuse to be worked to a really fine tilth (such as mine) sow the seeds thinly in a box or half-pot and plant out the seedlings when four leaves have developed; the proprietary composts based on peat are handy for this. This does not work for root crops, of course, and is not necessary for spinach, beans and peas, which do not need a very fine tilth.

In the vegetable garden, as in the orchard, it is quite vital to protect one's crops against pests and fungal disease. Part four deals specially with

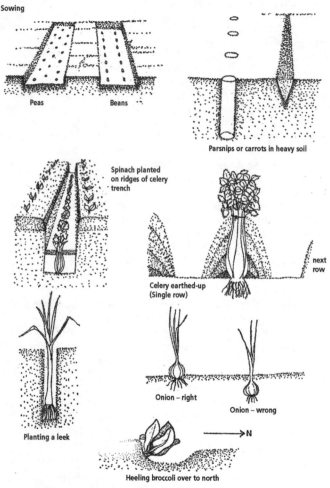

Vegetables: sowing, planting, etc.

the gardener's usual enemies, and references to them in this chapter are accordingly of a summary nature. But one may say that the afflictions one should specially guard against are birds, the pests of the soil, the little flies whose grubs attack the onion, the carrot, and the cabbage, the serious club-root disease of cabbages, the weevil that attacks the foliage of peas and beans, and the special maladies of the tomatoes and potatoes.

SPECIAL FAMILY NEEDS

For gardening purposes it is convenient to classify vegetables according to the portion of it that we generally eat; e.g. brassicas (cabbage, cauliflower, etc.); root crops (carrots, parsnips, beets, etc.); legumes or pulses (peas and beans); tubers (potatoes and Jerusalem artichokes); salads; and bulb crops (onions, shallots, leeks). In order to avoid constant repetition in the following cultural notes, I give here, for some of these groups, some general notes which must be followed for all members of their families and which will not be repeated in the individual notes.

Brassicas

For spring plantings, dig the ground deeply in autumn. Early digging allows the soil to settle, and it is essential for all brassicas to have a firm, well-consolidated bed. The ground should have been dressed in the previous or current year with manure or other organic food. It should contain lime. Before planting out, the rows should be well trodden down by foot, but the top inch or two hoed to prevent caking. Finally the seedlings should be *firmly* planted. Where greens are put out at times other than the spring the same rules apply – a deep bed rich in nitrogen, dug well ahead of planting-out time, a firm, consolidated bed, the presence of available lime, firm planting.

Brassicas are usually sown in a nursery seed-bed or in a seed-box and pricked off. Sow sparsely; twenty Brussels sprouts go a long way. If planting out has to be done in dry weather, 'puddle' the roots in a thickish mixture of clay and water. Pick off any leaves that turn yellow in autumn and consign at once to the compost bin. About the beginning of November earth up the stalks of winter-standing greens several inches, except the cauliflower type of broccoli.

Dress all seed-beds with Growmore a few days before sowing.

The particular nuisances of the brassica family are the clubroot fungus (especially in acid soils), the cabbage root-fly and caterpillars. *See* Chapter 23 for all. Practise crop rotation.

Root crops

These prefer a light or medium soil, reasonably stone-free. Heavy soils should be lightened with sand. Root crops must *not* be sown in ground recently manured; this causes the roots to split into distorted fangs. Therefore use a piece of ground which was manured for a *previous* crop; e.g. leeks or brassicas, which they may follow. Do not neglect, however, to treat the seed-rows with Growmore before sowing; give another dressing at 1 oz. per 6 ft. (35 gm. per 2 m.) run after thinning, and repeat a month later.

Root crops are almost invariably sown *in situ*, as they do not transplant, and the easiest method is to sow at stations. Parsnip seed does not germinate well, and should accordingly be sown fairly thickly. For carrots and beets you can sow at half-stations, pulling every other one for the table when small and tender.

After picking for current use, those crops which cannot stay in the ground all winter are lifted and stored before the frosts. Lift with a fork carefully so as not to cause damage, especially beetroot. Clean off clods of earth. Store in a frost-proof place between layers of slightly damped sand. Do not store any diseased, damaged or pest-bitten plants.

Root crops are liable to be bothered by underground pests, especially wireworms, which can be controlled using the nematode *Heterorhabditis megidis.*

Legumes

Peas and beans have long roots, and therefore need deeply dug soil. They are also greedy feeders, and so need plenty of organic manure, and should have the first feed of it, for preference, before the brassicas, for which, moreover, they will supply the nitrogen brassicas need so much. They also like lime. Treat the rows with Growmore before sowing, and dress with it again at 2 oz. per 6 ft. (65 gm. per 2 m.) run when the plants are well away.

Legumes are generally sown direct *in situ*, and usually in broad drills made by the draw-hoe or spade. In these broad drills the seed is often sown in staggered rows, thus: .· .· .· Distances vary, but don't crowd them. Water thoroughly in dry seasons. Foliar feeds or weekly feeds of liquid manure greatly improve crops, as do mulches of manure, lawn mowings, etc., after rain or watering; but don't overdo things.

When a crop of peas or beans is finished, cut off the stems at ground level, but leave the roots with their present of nitrogen for the next crop. The tops, or haulms, are valuable for the compost if cut when still green.

ROTATION OF CROPS

It is a general agricultural rule over all the instructed world that the same crop, or one too nearly related to it in genus, must not continually be planted in the same piece of ground. Expressed in simple terms, the main reason is that one genus of plants takes out of the soil more of one of its constituent qualities than another. Another reason is that continued cultivation of one crop on the same piece of ground encourages the pests and diseases particular to that crop. It is from neglect of these principles that so many allotments are riddled with clubroot through over-planting of brassicas. For some odd reason, onions seem to be an exception to what is a general rule, and many old gardeners, having found a spot that onions like, grow onions there always.

Some method of crop rotation also saves the gardener labour, in that he digs in manure only in those parts needed, year by year; and the same with lime. Thus it may be taken as a useful rule of thumb that in any one season you manure only those plots needed for potatoes, legumes, celery, and bulb crops. These crops are followed by the brassica family, which specially like the nitrogen left in the soil by the roots of legumes, and the brassicas are then followed by root crops, which must not have manure.

Crop rotation is a scientific subject, but all that the small gardener need concern himself with is the general principle of sowing each kind of crop in a different part of the garden each year, and a rotation on the broad lines of the previous paragraph will do well. For this purpose the ground should be divided up into approximately equal portions, either three or four, however small.

LAYOUT AND MANAGEMENT

The site of the kitchen garden should be in full sun as far as possible, though some shade is valuable for a few crops.

Ease of working is the next consideration. All plots should be rectangular, or some other straight-edged shape. Avoid a lot of fussy little beds. Paths should be laid out on strictly utilitarian lines, going from A to B directly in a straight line.

Then broadly apportion the uses of each part of the garden. The most precious site – the wall or fence facing south – will be for tomatoes and the more tender fruits. Next site the permanent crops – those that do not have to be sown every year, such as rhubarb, seakale, asparagus, Jerusalem artichokes if you grow them. Rhubarb and horseradish, being tough fellows, can go in an east border, artichokes in the coldest NE corner; but asparagus must have full sun in the centre. So also must strawberries if grown, for, though a fruit, they are best fitted into the vegetable rotations. Spinach sowings can alternate between sun and shade. Scarlet runners, if you like, can climb a fence or trellis at the sides, somewhere in the sun. The rest of the central space can be apportioned as you like for easy management on broad rotational principles in three or four roughly equal plots.

Remember a little space for the herbs, and site them if possible close to the kitchen; but all must be in full sun, though mint, rhubarb and horseradish do not mind shade.

It will be seen, therefore, that a certain amount of forethought and management is needed to get good results out of a small space. Work out well in advance what is to follow early potatoes and peas when they are lifted, what space shall be reserved for celery trenches and what for marrows, where you will work in your successional sowings of lettuces and peas, what you will be able to pop in as inter-crops and catch-crops. If some such general planning is not done ahead, you are likely to find either that large pieces of ground are lying idle for long periods, or that you have got masses of seedlings on your hands for which you have no room.

FRAMES AND CLOCHES

A greenhouse enables you to raise from seed plants you would otherwise have to buy, and to grow tomatoes with success; and a frame is also a good stand-by for many jobs. But the great thing in the vegetable garden is the cloche (*see* Chapter 9). Even a very few are a godsend. Cloche gardening is now a specialised subject, but the apprentice may employ them in general terms to ensure the success of early spring sowings and to prolong the growing season into the autumn, especially for early and late lettuces, peas, French beans, and so on.

SELECTIONS

I propose to give only a very few, being the one or two generally found to be the best. It is always sound to take the local advice of an old hand. Too many seedsmen have the exasperating habit of giving their own fancy name to a variety that scarcely differs from the standard, but as a rule good catalogues will give, if not exactly the names used, something recognisable as the same. Many of the varieties I give are standard ones, obtainable in inferior strains as well as superior ones. Your safeguard is to go to a specialist seedsman. Get several catalogues and compare them. As in flower seed, the F1 hybrids are usually good value.

In reading the cultural notes that follow remember in each case to refer to the Special Family Needs for all Brassicas, Legumes and Roots on page 237.

Note. Sowing times are given as for the South and Midlands; for Northern gardens times should generally be some three weeks later for spring sowings and three weeks earlier for autumn sowings. All timings given are subject to conditions of weather and soil. Depth of sowings are as for medium loam. Sow a fraction deeper on light, sandy soils, less deeply on heavy clays.

Artichoke. There are the Jerusalem and the globe. The former is the tuber resembling a deformed potato considered by a few misguided people to be edible. It is not an artichoke at all and has no affiliation to Jerusalem, being merely the root of a wild American sunflower. If you really do like these things try to get the cultivar 'Fuseau'. They come in usefully in a cold NE corner, when their tall growth will hide an unsightly spot. Plant 6 in. deep and 15 in. apart. Lift the tubers as required.

The globe or true artichoke, which you nibble delicately in expensive restaurants, is part of the floral adornment of a large ornamental herbaceous plant; not suitable for small gardens.

Asparagus. In a garden of half an acre, room can be spared for this special delight, but 100 plants is about the minimum to give you several good feasts. It is perennial and lasts many years. It prefers a light soil, and cold, ill-drained clays are useless.

Trench deeply and dress lavishly with well-decayed manure or compost. Make built-up beds, 4 ft. wide and about 9 in. high, using the top spit

Asparagus

Path   Path

Planting asparagus. Note the 'saddles'.

between each pair of beds for the building-up; the space between each bed constitutes a path, say, 18 in. wide. Buy three-year-old plants for preference, and have the beds ready in good time. Insist on male plants. Plant the crowns (early April) quickly the moment they arrive in three rows 15 in. apart and 15 in. between plants in the row Make holes of ample size, shape the soil into a ridge or saddle, and plant the spidery roots astride it, with the crown at least 4 in. below the surface. The part you eat is a young stem shooting up from the soil. Take nothing from two-year-old plants till the second season after planting, but a light cutting may be taken from the three-year-olds the next year after planting. Cut the shoots when about 3-4 in. above ground about the end of April; use a sharp knife and cut just below the surface. Don't cut after mid-June, but leave the remaining shoots to develop. Cut these down when they turn yellow in autumn. Dress the beds in January, or February with seaweed if you can get it, or with manure or compost early in March. Rake the beds clean in autumn and spring, but never dig them, nor the paths between.

The standard variety in this country is 'Connover's Colossal.'

Bean, broad (legume). In all except the coldest counties it is profitable to sow in October, leaving the plants to stand through the winter for an early crop. Other sowings can be made in March. Sow 3 in. deep in double ranks, 6 in. apart and 9 in. between ranks, with a space of 2 ft. to the next double row. A position sheltered from winds is best, to avoid staking. Earth-up autumn sowings about 6 in.

Pinch out the top 3 in. of each shoot when the lowest flowers begin to set their pods and spray with pyrethrins, derris or insecticidal soap to keep down the wretched black-fly.

Varieties. Go for the excellent dwarf varieties such as 'The Sutton', in single rows. For top flavour 'Red Epicure' (not a dwarf). In October sow 'Aquadulce Claudia' to over-winter. Of others, the long-pods, e.g. 'Imperial Green Longpod', are the hardier and the Windsors, e.g. 'Imperial Green Windsors' and 'White Windsor', the tastier.

Bean, flageolet (legume). These delicious beans, very popular in France but almost unknown here, are eaten in the green stage, shelled, just like peas or broad beans. Culture is exactly as for dwarf French beans. Pick when the beans within the pod are swollen but the pods still green. Also very good as an ordinary French bean and as a haricot.

Varieties. 'Chevrier Vert'.

Bean, French or kidney (legume). Nothing else gives such good returns for a small place as this delectable and easily grown dwarf bean. Sow outdoors in full sun in mid-May, in drills 2 in. deep, 4 in. between seeds, 2 ft. between rows. Thin to 8 in. apart in the rows. Beware slugs. Spray with water after flowers appear to help setting. Pick early and pick often. Make two or more successional sowings at a fortnight's interval until July.

Varieties. The stringless round-podded or 'pencil-podded' varieties are challenging the old flat-pods; e.g. 'Kinghorn Wax' (yellow beans easily seen among foliage), 'Sprite' and, for an early, 'Tendergreen'. Traditional varieties are 'The Prince' and 'Masterpiece Stringless', but they must be picked young.

Bean, scarlet runner (legume). Following normal amateur practice, sow 3 in. deep in May in double rows 9 in. between seeds, and 6 ft. from the next double row. Plant tall bean poles, 7–8 ft. long in two rows 18 in. apart, up which the plants will climb. Spray flowers with water to help setting. *Pick while small and tender.* The more you pick the more will come. Further sowings can be made fortnightly till late June.

Varieties. 'Enorma', 'Kelvedon Marvel' or 'Scarlet Emperor'.

Beetroot (root). An easy vegetable but required by the family only in small quantities. Omit from very small gardens, and buy the few needed from the shops, ready cooked.

If you do grow them, sow mid-April onwards in permanent quarters in drills or at stations 1 in. deep and in rows 1 ft. apart. Thin out to 8 in. apart in the row. For current use, make limited sowings only, and make successional sowings every three weeks up till the end of June. For winter storage, make a maincrop sowing in June or late May.

Lift for the table as required, using great care not to break or bruise either the skin or the roots, else the beet will 'bleed'. For the same reason use care when hoeing. For storage, lift before frost; twist off the leaves (do not *cut*) 2 or 3 in. above the crown, using two hands.

Varieties. 'Detroit 2' or 'Detroit 3'

Borecole. *See* Kale.

Broccoli (brassica). There are two groups: the sprouting, and the cauliflower-headed. Better than real cauliflower for the amateur, and do well on heavy soils but take up a lot of space. There are varieties which provide fare for autumn, winter, and spring. The sprouting types – green, purple or white – throw out a lot of small side-shoots, tender and rich in vitamins.

Sow seed for all types late April. Plant out finally into permanent beds from late May to July – 2 ft. apart for the cauliflower types and 6 in. more for the sprouters. When frosts are likely to become hard, snap a couple of the large leaves over the heads of the cauliflower sorts for protection, and in November heel them over to the north – loosen with a fork, push the plant well over, gently, take out a shallow trench on the north and heap the soil over the disturbed roots on the south side.

Cauliflower or 'heading broccoli' variety. 'Arcadia'.
Sprouting varieties. Green sprouting broccoli is a most desirable vegetable for late summer and autumn. After taking the central head pick the delicious side-shoots before they flower and treat like asparagus. Choose Italian Sprouting. For winter, the very hardy Purple Sprouting. Cut them with 5 in. of stem.

Brussels sprouts (brassica). Sow towards the end of March. Plant seedlings into permanent quarters firmly and as deep as the first pair of leaves, a good 2 ft. apart and the same between rows; a little less for dwarfs. When ready, gather the sprouts from the bottom upwards. When the stalk is cleared, the tuft of leaves at the top – known as 'Brussels tops' – makes excellent eating.
Varieties. 'Peer Gynt' (dwarf). 'Igor' for the small, French-style sprout, 'Bedford Fillbasket' for whoppers.

Cabbage (brassica). The numerous varieties available will provide cabbages nearly all the year round if wanted.

Sow in March or April for summer and autumn sorts; late April for winter sorts, including Savoys; and at the end of July in Northern gardens and early August in Southern gardens for spring cabbage the following year. Spring varieties are liable to bolt if sown too early.

Planting distances depend on the ultimate size of the plants, but in general put them 2 ft. each way; where space is limited they may be put closer, and every alternate one cut for use as required. Take precautions against cabbage root fly, clubroot, the caterpillar of the 'cabbage white' butterfly etc. (Chapter 23). Where there are wood pigeons the cabbages will be ruined unless protected by nets.
Varieties. The following are well-tried traditional sorts. For summer: 'Velocity'. For autumn: 'Greyhound' (18 in. spacing only). For winter: 'Christmas Drumhead', 'January King 3', and all the Savoys (especially the dwarf varieties for small places). For spring: 'Flower of Spring'.

Carrots (root). In stiff clays attempts to grow carrots are a waste of time. Light, sandy soils are best, soils on the heavy side should be lightened with sand.

The proper way to grow carrots is to make small sowings every three or four weeks from the end of March till July. In this way there will be a constant supply of tender young roots. For winter storage a maincrop variety is sown in early June.

Sow direct into permanent quarters, preferably at stations or half-stations, in dry weather on a surface reduced to a fine tilth. Sow only ¼ in. deep in rows 9 in. apart. Thin out as necessary. Final distances apart should be from 4 to 8 in., according to variety. Do any thinning out and pulling when the soil is moist if possible and firm the soil afterwards, or else water the soil well; do not leave any thinnings lying about.
Varieties. We have three groups: (*a*) the Short, which are early, sweet and small; (*b*) Intermediates, which you pull as you want and store the rest; and (*c*) the long-rooted, such as 'Saint Valéry', which are for exhibitors and not

us. For (*a*) choose 'Little Finger' or 'Nantes 2', for (*b*) 'Chantenay Red Cored 3'.

Cauliflower (brassica). Not advised. The true cauliflowers are not hardy, need a very rich soil, are quite unsuitable for dry soils and hot summers, and tend to ripen all together, so that there is a sudden glut and then no more. Cauliflower-headed broccoli is to be preferred. If grown, get a couple of dozen seedlings from a good nurseryman in May, or sow the variety 'All the Year Round' outdoors under cloches, making three or four sowings at about ten-day intervals from mid-March, and plant out in May 2 ft. apart. A lavishly manured soil is needed, with fertiliser ten days after planting out and copious water thereafter.

Celeriac. Very useful for soils that are too hot and dry for celery. Is a bulbous root plant, closely resembling celery in flavour. Good for soups, or grated or sliced for salads, or boiled like beetroot. The leaves, if hung upside down and dried, are good in stews and soups. Raise seed exactly as for celery, but plant out late May into a heavily manured flat bed, not a trench. No earthing-up. Space 1 ft. apart and 18 in. between rows.

Variety. 'Prager Reuzen' (syn. 'Giant Prague').

Celery. It is not much use attempting to grow good celery unless you give it rich, deeply dug, heavily manured soil, and take a bit of trouble over it. Seed is best raised in heat, but in mild districts can be sown very shallow under cloches or in a frame in March; or young plants can be bought from a nurseryman.

Most amateurs who have to earn a living will be satisfied with the 'self-blanching' celery, such as 'Lathom Self Blanching' and the very early 'Gigante Dorate 2' (syn. 'Golden Self Blanching 2'). Their flavours are quite good but not top-class. They must have the same rich soil as traditional celeries but, instead of being grown in trenches and earthed up as they go, they are grown on the flat and in solid squares at 9 in. spacing. They are pretty care-free but need a lot of water and are *not winter-hardy*.

For gardeners who want the real thing the drill is as follows. Dig a trench in late winter about 18 in. deep, taking out all the soil and breaking up the bottom with a fork, and leave it open for some weeks for the elements to work on it. On heavy soils something shallower suits. For a single row of plants the trench should be 15 in. wide, for a double row 18 in. Throw the soil out on each side and spread it out as a flat raised bed between each pair of trenches; on this bed can be grown 'inter-crops' of lettuce, summer spinach, radishes, etc., before the soil is used for the subsequent earthing up. Trenches should be 3 ft. apart.

Before planting out, spread a thick layer, 6 in. deep, of farmyard manure in the bottom of the trench, mix it with about half as much again of good top-spit soil, and tread it lightly down; then fill up to within about 3 in. (or, say, 6 in. on light soils) of the top of the trench with good friable top soil. Plant out the seedlings late May or early June, 10 in. apart. If in a double row, plant side by side, not staggered. Water in each plant as you go, or give the whole trench a good soaking. Subsequent cultivation consists mainly in frequent flooding of the trench in dry weather; removal of side-shoots from the base of the plant.

To blanch. This is done by periodically earthing up the soil on to the plant. Do it when the plants are dry, but the soil a little moist and crumbly. Start when they are 6 in. high, repeat at 1 ft. and finally at 18 in. Hold each plant bunched up with one hand, and with the other draw the soil up loosely round the plant, taking care that no soil trickles down into the heart of the plant you are holding. Repeat at least twice at fortnightly intervals. Finally, tie up the topknot of leaves and give a *gentle* patting with the spade (never beat it hard) to the now steep sides of the ridge, to help shed winter rain. The practice of using paper collars for blanching does not give as good results as earthing up.

Varieties. The red and pink sorts are hardier and easier than the white.

Chives. Of the onion family, producing tufts of neat foliage. Acquire a dozen or so of the tiny bulbs. Plant out about 6 in. apart, and use as an edging. The leaves are snipped off with scissors as required. Snip off the flower-buds, too, to promote increase. Lift, divide, and replant the clumps every three or four years in autumn or spring. They are of the easiest culture and multiply rapidly.

Courgettes are simply small marrows. If you want to appear modish, order 'Zucchini' or 'Golden Zucchini', but English marrows, cut small, have a much better flavour.

Cucumber. Another vegetable that can be omitted with little loss. One wants only one at a time, and the greengrocer will oblige. However, for those who like to grow their own, the 'ridge' or prickly type of cucumber is quite easy. Soak the seeds in water overnight. Sow them in 3 in. peat pots in late April for planting out about 1st June. They hate root disturbance. Lacking a greenhouse, sow direct outdoors in late May. Provide a very rich soil in full sun, screened from strong winds. Plant out the seedlings 2 ft. 6 in. apart. When about seven leaves have formed, nip out the tops of the plants. Later all shoots which form may also be so stopped if desired after one fruit has formed on each. Water abundantly and give liquid manure every week after the first fruits are 3 in. long. Cut as soon as fruits are of usable size, and keep on cutting.

Varieties. The small, oval, yellow-flecked 'Crystal Apple', the size of a duck's egg, is outstanding for flavour and juiciness. Otherwise, use 'Birgit' or 'Femdan'.

Endive. A valuable winter salading. There are two sorts – the Batavian, with broadish leaves rather like cos lettuce, and the 'mossy' or curly, with lacy leaves (the *chicorée frisée* of France). Any soil in good heart and well tilled should do. Sow ½ in. deep in the nursery seed-bed or in a seed-box, the curly sort from April to July, the Batavian from July to October.

Transplant 9 in. apart. Germination is slow. The plants have to be blanched, a few at a time, being otherwise too bitter. The usual method for the curly kind is to cover them with an inverted pot when about three-quarters grown. Leaves of the Batavian should be tied up like cos, while dry, using raffia.

Horseradish. Very tough and very invasive, horseradish should be kept well away in a remote, cold corner. Digging up the deep roots on a winter's day is no fun. It is really best to build up a mound, about 2 ft. high. Buy or cadge some thick roots about 6 in. long in March, make a very deep hole with a dibber, and plant the roots with their crowns 5 in. below surface. In November lift the whole of the crop and store in sand, etc. Some will be used in the house and some kept for planting out again next March.

Kale (brassica). Also called borecole. Very easily grown in poor soils, kale is a winter vegetable and one of the very hardiest. Good for very cold places and of high nutritional value. For a maincrop sow late April in the seed-bed, rather thin and shallow. Except for the dwarf sort, transplant firmly a good 2 ft. apart. Avoid nitrogenous fertilisers. On Scotch kale the leaves are eaten; on others, after the top has been used, side-shoots sprout from the stem, and these should be eaten while young and tender. The best variety is 'Dwarf Green Curled'.

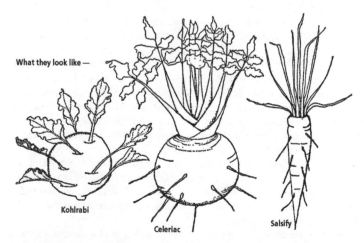

What they look like —

Kohlrabi

Celeriac

Salsify

A gallery of oddments: left to right, *kohlrabi, celeriac, salsify.*

Kohlrabi. This rather queer-looking vegetable is a cabbage with a bulbous stem, turnip-flavoured, and a useful substitute for turnips in very dry soils. Eat it when it is no bigger than a tennis-ball, when it is tender. Sow in April in rows 2 ft. apart, and thin to 1 ft. apart in the rows. 'Wener Witte' (White Vienna) is perhaps the best variety.

Leek. Member of the onion family, very hardy and subject to few diseases. One of the best winter vegetables. Southern gardeners are backward in its cultivation as compared with Northerners and Scotsmen.

The tastiest leeks are small ones, not whoppers. Even so, they are greedy, and you must dig quantities of manure deep into the soil. There are many ways of growing them, the best being as follows.

About 1st April sow seed very sparsely in a nursery bed or deep seed-box. About 1st June make holes 6 in. deep and apart in the permanent bed with a blunt dibber, drop in the nursling plant and fill the hole with water – that is all. Don't firm the plant; as it grows it swells to fill up the hole and is automatically blanched. You can earth-up further if you like after the plants have filled up their holes and are going ahead strongly. Snip an inch or two off the tips of the longest leaves from time to time.

Varieties. 'Musselburgh', 'Blauwgroene Winter Laura' and 'Winterreuzen 3'.

Lettuce. Though very long-suffering, lettuces benefit enormously from a little manure or compost, not only as food but also as a check to their bolting to seed in hot weather. The way to grow them is to sow seed at about three-week intervals, being careful to choose a variety suitable to the season. Even without heat they can be grown over a very long period.

Start early March with 'Suzan' or 'Maikönig' (May King). A little later make the first of successional sowings up to midsummer (not later) of 'Tom Thumb', a dwarf of excellent quality, spaced at about 6 in. For the main-season crops, begin early April with 'Buttercrunch' and 'Little Gem' and 'Suzan' again. In July change to 'Avondefiance' for autumn use. In mid-September sow 'Val d'Orge' (syn. 'Valdor') or 'Maikönig' again to over-winter and mature in early spring. If you want to stick to one variety only for spring, summer and early autumn cutting, use 'All the Year Round'. The 'crisphead' lettuces need hot weather. Of these 'Webb's Wonderful' is an old favourite; sow April to June. Some people like the loose-leaf varieties, such as 'Salad Bowl' and 'Grand Rapids', of which, like spinach, you pick only a few leaves at a time.

For small quantities the most convenient method of using lettuces is to sow in a seed-box or wide pot and transplant. Twenty-four plants at any one time are quite enough for small households. Feed them at intervals with, say Growmore, or a foliar feed. In prolonged dry summer spells water them copiously.

Lettuces are hungrily preyed upon by birds, slugs and soil pests. Take precautions accordingly.

Marrow. Only three or four are needed by the average family. Buy seedlings from a nurseryman the first week of June, or sow seed (on edge) single in small pots in mid-April in the greenhouse or kitchen and plant out in June; they are not hardy.

Choosing a sunny position, dig a deepish trench in May 18 in. wide, and enrich the soil with lavish quantities of manure or compost. Build a low ridge round the bed so that it can be flooded. Don't grow marrows on a mound.

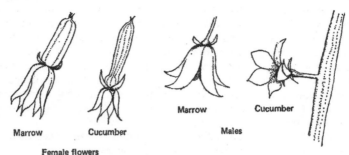

Female flowers

Marrow and cucumber.

Plant out a yard apart. Water copiously at all stages. On the trailing sorts nip off the tip of the main shoot before it is 3 ft, long; nip off the resultant side-shoots also at seven leaves if too rampant. Fertilise each female flower (recognisable by a bulbous swelling at the base) by stripping a male blossom of its petals and thrusting the pollen-bearing core into the female. Don't attempt to grow large marrows. Small ones are far more succulent. If cut when about 6 in. long and cooked whole, they constitute courgettes. The most recommended variety is 'Long Green Bush 2', but, if you have room for a trailer, 'Table Dainty' is the one for flavour.

Mint (herb). A few roots will suffice. Spreads rapidly, and invades other crops unless planted in an isolated bed. Prospers in sun or partial shade. Plant roots in March or autumn. For winter use dry off the stalks (well spread out) in an airy, dry, warmish place. When dry, strip off the leaves, powder through a sieve and store in an air-tight bottle.

Mint rust (tiny orange spores) is a nuisance. If it appears, pluck out the whole stem from the ground and burn. In October lay straw on the ground and burn off the whole crop; the roots will sprout afresh.

The most commonly grown type is spearmint (*Mentha spicata*), but by epicures the apple-mint (*Mentha* x *villosa*) is more valued; for herb fans there are several other mints.

Onion. This is not really an easy vegetable. It needs plenty of hot sun, a light, rich soil, and a really firm bed. Undoubtedly the easiest way to grow them nowadays is from 'sets', which are tiny bulbs raised under crowded conditions. A pound, or ½ kg., is enough for a small family.

Thoroughly manure the soil in November to ensure settlement and consolidation. In March make a seed-bed which is very firm, but with a fine tilth by repeated treading and raking in dry weather. Rake in some Growmore. Plant the bulblets at 5 in. spacing, in rows 12–15 in. apart, by pressing them into the soil so that their tips just peep out of the surface.

Firm the soil around each bulb and watch for any that jump out. Protect
against birds.

In August bend the stalks down to the ground, towards the north, to
hasten ripening. Harvest in September by lifting the bulbs with a fork and
leaving them on the ground a few days to dry in the sun (under glass if
wet) before roping and storing. Use early any with thick, soft necks.

By seed. Sow when the soil is dry in early March very sparsely in drills only
¼ in. deep. Thin out finally to 5 in. apart, using the thinnings as 'spring
onions'. After thinning and weeding firm the soil to discourage the onion
fly (*see* Chapter 23). Don't leave any thinnings lying about. The fly does not
attack sets. Snap off any seed-heads that form.

In the North it is often preferred to sow in boxes in the greenhouse or
frame, or under cloches, and to plant out seedlings rather late in April. Plant
very firmly but *not* deeply – the soil level should come only half-way up
the little bulb.

Varieties. 'Ailisa Craig' leads the field, with 'Bedfordshire Champion'
runner-up. For salads, 'White Lisbon'. For pickling, 'Silverskin' (no
manure). For sets seedsmen use other sorts.

Tree onions bear a cluster of small bulbs at the top of the stem; good for
pickling or general use. Plant the mother bulbs in rows 18 in. apart. The
basal bulb can also be eaten.

The *Welsh onion* (*Allium fistulosum,* which does not hail from Wales) is
a perennial and, instead of a true bulb, has thickened leaf bases, like chives.
Use as spring onions. Strong flavour. Sow *in situ.*

Parsley (herb). Easy in some districts, stubborn in others. Use as an edging and give it fine soil. It likes lime and some shade. Sow sparsely ¼ in.
deep. Germination is slow but thinnings can be transplanted. In heavy soils
(like mine) sow in one of the proprietary composts in 5 in. pots, two or
three seeds to each, and transplant. For winter, use a similar compost in
large pots, four or five in each, in a frost-free glasshouse.

Parsnip (root). Sow very early – in February in the south if the ground
allows – in drills 15 in. apart. Sow fairly thickly, as the seed is uncertain (and
slow) in germination. Thin out to 9 in. apart. There are few troubles with
parsnips. On hard, heavy, and stony soils it is necessary to make holes 2 ft.
deep with a crowbar, fill with fine soil, sow two or three seeds in each and
thin out when necessary. Their flavour is best when they have been
touched by frost, which turns the starch to sugar.

Varieties. 'Avonresister' (very short) is an excellent all-rounder, especially in
poor soils. For flavour, 'The Student,' longer-rooted. 'Tender and True' is
choice but really too long.

Pea (legume). Having obeyed all the injunctions prescribed for legumes,
dress the bed before sowing with an all-round fertiliser. Sow in two
staggered rows 3 in. apart in a broad drill 2 in. deep made with a draw-hoe
or spade. Distances between rows of dwarf varieties should be 2 ft. or more,

and for taller sorts the distance should be the same as the height of the variety. Protect against birds at all stages. Except for the dwarf sorts, plant pea-sticks generously when seedlings are about 5 in. high.

Nuisances. The pea and bean weevil scallops the margins of leaves. Tiny caterpillars of the pea moth eat the peas in the pods. Thrips cause a silvery discoloration of the pods. All can be treated with permethrin.

Varieties. There is a bewildering multitude. Note that the round-seeded varieties are the more hardy, but that the wrinkled seeds are the sweet and delicious marrowfats. The following are my choices for a succession, all being marrowfats except 'Meteor'.

Early dwarfs, sow early March: 'Kelvedon Wonder' or 'Little Marvel', both quite outstanding, 'Meteor' for cold districts (can be sown in November for May eating). Sow 'Kelvedon Wonder' again in June for September.

Second early, sow late March: 'Early Onward'.

Maincrop, sow April till June: 'Onward', 'Senator', 'Achievement'.

If you want one only, choose 'Kelvedon Wonder' and sow in succession all spring and summer.

A great treat is the true French *petit pois* (e.g. 'Waverex'). So also is the mangetout or sugar pea (e.g. 'Oregon Sugar Pod' and 'De Grace'). You pick them young, before the peas have swollen in the pod, top and tail the pods and boil whole, serving with a spot of melted butter. Both are maincrops and need staking.

Potato. Order 'seed potatoes' early and from first-rate suppliers only, preferably from Scotland or Ireland, for delivery January or February. In districts where the wart disease is prevalent you are bound by law to grow only those varieties certified as 'immune'. Five lbs. (2.37 kg.) will make a 30 ft. (9 m.) row, which should produce about 60 lbs. (27 kg.) of spuds.

Unpack immediately on arrival and stack in shallow boxes or trays in a light, frost-proof place, such as a brick garage or light attic. Stand them with their 'eyes', or 'rose' end, upwards – the end opposite to the little scar where the potato was attached to its root. This will induce early sprouting. Only two shoots are wanted at the rose end, but if others appear elsewhere the tuber can be cut in two at planting time and each part planted separately. Rub out excess sprouts.

Dig the soil at least 10 in. deep in autumn, laying in manure at one full barrow load per 10 sq. yd. They like peat, but not lime. Weather permitting, plant in April, after dressing the rows with Growmore at about 3 oz. per 10 ft. (85 g. per 3 m.) a few days beforehand. The early varieties go in at the beginning of April, the lates at the end. Allow 2 ft. between the rows for the earlies, 28 in. for the second earlies (if you have room for such a crop) and a good 30 in. for maincrops. Plant in drills a good 5 in. deep at these distances apart: 10 in. between earlies, 12 in. for second earlies, and 15 in. maincrop. Some people spread a layer of lawn mowings on the

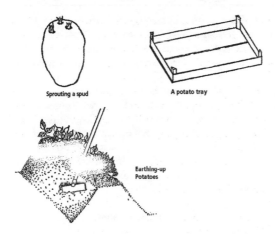

Sprouting a spud

A potato tray

Earthing-up
Potatoes

Potatoes.

bottom of the trench before planting. Alternatively, instead of drawing a deep drill, plant with a trowel, ensuring there is no air pocket beneath the spud.

As soon as the first leaves show, cover them with straw or bracken against frost, or draw some soil lightly over them, allowing a wee tuft of leaves to see daylight. When the haulms are 8 in. high, begin the process of 'earthing up', the purpose of which is to prevent the potatoes from coming to the surface and turning green and bitter. You do this by drawing the soil between the rows up to the plants with a draw-hoe, so that a trench appears between each row. Earth up again three weeks later. Carry the soil up to the lowest leaves, leaving not less than 6 in. of foliage above soil level, and making the ridge broad, not pointed. This traditional process of earthing-up is better than the slick one of using black polythene strips.

Spraying, with Bordeaux mixture or mancozeb, is a most desirable preventive measure against potato blight. In the SW, spray at the end of June, in the south the first week of July, in the Midlands and east the second week of July, in the north and west at the end of July.

The earlies can be lifted for the table as wanted in July, when the blossom is over. Use a broad-tined potato-fork. To ensure full maturity, leave the lates till the haulms have died down, about 1st October. Dig up on a dry day and leave the tubers on the ground for a few hours to dry. Big crops go into an outdoor clamp, but for small gardens storage can be done in any shed, attic, or cellar that is dry, cool but frost-proof and dark. Clean off any clods of earth and spread the potatoes out loosely. They may also be put into sacks. Look them over occasionally for signs of disease.

Varieties. Of the innumerable varieties the following is my pick for flavour, always subject to local advice: Earlies — 'Arran Pilot' (slow to bulk) and

'Epicure'. Maincrops – 'King Edward' has every excellence, whether boiled, baked or chipped, but has low resistance to disease. 'Golden Wonder' is an epicure's potato, splendid for baking, but needs rich culture, is not a big cropper and is hard to get. Flavour apart, 'Pentland Crown' and 'Désirée' are sound choices.

Radish. Choose a patch in partial shade that was manured for previous crops. Hoe to a very fine tilth. Broadcast a pinch or two of seeds, very sparsely indeed, and cover with a sprinkling of fine soil. Use when young and tender. Ample moisture is needed. For a continuous supply, sow at fortnightly intervals from early March till July. For mild flavour choose 'Cherry Belle'. The big winter radishes that you grate or slice for salads are sown in July. 'Rose d'Hiver de Chine' (syn. 'China Rose') and 'Noir Gros Rond d'Hiver' (syn. 'Black Spanish Round') are chosen.

Rhubarb. Can be grown on most soils, but to produce big juicy stems should have deeply dug, well-drained, and manured soils. A shady spot will do. It is a perennial.

Buy unforced crown from a nurseryman – only a few are wanted – and plant out in March a good 3 ft. apart, with the tops barely covered. Plant firmly. Do not pick stalks at all the first year, and very few the second. Picking can start April but must stop at midsummer. The stalks should always be *pulled* when gathering. If any flower stalks form, break off at ground level.

To force. The simplest method is to put a box or tub over the crown in December, and encase it with strawy manure and leaves to generate heat. Don't attempt to force young plants, nor weakly ones.

Sage (herb). Buy one or two plants, specifying broad-leaved sage, and plant out 18 in. apart. When established, one good plant is enough, and it is decorative enough to go anywhere.

Salsify (root). A hardy root vegetable, with a very distinctive flavour and oyster-like texture which many enjoy but others don't. Pronounce the y as in 'Rugby'. Sow late April ½ in. deep in rows 12 in. apart; or, in heavyish soils, make a 10 in. deep hole as for carrots or parsnips. Thin to 10 in. apart. Hoe and lift carefully, for, if damaged, they 'bleed', like beetroot. Roots become usable late October. Lift as required, and the remainder can stay in the ground. It is not my business to tell you how to cook them.

If left till spring they throw up flowering shoots called 'chards'. Cut these when 5–6 in. long and eat them like asparagus.

Scorzonera is a similar vegetable, but not quite so good.

Savoy. *See* Cabbage.

Scarlet runners. *See under* Beans.

Shallots. Easy in almost any soil, but do best in a firm bed on an old manured plot. Buy a few dozen bulbs (small ones are best) and plant them at about Christmas in the South, early March in the North. Space 8 in. apart with 12 in. between rows. Plant the bulb with one-third of it above soil level. From each bulb will grow a cluster of new ones. Allow none to go to seed. When the leaves wither, lift the clusters in dry weather, break them up, dry them outdoors or in an airy shed, and store in a cool, dry place.

Spinach. Of the several breeds of spinach, I shall deal only with the annual summer round-seeded, the winter prickly-seeded, and the 'perpetual' or beet spinach, which is the least trouble and the most useful. All are sown *in situ*.

Summer spinach. Very ephemeral, but succulent. Sow early March 1 in. deep in drills 1 ft. apart. Thin to 4 in. between plants. Make additional sowings every three weeks up till June, the later sowings in partial shade. Use the variety 'Medania'. You need to sow a lot to make summer spinach worthwhile, but it makes a good catch-crop, and you pick a whole row at a time.

Winter spinach. Sow from August to September in sun in drills 1 in. deep. Thin to 4 in. In colder districts use cloches. Do *not* pick winter spinach too hard, but take the large leaves first. Use 'Grodane' or 'Viroflay'.

Perpetual spinach (or spinach beet). A form of beetroot, easy and good. Less trouble than the frequent sowings of summer spinach, easier to pick and to cook, but a thought less succulent. For all-the-year crops, sow early April, and again mid-August, in rows 15 in. apart, and thin to 8 in. between plants. Pick regularly, but lightly, as soon as ready, taking the largest leaves first. It lasts a year, then goes to seed.

Swedes. Those who care for this vegetable should treat it just the same as maincrop turnips. Sow in May, good varieties being 'Acme' (syn. 'Acme Garden Purple Top') and 'Champion' (syn. 'Champion Purple Top').

Sweetcorn. Indian corn or maize is not really a crop for the small garden, but I have known people with only a quarter of an acre or so grow a useful patch. It likes ample rain, yet long hours of sun-baking. Therefore a risky crop in our climate but frequently successful in the South. Should not be ventured in very dry, sandy soils, nor in heavy clays. Cloches or polythene tunnels are a great help against birds, cold and insects.

Bastard-trench the soil, putting in ample organic food but not animal manure. Into the top spit work in some damped peat and Growmore just before sowing.

Seed may be sown direct outdoors in mid-May 8 in. apart and 1 in. deep. Thin to 16 in. Or steal a march on time by sowing in 3 in. peat pots in a warm glasshouse about 1st May and plant out in the first week of June. Aim at creating a tight rectangular block or clump rather than formally spaced rows, in order to assist pollination, which is effected by the pollen from the male 'tassels' at the top of the plant falling on the female 'ears' below. In drought, water thoroughly evening or morning and apply a mulch. Feed with liquid manure. If cloches and tunnels are used, remove them in early June. When roots develop above ground level, earth them up. Avoid hoeing. Do not remove any side-shoots that develop.

To test when the cobs are ready for use, strip back the tip of the sheath and press one of the grains with the thumb-nail. If a creamy substance, rather than a watery one, squirts out the cob is ready. An indication will be when the silky female sheaths turn brown and wither. Pop the cobs into boiling water as soon as they are picked and cook for ten minutes only. Cobs allowed to go hard can be fed to chickens.

Varieties. 'Kelvedon Glory' in the South; 'Northern Extra Sweet' in the North. Short, compact, early maturing varieties, with small cobs, are 'Sundance' and 'First of All.'

Thyme (herb). Must have full sun and prefers a light soil; in heavy ones work in sand or road grit. Buy two or three plants and put out a foot apart. Easy and decorative.

Tomato. The tomato is a native of hot climates, and, as with sweetcorn, the outdoor grower is a good deal in the hands of the weather. It likes heaps of sun and regular rain, but not too much of it.

Tomatoes are perfectly easy to raise from seed, but need a temperature of about 60°F (15°C). Lacking a heated greenhouse, demand permission of the appropriate authority to use the kitchen. When potted up, the seedlings must stay there for a couple of months, subject to what other facilities you have. A dozen plants more than suffice for the average family. The great benefit from raising your own is that you can choose varieties of superior flavour. Otherwise, you have to buy young plants from the garden shop and these are almost never of the best varieties.

Outdoor cultivation. The best site for planting out is close to a wall or fence facing south. Dig the site in autumn or winter, using no animal manure unless old and thoroughly rotted. Compost is excellent but there is nothing better than old turves roughly chopped or broken up. A week before planting rake a good general fertiliser into the top spit.

The seedlings having been hardened off, plant them in the first week of June (not before), 18 in. apart, with the soil-ball a trifle below ground level. Plant the supporting stakes, which must be stout and 4 ft. out of the ground, before planting the tomatoes. To ensure the essential regularity of watering, sink a 5 in. pot close to each stem, partly filled with stones. Fill this with water about every other day if no rain falls.

Tie up loosely, as the plant grows, with soft string. Persistently pluck out the side-shoots which grow in the leaf-axils. Be careful not to mistake other growing parts for these side-shoots – it is the growth in an angle or elbow to look for. (*See* illustration.) However, the main stem itself is also pinched-out or 'stopped' two leaves above the fourth truss of flowers (the third truss in Northern gardens). The purpose of this treatment and of taking out side-shoots is to centre the plant's energies on ripening a few good trusses in our short and uncertain summer.

Varieties known as 'bush' tomatoes (as in 'Sigmabush') need no staking, stopping or side-shooting. Their habit is low and spreading. Lay straw or old, permeable sacking beneath them (not plastic) to keep the fruits off the soil.

Begin dressings of a tomato fertiliser when the first fruits begin to set. If any leaves turn yellow, remove them. Do not remove healthy lower leaves, as sometimes advised, but tie them back if they mask the fruits from the sun.

Pick the fruits as soon as they are ripe. At the end of the season (before frost) pull up the whole plant (or the trusses only if space is limited) and hang up in a sunny place indoors to ripen the remaining fruits. Any that are obstinate can be sentenced to the chutney jar.

Glasshouse culture. In a greenhouse or glass porch more certain results and a longer season can be realized, but more attention is needed. So if you plan to take more than a week's holiday in summer, don't grow tomatoes indoors.

If the glasshouse is an unheated one, raise the seedlings as for outdoors but promote them to the glass in late April. Serious troubles can occur from growing always in a greenhouse border, so it is safer to use boxes or 9 in. pots. The proprietary composts are good for this. Alternatively, use a rich, friable loam treated with Growmore. If boxes are used, make sure that they will give a surface area of 9 × 9 in. per plant, with rather more in depth. Scrub the boxes clean and make sure of ample drainage.

If the glasshouse is a heated one, start the seedlings in early January and pot them on successively into their final receptacles in March.

Subsequent culture in both cases is as for outdoor plants, but a few other points need attention. Ventilate freely, but shut up the house at night until June. When the flowers open, lightly tap the stems or the canes, to disperse the pollen and so induce fertilisation. Water *regularly*, rather sparingly at first, more when the blossoms open and a good half-gallon (about 2 litres) per plant when the fruits begin to set. In hot weather splash the floor of the house freely with water and provide shade with a special, cloudy paint, with blinds or with close-mesh netting. Excessive heat and light cause 'greenback'.

Next year make up entirely fresh soil; never use the same twice.

A method of culture that saves some trouble and is favoured by some is the 'ring culture' method. At ground level or on the greenhouse bench make a bed of washed gravel or weathered ashes, 5 in. deep. On top of the bed place bottomless pots of about 9 in. diameter (available in the shops). Fill with John Innes No. 3 compost or a proprietary one. Plant the tomato seedlings in the pots, firmly. Water very thoroughly. Thereafter keep the gravel base always wetted; the roots spread down into this water bed. Feeding is done by liquid fertiliser, maybe into the gravel base only or, as some think, into the pots as well.

Tomatoes, especially under glass, are subject to various ailments. See blossom-end rot, greenback, potato blight, tomato leaf mould and whitefly in Chapter 23.

Varieties. In the glasshouse use 'Ailsa Craig', 'Alicante' or one of the delicious yellow-fruited varieties, such as 'Goldene Königin' (Golden Queen). For outdoors, the same or 'Outdoor Girl' (early), or a bush type.

Turnip (brassica). The turnip is a cabbage with a swollen root. For tenderness, which depends on quick growth, you must give it (especially the early varieties) a rich soil that has previously been well manured. Lime may also be needed at the proper season.

The most profitable turnips for small gardens are those which are grown especially for their excellent and highly nutritious leaves or 'turnip tops' as a winter or spring vegetable, notably the variety 'Imperial Green Globe'. Sow sparsely in early September and do not thin out. Pick the leaves when 5 in. high and cook as cabbage.

Otherwise, there are Early and Maincrop varieties, of which you eat the roots. Sow the earlies in succession, in small quantities, from April to midsummer for use in late summer and autumn. Thin to 6 in. Sow the maincrops in late July for late autumn and winter. Thin to 12 in. In cold and wet countries lift and store in November in dry peat or sand.

Besides the other maladies of the brassica family, turnips may be bothered by the flea-beetle, which eats holes in the leaves. Dust with derris as the seedlings emerge.

Varieties. The flat 'Purple Top Milan' for an early, 'Golden Ball' for maincrop.

PART FOUR: KNOW YOUR ENEMY

Not many amateur gardeners are likely to be carried away by the lure of bug-hunting or to have any interest in distinguishing one sort of mildew from another. All they care about is how to get rid of the brutes. But, since one doesn't treat measles in the same was, as toothache, one does need to be able to recognise broadly between one group of ailments and another, particularly between the bite of an insect and the growth of a fungus. This is not difficult as a rule, and, fortunately for the non-expert, we can reduce the problem to fairly simple terms and evolve a system of mass or group treatment; moreover, to quite an appreciable extent, we are able to apply the principles of preventive medicine instead of waiting for the attack to fall upon us.

In the arrangement of this Part, therefore, we shall first consider the enemy in general terms, and the most simplified possible routine method of dealing with him. Then we shall see how to deal with him *seriatim* and finally the last chapter will outline the chemical warfare weapons at our command.

In my restricted space I am able to give no more than a few potted notes on these matters. Readers hungry for a more extensive meal will benefit greatly from *RHS Pests and Diseases* by Pippa Greenwood and Andrew Halstead and from the Pesticides Safety Directorate website (www.pesticides.gov.uk) which lists all approved pesticides available to the amateur in the United Kingdom. The Royal Horticultural Society also has some good pamphlets and their skilled, professional staff, as always, is at hand to advise Fellows.

22

FRIEND AND FOE

Our friends are all too few, so that it is a pity that so many are needlessly slaughtered by the gardener who goes on the principle of killing 'every kind of bug'. No doubt this practice is partly due to the fact that many of our natural friends are a long way from conforming to our conventional ideas of beauty. On the one hand, we consider the most villainous butterflies and moths as pretty creatures, and, on the other, even Shakespeare brands the beneficent toad as 'ugly and venomous'.

Of recent years birds have become a serious problem in gardens. Perhaps we have become too sentimental about birds in general, for the bullfinch (handsome rascal), the wood pigeon and the house sparrow are now our serious enemies. We delight in the blackbird's sweet song but, like a naughty choirboy, he is a thief in the orchard. In some parts of the country deer have also become a serious and an aggressive menace. Rabbits maintain their age-old reputation. The seemingly innocent tortoise must never be given the freedom of the garden, or he will ruin it.

FRIENDS

Our most valuable, and indispensable, friend is, of course, the bee. Less obviously, the wasp is also an ally in early summer, preying on the greenfly and carrying pollen, but by August he becomes a despoiler of the orchard. The hedgehog, the toad, the frog, and the 'devil's coach horse' beetle are excellent handymen in killing slugs and other hostile creatures though the hedgehog can make an awful mess. The earthworm, though a pest in lawns, is valuable elsewhere for aerating the soil. Of our other friends to be noted, two are soil-dwellers and four are winged in their adult phase. The soil-dwellers are:

The **centipedes,** to be carefully distinguished from the quite different and destructive millipede. Note two kinds of centipede, both rather flat and very fast-moving and brisk. One is long, thin, yellow, or light-brown, intensely wriggly, with legs rather splayed out; the other shorter, dark-brown, fatter, a runner rather than a wriggler, with a pair of swept-back 'whiskers' in front and another pair at the tail. Be careful to distinguish these from the sluggish and very destructive millipede.

The friendly **ground beetle** larva is rather like a caterpillar; dull, dark-brown, light under-body, three pairs of legs in front, and two very pronounced whiskers or horns at the tail. Very nimble. Do not mistake this for the evil cutworm. The adult ground beetle may damage strawberries.

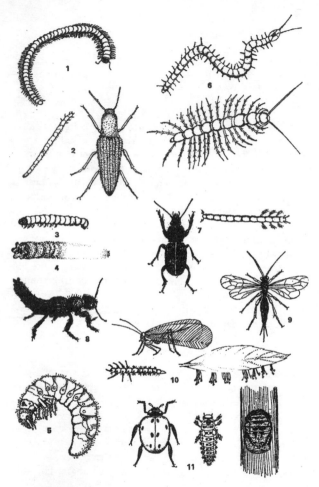

Foes: **a**, *millipede;* **b**, *wireworm with adult click-beetle;* **c**, *cutworm;* **d**, *leatherjacket;*
e, *chafer-grub. Friends:* **f**, *centipedes;* **g**, *ground beetle and larva;* **h**, *devil's coach horse;*
i, *ichneumon fly (one type);* **j**, *lacewing with larva and egg-cluster;* **k**, *ladybird with larva
and pupa (adhering to stem).*

Those friends that fly in the adult phase all prey on the greenfly.
They are:

The familiar **ladybird.** The larva, less well-known, is black or
near-black, agile, torpedo-shaped or resembling a minute crocodile. The
pupa or chrysalis is a small blackish blob that adheres to stems.

The **hover** or **serphid fly.** Wasp-like markings; hangs almost motion-less in the air in between quick darts. He does not sting you. The larva is an unpleasant leech-like creature, green, grey, or brown.

The **ichneumon fly.** An elongated creature whose plump abdomen is separated from its thorax by a thread-like tissue. Diaphanous wings. Pupa lives in a small yellow cocoon.

The **lacewing.** Thin pale-green body and two pairs of diaphanous wings, like a small dragon-fly. Larva is a fierce-looking little chap, very active, yellow, flushed brown, three pairs of legs, pointed tail, and a useful pair of nippers. A peculiarity of the lacewing is that it lays its eggs in a little bunch or cluster on thin stalks on the underside of a leaf.

Notice how many of these friendly little chaps are nimble and lively. When in doubt, it is quite a good general rule, especially in the soil-dwellers, to take the agile creatures as friends and the sluggish ones as foes.

ENEMIES IN GENERAL

Good husbandry is the first of garden commandments – not only good drainage and deep digging and liberal manuring, but also the annihilation of weeds which act as hosts for disease carriers, the cleaning out from hedge bottoms and odd corners of rubbish under which insects and fungi hibernate, the burning of waste wood and of leaves from trees that have carried disease and the scarifying of lawns. Overcrowding, stagnation, dirt, lack of light – these in particular may lead to one particular class of ailment known as physiological disorders, which are caused by some fault in what I have called the social science of plant life. Admittedly these diseases are sometimes obscure, as for instance those caused by the lack of some essential food in the soil. Thus a leaf with brown, burnt-looking edges suggests lack of potash; a yellow one lack of iron; brown patches between the veins a lack of magnesium. A good watering with a foliar feed often corrects these deficiencies.

Other physiological disorders, such as cold winds, frost and flood may be beyond our compass, and our main study here will be those visitations of predatorial forces that deliberately ravish our gardens with wilful intent. We can array these garden enemies into four categories, having in mind our intention of treating them as easily recognised classes or groups rather than by identification *seriatim*. First there is the very distinct category called PESTS; these are creatures of *animal* creation. Disregarding birds, deer, cats and rabbits, these comprise caterpillars, grubs, slugs, beetles, weevils, ear-wigs, flying insects, and so on.

The remaining three are classed as DISEASES and consist of
fungi
bacteria
viruses.

Bacterial and virus diseases are subjects for the expert only, but we may usefully note that any kind of malformation in a plant, any stunted growth, any unnatural streaking or mottling of foliage are probably due to some virus, and that the only way to arrest it is to burn the whole plant with its roots. Viruses are largely carried by aphids.

Thus the amateur is left to deal only with pests and fungi – and quite enough too. He must now distinguish between them. Fungi, or blights, manifest themselves mainly in

∞ mildews and fluffy moulds (but note the so-called 'American Blight', which is not a fungus);

∞ rusty discolorations of foliage;

∞ black or brown spots on leaf or stem;

∞ distortions of leaf;

∞ diverse cankers, rots, wilts and so on.

Pests classified. Insect pests, for our purposes, are of four sorts: soil pests, most of which feed on roots; and plant pests, of which one sort are biters, another borers and the third suckers. The distinction is extremely important.

The biters are betrayed by the eating away of leaf, stem, fruit, or flower. The culprits are generally to be found in the plant, though sometimes hidden. The more obvious ones are caterpillars. We attack these biters by contact poisons.

The suckers go to work with a fine proboscis, with which they minutely pierce the leaf or young stem-tip and suck out the sap, not the leaf-surface. The best-known are the aphids – greenfly, blackfly, cuckoo-spit etc. They are easily kept away by a preventive spray of a systemic insecticide.

The borers are the maggots of moths or beetles. Those that tunnel inside the stems of plants (leopard moth, goat moth, clearwing moth) are difficult, being invisible; the only evidence is a dying branch which you

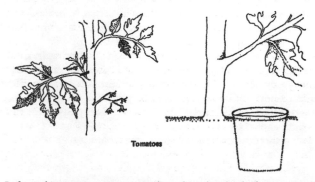

Tomatoes

Left, *pinching tomatoes: remove auxiliary shoots but not the fruiting spray.* Right, *a watering dodge.*

must cut right back to healthy wood. Other borers tunnel into fruits (e.g., codlin moth of apples and raspberry beetle) and are rather more vulnerable.

Some creatures create special problems. Chafers, for instance, are soil pests when they are grubs and plant pests when adult. Once loose in the air they are free, so we shall attack them in the ground. Others are difficult to tackle unless you get them at just the right moment, as for instance the apple sawfly and codlin moth, who will be safely inside the heart of the fruit if you are too early or too late. Likewise it is impractical to attack the 'flies' whose maggots ravage onions and carrots, and their damage is done before you see the result of it, so all we can do is to repel the fly from laying its eggs in those places.

REMEDIES IN GENERAL

The remedies to be applied are mainly chemical, either insecticides or fungicides, the majority applied either in liquid form through a syringe or sprayer or else in powder (or 'dust') form through a bellows, blower or 'puffer pack'.

Whether it be liquid or powder, make sure to cover the whole plant thoroughly, especially the under-surfaces of leaves by means of a curved nozzle which should be on every syringe. A fine mist or cloud should be delivered. Spraying is best done on a calm day in mild, dry weather, never in hot sun. When using the contact sprays, such as derris, drive the poison well into the heart of clusters of buds or fruitlets. The 'systemics', however, you use much more casually. For dusting, the air should be still, and the foliage slightly damp, so the best times are early morning, evening, or after showers. They are possibly less effective than liquids.

The gardener need not be fussed by the exaggerated propaganda against chemical pesticides, launched by people who like making our flesh creep. All those normally sold in shops are of low density and approved by Government, but there are a few caveats in the next chapter. Vegetables can be tainted by certain chemicals if eaten too soon after application. Read the label.

The broad and simple classification of nuisances in the last sections leads us to a similar simplification of remedies, which we can summarise thus:

Soil pests. No pesticides available except for plants in pots and containers for which imidacloprid can be incorporated in compost.

Plant pests – suckers and biters. Contact or residual pesticide such as insecticidal soap (fatty acids), pyrethrins, derris (rotenone) or bifenthrin.

Fungi. Many garden fungicides contain a systemic chemical such as myclobutanil, carbendazim or propiconazole while the protective, antisporulant penconazole is found in others. Sulphur and copper fungicides still have some important uses and are considered to be organic.

Fungi, being rooted in the tissues of a plant, can seldom be 'cured' once they have started, but they can be arrested and they can often be barred by preventive action.

Besides these chemical means, there is the basic method of 'finger and thumb work'. A pinch of the fingers for caterpillar or greenfly, a snip of the nails for millipedes, the weight of the foot for slugs, these are swift and effective methods. Anyone who cannot overcome squeamishness should collect the creatures and give them a quick mass death in boiling water or a concentrated insecticide.

The simplified system above will not, of course, deal with everything, but the busy amateur may have time to do little more. Special measures are necessary for fruits and some other crops. Besides the primary remedies I mention in this Part, there are also plenty of proprietary concoctions that combine two or more toxins.

Millipedes, in contrast to the friendly centipedes, have round rather than flat bodies, with a shiny, shell-like, dark-brown skin, equipped with innumerable tiny legs. Sluggish in movement and often found coiled up like little snakes, they feed mainly on decaying matter. When worried, they give off a slightly obnoxious smell.

Leatherjackets. See chapter on lawns.

Wireworm. Extremely slim, like a piece of glossy, yellow wire. Burrows into potatoes, carrots, etc.

Cutworm. Caterpillar-like, with *tucked-in tail*. Sluggish. Eats off small plants at ground-level at night. Bad in the vegetable plot. Do not confuse with the friendly grub of the ground beetle. Biological control with *Steinernema carpocapsae* nematodes is possible on moist, well-drained soils in summer.

Chafer grubs. Bloated, dirty white grubs with horny heads, half curled-up. The largest, with thickened tail, is the larva of the cockchafer. The garden chafer is a bit smaller and the vine weevil, often found in rock gardens, smaller still.

23

THE ENEMY IN DETAIL

The following are some condensed notes on how to deal with the commoner garden enemies *seriatim*. Descriptions and usages of the various medicines are given in the next chapter. When flowers are fully open do not use anything harmful to bees, but derris is safe.

Proprietary brand names of remedies are printed with a capital initial and the chemicals from which they are formulated with a small one. Thus Polysect is the maker's name for a brand of bifenthrin and Dithane of a brand of mancozeb fungicide.

SOIL AND GENERAL PESTS

Ants. Several proprietary antidotes.
Birds. For small plants a few strands of black thread stretched between twigs makes the birds suspect a snare as their feet touch them and they will keep away. For larger trees, such as cherries, a nylon net thrown right over protects most of the buds and fruit. For bush and cane fruits and strawberries the best thing is a complete cage of any sort of small-mesh netting.
Earwig. Make traps of hollow broad bean stalks or partially open matchboxes stuffed with hay or dry grass and suspended high in the foliage: shake out the pests into a cup of paraffin.
Slugs and **snails.** Pellets containing methiocarb are better than those containing metaldehyde, while formulations based or aluminium sulphate are considered to be organic and pose no threat to birds or pets. Biological control with *Phasmarhabditis hermaphrodita* nematodes works best on moist, well-drained soils in spring and autumn.

PLANT PESTS

Aphids (greenfly, blackfly, etc.). Suckers. Use a contact insecticide. A breed of aphid sometimes attacks lettuce and other roots; there is no currently available chemical control.
Big bud, on blackcurrants. Distinctive globular swelling of a dormant bud caused by mites in winter. Pick off and burn swollen buds.
Cabbage gall weevil. Small round swellings on the roots caused by tiny white maggot. Break open and crush maggot. Burn galled roots. Not serious, but compare with clubroot in fungus section.
Capsid bug. Sucker. Resembles large greenfly, but nimble. Distorted flowers, leaves, or stems. On apples a rough brown patch. Use a contact insecticide spray with pyrethrins or bifenthrin.

Caterpillars. Biters. On fruit trees, apply grease-bands and winter washes. Biological control with *Bacillus thuringiensis* is also possible.

Codling moth, on apples. Biter. The maggot usually enters the fruit at the eye about midsummer. The point of entry has a dry 'frass'. Treat with bifenthrin in mid-June and repeat two weeks later; also tie bands of hay or sacking round the trunk in July (in which caterpillars may pupate) and burn in autumn.

Cuckoo-spit, or spittle bug, or froghopper. Sucker. Inside a mass of frothy spittle is a curious soft creature which on disturbance will attempt to escape by weak hops. Handpick.

Eelworm. Microscopic creatures, each genus having its own worm. Shown in stunted, distorted or shrivelled growth. Curable only by experts. Lift and burn the plants and do not plant the same genus on that site for five years.

Flea beetle. Tiny, jumping beetle bites holes in brassica seedlings, especially turnips. A serious pest. Dust the ground with derris.

'Flies' – Cabbage-root fly, onion fly, carrot fly. These small creatures, seen only by the keen eye, are very widespread and destructive. Their maggots eat into the bulb of the young onion, into the carrot or into the roots of the cabbage. A wilting of the plant and, in carrots, a reddening or yellowing of the leaves are symptoms of them. Those of the onion and the carrot are attracted by the smell of the plant, especially when thinning is done. Infected plants must be pulled up and burnt. Remove seedlings when thinning.

Froghopper. Sucker. Pale yellow creature the size of greenfly on the underside of leaves. Leaf becomes mottled with yellow patches, later turning white. Adult phase of the insect that causes cuckoo-spit. Control by handpicking at cuckoo-spit stage.

Greenfly. *See* Aphids.

Leaf miner. Wriggly channellings within the tissue of a leaf, chiefly in chrysanthemums and celery. The maggot is at the extremity of the channelling. Burn infected leaves.

Mealy bug. Sucker. Tiny bug protected by coat of white mealy wax on hard-wooded greenhouse plants, especially vines. Spray tar-oil wash in winter (after rubbing off bark on vines) and spray with insecticidal soap or use biological control in summer with ladybird predator *Cryptolaemus montrouzieri*.

Raspberry beetle. The maggot eats out the hearts of raspberries, loganberries and blackberries. Spray or dust forcefully with derris at the earliest flush of pink on the fruits as a preventative; on loganberries when flowering is nearly over; on blackberries as the first flowers open.

Red spider. Suckers. Very difficult customers. A mere dot of red or rust scarcely visible to the naked eye. Encouraged by hot, dry conditions, especially in greenhouses. Often disclosed by grey mottling of leaf. Outdoors spray with bifenthrin, indoors use biological control with the predatory mite *Phytoseiulus persimilis*, introduced when temperatures are warm but before infestation has become heavy.

Sawfly, apple. The maggot makes characteristic ribbon scars of rough skin, and its point of entry into the fruit is wet and rank. Remove and burn affected fruitlets, including those that have fallen around the tree.

Slugworm. Biter. Its sign-manual is a leaf eaten to a papery skeleton. Use a contact insecticide.

Spittle bug. *See* Cuckoo-spit.

Thrips (thunderflies). Suckers. Tiny, slightly hairy, louse-like, nimble; adults winged. Encouraged by hot, dry conditions, especially in greenhouse. Pea and bean pods distorted, with mottled, silvery streaks. Rose petals speckled. In the greenhouse white patches on leaves, dark secretions on under-surface, blossoms distorted. Spray with pyrethrins; indoors use the predatory mite *Amblyseius degenerans* as biological control.

Weevils (long-snouted beetles). Biters and borers of several sorts. Ragged holes in foliage; scolloped edges of bean and pea leaves; ribbed bark of young trees; most serious in apples, blossom turning brown and failing to open. Spray with bifenthrin; on apples at bud-burst stage.

Whitefly. Sucker. Clouds of minute white flies in the greenhouse. Use biological control with the parasitic wasp, *Encarsia formosa*.

Woolly aphid (American blight). An aphid that protects itself with a covering like cotton-wool. Scrub with a stiff brush and methylated spirit.

FUNGUS DISEASES

Black spot. Black patches on rose leaves, sometimes on stems also. A menacing disease. Spray with penconazole or mancozeb. *See* Chapter 14.

Botrytis, or **grey mould**. A fluffy mould, affected parts going soft and black. A difficult disease, flourishing in damp, cold conditions. Burn all infected parts.

Brown rot. Apples, pears, and some other fruit go brown, putrid and mummified on the tree, often dotted with small white pustules in concentric rings. Burn all infected fruit.

Cane spot. Purplish patches on raspberry and loganberry canes, later turning grey. Burn all infected canes.

Canker. Deep oval wound, typically on apples, pears, and roses, with gnarled, corky edge, exposing smoother wood below. Starts with a number of small depressions. Cut off and burn diseased twigs. Spray with Bordeaux mixture.

In the bacterial canker of plums the leaves look as though eaten by caterpillars, then a gum exudes from elongated cankers on the branches. Use Bordeaux mixture three times at monthly intervals, starting mid-August.

Clubroot. Grotesque and evil-smelling swellings on the roots of the cabbage family. A serious disease. Thrives on soil deficient in lime. Cf. Cabbage gall weevil. Burn all diseased plants, dress the ground heavily

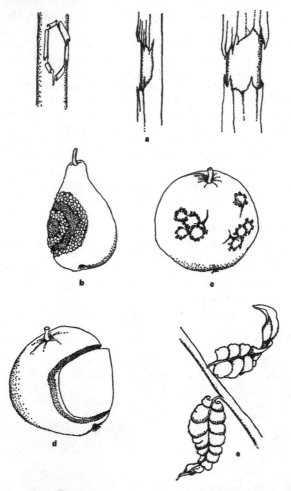

Some fruit afflictions: **a**, *stages of canker – the peeling bark, the gaping wound, death;* **b**, *brown rot;* **c**, *the cracks and dry, round scars of scab;* **d**, *the ribbon scar of the apple sawfly;* **e**, *peach-leaf curl.*

with lime at 14 oz. per sq. yd. (400 gm per sq. m.) and do not use it for any brassica for four years.

Coral spot. A speckling of bright coral pustules on branches, especially dead wood. Burn all infected wood.

Damping-off. Kills small seedlings at ground level, especially in the greenhouse. Treat the soil with Cheshunt compound when sowing seed or when pricking out.

Fireblight. Very serious disease that may attack apples, pears, cotoneasters and pyracanthas. *See* Apples, Chapter 20.

Leaf curl. The leaves of peaches, nectarines, and almonds are twisted and distorted, with red or yellow blisters. Burn all infected leaves. Spray with any copper-based fungicide in February and just before leaf-fall in autumn.

Mildews. White or grey, powdery growth on leaves and stems, sometimes on fruit also, as on gooseberries. Dust or spray with carbendazim, mancozeb or sulphur. 'Downy' mildew is a different fungus, which shows on the reverse surfaces of leaves. Burn these and treat with mancozeb.

Potato blight. Very serious. Symptoms are brown patches on leaves, turning black, with white, mouldy rings on the under-surface. Take prophylactic measures with copper fungicide or mancozeb. *See* Chapter 21.

Potato blight on tomatoes. Brown patches on leaf edges, brown patches on fruits, which turn rotten. Take protective steps with copper fungicide or mancozeb.

Rots. Various rots attack celery, lettuces, onions (wet rot) and others. Plants go soft and slimy, sometimes covered with fungus. May not appear till crop is in store. Burn them all and add potash to the soil.

Rusts. Rusty pustules on the undersides of leaves (brighter orange on roses). Burn infected leaves. Spray with myclobutanil, penconazole or mancozeb.

Scab, of apples and pears. Small, black, hard, dry patches develop with deep cracks and distortions of fruit, rough and broken surface on twigs; black spots under leaves. Very prevalent. Spray with carbendazim or mancozeb before blossoms open, and when they have fallen. Prune out and burn infected twigs and burn all fallen leaves of infected trees.

Silver leaf. If a dull, metallic silvering (not mere whitening) occurs on the leaves of stone fruits, better get in an expert. If it is silver leaf you are liable to prosecution if the infected bough is not removed. Cut cleanly back to the parent limb with no snag; burn all infected parts.

Spur blight of raspberries and loganberries. Dark, purplish patches around the nodes of the canes become silver then a mass of minute black fungus. Burn all diseased canes.

Tomato leaf mould. Patches of brown-grey mould on undersides of leaves with yellow blotches on surface. Encouraged by lack of ventilation. Spray with mancozeb or carbendazim and burn infected leaves.

Wart disease of potatoes. Large wart-like growth, the whole tuber becoming an evil mass. A notifiable disease, avoided by buying immune varieties.

PHYSIOLOGICAL AILMENTS

Blossom-end rot of tomatoes. A dark, sunken patch at the blossom end of the fruit spreads and blackens. Now known to be due to lack of calcium. Burn affected fruits and dress soil with lime at 4 oz. per sq. yd.

Chlorosis. A yellowing of foliage caused by lack of chlorophyll. Due to shortage of iron in the soil, which may in turn be due to excess lime. Water with iron sequestrene or a foliar feed.

Greenback on tomatoes. A band of hard green or yellow flesh round the stalk refuses to ripen. Due to excessive heat and light. Paint the greenhouse glass with 'Coolglass' or fix blinds or close-mesh netting.

Gumming (bacterial canker) of plums, cherries, and other stone fruits. Is an excretion of resinous gum; preluded by spotty leaves. If branches begin to die, cut back to healthy wood.

Reversion of blackcurrants. Is a virus. If a new sort of leaf appears – smaller and more elongated than the cultivated leaf, and lacking the basal lobes – burn the whole bush. No cure.

24

THE MEDICINE CUPBOARD

In this chapter is some outline information on insecticides and fungicides of the more usual sorts only. The more complicated ones and those requiring the use of protective clothing are omitted. Readers who have no chemical knowledge are advised to buy proprietary articles; not, for example, nicotine and pyrethrum in their pure chemical forms.

Very few of these concoctions are 'dangerous', but it is common sense to keep them out of the way of children and pets. A few affect tender skins and noses. Some will taint vegetables and fruit if used too soon before picking. Bifenthrin and derris kill fish and pyrethrins and most synthetic fungicides are harmful to them. ALWAYS READ WHAT THE LABEL SAYS, but do not take fright at the 'warnings' often given.

For the instant job that you spot as you go around the garden, keep the following ready to hand always: a slug-killer, and a small puffer or blower ready filled with derris dust for insect pests.

For the hard-pressed gardener, all-purpose mixtures of insecticide-cum-fungicide are handy but lack intensity if there is a serious attack of either. Roseclear 3 and Multirose Ready to Use are suitable for a wide range of plants.

For fungus diseases collectively, ICI's General Garden Fungicide is very good, but needs renewal after much rain.

Observe what is said below about copper brews. For fear of killing bees, do not spray any *open* flowers with any insecticide. Wait till the bees have gone to bed. Fungicides and soil pesticides are all right.

Remember also, Reader, that, even as I write, the scheming chemist is concocting fresh brews which will make the wonder of today the scorn of tomorrow. In any difficulty consult the Royal Horticultural Society or check the Pesticides Safety Directorate website (www.pesticides.gov.uk).

Bifenthrin. A contact and residual pyrethrin–like acaricide and insecticide.

Copper fungicides. For spots, rusts, botrytis, peach-leaf curl, potato and tomato blight etc. There are now various improvements on the traditional Bordeaux mixture, in liquid and dust forms, and copper is often married to other substances.

Do not put copper preparations in any iron, galvanized or tin vessel; use glass, earthenware, plastic or copper.

Cheshunt compound. Fungicide for protecting seedlings against damping-off disease. Apply to the soil before sowing and when pricking out. Use no iron, galvanized or tin vessel, as it contains copper sulphate.

Derris (rotenone). Safest all-round insecticide, for both biters and suckers. Great stand-by for general use. Obtainable as powder or liquid.

Insecticidal soap (fatty acids). Contact insecticide and acaricide approved for use by organic gardeners.

Mancozeb. A protectant fungicide useful against a wide range of diseases if used before they are well established.

Penconazole. A protectant fungicide with antisporulant activity, useful for control of powdery mildew in apples and ornamental trees and rust in roses.

Pyrethrum (pyrethrins). Insecticide for suckers often incorporated in pro-prietaries, as in the 'Py' products; harmless to man and his friends.

Sulphur. Essential fungicide available in several forms. Flowers of sulphur for dusting against mildews, harmless to the most tender plants and fruits; available in a green tint. Colloidal sulphur is a liquid for scab on apples and pears; may scorch foliage.

Sulphurs, like coppers, are preventatives and 'controls' for mildews, etc., rather than cures.

Systemic fungicides. Though systemic insecticides are no longer available to the amateur, these are several systemic fungicides that are effective against a wide range of diseases. Foremost among these are myclobutanil, propiconazole and carbendazim, all of them both protectant and curative.

PART FIVE: THE YEAR'S WORK

The following notes are intended to serve as reminders – and reminders only – of work that should be done month by month, so that the gardener may always be thinking a little ahead. The programme is based on a normal season, and on the assumption that weather and soil conditions are satisfactory. If in fact they are not, then delay the operation till they are. Thus seed-sowing outdoors must wait until the surface of the soil is tolerably dry, and planting out till it is tolerably wet (though this can be corrected by watering). Likewise spraying cannot be done on a windy day, but pruning may.

In the mildest climates operations scheduled for spring and early summer can be advanced a week or two, and those for late summer and autumn delayed a little; but in hard climates the opposite applies in both instances.

A programme of this sort cannot, of course, be all-embracing. Out-of-season jobs and those needing heat are generally excluded. So also are reminders of the obvious that the gardener ought to see for himself, such as pricking off and planting seedlings and cuttings as they come ready. Usually the first normal date for an operation is given and if not done at the time stated it should be done soon afterwards, or otherwise as stated in the appropriate cultural notes.

Despite what is said in Holy Writ, the gardener should always 'take heed of the morrow'. Read the calendar a month in advance, so as to be ready for the job due.

JANUARY

General. In the South begin pruning roses. Write your orders for seeds of vegetables and flowers, including seed potatoes if not already done; also gladioli, and other summer bulbs for spring plantings. Make vegetable cropping plan in conjunction with seed order.

Flowers. Sow schizanthus in greenhouse. Also tomato seed if the greenhouse is heated.

Vegetables. In the South and Midlands make a sowing of broad beans late in the month and plant shallots if not done in December.

Dress asparagus with seaweed if obtainable now or February.

Towards the end of the month set out potatoes for sprouting.

Fruit. Prune all fruit trees and spray with tar-oil wash if not done last month – apples last.

Dress strawberries with potash.

Root-prune overgrown trees if necessary.

FEBRUARY

General. Dress light soils with lime if needed, and any soils that were manured in autumn. Don't get behindhand with anything this month, as March is going to be a busy time.

Flowers. Early in the month prune clematis. Late in the month, or early March, prune *Buddleja davidii*, hypericums, wisteria, winter jasmine. Remove old wood and thin branches of deciduous berry shrubs.

In a greenhouse with some heat, sow antirrhinum, and start dahlias into growth for cuttings in boxes of soil. Pot up early rooted cuttings of chrysanthemums. Sow sweet peas in pots or boxes for early results.

Vegetables. Prepare seed-beds for first outdoor sowings.

Sow parsnips.

In districts unfavourable to early outdoor sowing, sow brussels, onions and leeks in boxes or frames or under cloches.

Prepare celery and leek trenches at the end of the month or early March.

Fruit. Shorten tips of summer-fruiting raspberries. Cut late-fruiting ones, and all newly planted canes, down to 6 in. of the ground. Spray peaches, etc., against leaf curl. Top-dress fruits with manure if needed or with bone-meal and compost. Dress apples, pears and plums with sulphate of potash.

MARCH

General. Complete preparation of seed-beds. Treat paths, etc., with Clearpath and beds with weed suppressants.

Flowers. Plant out (or transplant) all herbaceous perennials if not done in autumn. Also plant now those that dislike autumn planting – pyrethrum, scabious, gaillardia, etc. Plant gladiolus, montbretia, Caen and other hybrid anemones, schizostylis, water-loving iris; or early April.

Take delphinium, chrysanthemum and lupin cuttings.

In the South all roses should have been pruned by now. Where required, top-dress at the end of the month with manure, etc., all beds of *established* roses (after pruning), flowering shrubs and climbers and herbaceous borders.

Prunings. Early in the month prune deciduous shrubs that flower late in the year on new shoots that will result from such pruning (e.g. *Buddleja davidii*, ceratostigma, indigofera, *Hydrangea paniculata* 'Grandiflora', *Ceanothus* 'Gloire de Versailles'); also shrubs grown for stem and leaf effect (*Cornus alba* cultivars and *Berberis thunbergii* 'Rose Glow', etc.); also hypericums, especially the dwarf 'Tricolor', hard. Also prune passion flower.

Sow sweet peas and other hardy annuals in the open late in the month, or early April.

In the greenhouse sow China asters and summer stocks; also clarkia and other annuals for greenhouse decoration. Plant Scarborough lily.

Sow new lawns at the end of the month (or, better, prepare it now for August sowing). Begin work on old lawns by raking and brushing. Rake and re-sow any bare patches. Begin mowing, according to growth.

Vegetables. Having prepared proper seed-beds in both nursery and main gardens, make the following sowings: early lettuces (first week), onion, early potatoes (end of month), summer carrots, parsley, early dwarf peas (early in month), spinach, leeks, parsnips, early cabbages and onion sets. From now onwards lettuces, carrot and radish can be sown in succession. Under glass sow celery.

Late in the month plant out seedlings (after proper hardening off) of varieties previously raised under glass, including autumn-sown onions.

Plant rhubarb, seakale thongs, horseradish roots. Divide clumps of chives. Plant shallots in the North.

Fruit. Prune *new* blackcurrants down to three buds above ground level. Plant greenhouse grapes.

From now onwards carefully watch the bud development of apples and pears (green cluster, pink, or white bud, and petal-fall). Spray apples and pears for scab at bud-burst and again at green cluster. Spray plums and cherries for aphids and caterpillar at bud-burst. Spray blackcurrants at grape stage for mildew and grey mould and at late grape stage for big bud (and again 3 weeks later). Spray gooseberries for gooseberry mildew just before flowers open and 3 weeks later.

APRIL

Flowers. Plant out sweet peas raised in pots. Plant or transplant evergreen shrubs in the middle of the month.

Sow delphinium, lupin and other hardy perennials. Continue sowing annuals.

Apply lawn-sand etc. to lawns in a dry spell.

Prune forsythia, flowering currant and other early-flowering shrubs as soon as blossom is over (cut back generally to within three buds of the old wood). Trim winter heathers late in the month. Pick off seed-pods of bulb plants and hydrangea heads (late).

In the greenhouse, 'start' begonias, 'stop' chrysanthemums, and sow seed of zinnia, and African and French marigold. Start dahlia tubers for division if not done earlier under heat.

Vegetables. Plant new asparagus beds. Finish planting potatoes. Take precautions against soil pests.

Celery and leek trenches must be completed by now. Prepare marrow and cucumber beds.

Sowings for this month: Broccoli for all seasons, winter cabbage and savoys, salsify, kale, kohlrabi, pickling onion, late in the month. Limited sowings of beetroot, summer turnip (and afterwards in succession) and swedes. A further sowing of broad beans. Continue successional sowings of summer cabbage, lettuce, summer spinach, summer carrot. Sow a few seeds of vegetable marrow and ridge cucumber in pots under glass.

Peas: make a second sowing of earlies and the first sowing of maincrop variety early in the month, and a second sowing of maincrop at the end of the month.

Tomatoes: if not raising your own seed, order plants late in the month for the greenhouse (not for outdoors yet).

Begin picking rhubarb on established plants.

Fruit. Plant strawberries if not done in August. Continue spraying of all fruits against caterpillars; apples and pears against scab, mildew and aphids; blackcurrants again against big bud, mildew, grey mould and leaf spot; plums for sawfly 8 days after flowering.

MAY

General. Be specially on the lookout for the treacherous late frosts, which may occur at night right up to the last week. Give night protection to anything not hardy, and replace losses by fresh sowings. Spray early against fungus diseases, aphids, etc.

Flowers. Begin hardening-off half-hardy plants (antirrhinum, etc.) of your own raising. If not raising your own, order plants for putting out end of month or first week of June.

Spray roses early in month with insecticide.

Plant out early chrysanthemums about the second week and pinch tips end-May. Stand greenhouse sorts outdoors in the last week. Plant dahlia tubers (not growing plants) mid-month in mild places where it has not been possible to start them earlier under glass. Bed out any hardy annuals started in boxes.

Sow seed of perennials (delphinium, lupin, campanula, hollyhock, foxglove, pinks, etc.). Sow *Primula malacoides* for the greenhouse.

Prune early-flowering shrubs as they cease to bloom. Trim back rock plants that have finished flowering.

Evergreens may still be transplanted.

Vegetables. Outdoor sowings for this month: dwarf French beans, scarlet runners, haricot bean, flageolet, all mid-May; first sowing of endive and final sowing of maincrop peas, end of month. A second sowing of French beans in the third week; sweetcorn in the last week.

Earth up potatoes.

Plant out early sowings of brassicas; leeks, celeriac and celery (end of month or earliest June).

Tomatoes: if not raising your own, order plants for outdoors for planting first week of June. The same for marrows, cucumbers and celery.

Look out for blackfly on broad beans and pinch out top 3 in. (7.5 cm.) when lowest pods set.

Fruit. Watch for bugs and diseases. Spray – apples for sawfly and capsid; pears for scab at petal-fall; gooseberries for mildew and leaf spot; raspberries after flowering for cane-spot; strawberries for mildew just before flowering.

Thin fruits of peach, nectarine, apricot when the size of a pea. De-flower 'perpetual fruiting' strawberries and spring-planted summer ones.

JUNE

Flowers. The big job of the first week or two is to clear out the early flow-ering, non-perennial stuff (wallflowers etc.,) to fork over and feed the beds, and to plant out their successors. Lift tulips, if necessary, with a ball of soil and heel-in. Plant out antirrhinum, stock, zinnia, scarlet salvia, begonia and dahlia.

Spray roses with systemic fungicide and repeat once a fortnight until September.

Divide and transplant bearded flag irises after they have flowered (the best time). Plant belladonna lily.

Pick off dead blossom everywhere. Prune early-flowering shrubs as they cease blooming, e.g. broom (very hard), lilac, philadelphus, deutzia, laburnum, rhododendron. Do second 'stopping' of indoor chrysanths if desired.

Begin feeds of liquid manure, soot-water, etc., as appropriate. Begin staking in the herbaceous border.

Sow biennials – wallflower, sweet William, Canterbury bell, polyanthus, pansy, forget-me-not, Brompton stock, etc. – for next year; remember to transplant them into nursery rows when going ahead well.

Take cuttings of pinks and helianthemums.

Carefully watch ventilation and watering in greenhouse.

Vegetables. Plant out tomatoes, marrows, ridge cucumbers in the first week. Transplant brassicas as ready; Brussels should be in final quarters by third week.

Sowings: Maincrop beetroot and carrot for storing; final sowings of French beans and scarlet runner; sowing of dwarf early pea for September (end of month); successional sowings of lettuce.

Stop cutting asparagus mid-June. Earth up potatoes as necessary, and spray against potato blight with copper fungicide or mancozeb in the SW (other areas in succession).

Fruit. Root strawberry runners, and prepare new bed for their planting in August.

Spray apples against codlin moth, mid-month and again against scab and mildew. Anticipate the 'June drop' by thinning heavy-cropping apples. Spray raspberries against the beetle when most of blossom over and again 14 days later. Watch for caterpillar on gooseberries.

Begin summer pinching on stone fruits and select the new shoots on wall-trained peaches, nectarines and cherries to be tied in for next year. Summer-prune gooseberries and redcurrants.

Lay straw under strawberries, and spread nets when fruits set.

JULY

General. Bad month for diseases and pests.

Flowers. Prick out into a nursery bed the nurselings of wallflower, etc., sown earlier. Continue spraying roses with a systemic fungicide.

Plant: Madonna lily, snowdrop, autumn- and winter-flowering crocuses, meadow saffron and sternbergia.

Layer border carnations late in month. Take cuttings of shrubs and of pinks and violas.

Lift any tulips and ranunculus still in ground, dry off and store.

Prune early-flowering shrubs and climbers, e.g. philadelphus and weigela. Summer-prune wisteria and Japanese quince early. Feed roses after first blooming.

Clip non-flowering evergreen hedges in the last week or early August. Sow cineraria seed end of month.

Vegetables. Some early potatoes may be lifted for the table as required. Sow spring cabbage and kale late this month in Northern gardens (early August elsewhere).

Sow winter prickly seeded spinach at the same time. Spray potatoes again, against blight.

Fruit. Summer-prune apples and pears if required – pears about the middle of the month, apples at the end. Spray apples again for codlin moth, early in the month and tie sacking bands round apple trunks.

AUGUST

Flowers. Plant daffodils. Sow new lawns late in the month. Cut back and top-dress violas. Cut down the foliage of bearded flag irises by about a half. Disbud chrysanths as necessary. As gladioli fade cut off the stalks, not lower than the lowest blossom, or pluck off buds. Cut out feeble new stems of rambler roses.

Continue to take cuttings of flowering shrubs.

In the greenhouse: begin planting freesias in pots. Take pelargonium ('geranium') cuttings. Sow schizanthus, and clarkia, antirrhinum, etc., for spring display.

Vegetables. Keep celery and leeks copiously watered and earth up. Mulch peas and beans.

Sow: lettuce 'Avondefiance' for late autumn use; spring cabbage in Southern gardens; pickling cabbage; winter (prickly) spinach or perpetual spinach.

Stop outdoor tomatoes after fourth truss and spray against blight; spray again two weeks later.

Towards the end of the month bend over onion tops to hasten ripening. Lift and dry shallots. Watch out for cabbage-white butterfly on brassicas and spray with derris.

All winter greens should have been planted out by now.

Fruit. Cut down all canes of raspberry and loganberry that have finished fruiting this summer to within 6 in. of the ground, and cut out weakly new shoots (late-fruiting raspberries wait till February). Prune blackcurrants when fruit has been picked.

Plant out rooted runners of strawberries in their new beds soonest.

Pick early varieties of apple and pear, and remember that they will not keep.

SEPTEMBER

General. This is like May in reverse, and early frosts have to be guarded against late in the month in the North. It is also the beginning of the digging, harvesting, and bulb seasons. Special attention to compost bins. Order new fruit trees, roses, shrubs, herbaceous plants, etc., if not already done. Order manure, peat, lime, etc.

Flowers. If a new herbaceous border is planned, dig it now; the like for new rose-beds, and for spring bedding.

Prune rambler (but not climber) roses early. Take cuttings of violas from those cut down last month.

Plant bulbs of hyacinth (late), spring crocus, muscari, bulbous iris, scilla, chionodoxa, anemone species, hybrid anemones if not done in March, etc. (*not* tulips yet). Plant bulbs in bowls and pots for the house. Plant peonies, red-hot pokers, and clematis; and flag irises if not done in the summer.

Late in the month bring pot-grown chrysanths into the greenhouse.
Also lift, pot and bring in pelargoniums and heliotrope.
Vegetables. Harvest: tomatoes (end of month), potatoes, onions, haricot
beans, marrows.
Sow turnip 'Imperial Green Globe'. Plant out spring cabbage.
Cloche late-sown peas and French beans third week.
Begin to blanch endives late in month.
Fruit. Grease-band all tree-fruits. Harvest apples and pears as they become
ready, leaving late varieties till next month. Protect 'perpetual' strawberries
with tunnel cloches.

OCTOBER

General. Frost-sensitive plants must now all be out of the ground unless
protected. Push on with the digging. The end of this month is the ideal
time for planting trees and shrubs (including roses and fruits) and most
herbaceous plants (not scabious, gaillardia, pyrethrum and the amellus
group of asters until the spring).
Flowers. Lift, dry and store dahlias and begonias at the first touch of frost.
Divide and re-plant overcrowded herbaceous plants (Michaelmas daisies,
heleniums, etc.).

Deploy your spring bedding plants (wallflowers, sweet William,
polyanthus, Canterbury bell, etc.). Sever carnation layers early in month
and plant out a week or two later.

Complete bulb plantings, but not tulips till end of month or early
November.

Take cuttings of roses late in month. Also of bedding verbenas.
Vegetables. If the digging programme is going to be a big one, start
towards end of this month. Clear all decaying crops, cabbage leaves and
rubbish.

Harvest: carrots, beet, turnips (except sorts to stand out in the winter).
Sow: broad beans to stand the winter; lettuce 'Maikönig' or 'Val
d'Orge'.

Give celery final earthing up. Cut down asparagus when foliage turns
yellow. Protect cauliflowers by breaking a leaf over the curds.

At the end of month cut down spearmint and dry off.
Fruit. Prune gooseberry, redcurrants and blackcurrants and take cuttings.
Apply grease-bands to apples and cherries.

NOVEMBER

General. For the next few weeks the dreary business of cleaning up
confronts you. Do it thoroughly. Burn everything not suitable for the compost bin. Meanwhile push on with the planting. Begin to withold water in
greenhouse and frame. Send secateurs to be sharpened.

Flowers. Plant tulips, turban ranunculus, lily-of-the-valley; divide and re-plant old overcrowded stock.

Lift stock plants of early chrysanthemum and plant under glass. Lift, dry and store gladioli.

Mulch shrub and herbaceous borders with leaves (not manure).

Vegetables. Dig areas cleared of crops and treat as necessary for next planned crop.

Begin forcing rhubarb and seakale if grown, and continue forcing endives.

Heel 'heading' broccoli over to north in exposed regions and earth up all other winter greens. Lift horseradish.

Fruit. Plant all species of fruit if not already done.

Take cuttings of gooseberry and red- and blackcurrant.

Take down and burn sacking bands on apples.

Begin pruning apple, pear, gooseberry and redcurrant, and outdoor grapes towards end of month if there are many to do.

Lower rods of greenhouse grapes; clean bark if necessary.

DECEMBER

General. Send mowers, shears, etc. to be sharpened (secateurs should have been done earlier).

Flowers. Roses, deciduous trees, climbers, etc., and herbaceous plants may still be planted if the weather is open.

Aerate damp lawns with a fork or special spiked tool.

Dress trees, shrubs and hedges with bonemeal.

Vegetables. Protect celery heads towards end of month with loose straw, etc.

Fruit. Prune apples, pears, etc. Grapes, indoors or out, *must* be done before end of month.

APPENDICES

I. SOME MEMORANDA

A linear rod, pole or perch = 5½ yd. (5.03 metres).
A square rod, pole or perch = 30¼ sq. yd. (25.50 sq. metres).
160 square rods to the English acre (4,840 sq. yd.); the
Scottish acre is 6,150 sq. yd.
2 tablespoons = 1 fluid oz.; 20 fluid oz. (480 minims) = 1 pint.
1 oz. per gallon = 60 minims per pint.
1 bushel of J.I. Compost fills 12 2-in. seed-boxes or 48 pots size 48 (4½ in.
diameter).

2. METRIC CONVERSIONS

The following tables give more or less precise equivalents. Gardening,
however, is not an exact science and in practice it will usually be sufficient
to use approximate equivalents. Thus, in weights, one would use 30
grammes per linear metre for granular or powdered fertilisers (a trifle more
for square metres) and, in liquid measure, 30 millilitres per 5 litres or (using
the standard watering-cans made to hold gallons) 25 ml. per 4 1. Likewise,
one would interpret '1 fluid ounce per gallon per sq. yd.' for a weedkiller
etc., as '30 millilitres per 5 litres per sq. metre', instead of the ridiculous
'28.4 ml. per 4.5 1. per .9 sq. m.'

Linear

1 inch	= 2.54 centimetres (say 2½ cm.)
1 foot	= 30.5 centimetres
1 yard	= 0.914 metres
10 yards	= say 9 metres
1 *millimetre*	= 0.039 *inch*
1 *centimetre*	= 0.3937 *inch*
1 *metre*	= 1.0936 *yards*

Weight

1 ounce	= 28.35 grammes
1 pound	= 0.4536 kilogrammes
1 hundredweight	= 50.802 kilogrammes
1 *milligramme*	= 0.0154 *grain*
1 *gramme*	= 0 0353 *ounce*
1 *kilogramme*	= 2.2046 *pounds*

Liquid

1 fluid oz. (8 fl. drachms)	= 28.4 millilitres
1 pint (20 fl. oz.)	= 0.568 litres

1 gallon	= 4.546 litres
1 *centilitre* (10 *millilitres*)	= approx 2¾ *fl. drachms*
10 *centilitres* (100 *millilitres*)	= approx 3½ *fl. oz.*
1 *litre* (10 *decilitres*)	= 1.76 *pints or say* 35 *fl. oz.*

Capacity

1 bushel = 36.37 litres

Square measures

| 1 square foot | = 0.09 sq. metre |
| 1 square yard | = 0.836 sq. metre |

Temperatures

Centigrade	Fahrenheit
0	32
5	41
10	50
15	59
20	68
25	77
30	86
35	95
40	104

3. SEED AND POTTING COMPOSTS

John Innes seed compost

2 parts by bulk sterilised loam
1 part by bulk peat (moss or sedge)
1 part by bulk sharp lime-free sand

To these are added, per bushel, 1½ oz. superphosphate of lime and ¾ oz. ground chalk or limestone.

John Innes potting for cuttings

7 parts by bulk medium loam
3 parts by bulk moss peat
2 parts by bulk coarse silver sand

To this is added a special fertiliser compounded of 2 parts by weight of hoof-and-horn meal, 2 parts superphosphate of lime, and 1 part sulphate of potash. For pots up to 4½ in. size, 4 oz. of this fertiliser is added per bushel of compost; for pots from 4½ to 8 in., 8 oz.; over 8 in., 12 oz.

Compost for cuttings

1 part by bulk medium loam
2 parts by bulk peat
7 parts by bulk sharp sand
No fertiliser.

4. THE NORTH WALL AND BORDER

The following is a short selection of plants that succeed on the shady north side of a wall, fence or hedge.

For the wall or fence itself (according to height), provided there are no overhanging trees–

'Morello' cherry, 'Kentish Red' cherry, and some sweet cherries; redcurrants and gooseberries, either trained or as bushes; loganberries and blackberries on fences.

Pyracantha, cotoneaster, *Hydrangea anomala* subsp. *petiolaris*, Virginia creeper, winter jasmine, *Forsythia suspensa*, flowering quince.

Clematis: especially 'Nelly Moser' and 'Barbara Jackman'.

Climbing roses: 'Mermaid', 'Madame Alfred Carrière', 'Madame Grégoire Staechelin', 'Gloire de Dijon'.

For the border –

Lilies: *regale, henryi, hansonii, monadelphum*, and many others.

Campanula (border varieties), woodland anemones and *Anemone* x *hybrida*, foxgloves, lily-of-the-valley (extra good), snake's-head fritillary and any small bulbs of early spring, cyclamen, peony, mossy saxifrage, lupins, columbine, primrose, dicentra, Solomon's seal (*Polygonatum multiflorum*), forget-me-not.

Some shrubs other than wall-climbers: mahonias, hypericums, elaeagnus, camellias, *Daphne mezereum* and *D.* x *burkwoodii*, forsythias, flowering currant, the flowering bramble, *Rubus deliciosus* (easy and useful).

5. SOME PLANTS FOR DRY SOILS

Shrubs and trees

Gorse (for dry, arid banks).
Brooms (*Cytisus, Genista, Spartium*).
Cistus (mild counties).
Helianthemum.
Lavender.
Potentilla.
Laburnum.
Syrian hibiscus.
Tree lupin.
Olearia x *haastii.*

Buddlejas.
Brachyglottis (Dunedin Group) 'Sunshine'.

Border and rock plants

Stonecrops and house leeks.
Everlasting pea (*Lathyrus rotundifolius*), 4 ft., pink flowers at midsummer,
 good for an arid bank.
Valerian (*Centranthus*).
Cranesbill (true *Geranium*).
Catananche.
Thymes.
Arabis.
Anchusa (if not over-dry).
Baptisia australis (as substitute for lupins).
Belladonna lily and *Nerine bowdenii* in warm spots.
Soapwort.
Aurinia saxatilis.

6. SOME PLANTS FOR MOIST SOILS

Shrubs and trees

Willows, alders and bamboos.
Hydrangea.
Some spiraeas.
Diervilla.
Deutzia.
Nearly all lime-hating shrubs if the moisture is not excessive and the
 drainage good – rhododendron, eucryphia, kalmia, azalea, etc.
Cornus alba, a waterside dogwood grown for its brilliant bark.
Thujas.

Border plants

Astilbe and most of the herbaceous spiraeas.
Iris ensata, if you can! *Iris laevigata* (standing in water). Siberian iris.
Rodgersia pinnata (plumes of deep pink, 3 ft., resembling astilbes and the
 popular notion of spiraea).
Marsh marigold (*Caltha palustris*), standing in water.
Loosestrife (*Lysimachia*) and purple loosestrife (*Lythrum*).
Forget-me-not.
Bergamot (*Monarda*).
Ranunculus.
Mimulus (shallow water, waterside or bog).
Monkshood (*Aconitum*).
Phlox, if not excessively wet.

Many primulas, generally the 'difficult' ones, such as *P. florindae*, *P. japonica*,
  P. pulverulenta, etc.
Daylily (*Hemerocallis*).
Trollius.
Lychnis chalcedonica, good also for waterside and bog.
Salvia uliginosa.

7. TOWN GARDENS

The following is a selection of some plants that, subject to soil conditions,
are generally found to succeed even in the atmosphere of large towns. Give
them plenty of space and spray or hose them overhead occasionally with
water. In old town garden soils, lime dressings are often called for.

Trees and shrubs

Catalpa bignonioides, extra good.
Daphne mezereum, extra good.
Koelreuteria paniculata, extra good.
Hawthorns of all sorts.
Flowering almonds, peaches and cherries.
Sumacs.
Brachyglottis (Dunedin Group) 'Sunshine'.
Buddlejas
The bladder senna (*Colutea arborescens*), very useful.
Barberries, nearly all.
Hypericums, especially 'Elstead'.
Forsythia.
Diervilla.
Syrian hibiscus.
Philadelphus (mock orange).
Spindle tree (*Euonymus europaeus*).
Kerria japonica.
Pyracantha.

Climbers

Virginia creeper and *Vitis coignetiae*.
Some honeysuckles, as *Lonicera japonica* 'Halliana'.
Wisteria.
Clematis.
Hydrangea anomala subsp. *petiolaris*.
Ivy.
Fallopia baldschuanica.

Roses

A great many succeed in towns and in the industrial ones escape the
black-spot disease.

Some border plants

Most bulbs, especially the small ones.
Chrysanthemum.
Hellebores.
Thrift.
Michaelmas daisy.
Bergamot (*Monarda*).
Catananche.
Anchusa.
Catmint.
Viola.
Hollyhocks.
Lavender.
Lily-of-the-valley (dense shade).
Solomon's seal (dense shade).

8. SOME GOOD NURSERIES AND SUPPLIERS

The following is a small selection of nurseries and suppliers, to serve as an introduction, not arranged in any significant order.

General

Hillier Nurseries Ltd,
Ampfield House, Ampfield, Romsey, Hampshire SO51 9PA
01794 368733
www.hillier.co.uk

Notcutts Nurseries
Woodbridge, Suffolk IP12 4AF
01394 445400
www.notcutts.co.uk

Sunningdale Nurseries (Hiller Garden Centre)
London Road, Windlesham, Surrey GU20 6LQ
01344 623166
www.hillier.co.uk/gc/HGC_Sunningdale.html

Treasures of Tenbury (Burford House Gardens)
Burford House, Tenbury Wells, Shropshire WR15 8HQ
01584 810777
www.burford.co.uk

Trees and shrubs (in addition to several of the above)

Glendoick Gardens Ltd
Glencarse, Perth, Scotland PH2 7NS

01738 860205
www.glendoick.com

Hydon Nurseries
Clock Barn Lane, Hydon Heath, Godalming, Surrey
(especially for rhododendrons)
01483 860252

G. Reuthe Ltd
Crown Point Nursery, Sevenoaks Road, Ightham,
Nr Sevenoaks, Kent TN15 0HB
01732 810694

R.V. Roger Ltd
The Nurseries, Pickering, North Yorkshire YO18 7JW
01751 472226
www.rvroger.co.uk

Scotts Nurseries Ltd.,
Merriott, Crewkerne, Somerset TA16 5PL
01460 72306

Herbaceous plants

Claire Austin Hardy Plants
The Stone House, Clamp Pool, Shifnal, Shropshire TF11 8PE
01952 463700
www.claireaustin-hardyplants.co.uk

The Beth Chatto Gardens Ltd
Elmstead Market, Colchester, Essex CO7 7DB
01206 822007
www.bethchatto.co.uk

Bressingham Gardens (incorporating Van Tubergen UK)
Bressingham, Diss, Norfolk IP22 2AG
01379 688282
www.bressinghamgardens.com

Kelways Ltd
Langport, Somerset TA10 9EZ
(especially for peonies)
www.kelways.co.uk

Rock plant specialists

W.E.Th. Ingwersen Ltd
Birch Farm Nursery, Gravetye, East Grinstead, West Sussex RH19 4LE
01342 810236
www.ingwersen.co.uk

Inshriach Alpine Nursery
Aviemore, Inverness-shire, Scotland PH22 1QS
01540 651287

Roses

David Austin Roses
Bowling Green Lane, Albrighton, Wolverhampton WV7 3HB
01902 376300 or 376307
www.davidaustinroses.com

Peter Beales Roses
London Road, Attleborough, Norfolk NR17 1AY
01953 454707
www.classicroses.co.uk

James Cocker & Sons
Whitemyres, Lang Stracht, Aberdeen, Scotland AB15 6XH
01224 313261
www.roses.uk.com

Cants of Colchester
Nayland Road, Mile End, Colchester Essex CO4 5EB
01206 844008
www.cantsroses.co.uk

R. Harkness & Co. Ltd
The Rose Garden, Cambridge Road, Hitchin, Hertfordshere SG4 0JT
0845 331 3143
www.roses.co.uk

Mattock's Roses
Notcutts Ltd. Ipswich Road, Woodbridge, Suffolk IP12 4AF
01865 343454
www.mattocks.co.uk

Bulbs, etc.

Avon Bulbs

ARTIhaut

Burnt House Farm, Mid-Lambrook, South Petherton,
Somerset TA13 5HE
01460 242177
www.avonbulbs.co.uk

Bloms Bulbs, Primrose Nurseries, Melchbourne, Bedfordshire MK44
1ZZ
01234 709099
www.blomsbulbs.com

Broadleigh Gardens
Bishops Hull, Taunton, Somerset TA4 1AE
01823 286231
www.broadleighbulbs.co.uk

Seeds (flower and vegetable)

Samuel Dobie & Son
Long Road, Paington, Devon TQ4 7SX
0870 112 3623
www.dobies.co.uk

Suttons Seeds
Woodview Road, Paington, Devon TQ4 7NG
0870 220 2899
www.suttons-seeds.co.uk

Thompson and Morgan
Poplar Lane, Ipswich, Suffolk IP8 3PU
01473 688821
www.thompson-morgan.com

Unwins
Wisbech, Cambridgeshire PE13 2BR
01945 588522
www.unwins-seeds.co.uk

INDEX

Note: Plants are entered under both their botanical names and their common names (where they exist). Page references in **bold** type indicate the main source of information. References to pages with line drawings are in *italics*. 'The Year's Work' is not covered in the index.